D1555559

ETYMA II

An Introduction to Vocabulary-building from Latin and Greek

Cecelia Eaton Luschnig
and
Lance J. Luschnig

Hamilton Books
An Imprint of
Rowman & Littlefield
Lanham • Boulder • New York • Toronto • Plymouth, UK

This book is dedicated to all those grown-ups who wish they had had a chance to study Latin. It is not too late to start.

CONTENTS

ABBREVIATIONS AND SYMBOLS

*	Indo-European root
<	is derived from
>	produces as derivatives
abl.	ablative
acc.	accusative
adj.	adjective
adv.	adverb
dat.	dative
decl.	declension
Engl.	English
ex.	example
exer.	exercise
f.	feminine
FAQ	frequently asked question
freq.	frequentative
gen.	genitive
I-E	Indo-European
inf.	infinitive
Lat.	Latin
lit.	literally
m.	masculine
n.	noun
neut.	neuter
nom.	nominative
O.F.	Old French
PIE	Prot-Indo-European
pl.	plural
PPP	perfect passive participle
pres.	present
sg., sing.	singular
Vocab.	vocabulary list

AHD	American Heritage Dictionary
NPR	National Public Radio
OCD	Oxford Classical Dictionary
OLD	Oxford Latin Dictionary
OED	Oxford English Dictionary
RSV	Revised Standard Version (of the Bible)

FOREWORD

I WHY ENGLISH WORD ORIGINS?

What is so special about English that we need a whole college course to learn the sources of its words? The number of words in English is vast, with new ones being coined every day, to name new discoveries, inventions, or products, new ways of doing things, new ways of interacting in the world, new political, sports, or celebrity scandals, even new ways of talking about words. English is also a melting pot language with words being accepted readily from other languages. It has so many foreign words, words from hundreds of living languages and even more words from ancient Latin and Greek, that unless we have studied other languages, much of English is a foreign language even to its native speakers. It has been estimated that as much as ninety per cent of the English word stock comes from Latin and Greek. So much of English comes from Latin directly and from Latin through French that—though English is basically a Germanic language in its structure—in vocabulary it can also be considered a Romance language. The purpose of this book and course of study is to help you organize the magnificent vocabulary of Modern English, which is one of the many human-made wonders of the world.

II ENGLISH AND ITS KIN[1]

English belongs to the Indo-European (I-E) family of languages. This is a group of languages that traces its ancestry back to the reconstructed Proto-Indo-European (PIE). There are eight major divisions of I-E: GERMANIC which includes German, Yiddish, Dutch, Flemish, English (in the basic words-of-one-syllable department and in its grammatical structure), and the Scandinavian tongues: Icelandic, Norwegian, Swedish, and Danish; CELTIC (also called Gaelic): the Irish, Scots, Welsh, and Cornish languages; ITALIC, the languages both ancient and modern that were spoken on the Italian peninsula and spread from there: Latin, and its ancient kin, Oscan, and Umbrian, and the descendants of Latin (called the ROMANCE languages because of their Roman origins): Italian, French, Spanish, Portuguese, Romanian, Catalan,

Provençal are the main ones; HELLENIC or Greek (both ancient and modern); BALTO-SLAVIC: the Baltic tongues, Latvian and Lithuanian, and the Slavic languages, including Polish, Czech, Slovak, Serbo-Croatian, Bulgarian, Russian, and Ukranian; ALBANIAN; ARMENIAN; and INDO-IRANIAN which includes the two branches, Indic: Sanskrit, Romany, Urdu, Hindi, Bengali; and Iranian which includes Avestan, Kurdish, Farsi, Pashto, and Tajiki. English has borrowed from most of these languages and from many others that belong to other families.

III SOME DEFINITIONS AND GENERAL PRINCIPLES[2]

ROOT: the most basic element of a word that carries its meaning and to which prefixes and suffixes may be added. Often English words can be traced to an Indo-European root. For example, the English word *stand* is from the I-E root, *stā-, (stand), which has forms in Latin: *stare* and *sistere* (a derivative of *stare*) and in Greek: *histanai*, as well as in other branches of the family.
COGNATES: words that share the same root. For example, English *stand*, Latin *stare*, Greek *histanai*.
MORPHEME: a meaningful linguistic unit which can be a word or a word part, but cannot be divided further into meaningful units. Example: *eat* is a morpheme, as is *-ing*.
BASE: the element from which other words are formed by adding prefixes and suffixes. Example: Latin *caput*, base *capit-*, head > capital, decapitate.
CONNECTING VOWEL: sometimes a vowel is added to join the parts of words. In Latin the most common connecting or combining vowel is -i-; in Greek it is -o-. Example: hom*i*cide; heter*o*dox.
PREFIX: a meaningful word element fastened to the beginning of a base to form a compound. Example: *con-* added to the base *-sist-* gives consist.
SUFFIX: a meaningful word element fastened at the end of a base to form a compound. Example: base *sta-* plus suffix *-nce* gives stance.
COMPOUND WORD: a word with a base and at least one prefix or suffix. Example: persistence.
NATIVE WORDS: those belonging to a language at its earliest state. The native words in English are Germanic and form the backbone of the language. Example: English *hair* cognate of German *Haar*.
LOANWORDS: words borrowed from other languages. Example: *muezzin* < Arabic.
DERIVATIVES: words formed from other words. Example: *consistency*, a derivative of Latin *sistere*.
ETYMOLOGY: (1) the study of word origins and (2) the origin of a particular word. Example: *etymology* < Latin *etymologia* < Greek *etumologia* < *etumos*, true + *logos*, word + suffix *-ia*. ETYMA (singular: *etymon*) are word elements from which derivatives are formed.

When we dig into the etymologies of words we find that they sometimes change meanings. They may become more GENERALIZED, that is, they refer to a broader range of things than they originally did: for example, *farrago*, originally "mixed fodder for cattle" is now used for any hodgepodge whether edible or not (as in "the farrago of courses called the core curriculum"). Sometimes they become more SPECIALIZED, that is, they refer to a narrower, more specific range: for example *marsupium*, a pouch in Latin, has narrowed from general to particular usage and now refers to a pouch found in certain mammals (called marsupials) or fish. Sometimes words change fields, as it were: for example *delirium* < Latin *lira*, furrow + *de*, off, was an agricultural term referring to sowing away from the furrow. Now it is used metaphorically to mean "the condition of being off one's rocker." Latin and English as well as other languages are full of colorful expressions.

IV HISTORY IN WORDS:
A brief overview of the forces that brought foreign words into English[3]

Some of the earliest Latin loanwords come from the contact between the Roman legions and the Germanic tribes in northern Europe before the masses of these tribes, mostly Angles, Saxons, and Jutes, migrated to England from the continent. Such a word is PEPPER [< Latin *piper* < Greek *peperi* perhaps < Sanskrit *pipali*]. Evidence that this is a very early loan-word in English is the fact that there are similar words in other Germanic languages and dialects: German *Pfeffer*, Dutch *peper*, Swedish and Norwegian *pepper*, Yiddish *fefer*, for example.

After the Angles, Saxons, and Jutes arrived in England from the European continent throughout the fifth and sixth centuries, the chief source of Latin words was from the Romano-Britons (Romanized Celts) in the towns or *castra* (settlements fortified by the Roman legions), which is the origin of English place names in -CHESTER, -CESTER, and -CASTER. Such a word is MONGER from Latin *mango*, dealer, which survives in such compounds as fishmonger, ironmonger, warmonger, costermonger, whoremonger, some of which show the negative connotation the word has had since its Latin days when it meant a "dealer in slaves." *Mercator*, trader, is classier and was even applied to the Tiber River because of its use in commerce. The word comes ultimately from *merx*, commodity, goods, sale, and has given us numerous loanwords, including merchant, merchandise, commerce, mercenary, mercantile, mercatorial; Gerardus Mercator (originally Gerard de Kemper), the famous cartographer, is known by the Latin version of his surname. Many early, and later, loanwords have to do with trade and its products, establishing lowly merchants and mongers among the earliest heroes and sometimes villains of vocabulary.

The period of the conversion of the Anglo-Saxons to Christianity at the end of the 6th century C.E. is another source of words, especially those having to do with religion and scholarship. *Church* is an early word to enter English from Greek: Old English *circice* from Greek *kuriakon* [*doma*] *the Lord's* [*house*] from *kurios* (κύριος, lord / the Lord; as an adjective, authoritative, appointed) from the root

keuə-, swell (designates an I-E root). The *Kyrie* (*Kyrie eleison*) is a liturgical prayer and song, "Lord have mercy" as well as a song by Mr. Mister, an American rock band. In Modern Greek *kurios* means mister; the vocative, *kurie*, is used in formal address to a man (*kuria*, Mrs./Ms., to a woman). *Kuriakē* is Sunday. Other words from the same I-E root include cave, excavate < Latin *cavus*, hollow; -cele, celiac < Greek *koilos*, hollow, *koilia*, belly; codeine < Greek *kōos*, hollow > *kōdeia*, bulb, poppy head; cumulus, accumulate < Latin *cumulus*, heap; cyme, kymograph < Greek *kuma*, wave.

The Norman Conquest, the coming of Northmen (Scandinavians) to England from France, where they had settled around 900 and become Francophone, is dated to 1066, the date of the defeat of the English in the battle of Hastings, but the influence of French on English began long before that. One result of the conquest was an enormous increase in English vocabulary in all areas of speech and life: food and cooking, entertainment, nature and science, kinship, class, war, law, religion, business. Many doubles, such as *will* and *testament*, *safe* and *sound*, *erred* and *strayed*, one in each set from Anglo-Saxon, the other from French, can be traced to this period. These show the willing acceptance of foreign words into English, and perhaps a desire to communicate with speakers of both English and French.

And so it goes. Words are constantly borrowed from other languages and become part of English, whether from trade, war, or other cultural exchange. New scientific and scholarly words are coined using Greek and Latin (and other) elements whenever something new is found, made, or thought of. Such inventions are sometimes called INKHORN words, especially if they are more pedantic than practical. The naming of things is a human prerogative. With the help of this course you will gain more tools to do it, too. I have done it myself. My brother remarked, referring to the administration then in power, "They show a hardening of ideas." "Ideo-sclerosis," I said. I am still waiting for this useful word to gain wider currency. The general term for a newly coined word is NEOLOGISM. I recently heard a new one on a morning news program: *murderabilia*. This is what Lewis Carroll called a PORTMANTEAU WORD, made up by combining two words (like a folding suitcase), in this case *murder* and *memorabilia*. It refers to the gruesome trade in items associated with notorious murders.

V. USING THIS BOOK

The purpose of *ETYMA* is to help the many students, who have not had the opportunity and pleasure of studying Latin and Greek, to organize the vast word stock of English (over eighty per cent of which is derived, whether directly or indirectly, from the classical tongues) by introducing the tools of vocabulary-building as well as the fascinating study of word origins. For variety, in addition to practical aspects of word formation (the nuts and bolts), we treat the interesting histories of words and groups of words, including words derived from the names of people and places, words that give insights into history, culture, literature, or mythology.

Section One deals with the history of foreign influence on English. This may be treated in class or used for students' projects or as a break from the drier more practical exercises. Sections Two and Three explain how Latin and Greek words are Englished and how compounds are formed in those two languages. Attention is given to both everyday and technical English words.

Advice for Doing the Exercises

1. In defining a word always define it with a word or phrase that can be substituted for it in a sentence. Keep the same part of speech.

For example: magnanimity is a noun [< *magn-* great + *anim-* spirit + *-ity* condition of being/-ness]. You could define it as *generosity* or *greatness of spirit* or *big-heartedness* or *the condition of being great in spirit*, all of which are nouns or equivalent to nouns. But it will vex your teacher and fellows if you say "it means to be generous" or "it's like generous." Some of the suffixes are used for a specific part of speech, but others may be used for more than one part of speech. A further complication arises because English is very flexible in using nouns as adjectives, verbs as nouns, phrases as verbs, etc.

2. In forming compounds do not just add English elements like -s, -ed, -ing, -ly, but make up different words using prefixes and suffixes from Latin or Greek.

For example: Latin: *errare*, to go astray > English err [but erring, errs, erred do not count as separate words], error [but not errors], aberrant, aberration, erratic, erroneous [but not erratically, erroneously, erroneousness], erratum [pl. errata], inerrant. Errant itself is influenced by Latin *iter*, road, journey > *iterare* to travel and can mean both *roving* as in "Knights errant" and *straying* as in "errant ways." If in doubt about a word's etymology look it up in a dictionary that gives this information. For example, *errand* does not come from *errare* even though it may seem to fit in with the meaning, especially if you have a lot of errands to run in different places. *Errand* actually comes from Old English.

3. In the units that follow always give special attention to the vocabulary lists in Latin or Greek. At the end of each unit is a checklist of what you should know. Some of the exercises are designed for group work or in-class practice, others for review.

Suggestions for Instructors

Pre- and Post-Test

When I taught English Word Origins, on the first day of the semester, I gave the class a test of fifty words derived from Latin or Greek, some sesquipedalians, some often misused or mistaken words, all or most of which would come up in the course. I corrected these but did not return them. On the last day of the course I gave the students the same test, which I returned as they were handing in their finals. This was suggested by a student early on, so that they could see how much they had progressed. It nearly always worked: significant progress was made.

Project: Word Journal or Subject Vocabulary

Submit a word journal of 20–25 interesting words with their sources (where you found them), a quotation using each (or a sentence of your own invention), the meaning of each in brief, and its origin (etymology) *or* a list of 20–25 important or interesting words in your major, hobby, or a field you are interested in, with brief definitions, sources, etymologies, a sentence using each word, and a brief explanation of why it important in its field. This project may be started at any time during the course once you have learned some of the basic principles of taking apart words and explaining etymologies.

The format is open. The journal may be a notebook with drawings, index cards neatly tied together, a typed list, a wall chart, a Web page, or something else you have developed.

Try to include the following information for each entry:

Word
Meaning
Sentence and source
Etymology[4]

Sample entries:

WORD: floccinaucinihilipilification
MEANING: *The act of making something worthless.*
SENTENCE AND SOURCE: I first encountered this word in an interview (published in a newspaper called at that time the Moscow *Idahonian*) with the editor of the *Oxford Collegiate Dictionary of the English Language* in which it was said that *floccinaucinihilipilification* was the longest word in that dictionary.
The example in the *OED* is "I admired him for nothing so much as his *floccinaucinihilipilification* of money."
ETYMOLOGY: from Latin elements, *floccus*, a tuft of wool
  nauci- is related to *nugae*, trifles, trivial things
  nihil, nothing
  pilus, hair
  -fic- < *facere*, make
  -ation, the act of

WORD: ucalegon
MEANING: *a neighbor whose house is on fire*
SENTENCE AND SOURCE: Once in my word origins class a student asked, "What is that word that means *a neighbor whose house is on fire?*" I was perplexed. "Give me a clue," I said. Later I found it and realized I should have known it at once. It comes from Vergil's *Aeneid* (2, 312): *proximus ardet Ucalegon* ("Ucalegon, next door is on fire," that is, his house is on fire). In July 2016, Will Shortz, NPR's Puzzle Master and Crossword Puzzle Editor for the *New York Times*, was asked if he had a favorite word in English. He does. It is *ucalegon*.

ETYMOLOGY: Ucalegon was one of the Trojan elders, mentioned both in Homer's *Iliad* and Vergil's *Aeneid*.

And now, as the poet and lover of words, John Ciardi, used to say at the end of his etymological radio messages, "Good words to you."

WEB PAGES OF INTEREST

Wiktionary: http://en.wiktionary.org/wiki/Wiktionary:Main_Page
American Heritage Dictionary of the English Language: https://ahdictionary.com/
    Indo-European Roots Appendix:
    https://ahdictionary.com/word/indoeurop.html
Bartleby: Reference Books online: http://www.bartleby.com/61/
Oxford English Dictionary: http://dictionary.oed.com/
Free On-line Dictionaries: http://www.lib.washington.edu/research/dic.html
Behind the Name:
    History and Etymology of first names: http://www.behindthename.com/
Alpha Dictionary – various on-line dictionaries:
    http://www.alphadictionary.com/index.shtml

Free Rice for the Hungry
Help feed the hungry with the help of words: there is a web site through which for *every word you get right* a donation is made to the United Nations to help end world hunger: http://www.freerice.com/index.php.

Words migrate like goods
across lands, seas, and deserts
from lips into ears.

NOTES

1. The material in this section is treated more fully in Section One, Chapters One and Two.

2. More definitions and exercises using this material are found in Section One, Chapter Three.

3. This material is covered more fully in Section One, Chapters Four through Six.

4. Sometimes the etymology of a word is not known. For such words simply write "unknown" or "obscure." Sometimes, if you cannot find the etymology of a word, you can figure it out from the elements (or *etyma*).

SECTION ONE: HISTORY IN WORDS

CHAPTER ONE: FAMILIES OF LANGUAGES

Nearly seven thousand languages are spoken in the world today. These, along with their ancient ancestors, can be grouped into several hundred families of languages, each family descended from a common ancestor, which—though it may no longer be fully recoverable as a language—is known to have existed from the common roots and structures in known languages both ancient and modern. By comparing words and grammars, family relationships are recognized. Descent from a common ancestor is the criterion for placing a language in a given family.

The families of languages vary in size from as few as two distinct members to several hundred. INDO-EUROPEAN (I-E), the group to which English belongs is the largest, both in numbers of speakers (Spanish and English are the most widely spoken of its members) and in the number of its languages. Its name comes from its geographical range, extending across Europe in the West all the way to India in the East.[1] Not only does Indo-European include most of the languages of India, Persia, and Europe,[2] extending from Iceland, Ireland, and the Hispanic peninsula all the way to Sri Lanka (formerly called Ceylon), but through colonization it covers the Americas, Australia and New Zealand, and parts of Africa.

NOTES ON THE CONTRIBUTION OF NON-INDO-EUROPEAN LANGUAGES TO ENGLISH

This is not the place for a long description of the other families of languages, but a few remarks on words that have come into English from some of them will add to our appreciation of the diversity of English.[3]

1 AFRO-ASIATIC (also traditionally called Hamito-Semitic[4]): this family includes about three hundred living languages in a number of sub-groups. Among its languages are Arabic (the most widely spoken), Hebrew (both Biblical and Modern), Amharic (the official language of Ethiopia), Aramaic, Syriac (a dialect of Aramaic),

Akkadian (an extinct language of ancient Mesopotamia), ancient Phoenician, ancient Egyptian and its descendant Coptic, the Berber languages of North Africa, Hausa (a major language of West Africa).[5]

English has borrowed a number of words from this family. From Hebrew, words like amen, shibboleth, manna, rabbi, seraphim; from Arabic, admiral (from *emir*), saffron, mattress, hazard, zero, alcohol,; from Aramaic, Messiah (the anointed), mammon (through Latin and Greek from *mamona*, riches); from ancient Egyptian (through Latin and Greek), ebony, barge, elephant, ibis, Pharaoh; from Coptic, oasis (from *ouah*, to dwell).

Most of the words taken into English from Hebrew come from the Bible, though some were first borrowed by Greek or Latin and by English at second hand. Many Arabic words begin with *al-* which is the word for *the* (the article) in Arabic: for example, alfalfa, algebra, alcove, alchemy (the element *-chemy* is from Greek), elixir (< *al-iksir*, also from Arabic and Greek), artichoke (< *alkharshuf*), albacore. A large number of the entries from Arabic recall the splendor of classical Arabic culture and the contribution of Arabic scientific and mathematical discovery: of the latter, zero, cipher, algebra (literally, "the putting together of broken parts"); of the former, sofa, mattress, harem, mufti (meaning "civilian dress," but originally it meant a "legal scholar"), arsenal (originally, "a workshop").

The stories behind words are often fascinating, revealing aspects of history, culture, and religion.

SHIBBOLETH is such a word. It first came into English as a transliteration of its Hebrew original in Wyclif's 1382 translation of the Bible. The modern meaning of *shibboleth* is "a password, test, or watchword of a party or faction, that is distinctive of that particular group." Its meaning in Hebrew is "an ear of grain" or "a stream in flood." How did a word meaning "an ear of grain" or "a stream in flood." come to mean "a password"? The answer can be found by reading the passage in which the word occurs, *Judges* 12.4–6:

> Then Jephthah gathered all the men of Gilead and fought with Ephraim; and the men of Gilead smote Ephraim, because they said, "You are fugitives of Ephraim, you Gileadites, in the midst of Ephraim and Manasseh." And the Gileadites took the fords of the Jordan against the Ephraimites. And when any of the fugitives of Ephraim said, "Let me go over," the men of Gilead said to him, "Are you an Ephraimite?" When he said "No," they said to him, "Then say Shibboleth," and he said "Sibboleth," for he could not pronounce it right; then they seized him and slew him at the fords of the Jordan. And there fell at that time forty-two thousand of the Ephraimites. (RSV)

The word *shibboleth* was, as you see from the context, used by Jephtha to distinguish the fleeing Ephraimites, who could not pronounce the *sh*-sound, from his own men. For want of proficiency in their enemy's tongue, 42,000 men are reported to have perished in that genocidal slaughter. The meaning gradually extended from reference to this passage to more general use, and came to mean "any word or sound which can be used as a test to detect outsiders": for example, "They had a

Shibboleth to discover them, he who pronounced *Brot* and *Cawse* for *Bread* and *Cheese* hat his head lopt off" (John Cleveland, 1658). Later it extended to an even looser use: a custom, mode of dress or speech that distinguishes a class or group of persons; a password or formula adopted by a group to recognize its own members and exclude others.

2. SINO-TIBETAN is a large Asian family of over four hundred languages, including the Chinese languages, Burmese, and the tongues of Tibet. It has sometimes been divided into Sinitic (Chinese) and Tibeto-Burman. Most of the words from these languages that have come into English refer to items special to the culture of its speakers. From Chinese, we have borrowed such words as ginseng, tea (from the Amoy dialect; the Mandarin word is *ch'a*) and several of its varieties, pekoe, souchong, oolong, as well as tong, ketchup, japan (a kind of varnish, from the Chinese name for Japan [*Jihpun*, meaning sunrise]), tai chi, feng shui, wok, yin and yang, tofu. From Tibetan, lama (a Buddhist monk), Dalai Lama, yak. The word SILK has a connection to China and the Chinese: it shows numerous permutations in its passage along the linguistic silk road. It comes via Latin *sericum* from the Latin and Greek names *Seres* used to refer to an Asian people (possibly the Chinese) from whom they first obtained silk. Other words were borrowed first through translations and transliterations by missionaries, scholars of China (sinologists), maritime merchants, and later by immigrants from China to English-speaking countries, and by European colonization of Shanghai and Hong Kong, and, most recently, through globalization.

The JAPANESE language does not belong to this Asian family, but is on its own. English loanwords from Japanese were very rare until the opening of Japan to the West in the nineteenth century. Among the familiar Japanese words in English are kimono, sake, samurai, hara-kiri, gingko, geisha, origami, kamikaze (divine wind from *kami-*, divine and *kaze*, wind), as well as a number of Chinese words that Japanese borrowed before lending them to English, such as, soy, tycoon, jujitsu.

3. The URALIC family has two main sub-divisions: Finno-Ugric, which includes Magyar (Hungarian), Estonian, Finnish, and Lapp; and Samoyedic, the languages of the Samoyeds who inhabit the Eurasian tundra around the Ural mountains in Russia. English has borrowed from several languages in the group: from Finnish, sauna; from Lapp, lemming; from Magyar hussar, goulash, paprika, coach.

COACH, in all its meanings, comes to us from Magyar, the language of Hungary. It is derived from *kocsi*, meaning "of Kocs," a place near Buda in Hungary. Forms of the word—which came into use in Hungary in the late fifteenth century when a new kind of vehicle (a coach) was first built at Kocs—appear throughout Europe from the sixteenth century, in England as early as 1556. Its original name was *kocsi szeker*, "Kocs-cart" or, in Latin, *cocius currus*. The first meaning was a "large closed carriage," usually a state conveyance for royalty or high-ranking officials of the government (as "the Lord Mayor's coach"), or "a public carriage or stage-coach." Its use has extended to a railroad car, a bus, and the economy section of an airplane. The use of the word *coach* to apply to a private tutor who helps students prepare for examinations began as university slang in the nineteenth century: "Besides the regular college tutor, I secured the assistance of what, in the slang of the day, we irreverently termed 'a coach'" (1850). Some years later *coach* began to be used to mean an athletic trainer.

4. The ALTAIC[6] family includes Turkic (Turkish, Turkoman, Tatar, Uzbek), Tungus (spoken in Eastern Siberia), Mongolian, and, possibly, Korean. English words from this group include khan, horde, tulip, odalisque, turban, caftan, turquoise, yogurt, kiosk, pasha, fez, pilaf, balaclava, coffee, kimchi.

5. OTHER LANGUAGE GROUPS FROM WHICH ENGLISH HAS BORROWED

AUSTRONESIAN (once also called Malayo-Polynesian, but this is now considered a sub-group of Austronesian) includes Indonesian, Melanesian, Micronesian, Polynesian[7] (including Hawaiian).

Although there are no early loanwords from these languages and most have entered English since the latter part of the sixteenth century, some have become very familiar. As with many of the loanwords that have come to English through commerce, colonization, and travel, most of the words from these groups describe plants, animals, and products made from them that are characteristic of the area. For example, among the borrowings from Malay are sago, bamboo, gong, gingham, cockatoo, launch (a boat), bantam, caddy (for tea < *kati*, a weight), junk (the boat), rattan, raffia, batik, kapok, cootie, orangutan (or orangoutang < *orang hutan*, "man of the jungle"), amok (< *amuk*, "rushing in a frenzy to murder").

In the late eighteenth century, among Captain Cook's discoveries, are the first Polynesian words to come into English. Besides various names for new kinds of plants and parrots are words that have found a place in everyday English, such as, tattoo, taboo (also spelled tabu), poi, ukelele, luau, lanai, lei, hula, aloha, and wiki (meaning "fast," as in *Wikipedia*). The first word borrowed from aboriginal peoples of Australia was *kangaroo*, used by Captain Cook in his *Journals* for August 4, 1770. Others from the eighteenth and early nineteenth centuries are koala, boomerang, wombat and a number of other words describing native animals, plants, and trees.

KANGAROO: an amusing, if apocryphal, story is attached to this marsupial. Captain Cook writes, "The animals which I have before mentioned, called by the Natives Kangaroo or Kanguru" (1770). Clearly the worthy captain believed that this was the name given it by the natives of Queensland, Australia, but other explorers did not find the word in use. Thus the story grew up that when Captain Cook pointed at the remarkable creature and inquired, "What is that?" the bewildered native responded, "Kangaroo," meaning "I don't know." The debate over the name of the beast can be seen in diaries of later travelers. For example, as late as 1850, "It is remarkable that this word [kangaroo], supposed to be Australian, is not found as the name of this singular marsupial animal in any language of Australia" (Wilson). Such is the information to be found in the Oxford English Dictionary (*s.v. kangaroo*).

Whatever the origin of the word, whatever the aboriginal name for the being, it is now called kangaroo by all the Australian tribes, thanks to the English explorers, Captain James Cook and Sir Joseph Banks, and their anonymous knowing or inventive native informant.

NORTH AMERICAN: from North American native languages words began to come into English after 1607, the date of the refounding of the colony of Virginia. Later settlements brought the English language into contact with dialects further up the coast. Some of the native American words remain as resident aliens even in their native American land, used only to describe customs and objects of Native American culture, such as wigwam (from the Ojibwa language), wampum, tomahawk, and papoose (from Algonquin), tepee (from Sioux). Others are in more general use by English speakers: racoon, opossum, persimmon, moose, hominy, hickory, woodchuck, catalpa, pecan, caribou, succotash, tamarack, chipmunk, catawba, toboggan, moccasin, camas, chinook, kiva, potlatch; and from Eskimo kayak, umiak, igloo. Others, like the now obsolete mugwump, used to refer to a reform-minded but also rather sanctimonious American political movement of the nineteenth century (from Natick *mugquomp*, great chief) and powwow (from the Narragansett word for "shaman," but later, "conference") have been generalized to refer to the culture of English speakers.

SOUTH AND CENTRAL AMERICAN: once again we have many plant and animal names and the names of some very important foods, as well as some imported objects now in everyday use from the languages of South and Central America and the Caribbean. Plants and animals include iguana, yucca, petunia, tobacco, llama, condor, jaguar, coca, vicuna, ocelot, coyote. Foods include some we would not want to do without: cocoa, cayenne, potato, maize, chocolate, tomato, chili, avocado, cashew, tapioca; objects, etc.: canoe, hammock, poncho, barbecue, buccaneer.

AFRICAN languages have also contributed some important words to English. Among them Bantu (meaning "people," from the large Bantu family which includes Congo, Swahili, Zulu, Luba, Kikuyu, Luganda, and Nyana: < *ba*, a plural prefix + *ntu*, man). Common words from various African languages are zebra, gnu, gumbo, voodoo, banana, okra, yam, cola, chimpanzee, banjo, mojo, and zombie.

DRAVIDIAN languages are spoken by pre-Indo-European peoples of southern India and Sri Lanka and include Tamil, Telegu, and Malayalam. Words from these languages that are used in English include candy, teak, pariah (outcast, originally, a drummer).

EXERCISES

I.1 NON-INDO-EUROPEAN WORDS ADOPTED INTO ENGLISH

Choose a word from the list below and try to find the story behind it by answering the following questions. The best source for this information is the Oxford English Dictionary (OED).

1. What language does it come from? What family does that language belong to?
2. What does the word mean in its original language?
3. What does it mean in English?
4. If it has changed significantly in meaning, try to find out how it got from 2 to 3.
5. When did this word make its first appearance in English? Write down the date of and the quotation given for the first citation in the OED.
6. Consider the significance of the date of this entry into English: was it borrowed during a period of commercialism, exploration, imperialism, war? Or is it a religious or literary word?
7. Would you say that this word is a "naturalized citizen" in English, extended and used for something in our everyday lives, or is it a "resident alien," still used primarily to apply to an aspect of its native culture. Did we borrow an object with this word or have we applied it to something we already had? For example, for many Americans *couscous* is a delicious, but exotic food, but *sherbet* is right at home in our freezer and can be found at any supermarket.

The Words:

barge	admiral	hazard	mammon	sirocco	assassin
kosher	ghoul	safari	azimuth	nadir	gingham
minaret	jar	tunic	arsenal	caliber	alchemy
alfalfa	gnu	hegira	muezzin	harem	cinnamon
sherbet	candy	goober	mattress	potato	burnoose
mohair	elixir	fakir	Messiah	syrup	elephant
oasis	amen	rabbi	kimono	soy	couscous
lama	japan	ketchup	magazine	shekel	Pharaoh
tong	cabal	sash	jubilee	babel	behemoth
juke	launch	voodoo	macrame	gorilla	odalisque
tulip	amok	horde	pariah	tapioca	artichoke
mufti	zenith	tycoon	boogie-woogie		

Word Games

I.2 Match the words in column A to those in column B that are from the same Arabic root.[8]

A	B
1. admiral	a. Alcatraz
2. albatross	b. azimuth
3. assassin	c. cipher
4. syrup	d. emir

5. zenith   e. hashish
6. zero   f. sherbet

I.3 Match each word in column A with a word or phrase in column B that translates its original meaning. You may have to look some of these up, but first see if you can guess right.[9]

A	B
1. algebra	a. hereditary drummer
2. amok	b. striped
3. arsenal	c. the brine of pickled fish
4. assassin	d. great lord or chief (use twice)
5. Bantu	e. a die for coining
6. fakir	f. I do not know
7. gingham	g. ear of corn/stream in flood
8. japan	h. dwelling place
9. kamikaze	I. the people
10. kangaroo	j. man of the forest
11. ketchup	k. sun's origin
12. macrame	l. divine wind
13. magazine	m. a turban
14. mattress	n. the anointed
15. Messiah	o. a towel
16. mufti	p. shaman or medicine-man
17. mugwump	q. a storehouse
18. oasis	r. wine or other drink
19. orangutan	s. place where something is thrown
20. pariah	t. putting together of broken parts
21. powwow	u. eater of hashish
22. sequin	v. workshop
23. shibboleth	w. an Islamic scholar
24. syrup	x. a poor man
25. tulip	y. rushing in a frenzy to murder
26. tycoon	

NOTES

1. The term *Aryan*, from a Sanskrit word meaning "noble," was once used for Indo-Iranian, a sub-group of I-E, or for the whole Indo-European family, but for obvious reasons that term has fallen into disrepute and is now obsolete.

2. Most, but not all. There are European languages like ancient Etruscan and possibly Minoan, as well as the living languages, Basque, Hungarian, Estonian, and Finnish, that are not Indo-European; in India and Sri Lanka, the Dravidian languages are pre-Indo-European.

3. A useful website on English words from different languages is:
http://en.wikipedia.org/wiki/Lists_of_English_words_by_country_or_language_of_origin
Before citing information on individual words, check for accuracy in a good etymological dictionary. A fine book on the subject from the last century is Mary S. Sarjeantson. *A History of Foreign Words in English*. New York: Barnes & Noble, 1961.

4. Semitic, adj. of Semite, "a descendant of Shem" (the first son of Noah); Hamitic, from Hamite, "a descendant of Ham" (Noah's second son).

5. The famous Cleopatra, the last of the Ptolemies (whose native tongue was Macedonian Greek, but who also spoke Egyptian), was fluent in several languages in this group. According to Plutarch's *Life of Antony* she spoke to "Ethiopians, Troglodytes [or Trogodytes, peoples mentioned by various Greek historians and geographers in different locations, probably referring to an Ethiopian people in this passage], Hebrews, Arabians, Syrians, Medes, Parthians [these last two are in the Iranian or Persian group of I-E], and many others" without an interpreter.

6. Not long ago linguists made connections between the Uralic and Altaic families in a hypothetical group referred to as Ural-Altaic, but this term and the kinship it implies is now considered obsolete.

7. -nesian is from Greek *nēsos*, "island."

8. Answers to I.2: 1. d 2. a 3. e 4. f 5. b 6. c

9. Answers: I.3 1—t; 2—y; 3—v; 4—u; 5—I; 6—x; 7—b; 8—k; 9—l; 10—f; 11—c; 12—o; 13—q; 14—s; 15—n; 16—w; 17—d; 18—h; 19—j; 20—a; 21—p 22—e; 23—g; 24—r; 25—m; 26—d

SECTION ONE: HISTORY IN WORDS

CHAPTER TWO: THE INDO-EUROPEAN FAMILY OF LANGUAGES

The Indo-European family tree has eight main branches.[1] English belongs to the *Germanic* (or Teutonic) branch in its most basic vocabulary and grammatical structure, but has borrowed words from all the others, as well as from many languages that do not belong to the I-E family at all. Of the other branches, two will be considered in some detail in this book: *Italic*, which survives in Latin and the modern Romance languages (Italian, French, Spanish, Portuguese, Romanian, Catalan, Rhaeto-Romance, and Provençal[2]) and *Hellenic* (which is known from ancient Greek and Medieval texts and both spoken and written Modern Greek). Languages from these groups, especially Latin, Greek, and French, have greatly influenced and enlarged the vocabulary of English.

I ENGLISH AND OTHER GERMANIC LANGUAGES

That English belongs to the Germanic family is clear from a comparison of native words in some of the other languages in that branch.[3]

ENGLISH	GERMAN[4]	DUTCH	SWEDISH	NORWEGIAN	ICELANDIC	YIDDISH
good	gut	goed	god	god	godr	gut
thirst	Durst	dorst	törst	tørst	þorsti	darscht
book	Buch	boek	bok	bok	bók	buch
flask	Flasche	fles	flaska	flaske	flaska	flasch
arm	Arm	arm	arm	arm	armr	orm
kiss	Kuss	kus	kyss	kyss	kyssa	kisch
life	Leben	leven	liv	liv	lif	leben
knee	Knie	knie	knä	kne	kné	knie
learn	lernen	leren	lära	laere	laera	lernen
milk	Milch	melk	mjölk	melk	mjólk	milch
warm	warm	warm	varm	varm	varmr	varim
glass	Glas	glas	glass	glas	glas	glos

| son | Sohn | zoon | son | sønn | sonr | suhn |
| daughter | Tochter | dochter | dotter | datter | døttir | tochter |

These words are recognizable or almost recognizable to an English speaker. Many more German words can become familiar if you learn a few rules of consonant correspondence between the two languages.

1. English *t* usually shows up in German cognates as *z* at the beginning or end of a word, as *ss* in the middle of a word.

English	German
to	zu
tongue	Zunge
heart	Herz
(to) let	lassen
street	Strasse

2. English *p* appears in German as *pf* at the beginning of a word, as *f*, *ff*, or *pf* in other positions.

English	German
pepper	Pfeffer
harp	Harfe
plum	Pflaume
ape	Affe

3. Where English has *k*, German often has *ch*.

English	German
seek	suchen
cake	Kuchen
break	brechen
week	Woche

4. Where English has *d*, German has *t* or *tt*; where English has *th*, German has *d*.

English	German
do	tun
deed	Tat
death	Tod
bed	Bett
bread	Brot
thumb	Daumen
then	dann

The pairs in these lists are called COGNATES ("born together" < Latin *co-*, with, together + [*g*]*natus*, born).
Definition:

COGNATES are words in different languages that are derived from a common ancestor. It is possible to show correspondences not only among words in the various Germanic languages, but among all the languages in the Indo-European family.

II INDO-EUROPEAN CONSONANT CORRESPONDENCES

The discovery of the laws of consonant correspondence was the heroic feat of linguists of the nineteenth century, notably Jacob Grimm, a German philologist (one of the brothers Grimm who collected the famous fairy tales), and Karl Verner, a Danish philologist, who gave us, respectively, Grimm's Law and Verner's Law. These laws show how words in the language groups of the I-E family are related according to a regular pattern of change in consonants that are (generally speaking) produced in the same part of the mouth. Most often, for example, labials will correspond to labials, dentals to dentals, palatals to palatals.

Definitions:

LABIALS are those sounds formed with the lips closed, as p, b, f, v, ph (< Latin *labium*, lip).

DENTALS are those sounds formed with the tongue in the region of the teeth, as t, d, th (< Latin *dens, dent-*, tooth).

PALATALS are formed in the region of the hard or soft palate, as k, g, ch, y (< Latin *palatum*, palate).

Some Examples:

An original I-E *p*, which remains *p* in most of the other groups, changes to *f* in most of the Germanic tongues (in German the *f*-sound is represented by the letter *v*) and *v* in Dutch.

English: father

> German *Vater*; Dutch *vadar*; Swedish and Danish *fadar*; Norwegian *far*; Yiddish *foter*; Plautdietsch *Foda*
> Latin *pater*; French *père*; Spanish and Italian *padre*; Portuguese *pai*
> Greek *patēr*
> Sanskrit *pita*

I-E *s*, which remains *s* in most of the languages sometimes changes to *h* in Greek (*s* also becomes *h* in Avestan, Old Persian, and Armenian).

English: *stand*

> German *stehen*
> Latin *stare*
> Greek *histanai*

Sanskrit *stha*
Russian *stoyat*; Czech *stati*; Serbo-Croatian *stajati*; Polish *stać*

I-E *bh* remains *bh* in Sanskrit, but changes to *ph* in Greek, to *f* (or *b*) in Latin, to *b* in the Germanic languages and to *p* or *b* in the other branches.
English: BEAR (verb, to carry) and BRING
  German *bringen*
  Sanskrit *bhri*
  Old Irish *indber*
  Greek *pherein*
  Latin *ferre*
Or, to take another example, from the I-E root *bha-, to speak
  Old English *bannan* (to proclaim) yields Modern English ban, banns
  Latin *fari/fatum* (to speak), gives us infant, fate, fable, preface
  Greek *phanai* (to speak), *phēmē* (sound), *phōnē* (voice) give phone, telephone, phonetics, euphemism, cacophony and many others.

I-E *i/y* appears variously as *y, j* in most groups, but in Greek as *h* or *z* and in Old Engish and Middle Dutch as *g*. From the I-E root *yeug-, to join:
  Old English *geog* > Modern English yoke
  Latin *iugum* (yoke), *iungere* (join) > jugular, conjugate, subjugate, join, junction, adjunct.
  Greek *zugon* (yoke) > zygo-, syzygy, zeugma
  Sanskrit Yoga (union, yoking)

III SOME THINGS THAT ARE KNOWN ABOUT THE INDO-EUROPEANS

Indo-European is the relationship of all these eight branches—both ancient and modern—to each other: a relationship that indicates a common ancestor called Proto-Indo-European (PIE). PIE was in use long before the advent of writing and so left no direct trace, no hard copy, as it were. Writing has preserved for us some of the classical languages, Latin, Greek, Sanskrit, among them, ancient languages of which knowledge has never been lost. They were passed on from generation to generation in the natural way with the tongue (*lingua* > language), and when they ceased to be spoken in their classical forms, they continued to be preserved in the schools, much as they are today. It is not right to call these "dead languages." The death of a language comes hard and twinges of life appear again and again. Ancient Greek is not spoken as it was two and a half or three millennia ago, but its direct descendant, Modern Greek, closely preserves its roots and grammar, though the latter in a simplified form. Sanskrit is preserved and read by educated Hindus and scholars of the ancient religious texts, the Vedas (*Veda*, meaning "knowledge" comes from the PIE root *weid-, to see > English wise; Latin *vidēre*, to see; Greek *idea, historia*) and is preserved in languages spoken by millions, such as Hindi,

Urdu, Punjabi, Bengali, and Romany. Latin has left its mark through the classical texts, the basis of the Western Humanities, and through its linguistic impact not only on its direct descendants (the Romance languages), but also on English and many other languages.

From the relationship of words in the various members of the I-E family, linguists have come up with basic I-E roots, a dictionary, as it were, of the roots that can be reconstructed. These relationships are revealed through understanding sound correspondences among the scattered children of the Proto-Indo-European language and vowel gradation peculiar to individual offspring, studying the complex histories of the languages that have survived in spoken and written form, and delving into the histories of the people who spoke or speak them. The study of linguistics is the study of change. All languages change constantly, though the changes are often imperceptible to their speakers. NEOLOGISMS (newly coined words or phrases) are sudden changes that may seem outlandish at first.[5]

Though PIE cannot be known in its entirety and cannot be spoken, we use its roots every time we speak any of the many languages that belong to the family. In the early days of comparative linguistics, scholars sought religiously to find the pre-Babel mother tongue of the human race. Some thought is was Sanskrit. And Sanskrit did play a crucial role in the discovery of the parent of the I-E group. An English judge and philologist, Sir William Jones, noticed similarities among Sanskrit, Greek and Latin, Gothic, Celtic, and Old Persian, and realized that they must have sprung from a common source that no longer existed. The linguistic connection between East and West had been noticed before, but Jones' work with Sanskrit was a new starting point which—in the hands of a series of brilliant scholars—has shown the branches to be siblings, rather than descendants of Sanskrit, their related native words to be cognates rather than derivatives.

When we apply the term *family* and other words implying family relationships—kinship, mother-tongue, descendant, even cognate—to languages, we are using a metaphor, which makes a strange and distant concept more familiar and, in this case, homely. The family is an ancient institution known to the Indo-Europeans and the transference of terms indicating family relationships to other aspects of life and thought is an ancient Indo-European metaphor. The study of the common words in the various languages has not only made it possible for us to know I-E roots, but it has also told us some things about the nature of I-E society and environment. Language may be the most important and enduring aspect of culture and the aspect of language that offers the clearest and most cogent guide to what its users thought about and how they lived and perceived the world is vocabulary. The vocabulary of a language for a linguist is what potsherds and soil samples are for an archaeologist. The vocabulary of a language tells us what foods its speakers eat, what kinds of trees and animals they distinguish, what seasons and colors they recognize, what climate and economy they have, what they wear, what degrees of kinship they recognize as integral to the family unit, what gods they worship. Word study is the archaeology of a language. And—where archaeology is left behind—we can learn something about the minds of the speakers, how they perceive and think and feel about the world, how they define knowledge, and even how they perceive language.

Some Examples

1. Religion: The I-E word for *god* has been reconstructed as *deiw-os and the name of the chief god as *dyeupǝter. In Latin, he is called *Juppiter*, in Greek *Zeus patēr*, in Sanskrit, *Dyaus pitar*. However it is spelled, the pǝter element in these names means "father" and indicates a patriarchal society. It also shows the transference of an aspect of human society to the divine and suggests that the idea of "God the Father" is very old.

The meaning of the root *deiw- is "to shine" and it shows up in many words meaning "sky," "heaven," or "god," indicating that the chief god in the I-E pantheon was a sky and weather god, one who had to be propitiated by an agricultural people, dependent upon nature and the weather. Words from this root and their English derivatives include:

Germanic *Tiwaz* (Old English *Tiw, Tiu, Tig*), the god of war and sky, preserved in the word Tuesday. Latin *deus*, god, which survives in many English words, in-cluding: deity, Deism, adieu, joss, deification, deify. Latin divus, divine > divine, diva, divinity, divination. The name of the Latin goddess Diana (the luminous one or moon goddess) is from this root. So is the Latin word for "day," *dies* from which English has borrowed or developed dial, diary, dismal, diurnal, journal, adjourn, journey, sojourn, quotidian, meridian, a.m. and p.m. From the name of Juppiter (as it is spelled in Latin), besides the planet Jupiter, we get the name Julius ("descendant of Juppiter") and the name of the month *July* which was named after Julius Caesar. From the variant *Jove* the cheerful word *jovial* is derived, "born under the sign of Jove" (the source of happiness). The word *deiw-os itself with its association with brightness and day tells us as much about the Indo-European view of deity as would the discovery of temples, offerings, and other artifacts.

2. Family: Other words give evidence that the Indo-Europeans were a patriarchal society. The word *pǝter (Latin *pater*, Greek *patēr*, Sanskrit *pitar*, German *Vater*) means "father" in the sense of "adult male head of the household," as in the Latin expression *pater familas*. There are names for the in-laws of the bride, but not for the in-laws of the husband, indicating that she entered his home and became part of his family, as can also be seen in the Greek and Latin literary and artistic record. The social unit was probably the extended family: the root *bhrater (cf. English brother, Latin *frater*) seems to mean "fellow male member of the clan," and would extend to male relatives beyond those with common parents, as the Greek cognate *phratēr* ("fellow clansman"; cf. phratry) suggests. Likewise *swesor (cf. Latin *soror*, German *Schwester*, English sister) seems to mean a "female member of one's own group") and probably stems from the root *seu-, reflexive pronoun (that is, -self), referring to the members of a social group distinguished from outsiders. The significance of this root can be seen in a number of English derivatives, both native and borrowed:

Native English: self, sib ("related by blood"), sibling, gossip, swain (original meaning: "servant").

From Latin: suicide, per se; the prefix se- (without, apart, i.e., by onself) as in secede, seduce, secret, secure; possibly Latin solus (alone) as in solo, solitude, soliloquy; sodality (from sodalis, companion); suescere (to become accustomed, i.e., "to make one's own") > custom, consuetude, mansuetude.

Related to this root in Greek: *ēthos* (custom) > ethic and *ethnos* (people, nation) > ethnic.

From Sanskrit: Swami (originally "one's own master").

Words for community include *dem-, both "house" and "household":

Latin *domus, dominus* (house, master, head of the house) > domicile, domain, dominion, dominate, domestic, don, donna. In Greek *despotēs* (master of the house) > despot. Possibly English timber, i.e., "material for building a house."

*weik- represents the next unit, the village or clan:

Latin *vicus* (quarter of a town, neighborhood) and *villa* (farmhouse) > vicinity, villa, village, villain (originally, "a feudal serf"), wick. In Greek *oikos, oikia* (house, dwelling) > English words in eco- like economy, ecology; diocese, parish, monoecious, ecumenical.

Also *da- "division of society" gives Greek *dēmos* (the people) > deme, demos, democracy, demagogue, pandemic, epidemic, endemic.

3. Economy: The early Indo-Europeans were agricultural. They practiced stock-breeding and cultivation of cereals. The I-E word stock distinguishes several types of grain: corn (the predominant grain of a region), wheat, spelt, barley, rye: respectively *grano-, *yewo-, *puro-, *bhares-, *wrughyo-. There are words for ploughing, sowing, gathering, grinding, and for pasture land. We know what animals they bred: pigs (*su- and *porko-; cf. pork and swine); sheep and lambs (*owi- and *agwhno-; cf. ovine, Agnus Dei); goats (*aig- and *ghaido-; cf. aegis, Athena's goat-skin shield), cattle (or kine) (*g^{w}ou-, the root of Latin *bos, bov-* and Greek *bous* which give us such words as bovine, bucolic, butter, bugle). The dog (*kwon- > cynic from Greek, hound from Germanic; cf. *Hund*) was domesticated and may be the ancestor, liguistically speaking, of the horse (*ekwo- > Latin *equus* > equine, equestrian), which the Indo-Europeans were familiar with by the end of the third millennium B.C.E., a time of expansion and migration. They also knew metals and metallurgy: gold, silver, copper, bronze, and ore are common to the various groups, but words for iron, known to be a late-comer, vary in the different dialects. There are also words for a variety of household activities: weaving, crushing, cooking, sewing, spinning, shaping (both of dough for bread and mud or clay for building).

4. Environment: Some words for plants and animals and climate are particularly significant because they can help us locate the geographical borders of the I-E

peoples. Among the trees for which there is an I-E root is the beech, *bhago- (Latin *fagus*, Greek *phēgos*, Russian *buziná*, Serbo-Croatian *bâs*, Polish *bez*, Old English *bok*). Unfortunately these cognates may refer to different types of trees. Other trees that were known to the Proto-Indo-Europeans are birch, pine, aspen, poplar, willow, maple, alder, elm, ash, yew, and oak. Among the animals known to them were wolf, bear, beaver, mouse, hare; there are also generic names for wild beast and fish. Specific named fish include salmon and eel. The birds (*awi-: Latin *avis* > aviary) definitely known and named are crane, eagle, thrush, starling, sparrow, finch, woodpecker. Among insects are wasp, hornet, fly, bedbug, louse, and, of course, the bee and its honey, a source of sweetening and the base of the first certain I-E alcoholic beverage, mead (*medhu-; related to Greek *methu*, wine > amethyst[6], methylene). From the lack of a common word for *sea*, the I-E are believed to have lived inland, though they had boats and a word for rowing. There is a common word for *snow*, but, strangely, a variety of roots for *rain*.

5. Numbers: I-E speakers counted according to the decimal system. Common roots exist for the numbers *two* through *ten*, but words for the number *one* vary from dialect to dialect.

	I-E	Latin	Greek	German
2	*dwo	duo	duo	zwei
3	*trei	tres, tria	treis, tria	drei
4	*kwetwer	quattuor	tessares	fier
5	*penkwe	quinque	pente	funf
6	*sweks	sex	hex	sechs
7	*septm	septem	hepta	sieben
8	*okto	octo	oktō	acht
9	*newn	novem	ennea	neun
10	*dekm	decem	deka	zehn

The ways of expressing 11 and 12 in the vaious languages show that their speakers based their counting on tens:
English: *eleven* means "one left"; *twelve* means "two left," that is, left over after ten.
Latin: *undecim* is one (*unus*) + ten (*decem*); *duodecim* is *duo + decem*.
Greek: *hendeka* is one (*hen*) + ten (*deka*); *dōdeka* is *duo + deka*.

6. Mind, Memory, and Madness: The root *seu- (self) shows some degree of self-consciousness and awareness, both of the individual and the social group as an entity discrete from others, a *sine qua non* for much that we recognize as religion, history, philosophy, and art. The I-E root *men- (to think) has derivatives referring to different kinds of mental activity. English words from this root include the native *mind*: in the Germanic tongues one of the meanings of the root was "to love" and one of the words derived from it is minion (a favorite, a subordinate), an interesting alignment of meanings, especially taken with the Greek *mania* (madness, considered

a gift of the gods) that also comes from the same root. In addition to an ever-expanding list of manias we have borrowed maniac, manic, mantic, and maenad (an uninhibited worshiper of Dionysus) from the Greek side. From Latin *mens* (mind) are derived mental, demented, mention. The same root produces the verb *meminisse* (to remember) > memento, comment, reminiscent. It is an easy step from thinking to remembering: in Greek mythology and poetry, Mnemosyne (Memory, personified) is the mother of the Muses, patronesses of all the arts. Related words include mnemonic (aiding memory) < *mnēmē* (memory), amnesty, and amnesia (with the negative prefix a-).

Other roots for mental and perceptual activities are *gno- (to know) and *weid- (to see). The former has given us our native know, knowledge, cunning, and uncouth; gnome (a maxim), gnostic, agnostic, prognosis, diagnosis from Greek; notice, noble, recognize, and many others from Latin. From the latter English has many native Germanic words including wise, wisdom, wiseacre, wit. In Greek different forms of the same root mean both "to see" and "to know" and are the origin of idea, ideo-, kaleidoscope, idol, psychedelic, history, story. The Sanskrit sacred texts, the Vedas, are named from this root: *veda* means "knowledge." From Latin *vidēre* (to see) we have borrowed video, television, view, vision, advise, and many other common words.

Among roots relating to other-worldly matters are *wegwh- (to preach) which comes to us in vow, votive, devout, devotions, vote, from Latin; *gwer- (to praise) which yields grace, gratitude, gratify, ingrate, congratulations from Latin and bard from Celtic; *aiw- (life-force, age) > from Greek eon and from Latin longevity, medieval, primeval, coeval, eternity, eternal, sempiternal.

IV THE ITALIC BRANCH

The similarities among the modern languages, French, Italian, Spanish, Portuguese, and Romanian make it obvious that they are closely related. They are descended from Latin, the language of the ancient Romans and are called the Romance languages. Latin, itself, is a widely studied language with a great and unique literature and a continuous tradition. It is still in use as an official language of the Holy See. The reconstruction of Proto-Romance, the immediate ancestor of the modern Romance languages is very like the written language of Classical Latin texts, with some variations accounted for by the fact that Classical Latin is known primarily from literary texts that are somewhat more formal than the language people spoke (Vulgar Latin). The spoken language had a greater effect on the formation of the modern languages than did the written language. We do have surviving samples of writing that is close to Vulgar Latin in the dialogue of comedies, fiction, personal letters, some lyric poetry, and handwriting on the walls (graffiti). Written Latin is still a source of learned words, words adopted or coined by scholars and scientists.

LATIN AND HER CHILDREN

A few examples will give an idea of the relationship between Latin and her children.

Latin & Romance	English Derivatives from the Latin
1. MATER, mother	maternal, maternity, matrix, matron
Italian: madre	matriculate, matrimony, matricide,
French: mère	matrilineal, matter[7]
Spanish: madre	
Portuguese: mãe	
Romanian: mamă	

Fill in additional derivatives for each Latin word:

2. PATER, father   paternal
Italian: padre
French: père
Spanish: padre
Portuguese: pai
Romanian for *father* is not from this root

3. SOROR, sister[8]   sorority
Italian: sorella
French: soeur
Romanian: soră

4. FRATER, brother   fraternity
Italian: fratello
French: frère
Spanish and Portuguese are from a different Latin word, the adj. *germanus*.
Romanian: frate

5. FILIUS, son; FILIA, daughter   affiliate
Italian: figlio, figlia
French: fils, fille
Spanish: hijo, hija
Portuguese: filho, filha
Romanian: fiu, fiică

6. NOX, base: noct-, night   nocturnal
Italian: notte
French: nuit
Spanish: noche
Portuguese: noite
Romanian: noapte

7. CAELUM, sky   celestial
Italian: cielo
French: ciel
Spanish: ceilo
Portuguese: céu

    Romanian: cer

8. DEUS, god   deity
    Italian: dio
    French: dieu
    Spanish: dios
    Portuguese: deus
    Romanian: dumnezeu

9. PRIMUS, first   primordial
    Italian: primo
    French: premier
    Spanish: primero
    Portuguese: primeiro
    Romanian: primul

10. HOMO, homin-, human being   homunculus
    Italian: uomo
    French: homme
    Spanish: hombre
    Portuguese: homem
    Romanian: om

11. PAX, pac-, peace   pacifist
    Italian: pace
    French: paix
    Spanish: paz
    Portuguese: paz
    Romanian: pace

12. DORMIRE, sleep   dormitory
    Italian: dormire
    French: dormir
    Spanish: dormir
    Portuguese: dormir
    Romanian: dormi

13. FOCUS, hearth (with derivatives meaning *fire*)   focal, curfew
    Italian: fuoco
    French: feu
    Spanish: fuego
    Portuguese: fogo
    Romanian: foc

14. NOMEN, nomin-, name   nominate, noun
    Italian: nome
    French: nom
    Spanish: nombre
    Portuguese: nome
    Romanian: nume

15. PISCIS, fish   pisces, piscivorous
    Italian: pesce
    French: poisson
    Spanish: pescado
    Portuguese: peixe
    Romanian: peşte
16. BIBERE, drink   bibulous
    Italian: bere
    French: boire
    Spanish: beber
    Portuguese: beber
    Romanian: bea

EXERCISES

EXERCISE II.1.A. — ENGLISH/GERMAN: following the rules of consonant correspondence between English and German, try to figure out the English equivalents of these German words. The vowel in brackets is given as an added hint for those words with a different vowel in the English word.

Examples: German *Pfeife* (whistle) ~ English pipe

German *Wasser* ~ English water

Nouns & Adjectives:	Verbs:
Milch	danken
Pflanze	denken [i]
Salz	trinken
Zoll	machen
Apfel	baden
Dorn	pflücken
Pfad	brechen [ea]
besser	vergessen [ver: for]
Bad	helfen
tief [ee]	
Durst [i]	
Wasser	
Bruder [o]	
Kupfer [o]	

EXERCISE II. 1. B. — ENGLISH/GERMAN COGNATES: match the German word with its English equivalent:[9]

German	English
1. Blatt	a. clothing
2. vierzig	b. door

3. zwei	c. eat
4. Tür	d. forty
5. tief	e. two
6. essen	f. beard
7. Kleidung	g. blade
8. Bart	h. deep
9. schlafen	I. hind (behind)
10. hinten	j. sleep
11. Geburtstag	k. blood
12. Blut	l. dream
13. Tanz	m. birthday
14. Traum	n. forbidden
15. verboten	o. hate
16. hassen	p. thick
17. dick	q. dance

EXERCISE II.1. c. — COGNATES: Try to think of English words that are cognate to these German Words. The meaning of the German word is given as a clue: think of an English synonym or related word that sounds more like the German word.

German Word	Definition	English Cognate
Ex. schwarz	black	*swarthy*
Busen	breast	*bosom*
Be*grab*nis	funeral	*grave*
*Burg*er	citizen	*burg*
1. unten	below	
2. Gürtel	belt	
3. Vogel	bird	
4. Kessel	boiler	
5. Knabe	boy (In playing cards, an alternate for "Jack.")	
6. Wagen	car	
7. Vorsicht	caution	
8. Fracht	cargo	
9. tragen	carry	
10. Jahrhundert	century (Use two or three words.)	
11. Stuhl	chair	
12. Glocke	bell, chime	
13. Mantel	coat	
14. richtig	correct	
15. Zollhaus	customs house	
16. Worterbuch	dictionary (Use two words.)	
17. Hund	dog	
18. Esel	donkey	
19. nieder	down	

20. Mehl	flour
21. Kalbflesch	veal (Use two words.)
22. Blume	flower
23. Handschuh	glove (Use two words.)
24. wachsen	grow
25. Hafen	harbor
26. Landstrasse	highway (Use two words.)
27. Sprache	language
28. mittags	noon
29. Schweinefleisch	pork (Use two words.)
30. riechen	smell
31. Ofen	stove
32. Wert	value
33. Mittwoch	Wednesday

EXERCISE II. 2. A.—I-E NOTIONS: using an etymological dictionary and a dictionary of I-E roots (the most convenient is Appendix I of the *American Heritage Dictionary of the English Language*), chose three of these words and roots. Find out the original meaning of the roots and try to figure out how the words came to mean what they do today. Give two or more related English words.

1. pastor — root *pa-
2. pecuniary — root *peku-
3. wagon — root *wegh
4. wheel — root *kwel-
5. textile — root *teks-
6. dough — root *dheigh-
7. mere (a body of water) — root *mori-
8. demon — root *da
9. mind — root *men-
10. know — root *gno-
11. wise — root *weid-

EXERCISE II. 2. B. I-E ROOT CANALS: following the simplified chart of consonant correspondences, choose an English cognate from column I and an English derivative from column II to match the Greek [G] or Latin [L] word(s) at the left.

SIMPLIFIED CHART OF CONSONANT CORRESPONDENCES

I-E	Greek	Latin	Germanic	Old English	Modern English
p	p	p	f	f	f
t	t	t	th	th	th
k	k	c	h	h	h
kw	p/t/k	qu	hw	hw	wh
b	b	b	p	p	p

d	d	d	t	t	t
g	g	g	k	k	k
gw	b/d/g	v/gu	kw/k	cw/k	qu/c
bh	ph	f (b)	b	b	b
dh	th	f (d)	d	d	d
gh	kh/ch	h	g	g	g/y
gwh	ph/th/ch	f	gw	w	
s	h	s	s	s	s
m	m	m	m	m	m
n	n	n	n	n	n
r	r/rh	r	r	r	r
l	l	l	l	l	l
i/y	h/z	j	j	g/y	y
w/u		v	w	w	w

Latin/Greek	English Cognates I	Derivatives II
(1)[10]		
1. AD to [L]	1. who, which	1. quiddity
2. TO the [G]	2. harvest	2. cornucopia
3. PORTUS harbor [L]	3. the	3. tautology
4. CARPERE to pluck [L] (cf. Greek KARPOS fruit)	4. horn	4. addition
5. CORNU horn [L]	5. wheeze	5. querulous
6. QUIS/QUID who/what? [L]	6. at	6. carpet
7. QUERI complain [L]	7. ford	7. opportune
(2)		
1. BACULUM rod, stick [L]	1. tusk, tooth	1. symbiosis
2. BULLIRE boil [L]	2. kind	2. revenue
3. DENS, DENT- tooth	3. kneel	3. palindrome
4. DROMOS a running [G]	4. peg	4. geranium
5. GENOS race, family [G]	5. puff, poach	5. genuflect
6. GERANOS crane [G]	6. come	6. ebullient
7. GENU knee [L]	7. queen	7. genealogy
8. VENIRE come	8. quick	8. gynecocracy
9. BIOS life [G]	9. crow, crane	9. dentures
10. GYNE, GYNEC- woman [G]	10. tread	10. bacillus
(3)		
1. PHAINEIN bring to light [G]	1. bite/bit	1. habitat
2. FAR spelt [L]	2. drone	2. chlorophyll
3. FINDERE/FISSUS split [L]	3. give	3. efficiency
4. FACERE do [L]	4. gape	4. fission
5. THRĒNOS dirge [G]	5. do	5. threnody

6. FORAS out of doors [L] 6. beacon 6. farina
 cf. Greek THURA door
7. HABĒRE have/hold 7. yellow (OE gealu) 7. chasm
8. CHASMA gulf [G] 8. door 8. forest
 cf. Latin HIATUS a gaping
9. CHLŌROS greenish yellow [G] 9. barley 9. phantasm
(4)
1. HORA season [G] 1. yoke 1. syzygy
2. JUVENIS young [L] 2. weight 2. horoscope
3. ZUGON yoke [G] IUGUM [L] 3. weather, wind 3. ochlocracy
4. VENTUS wind [L] 4. year 4. ventilate
5. OCHLOS mob [G] 5. youth 5. rejuvenate
 cf. Latin VEHERE carry

EXERCISE II. 2. C. MATCH RELATED WORDS:[11]

English Natives	Derivatives from Greek or Latin
1. wear	1. vespers [L]
2. way	2. heptad [G]
3. western	3. bucolic [G]
4. werewolf	4. vest [L]
5. dunk	5. quorum [L]
6. seven	6. cynic [G] < *kuon*, dog
7. yoke	7. convey [L]
8. cow	8. virile [L]
9. whom	9. tint [L]
10. hound	10. zeugma

EXERCISE II. 3. LATIN AND HER CHILDREN

II. 3. A. Look over the lists of Latin words in section III and fill in the blanks:
1. Filial duty is the obligation of the _____ to his/her parents.
2. Matrimony etymologically is the state of being a _____.
3. Patrimony is the inheritance from the _____.
4. Fraternities and sororities are associations of _____ and _____.
5. A nocturnal predator hunts at _____.
6. Celestial beings live in the _____.
7. A hominid resembles a _____.
8. To pacify is to make _____.
9. A dormitory is a place for _____.
10. Primeval forests are from the _____ age.
11. The Pax Romana was a time of relative _____.

II. 3. B. Find:
1. At least five derivatives of *pater* and *primus*.

2. At least three derivatives of *nox*, noct-; *pax*, pac-; *dormire*; *focus*.

III.3. C. Fill in Latin words or bases:
1. The killing of another human being is called _____cide.
2. The "Our Father" in Latin is called the _____ Noster.
3. The greeting "peace be with you" in Latin is _____ vobiscum.
4. The astrological sign of the fish is called _____.
5. Another word for *drink* is im_____.
6. A synonym for *brotherly* is _____nal.
7. A case to establish fatherhood is called a _____nity suit.
8. Our species is _____ *Sapiens*.
9. A synonym for *to name* is _____ate.
10. *In name only* can be expressed by the word _____al.

III.3. D. Choose one or two of the following Latin Words and try to find the Italian, French, Spanish, Portuguese, and Romanian forms and give three of more English derivatives.[12]
Example: 12. *frenum* (bridle, brake): Italian *freno*; French *frein*, Spanish *freno*, Portuguese *freio*, Romanian *frână*; English derivatives frenum, frenulum, refrain, fraise (a defensive barrier or a neck ruff).

1. totus (all)
2. mors, mort- (death)
3. corpus, corpor- (body)
4. lingua (tongue, language)
5. vita (life)
6. scribere (write)
7. annus (year)
8. vendere (sell)
9. manus (hand)
10. crescere (grow)
11. arbor (tree)
12. frenum (bridle, brake)
13. vetus, veter- (old)
14. liber (free)
15. alter (another)
16. saeculum (age)
17. oculus (eye)
18. dulcis (sweet)
19. vidēre (see)
20. altus (high, tall)
21. sanguis (blood)
22. venire (come)
23. nux, nuc- (nut)
24. rex, reg- (king)
25. bonus (good)
26. ovum (egg)
27. ventus (wind)
28. fumus (smoke)

NOTES

1. For a handy chart, see the end paper of the *American Heritage Dictionary*; online: https://web.cn.edu/kwheeler/IE_Main2_Centum.html.

2. Catalan is the language of Catalonia in northeastern Spain and in the nearby area of France; Rhaeto-Romance is spoken in northern Italy and southern Switzerland, named after the Roman province of Rhaetia; Provençal is a group of dialects spoken in southern France.

3. Other limbs of this branch are Frisian (used in the coastal areas of the Netherlands and Germany), Flemish (a Dutch language spoken in Flanders in northern Belgium), Faroese (spoken in the Faroe Islands), Afrikaans (an offshoot of Dutch used in South Africa and Namibia) and Low German. Some of the words listed here and in the next section as they occur in PLAUTDIETSCH, or Mennonite Low German (the language of the Mennonite community in the Vistula region, which they brought into Russia in the late eighteenth century and which is still spoken by the Russian Mennonites in Latin America, the United States, and Canada) are: good, *gout* or *goot*; thirst, *Darscht*; book, *Büak*; arm, *Oarm*; life, *Läwe*; knee, *Kjnee*; learn, *leare*; milk, *Malkj*; warm, *woam, woarm*; glass, *Glauss*; son, *Sän*; daughter, *Dochta*; heart, *Hoat*; tongue, *Tung*. Sources: http://www.mennolink.org/doc/lg/dict.ea.html and http://en.wikipedia.org/wiki/Plautdietsch_language.

4. Note that nouns are capitalized in German.

5. For example, some of the new usages in 2014 are *tweep* (a person who tweets), *crowd-funding, selfie, freegan* (someone who avoids spending money by scavenging for food), *hashtag, steampunk, to primary,* and *to second-amendment* (that is, to shoot someone, which I hesitate to call a euphemism). On the other hand, a festive neologism of 2013 is *Thanksgivukkah*, the once in a lifetime coinciding of Thanksgiving and Hanukkah. Of recent coinage is *Brexit*, the proposed and passed British exit from the European Union. Offensive neologisms are known as *Frankenwords*.

6. Amethyst < *a*-, not + *methu* (wine) was a cure for intoxication.

7. From Latin *materies,* tree trunk, i.e., the tree's source of growth.

8. The Spanish and Portuguese words *hermana* and *irma* are from Latin adj. *germanus, -a,* of the same stock, born of the same parents, i.e., "full (sister or brother)".

9. Answers: II.1.B 1–g; 2–d; 3–e; 4–b; 5–h; 6–c; 7–a; 8–f; 9–j; 10–I; 11–m; 12–k; 13–q; 14–l; 15–n; 16–o; 17–p.

10. Answers:II. 2. b (1) 1–6,4; 2–3,3; 3–7,7; 4–2,6; 5–4,2; 6–1,1; 7–5,5.
Answers: II. 2. b (2) 1–4,10; 2–5,6; 3–1,9; 4–10,3; 5–2,7; 6–9,4; 7–3,5; 8–6,2; 9–8,1; 10–7,8. Answers: II. 2. b (3) 1–6,9; 2–9,6; 3–1,4; 4–5,3; 5–2,5; 6–8,8; 7–3,1; 8–4,7. Answers: II. 2. b (4) 1–4,2; 2–5,5; 3–1,1; 4–3,4; 5–2,3.

11. Answers II.2. c.: 1–4; 2–7; 3–1; 4–8; 5–9; 6–2; 7–10; 8–3; 9–5; 10–6.

12. Try http://www.wordhippo.com/ for help with finding words in various languages. The *American Heritage Dictionary* will help with finding derivatives.

SECTION ONE: HISTORY IN WORDS

CHAPTER THREE: SOME DEFINITIONS

Now that we have worked with some examples of words in history, it is time for definitions.

> The ROOT is the most basic element of the word.

For many words in English, both native and foreign, we can trace the root back to an Indo-European word element. Large vocabularies grew up in the various languages after the dispersion of the original Indo-Europeans and later in the separation of the branches into the languages used today. It is not possible, however, to discover an I-E root for every native word. Roots are, nevertheless, very useful in finding cognates.

> COGNATES are words in different languages derived from the same root.

For example, English *know* is cognate with Latin *cognoscere* (to be acquainted with) and Greek *gignōskein* (to know) since they all share the same root *gno-.

> The BASE of a word is that element from which other words are formed by adding affixes, that is, prefixes and suffixes. AF-FIX (used for either prefix or suffix)"something fastened to": PRE-FIX "fastened before," SUF-FIX "fastened under" (i.e., after).

For example: the base of the word *diagnosis* is the Greek base *gno-* (base of the verb *gignōskein*); diagnosis breaks down to:

prefix: *dia-*, through, thoroughly
base: *gno-*, know
suffix: *-sis*, act or process of

Or its cognate *acknowledgment*:

prefix: *ac-* (from Old English), on
base: *know*, know

suffix: *ledg*(e) — of obscure origin

suffix: *ment*, act, state of < Latin *-mentum*: this is an early instance of the addition of this suffix to a native word.

The vocabulary of a language can be said to be made up of NATIVE WORDS and words borrowed from other languages, called LOANWORDS. In English, native words are those inherited from Anglo-Saxon (or Old English). These form the backbone of English and are the most commonly used words. Many of our native words have cognates in the other tongues of the Germanic branch, for example, English good, German *gut*, Dutch *goed*, Icelandic *goðr*. But the English language has also freely admitted words from other languages into its vocabulary. Sometimes these are words for new things picked up through contact with the speakers of other languages. Sometimes new words are borrowed from literature and learning: these are called LEARNED WORDS. The languages that have added the most words to our vocabulary are Latin (long the language of learning, culture, and religion), French (from long contact with the British Isles, through diplomacy, education, and conquest), and Greek (the source of many learned words including technical terms in all fields).

The borrowing of words from other languages has a long tradition in English: the vocabulary of Anglo-Saxon has a number of everyday words taken from the classical tongues. For example, the word *pepper* is borrowed from Greek, but the Greeks themselves had long before borrowed it from an Indic language. The exact transmission is not known, but Greek *peperi* is probably connected with Sanskrit *pippali* (berry). The word *street* is also a very early entry, this time from Latin (*via strata*, "a road or way [that is] paved"). Evidence that these words were borrowed before the Anglo-Saxons departed continental Europe, crossing the English Channel and breaking with their linguistic kin, is the fact that these words occur in slightly varied, but clearly cognate, forms in other Germanic tongues:

1. STREET — German *Strasse*; Dutch *straat* < Latin [*via*] *strata*
2. PEPPER — German *Pfeffer*; Dutch *peper*; Swedish & Norwegian *pepper*; Danish *peber*; Yiddish *fefer*; Plautdietsch *Päpa* < Latin *piper* < Greek *peperi* < (perhaps) Sanskrit *pippali*

In addition to countless loanwords from Greek and Latin, English has many COINED WORDS (made up words) and CONSTRUCTED WORDS (words put together from already existing elements). Such words often are put together using word elements from Greek or Latin, or both, and may include elements from other languages too.

Some examples:

ABSQUATULATE "to get up and squat elsewhere" was constructed from Latin prefix and suffixes + the English word *squat* (itself ultimately from Latin *cogere*, compress).

TELEVISION is from the Greek prefix *tele-*, from afar + *vision* from Latin *visio*, sight < *visus*, seen.

SOCIOLOGY from Latin *socius* (companion) and *-logia* < Greek *logos* (word, reason) The long and uncomely construction, a favorite of grade-school children as the longest non-technical word in an English dictionary,[1] ANTIDISESTABLISH-MENTARIANISM ("the doctrine of those opposed to the removal from the status of State Chuch") is built up from the base *-establ-* < Latin *stabilire*, to make firm < *stare*, to stand < I-E root *STA-, stand + two prefixes and an almost unseemly number of suffixes:

Prefixes:

　　anti- (<Greek *anti*), against

　　dis-, a Latin inseparable prefix indicating reversal

Suffixes:

　　-ish a verbal formant influenced by French

　　-ment, state of < Latin noun-forming suffix *-mentum*

　　-ari-, pertaining to from Latin *-arius*

　　-an-, one who (also of, belonging to) < Latin *-anus*

　　-ism, doctrine of < Greek *-ismos*

A word made up by the addition of prefixes and suffixes is called an AGGLUTINATIVE CONSTRUCTION. Clearly *antidisestablishmentarianism* is a word made up or coined from classical elements, but it does not represent a concept known to the ancient Romans or Greeks.

　　A newly coined or constructed word that has not yet gained wide acceptance is called a NEOLOGISM (< *neo-*, new + *log-*, word + *ism*, usage, all Greek elements).[2] Recent examples include to google, app, e-memes, staycation, metrosexual, ammosexual, chilax (a combination of chill and relax), stagflation (a situation of economic standstill with steadily rising prices), Obamacan (a Republican supporter of President Obama), Obamacare, Clintonomics (the economic policies of President Clinton; see also Nixonomics, Reaganomics), locavore (a person who avoids food produced on corporate farms, preferring to eat locally-grown products), freegan (a person who stays off the economic grid by availing him-/herself of whatever is free), affluenza (the defense, apparently successful in at least one case, that one's opulent and undisciplined up-bringing renders one incapable of telling right from wrong). All but the first two are also PORTMANTEAU[3] WORDS, words formed by blending the sounds and meanings of two different words, a phrase coined by Lewis Carroll in *Through the Looking Glass*: "Well," wrote Lewis Carroll, "'slithy' means 'lithe and slimy' . . . you see it's like a portmanteau—there are two meanings packed up into one word." A NONCE WORD is a new word created for a single occasion, "for the nonce". *Quark* started as a nonce word, coined by James Joyce in *Finnegan's Wake*, "Three quarks for Muster Mark" but came to be used for a new class of sub-atomic particle. Stephen Colbert's *truthiness* seems to be a nonce word with staying power. A GENERONYM is a particular commercial name that has come to be used for the whole type of product: kleenex, aspirin, xerox, zipper, granola, band-aid, jell-o, hoover are examples.

　　The science that studies word origins is called ETYMOLOGY (< *etymos*, true +

logos, word + *-ia*, an abstract-noun-forming suffix), that is, *etymology* seeks the truth of words from their origins. The word *etymology* is also used of the origin of individual words. When we ask "what is the etymology of this word?" we mean what are its origins, its component parts, what language(s) does it come from. In a broader sense the etymology of a word is its whole biography, not only its elements, but when and where it originated, how its form and meaning developed over the years. For some words this makes an exciting story.

Example: A short etymology of VERNACULAR: noun, "the standard native language of a country or region; the idiom of a trade or profession"; adjective, "native to or commonly spoken by persons in a country or region."

Origin: Latin *vernaculus*, adj. "having to do with a *verna*" i.e., native, domestic < *verna*, a home-grown slave (that is, a slave born in the household rather than bought) + *-ar*, of, adjective-forming suffix.

Usage: The earliest citation of the word vernacular in English is from 1601. In Latin the words *verna* and *vernaculus* occur in a variety of uses, but the English is restricted to language. This usage may come from the Roman writer, Varro (first century B.C.E.) who used the phrase *vernacula vocabula* (native words).

Contexts (cited in the OED):

1788: Brown . . . preferred polysyllabic expressions, derived from the language of ancient Rome, to his *vernacular* vocabulary.

1832: The congregation here being chiefly peasants and artisans, a sermon was delivered in the *vernacular* dialect.

1848: Low-born *vernacular* idioms were handed down to posterity as the poet's creation.

Useful Reference Works:

The dictionary that gives the most information about the life stories of English words is the *Oxford English Dictionary* [OED] in twenty volumes (but available on line and in a compact one-volume edition) which covers 1000 years, with over a million quotations to illustrate the first appearance and every notable point in the biography of each word. Another useful dictionary is the *American Heritage Dictionary of the English Language* which, though much smaller than the OED, offers a useful tool for finding cognates and derivatives in the list of Indo-European roots in Appendix I. Various etymological dictionaries are also available on line.

EXERCISES

EXERCISE III.1 — NATIVES AND NATURALIZED ALIENS

A. NATIVE ENGLISH WORDS: using the OED and other dictionaries, find out the history of one of these words, how did it develop, what other words are derived from it or related to it; has its meaning, spelling, or use changed over the centuries, can you find words cognate with it in the other I-E tongues, especially the other Germanic languages?

the	this	that	it	man	woman	son	daughter
and	love	will	have	be	by	for	or
he	she	if	a/an	not	in	to	then
there	tell	when	which	of	on	get	

B. NATURALIZED ALIENS: the following words are imports from various I-E branches. They have become so English that they do not need italics. Find out:
— when the word first entered English [use the OED]
— what it means in English
— what it means in its original language,
— what is the original language and which branch of I-E that language belongs to,
— whether there are native English cognates or cognates borrowed from other languages (the American Heritage Dictionary will help with this).

crooked	skill	very	wing	smelt
rich	picnic	wainscot	uproar	contraband
traffic	motto	zany	cargo	umbrella
ditto	gusto	cork	sherry	whisky
rodeo	druid	shamrock	massage	leprechaun
steppe	guitar	vodka	tiger	mammoth
karma	pundit	cot	jute	marmelade
mummy	magi	gremlin	boor	keen (lament)
rent (payment)				

EXERCISE III. 2 — HEROES AND VILLAINS OF VOCABULARY: An etymology is the biography of a word, its life history. The words in this list come from people's names (also called EPONYMS[4]). Choose one or two and find out:
—What does the word mean in common speech?
—Who was the person? How and why did his/her name become attached to this thing or act?
—Do you think the transference of the proper name to the common word was justified?

WILLIAM BURKE, a villain of vocabulary

Example: BURKE (v.) "to murder by strangulation or suffocation, originally for the purpose of selling the body for dissection in the laboratory."

BURKE, a word with a gruesome meaning and etymology, comes from the name of William Burke, hanged for murder in Edinburgh, Scotland in 1829. William Burke and his partner in crime, William Hare, inhabited a rather seedy section of Edinburgh in the early nineteenth century. One evening a visitor happened to pass away in their rooming house. Rather than going to the trouble of disposing of his mortal remains in the traditional manner, or risk reporting his demise to the authorities, the two men carted the corpse off to the university and sold it for the use of medical students, apparently with no questions asked. The receipt of seven pounds sterling for an otherwise useless carcass set the two on the road to crime. They began enticing men, with the offer of drink, to their rooms and no longer waited for the unlikely event of their dying of natural causes. Instead they carefully smothered them so as to leave their bodies intact for dissection in the anatomy lab without causing more suspicion than could be winked away.

Fifteen or more unfortunate wayfarers were sacrificed to science and avarice before the two murderers were caught and put on trial. On February 2, 1829, the day of Burke's execution, the *Times* of London contained this item:

As soon as the executioner proceeded to his duty, the cries of "Burke him,

Burke him, give him no rope" were vociferated. "Burke Hare too."

The meaning of *to burke* has been extended to include "to hush up, keep quiet." By 1840, this figuative use appeared, "The Age of Chivalry is *Burked* by Time."

PEOPLE WORDS for Exercise III. 2

bloomers	abigail	babbitt	batiste
Bessemer	billingsgate	bowdlerize	boycott
braille	camellia	chauvinism	cardigan
derrick	doily	dunce	thespian
Frankenstein	galvanize	gardenia	gargantuan
gerrymander	guillotine	August	lynch
macabre	macadam	mackintosh	martinet
bowie knife	maudlin	mausoleum	mercerize
mesmerism	nicotine	namby-pamby	graham cracker
quisling	quixotic	shrapnel	silhouette
simony	Melba toast	spoonerism	tweed
ampere	begonia	bobby	Ferris wheel
chesterfield	dahlia	derby	derringer
diesel	Fahrenheit	forsythia	fuchsia
greengage	hansom	leotard	lobelia
magnolia	masochism	maverick	napoleon
ohm	pasteurize	philippic	pickle
poinsettia	pompadour	Pullman	raglan
sadist	sandwich	saxophone	sequoia
sideburns	teddy bear	timothy	volt
watt	wisteria	zeppelin	zinnia
Levis	czar/Kaiser	mentor	axel
Bakelite	chartreuse	decibel	epicure
Faraday	galvanize	hector	iris
jackanapes	klieg	luddite	madeleine
newton	onanism	pants	quixotic
ritzy	salmonella	tantalize	petri dish
uzi	valentine	welly	

SPOONERISMS are phrases in which the sounds of two or more words are transposed, as in "Let me sew you to your sheet," for "Let me show you to your seat." The term comes from the name of the Reverend William Spooner, a nineteenth century cleric, who was alleged to have habitually committed such amusing errors. Examples include "at one fell swoop"; "three cheers for of queer old dean"; "the Lord is a shoving leopard"; "you've tasted this whole worm."

EXERCISE III.3 — NEOLOGISMS: newly coined words come and go. They must be collected on the wing, on the fly, or on the hoof. Look and listen for them, especially on the internet, in blogs, in magazines, on the radio and TV. Keep a list of the ones you see or hear with provenance (where you heard them), the meaning or a phrase using them, and date. These will be particularly widespread during political campaigns.
Examples:

> January 21, 2015: *Boston Globe* on-line — deflate-gate, the allegation that the New England Patriots used underinflated footballs to gain an advantage in the pre-superbowl game.
> February 13, 2015:
> (1) NPR *Morning Edition* — reformicon, a conservative allegedly interested in reform.
> (2) Facebook (*Portside* page) — testocracy, the privileging of the affluent through standardized testing.
> May 30, 2015: NPR *Weekend Edition* — eggcorn, a creative use of language that involves the use of a word or phrase that is a plausible alteration of another word or phrase that sounds similar but has been misheard or misinterpreted. (Actually coined in 2003.) Examples: *coldslaw* for *coleslaw*; *ten year* for *tenure*.

EXERCISE III.4 — ETYMOLOGIES OF SOME INTERESTING WORDS: the words in this list have interesting histories or origins. Choose one or two and find out what you can about them.
   —Where are they from?
   —What do they mean; have their meanings changed?
   —Find a sentence using each of your words.
   —Are there other English words related to them?
CHANGED WORDS:

rally	achieve	anguish	biscuit	canary	coin
dismal	engine	foreign	haughty	jest	matriculate
parboil	scourge	solemn	terrier	puny	retort
atone	romance	copy	auspices	host	buckle
dean	dozen	era	gamut	libel	umpire
noon	peculiar	revel	sergeant	sport	insect
alarm	bead	travesty	aisle	bugle	chapel

culprit	denizen	fairy	sincere	gin	preposterous
mischief	outrage	porpoise	person	dame	quintessence
supercilious	prevaricate	capitulate	bachelor	eliminate	miscreant
precocious	delirious	rosemary	Mass	usher	manipulate

NOTES

1. Before the arrival of SUPERCALIFRAGILISTICEXPIALIDOCIOUS, a word coined (or remembered) by the Sherman brothers for a song in the 1964 musical *Mary Poppins*. Another facetious coinage intended for fame as the longest word in the dictionary is PNEUMONOULTRA-MICROSCOPICSILICOVOLCANOCONIOSIS (pneumoconiosis is a real word for vaious occupational lung diseases, such as silicosis and asbestosis, caused by inhalation of metallic dust particles).

2. See the Rice Dictionary of neologisms:
http://neologisms.rice.edu/index.php?a=list&d=1&t=dict&w1=A

3. A portmanteau is a suitcase that opens into two compartments.

4. See http://www.alphadictionary.com/articles/eponyms/index.html for a dictionary of eponyms

SECTION ONE: HISTORY IN WORDS

CHAPTER FOUR: THE BEGINNINGS OF ENGLISH

Peoples on the Move

English is a melting-pot language. It has been shaped by political, social, and intellectual forces that took place not only in the British Isles, but also in Northern Europe, the Italian peninsula, and the ancient Middle East. Successive waves of migration and invasion which swept over England left indelible marks on the language. And, finally, when the English language and the people who spoke it seemed to coalesce, British imperialism in Africa, Asia, the Americas, and the South Pacific—a linguistic migration outward—brought new ripples of influence back to the mother country.

The most significant linguistic influences were exerted on English during the first thousand years of the language's development. In that time English grew out of a barely distinguishable group of Germanic dialects, first spoken in the northern reaches of Europe, into a magnificent amalgam of elements from Europe's rich linguistic storehouse. On a framework of Germanic syntax and vocabulary, the peoples of England shaped a new language by borrowing additional words and grammatical constructions from Latin, Greek, and other continental European languages. The resulting vocabulary is now so diverse in origins that some scholars question whether English can be considered a Germanic language at all. However it is classified, English, as it is today, is one of the most remarkable inventions of western civilization.

To gain an understanding of the historical events that shaped our language, we will take a brief look at the larger forces that went into the making of European history. During the Bronze Age the ethno-political geography of the continent was carved up predominantly among four large, and within themselves, loosely related groups of peoples. In the north were the Teutons, or Germans, a small grouping of land-starved tribes centered around the Baltic Sea. In the south the Greek and Italic speakers prospered in a climate conducive to agriculture and civilization. In the largest section of the continent, the vast heartland of Europe, Celtic tribes exerted a spreading influence, which at its zenith extended from Ireland to Spain and from northwestern Europe all the way to some tenuous plantings on the shores of Asia Minor. Needless to say our primary interest in these peoples is their languages and linguistic traditions. Within each of the groups there were separate dialects and even languages; so that, for example, Germanic tribes occupying different banks of the same river were further separated by linguistic habits that affected their ways of pronouncing and arranging the words in their language: a difference in dialect. The ancient peoples who inhabited the two major peninsulas of southern Europe, Greece and Italy, were separated by such a wide linguistic gulf that their languages belong to different branches of the I-E family, Greek and Italic, Latin being the best known of the latter group.

Some time about the fifth century B.C.E. the peripheral groups, the Germans to the north and the Greeks and Italians to the south, began to grow in numbers and power, and gradually pushed toward the center of the continent. Caught in the squeeze, the Celts migrated to the British Isles where they were eventually caught by the rapacious events of history. In the first century B.C.E. and, again, in the first century C.E., the Romans invaded Britain, and in the fifth century C.E. Germanic tribes turned in force on the island, pushing the Celts to more isolated spaces.

The implications of these distant historical events may seem remote at first glance. But some 2,500 years later, the Germanic expansion and Celtic flight still exert political and social pressure on western life. The causes and effects of the last three Europeans wars and the struggles in Ireland, recently, but not completely, resolved, should suffice as vivid examples that large historical events rarely die easy deaths. Moreover, the English language is a product of those distant migrations; its words are the artifacts of those remote events.

The British islanders (mostly Celts) and the Teutons of the continent, though at the time widely separated by geography and culture, are first mentioned in written history by a Greek merchant adventurer, Pytheas of Massilia (present day Marseille).[1] Around 325 B.C.E. he made a daring circumnavigation of the British Isles and other journeys in northern Europe. In the records of Pytheas' writings are to be found the first references to the Britannic Celts and the *Teutones*.

Britain solidly enters history in the year 55 B.C.E., when Julius Caesar, then a military commander in Gaul, undertook two retaliatory raids on the island in pursuit of Celtic safe havens for Rome's continental enemies. Caesar's expeditions ended in all but defeat at the hands of the Britons. But Rome's star was in the ascendency and the lure of a new province (rich in tin) was firmly affixed to the imperial imagination. In the zigzag play of history, Julius Caesar turned the force of his military and political genius to the affairs in northern Europe, planting the foundations of Roman power over the southernmost Germanic tribes. For the following seventy years, while the Roman legions pushed northwards through much of what today is Germany, Roman traders and merchants ventured sporadically into the British Isles to sell and buy. "No one goes to Britain without good reason, except the traders," opined Caesar, remembering his brief and unfortunate brush with the islanders (*Commentaries on the Gallic War* 4.20).

A picture of the advance from trading contact through military and political domination has been sketched out with the help of archaeology. A half century or so before direct Roman contact with Britain, Celtic chieftains on that island were being buried with grave goods of Roman manufacture. These goods, mostly ceramics, had reached Britain through continental Belgic traders. A decade before the Roman invasion of Britain actually began, small trading posts—not unlike those on the North American frontier which preceded western expansion—were established by the Romans. These were tentative ventures in a barbaric and hostile land. Nevertheless the influence of Roman goods spread quickly throughout the island. By the time the legions landed in Britain, there was hardly a Briton who had not come into contact with some object of Roman culture, even if the object was something as lowly as a common kitchen pot. It is no wonder, then, that the Latin words *mango* and *caupo* (dealer and huckster or small-time tradesman, respectively) were early entries into English. Both acquired a distasteful significance. Seneca says that the *mangones* (plural of *mango*) hide any fault in their merchandise through some artificial ornament, in the manner of pimps. Horace speaks of *perfidus hic caupo* ("this treacherous tradesman" *Sermones* 1.1.29), as if cheating or treacherous were the natural word to describe a huckster. Today these words survive in the English *monger* (as in fishmonger, warmonger, costermonger[2]) and *cheap, chap, chapman* (a traveling peddler), and *chapbook* (the classiest of the derivatives, a "booklet of poems, ballads, stories," sold by chapmen). In German, too, the influence of Latin *caupo* is seen in the verbs *kaufen*, to buy and *verkaufen*, to sell.

Merchants: Heroes of Language

The English, as Napoleon pointed out, are a nation of shopkeepers. The Corsican emperor was in fact paraphrasing and considerably shortening a remark Adam Smith made in *The Wealth of Nations*:

> To found a great nation for the sole purpose of raising up a people of customers, may at first sight appear a project fit only for a nation of shopkeepers. It is, however, a project altogether unfit for a nation of shopkeepers; but extremely fit for a nation governed by shopkeepers.

That English vocabulary reached its magnificent size and diversity in the mouths of such people is no accident. Mercantilism and its complement, consumerism, have played an immeasurable part in the development of the English language, from the time when our ancestors were unschooled tribesmen up to our present sophisticated age of consumerism, globalism, and e-commerce. To face the perils of sea and storm, of pirates, brigands, and unknown tribesmen, to journey to far-off lands to buy something or sell something may at first sight seem unworthy of humanity's highest efforts. But the contribution to the English language made by merchants should not be underestimated. Merchants as much as linguists are heroes of language. New lands, new worlds are discovered for them. Into these new lands merchants, tradesmen, dealers, peddlers, and even chapmen bring new things and new words for them and on the return journey they bring home new words for the things they find abroad. Behind, sometimes even ahead of, Rome's legions, came merchants, ever in search of new markets. The less worldly inhabitants of Britain and Germany naturally wanted to become more civilized. To them, probably, the most apparent aspect of the Romans' claim to greatness and higher culture was the fact that they had more things. What better way to acquire the envied civilization than through the possession of the things that were its outward sign? No less than ourselves, our rude forebears realized that standard of living is based on how much one has. And so they learned to want and need the new products. Among the earliest loanwords from Latin are the names for vessels: cup, chest, pan, pot, bin, box, sack. The Romans, because they had more things, naturally had to have more things to put them in. Many words for textiles and clothing were borrowed at this time too (sock, belt, mat, pall, purple, silk, for example) and words for good things to eat and drink such as wine, butter, cheese, pepper. We will see if the recent minimalist movement results in more people living with less.

Romans in Britain

Small civilian communities grew up around Roman military encampments all along the imperial frontier. In Britain alone there were nearly 200,000 Romans and Romanized Celts by the middle of the first century C.E. This rapid growth in Roman population and Romanization of the natives did not spring entirely from an influx of traders and the beguiling influence of their wares. By far the largest number of Romans to enter a new territory after it had been subdued were settlers of two types who shared one purpose—land. Perhaps the most numerous of the settlers were cashiered legionnaires, who, upon leaving the military were given a bonus in the form of conquered land. In the newly acquired territories, such as Britain and Germany, land could be had for the taking, which is just what the government did. This practice of distributing grants of land to ex-soldiers benefitted the imperial government in two ways: not only did it satisfy the payroll and pension problems with little actual expenditure, but the veterans' presence in the territory accelerated the pacification of the province. The other group of Roman settlers were underemployed peasants from the Italian peninsula, who, since the second century B.C.E., had been leaving their homeland in search of more arable lands to farm. Neither the veterans nor the frontiersmen farmers had any qualms about inter-marrying with the natives and so Romanization went apace.

Romanization did not go unchallenged, however. In 60 and 61 C.E. the affair of Queen Boudicca in Britain nearly brought an end to the earlier efforts at pacification of the island. Boudicca, the Celtic queen of York, had been widowed when Roman tax collectors murdered her husband as he resisted exorbitant and illegal levies that the provincial officials were trying to extort from his people. Not satisfied with murder, the Romans brutally humiliated the queen. But she escaped and raised a revolt. Long-smoldering dissatisfaction with foreign rule brought numerous Celtic tribes under her banner. In the course of two bloody years the armies of Boudicca leveled the three largest Roman towns in Britain, slaughtering 70,000 Romans and

Romanized Celts in a frenzy of revenge and revolt. Only by diverting a large number of troops from the continent was Rome finally able to maintain a hold on her new island province.

A small, but poignantly human incident which occurred during the Boudiccan revolt has been brought to light by British archaeologists. Just before the sack of London, a Romanized Celt, aided perhaps by family and friends, hurriedly drank off an amphora (approximately seven gallons) of imported wine—a Roman product that the tippler's father was probably unacquainted with. Whether this unfortunate Celt got drunk out of despair or to fortify his courage, the word he used for the beverage was the Latin *vinum*, which we still use today in the slightly altered spelling, *wine*.

After the events of 60–61 the Romans realized that a vigorously fair-minded policy of re-pacification was needed. Under the governorship of Agricola a crash program was instituted to build marketplaces and Roman temples in the native centers of population. "Now," wrote the governor's son-in-law Tacitus, "he began to school the chieftain's sons in the liberal arts, with the result that those who used to wag their heads at the Latin language now were beginning to aspire to eloquence. Then even our style of clothing was an honor and the toga was to be seen everywhere. Step by step they fell prey to the seductions of our vices: the portico and the bath and luxurious dining. Among the inexperienced [Britons] this was called *culture* (*humanitas vocabatur*), even though it was part of their slavery" (Tacitus, *Agricola* 21).

Physical evidence of this period that has been recovered by archaeologists proves the effect of these policies. Hardly a house of this period has been discovered that was not Roman in design. The largest were equipped with every luxury that could be found in Rome itself, while none but the poorest Briton used anything but imported Samian dinnerware produced in Roman Gaul and styled on Roman patterns.

The prevalence of Roman-style wearing apparel, Roman-style housing, utensils, and Roman cuisine created an environment in which Latin influence on the native Celtic languages was inescapable. Just as today's devotee of French cooking, who might live in Des Moines or Coeur d'Alene, is as apt to talk about a *bain-marie* and *pommes frites* as a double boiler or French fries, so the Romanized Celt found it easier and more dignified to use Latinate vocabulary for the newly imported wares and customs.

Bilingualism was widespread in the towns, especially in the southeast of the island. Latin was the first or second language of the foreign settlers; the language of government, commerce, and culture; the language that allowed social mobility. And at this time Latin was the language of the written word. Latin loan-words from this period survive not only in English, but in the Celtic tongues (Welsh,[3] Cornish, Breton).

One aspect of Roman culture that never gained acceptance was the semi-political state religion. Even when Britons in the cities and towns worshiped in typically Roman temples, they worshiped their own native deities there. Occasionally they gave their ancestral gods Latin names, but they did not give them Roman personalities. A strong example of this conservatism in religious matters is the name of Christianity's holiest feast day, Easter. *Eostre* was a Germanic goddess whose feast day roughly coincides with the Christian holiday. As for Christianity's influence at this early stage, the religion entered both Britain and northern Germany relatively early, though it did not become popular until well after Roman power had ebbed in those parts.

Thus far we have been dealing with what we might call the pre-natal stage in the development of English. Now it is time to bring together into one place the diverse elements that generated this great language.

Beginning in the third century, the Roman Empire started down the inexorable road to decline. The massive military and political machine centered in a central Italian city, which for three hundred years had held in check the various tribal pressures of Europe, began to weaken. Economic stagnation palled the empire; political disintegration loosened the bonds that previously had made the state cohesive; and social and spiritual malaise sapped the citizens' morale. While the core of the Empire suffered, however, the peoples on the periphery began to realize a new vigor. The Germanic tribes moved unhaltably south and west. At the same time, resurgent Celts pushed obstinately east and south.

By the year 287 Saxon German pirates were engaged in periodic raids on the British coast. A century later Saxons joined Celtic Scots in land-based attacks on Roman strongholds in Britain. By the beginning of the fifth century, all of the Roman legions were withdrawn from the island to defend the city of Rome itself. The death knell for Roman Britain was sounded a decade later when the Romano-Britons desperately besieged by both Celtic and Germanic hordes wrote to the Emperor Honorius begging his aid. His reply—known as the Rescript of 410—was to wish his harried subject well and commend them to their own devices.

> Rescript of 410
> Honorius to Britons: Drop Dead!

Some three hundred years after the Germanic invasion of Britain, an Anglo-Saxon monk in England, the Venerable Bede, recounted in Latin a legend about the coming of his forebears to the island.

In the year of our Lord 449 . . . the Angles or Saxons, sent for by the king, reached Britain in three long ships and received lands in the eastern part of the island on condition that they defend the country, but in fact their intention was to conquer it. *Historia Ecclesiastica 1.15*

Contrary to the neatness of the invasion implied by Bede's contracted tale, the Germanic invasion of Britain occurred over a long period of time and in piecemeal fashion. So gradual was the invasion that to an inhabitant of the island, the change from Romano-Celtic to German domination would have been so incremental as to seem nearly imperceptible. Again archaeologists have shown that in the mid-fifth century, when Bede suggests cataclysmic change was rending the island, Romanized

Britons were still confidently building country villas in the Roman style complete with running water and other civilized amenities.

Romanized Celtic Britain died hard. The cities lingered for decades, most of them never falling into disuse, where a population, basically unchanged, but a bit more impoverished, continued a Roman-like urban existence while the new settlers from the continent devoted their time to agriculture in the countryside. Gradually, in most parts of the island, through assimilation and political and economic domination, the German invaders became predominant and their language displaced the Celtic as the standard for popular communication. Latin influence, however, remained.

EXERCISES

EXERCISE IV.1—THROUGH THE ANGLO-SAXON INVASION: the earliest loanwords from Latin that entered an early form of English came through contact with the Roman legions in Germany. After the Anglo-Saxons arrived in England, the chief source of Latin loanwords was the Vulgar Latin[4] used by the Romano-Britons. Since it is not always possible to distinguish between words borrowed on the continent and those borrowed during the early years of Germanic settlement on the British isles, the two groups are treated together here. As normally happens when invaders enter a region for colonization and form a majority in the new land, acquiring political control over it, the language of the newcomers prevailed. Thus the language of the Anglo-Saxons gained the upper hand. The words they adopted from the inhabitants were mostly from the Romanized Britons of the market towns and villages. Though the Anglo-Saxons came with their language intact—the Romans had not colonized Germany to any great extent, nor had they become the majority—they already had some important loanwords from classical civilization.

After going over this list, choose one to look up and find its history in the English language. Using the OED and other dictionaries, find:

—Meaning of the word

—Meaning and form of the Latin or Greek original

—Earliest spelling in English

—The date of the earliest cited use in English (Jot down the quotation.)

—Any changes in meaning the word has undergone in its lifetime in English, especially new meanings acquired or any changes in its transition from Latin/Greek into English

—Any words in English that are related to it and any words derived from the same Latin or Greek base

street	mile	camp	cheap	monger	pound
toll	post	chalk	copper	belt	port (harbor)
mat	purple	pillow	sack	sock	candle
pipe	butter	cheese	wine	bin	pan
kitchen	kiln	line	pin	tile	wall

inch	pea	pepper	poppy	ass	fever
anchor	mortar	pot	fork	cat	trout

EXERCISE IV.2. ACH MEIN GOTT, EIN POT! The words in this list are for objects or creatures from everyday life, such items as would be brought by more experienced traders to a less experienced people. The most natural reason for one language to adopt a word from another is that the borrower has no word for the thing it names. Try to imagine the reception of the new article by uncouth (linguistic) ancestors of modern English. Take one of the words from the list and write a fable or a shaggy dog story about the reaction of the family members around the hearth when they first see the newfangled object and realize that mother or father has traded the family cow for a fork or a sack!

belt	sock	pin	tile	mat	pillow
sack	candle	butter	cheese	wine	bin
pan	pepper	pot	fork	cat	pipe
box					

EXERCISE IV.3. KITH OR KIN? In these pairs of words, some are related in meaning, others are just look-alikes. Choose a few and find out which are from the same Latin root and which are unrelated.

1. a) toll (The toll to cross the bridge is one dollar.)
    b) toll ("Ask not for whom the bell tolls.")
2. a) cheap (We have nothing cheap here!)
    b) chap (He's a nice enough chap.)
3. a) pin (straight pins for sewing)
    b) pen (fountain pen for calligraphy)
4. a) mint (U.S. Mint)
    b) mint (peppermint and spearmint)
5. a) street ("The sunny side of the street")
    b) stratum (the lowest stratum of society)
6. a) trivet (Put a trivet under the casserole.)
    b) tripod (The camera is on a tripod.)
7. a) kiln (a potter's kiln)
    b) culinary (culinary delights)
8. a) inch (an inch taller)
    b) ounce ("An ounce of prevention is worth a pound of cure.")
9. a) line (You have to draw the line somewhere.)
    b) linen (Don't wash you dirty linens in public.)
10. a) plum (A plum is an edible fruit with a single seed.)
    b) prune (A prune is a dried plum.)
11. a) prune (Prune the bushes in spring.)
    b) prune (He ate a surfeit of prunes.)
12. a) wine (A glass of white wine, please.)

b) vinegar (Mix vinegar and oil with a little mustard.)
13. a) kipper (Kippered herring is eaten for breakfast.)
    b) copper (Is that a copper bracelet?)
14. a) box (Take off the boxing gloves.)
    b) box (Thanks for the box of chocolates.)
15. a) mile ("A miss is as good as a mile.")
    b) millennium (*Millennium Approaches*)
16. a) fever (She had chills and a fever.)
    b) February (February is the shortest month.)
17. a) chalk (Is that a chalk drawing?)
    b) calcium (Calcium is good for teeth and bones.)
18. a) must (I must be going.)
    b) must (Must is unfermented grape juice.)
19. a) pound ("Give crowns and pounds and guineas / But not your heart away.")
    b) ponderous (That is a ponderous tome.)
20. a) post (The wire is held up by posts.)
    b) post (The Post Office is open on Saturday mornings.)
21. a) fuller (A fuller works with fabric.)
    b) fuller (For a fuller view of the stage, sit over here.)

IV. 4. Review Choose a word in column B that has the same Latin (or Greek) root as the word in column A.[5]

A	B
__ 1. copper	a. stratigraphy
__ 2. chalk	b. million
__ 3. cheese	c. uncial
__ 4. fork	d. menthol
__ 5. mile	e. bifurcation
__ 6. pound	f. imponderable
__ 7. street	g. interval
__ 8. mint (coinage)	h. cuprous
__ 9. mint (herb)	I. monetary
__ 10. ounce	j. calcination
__ 11. wall	k. casein
__ 12. chest	l. cistern

Celtic Words in English
Some Celtic words have come into English, though not very many compared to those from Latin.
BARD: *A poet.* Originally, "one of an ancient Celtic order of minstrel poets who composed and recited verses celebrating the legendary exploits of chieftains and heroes." (AHD)

Etymology: Middle English, from Irish and Scots Gaelic *bard* from the root *gwere-
(to favor) and so related to Latin *gratus* (pleasing).

Other Celtic words (and words of probable or possible Celtic origin) in English
include: andiron, basin, basket, bother, bran, brat (1), briar (1), bushel (1), budget,
butcher, charge, chariot, debris, decant, frown, javelin, lance, mine (1), piece, quay,
scourge, tunnel, vassal, whiskey, ambassador.

Some Celtic words come to us through Latin or French: for example, gladiator from
Latin *gladius* (of Celtic origin), sword.

OPTIONAL EXERCISE: Adopt one of these Celtic loanwords and find its story.

NOTES

1. Pytheas' work has not survived, but it is known through references in the writings of the
encyclopedist Pliny, the geographer Strabo, and the historian Diodorus Siculus.

2. A costermonger is someone who hawks fruits and vegetables from a cart or stand. The
coster- element comes from English costard, a type of cooking apple.

3. For example, Welsh for cheese is *caws* (from Latin *caseus*); Welsh *sach*, a cloth bag <
Latin *saccus* < Greek *sakkos*, ultimately from Egyptian.

4. *Vulgar*, that is, popular, everyday, as spoken by the people, rather than literary < Latin
vulgus, the common people, crowd, masses.

5. Answers for IV.4: 1–h; 2–j; 3–k; 4–e; 5–b; 6–f; 7–a; 8–I; 9–d; 10–c; 11–g; 12–l.

SECTION ONE: HISTORY IN WORDS

CHAPTER FIVE: THE ANGLO-SAXONS IN ENGLAND

The Anglo-Saxons found their progress in Britain neither swift nor spectacular. The native Celts and the Romano-Britons had discovered within themselves a new spirit of resistance and pride. Coincidental with their invigorated political systems, the natives of Britain reawakened their national religion, a pantheism of Celtic origin. Especially in the southeastern districts of the island, a new sense of purpose put steel into British determination to withstand the Angles and Saxons.

Around the year 500, the British won a pivotal military victory at a place called Mons Badonicus. For the next fifty years the invaders were held at a standstill. Still, the growing numbers of German immigrants eventually swung the balance against the natives. The last quarter of the century found the Anglo-Saxon invaders in the ascendance. After 571, when a new and larger army of confederated Anglo-Saxons routed the Britons, there was no doubt that the island would carry a Germanic stamp in culture, language, and politics.

During the same time, most, if not all, of Europe, which had previously fallen under Mediterranean Roman influence and power, came to be dominated by one or another Germanic tribe. Rome itself was the seat of Gothic rule. Britain was only one, peripheral, corner of the historical picture at the beginning of the Middle Ages.

While not escaping the political, cultural, and ethnic turmoil of the times, the oldest Roman provinces (in Italy, France, and Spain, for example) managed to retain their Latin based languages. But the newer western provinces, which had never been thoroughly Romanized, adopted or retained Germanic languages. In Eastern Europe, Slavonic peoples generally proved to be unyielding to outward pressures. Roman culture and religion, which now was Christianity, still remained in the eyes of the conquerors superior to their own, much in the way that European, especially French, culture used to be thought superior by those living on the peripheries of the Western world, for example North America and the Slavic countries.

In England, as we may now call the country after the Anglo-Saxons established hegemony there, Roman influence was carried mostly through religion. When they invaded the islands, the Germanic tribes worshiped a multitude of gods that embodied ancient virtues. Even today we recall these deities in the names of four of our weekdays: Tuesday, Wednesday, Thursday, and Friday. These are named after the old German gods, *Tiw*, patron of war, *Woden*, father of Tiw and supreme warrior, *Thor*, a rain and cloud god, and *Freyr*, god of fertility. Two other days, Sunday and Monday, are Germanic, but were translations of the names in Latin, *solis dies* (sun's day) and *lunae dies* (moon's day). Saturday (< Latin *Saturni dies*) is an eponym of the Roman agricultural god Saturn.

Early Christianity, which had gained a foothold on the island during the Roman occupation, vanished, it seems, with the withdrawal of the legions. A branch of the Church continued to exist in Ireland, where legend held that Joseph of Arimathea was the first to preach the Gospel. It was Celtic missionaries who first undertook the conversion of the polytheistic Anglo-Saxons in the far north of England. Their success was rapid. Within a short time they managed to establish a thriving series of monasteries in the kingdoms of Berenica and Northumbria.

The south was proselytized by Roman Catholic missionaries beginning with St. Augustine of Canterbury who was dispatched to England by Pope Gregory I (known as Gregory the Great, whose papacy lasted from 590 to 604) with instructions to use gentle persuasion. The southern kingdoms of England at this time were the center of English polytheism, both cultural and political. The early missions to that part of the island suffered disappointing setbacks and met with hostilities unknown to the Celtic missionaries in the north. As a result of the Roman policy of gradual conversion, religious practices in the south took on a mixed color, assimilating some of the earlier practices and vocabulary into the Christian rituals. English still uses words from the older tradition to refer to the two holiest seasons of the Christian calendar, Easter (as already mentioned, from *Eostre*, a goddess of spring or *eastre* a celebration of the dawn goddess) and Yule (as in yule log, Yuletide) from *geol* or *giuli*, an end of the year feast celebrating the winter solstice that roughly coincided with Christmas.

In time the two strains of Christianity came into conflict over theological and political matters, with the Romans prevailing over the Celtic Christians. The Roman alphabet won out over the runes used to write the Celtic languages. The quelling of religious opposition and the ascendency of the Roman alphabet opened England to the full force of continental European culture. Roman monastic houses were vigorously established throughout the island and monk-scholars traveled back and forth from England to European centers of learning. Within the climate of religious expansion at home, English monks felt it their fraternal duty to take Christianity to their Germanic homeland. For some half century, English missionaries pursued the conversion of the continental Germans with something bordering on fanaticism.

The high point of this phase of Anglo-Saxon culture came in the late seventh and early eighth centuries with the appearance on the scene of two north English monks, Bede and Alcuin in the kingdom of Northumbria. Alcuin made his career at the court of Charlemagne and is therefore considered more European than English, but Bede spent his life at the monastery of Jarrow writing Biblical and theological commentaries, studies that, at that time, were considered the highest form of scholarship. For his work in theology he earned the name the Venerable Bede. Another Englishman, St. Boniface, said of Bede that he was "the candle of the Church." Today we consider the most important work of this monk of Jarrow to be his *History of the Church in England* (in Latin, *Historia ecclesiastica*) which traces the history of the island up to his own time.

Bede and Alcuin—along with all their educated contemporaries—wrote in Latin. This is made less surprising by the fact that the Anglo-Saxon word *laedina* (their way of saying *Latina*) meant not only the Latin language, but also any literate language and even grammar itself. Since Latin was the universal medium of instruction and of learned writing at this time, most educated people were bilingual. They spoke of quotidian matters in their native tongue and of intellectual matters in Latin. Bede, in the *History of the Church in England*, tells us that in England there were four distinct groups of people and five languages spoken among them, the fifth and universal language was Latin. Throughout his *History*, however, Bede makes reference to vernacular literature, written in English, usually verse, by such authors as Caedmon and Cynewulf.

The age of Bede and that era of Anglo-Saxon culture was soon brought to an end by renewed migration. This time, the far northern Germanic tribes of Scandinavia were on the move, pushing south and west. During the respite from external threat, the English had built up a monastic establishment along the coast and on coastal islets because they could be most easily protected from secular intrusions and land-based brigands. These monasteries and towns were unprotected from the sea by either walls or a standing militia. The rich, undefended prizes of England were a magnet for the northern hordes who had been set roaming by the barrenness of their native fjords. The Norse began first to pick at England with small sporadic sallying raids, which year after year grew in intensity and ferocity. Within the three years 793–795, the three richest and most prestigious seats of monastic learning in England were sacked by the sea raiders. Lindisfarne, Jarrow, and Iona were each in turn obliterated. Within less than a century the Danish Vikings shifted from a pattern of seasonal raids to one of sustained attack. The Scandinavians began to look on England as a place to conquer and settle.

For over a century the island lacked both political stability and tranquillity of learning. But the period of Norse invasions was not entirely unrelieved. The Vikings, whose name has come to be associated with savagery and piracy, brought to the English language the word *law* and along with it a new concept of the law.

In the last decade of the ninth century a remarkable man ascended to the throne of the kingdom of Wessex in southern England. Hard pressed by the Danish menace, he manoeuvered his scanty forces cunningly, knowing when to retreat, when to compromise with the foreign enemy, and when to attack. In the end, by beating back the Danes, he earned the title that has followed him through history, Alfred the Great.

In his fortieth year after military and political victory were his, King Alfred began to study Latin; for the preceding times—fraught as they were with alarms—had not been conducive to study. And in his last years Alfred devoted his efforts to the revival of learning in England, as he wrote in the preface to his translation of Orosius' universal history.

Unlike his predecessors of the eighth and early ninth centuries, Alfred wrote the bulk of his works in Anglo-Saxon, concentrating mostly on translations of essential Latin works in order to facilitate the business of education in his country. Because the troubles of the previous hundred years had all but obliterated formal education on the island, Alfred felt he had to appeal to his subjects in a language they already knew, rather than in an alien tongue. Only by stepping over the niceties of classical education was he able to start a sizeable body of Englishmen back on the road to learning. His royal patronage lent authority to his educational reforms and imparted prestige to the particular dialect of Anglo-Saxon in which he wrote. Thus Alfred's Anglo-Saxon became the foundation of the standard English in use today.

The Alfredian renaissance did not revive scholarship in England immediately; it only started it on its way. Nearly a century later, Aelfric, a monk, schoolmaster, and author, tells us that the old priest who undertook to teach him Latin himself understood but "little Latin." At this time, the beginning of the eleventh century, England was caught up in a Pan-European reform of monasticism and learning. Monasteries, then as earlier, were the principal seats of learning, occupying a place in the intellectual life of their times something akin to universities today. English bishops, notably Oswald, Dunstan, and Aethelwold, brought a new spirit of educational excellence to the island. Aelfric himself took what we would call his college training from Aethelwold at the Cathedral School of Winchester, where the bishop took pleasure in personally teaching the students. As Aelfric later recounted, Aethelwold "exhorted them with pleasant words to do better things."

As the first age of Anglo-Saxon culture in the eighth century was characterized by the Venerable Bede, and the ninth century can be called the age of Alfred, so the tenth century is known as the age of Aelfric. He wrote many works, in both Anglo-Saxon and Latin, putting his peculiarly English stamp on Christian orthodoxy and European philosophy. Still he is most remembered for several small textbooks. One, a Latin grammar written in Anglo-Saxon, which Aelfric tells his readers can be used to teach either Latin or Anglo-Saxon. Another school book of Aelfric's is an elementary Latin language reader called the *Colloquy*. This book is made up of a series of short, witty, dialogues between the schoolmaster and various ordinary people, a fisherman, a baker, a farmer and so forth, concerning their day-to-day lives. It is still used to teach Latin conversation.

As a natural consequence of King Alfred's educational reforms in which Latin works were taught in translation, the vernacular became, alongside Latin, the language of scholars in England. England thus became the first country in Europe (since Roman times) where the intelligentsia was truly bilingual. Alfred and Aelfric, perhaps unwittingly, contributed to making the ordinary language of the people a respectable vehicle of intellectual communication. Owing to the way language was taught in the schools of that day, where English was never completely divorced from Latin in the classroom, changes were wrought upon the vernacular, giving it free access to the rich and varied vocabulary of Latin. In short order Latin words learned in school seeped into the students' everyday English conversation, and soon Latin derivatives seemed as natural to English speakers as were the words of Germanic origin.

EXERCISES

EXERCISE V.1 — WORDS FROM THE CONVERSION: The full-scale conversion of the Anglo-Saxons to Christianity beginning in 597 and the accompanying spread of scholarship brought many new words to English. Many of these words refer to ecclesiastical (< Greek *ekklesia*, assembly; church) matters, from which the list below is taken. Christianity existed among the Romano-Britons who inhabited the towns before the arrival of the Anglo-Saxons and some religious terms survived from this earlier period. A few words, moreover, were adopted from ecclesiastical Greek, perhaps first by the Goths, and then spread to other Germanic tribes.

Go over the words in the list and choose one to work on. Using the OED, try to find out:

1. When and where (if possible) did it first enter English?
2. What was its first spelling in English?
3. What was the original word in Latin or Greek?
4. What is the meaning of the original word?
5. Has the meaning changed?
6. Are there other words from the same Latin or Greek word?
7. As far as you can tell, has the word had a continuous history in English or was it reborrowed from Latin or French?
8. Does the word come from a specific work of literature?

angel	church	nun	alms	Mass	pope
cope	altar	cleric	deacon	passion	priest
monk	relic	creed	noon	abbot	paradise (<Persian)
apostle	cross	preach	devil	minister	Sabbath (<Hebrew)
bishop	disciple	offer	alb	acolyte	apostate
dean	martyr	saint			

EXERCISE V.2 (Recommended for in-class work)—WORDS FROM LITERATURE: Writing in the early eighth century in Latin, the Venerable Bede says, "At present peoples of Britain study and confess one and the same knowledge . . . in five tongues—equal to the number of books of divine law—English, British, Scots, Pictish, and Latin, which through study of the scriptures has become common to all," *Historia Ecclesiastica* 1.1.

The influence of literature on language should not be underestimated: the Latin translation of the Bible brought many coined words into standard Latin. The reading of religious and literary texts in Latin gave many new words to English. Bede himself, though he wrote in Latin, influenced English: in the Old English translation of Bede's *Historia Ecclesiastica* numerous learned words, mostly based on Bede's Latin, are found, for example, *antemn* (antiphon, anthem), *letania* (litany), *archidiacon* (archdeacon), *canon*, *capitol* (for chapter), *cometa* (comet), *eretic* (heretic), *subdiacon* (subdeacon) and many of the words listed in exercise V.1.

Many of these early literary loanwords did not survive. Some ceased to be used in English, but others were replaced or reborrowed either directly from Latin or Greek, or through French. Words borrowed from literature usually come into the language in its written form and though some such words pass into the spoken language and become fixed there, most remain *learned* words and never reach the lips of the average speaker.

In the list below are some early loanwords from Latin. These have dropped out of English and been replaced by other words. Give the modern English word for the Old English word or if no word from the same source has replaced it, give an English word derived from the same source (see examples).
Examples:

1. *plaetse, plaece* < Greek *plateia hodos*, broad street, from *platus*, broad (cf. the element *platy-* in platypus), was replaced by PLACE from the Latin version (*platea*) of the Greek word, under French influence, with the meaning "an open space in a town." The word PLACE has become so generalized that it means any space, spot, or area and so has led to the borrowing of the Spanish and Italian words *plaza* and *piazza* for the original meaning of "a public square."

2. *fenester* (window), on the other hand, has dropped out of everyday English and has not been reborrowed. We do have some derivatives of the Latin word *fenestra* in words like fenestrated (having windows) and fenestration (in architecture, "the design and placement of windows in a building" and in surgical terminology, "the cutting of an opening from the external auditory canal to the labyrinth of the internal ear to restore hearing") and defenestration ("the act of throwing something or someone out the window"), and in scientific terminology, we have the Latin *fenestra* ("a window-like opening" or "a transparent marking on an insect's wing").

Early English form   Meaning   Latin
    English replacement or derivatives
Examples:
    plaetse, plaece   open place in town   *platea* < Greek *plateia*
        Replaced by: place, plaza, piazza
    fenester   window   *fenestra*
        Derivatives: fenestrate, defenestration

1. milite   soldiers   *miles*, pl. *milites*
   Derivatives:
2. fers   a line of poetry   *versus*
   Replaced by:
   Derivatives:
3. ymen   a song of praise   *hymnus*
   Replaced by:
4. carte   paper, deed   *chartes*
   Replaced by:
   Derivatives:
5. punct   dot   *punctus*
   Replaced by:
   Derivatives:
6. titol   superscription   *titulus*
   Replaced by:
   Derivatives:
7. calend   month   *calendae* (the first of the month)
   Derivatives:
8. studdian   see, take care of   *studēre*
   Replaced by:
   Derivatives:
9. castel   village, town   *castellum*
   Derivatives:
10. clauster   enclosure   *claustrum*
    Replaced by:
11. columne   pillar   *columna*
    Replaced by:
12. antefn   sung response   *antiphona*
    Replaced by:
13. cantere   singer   *cantor < canere, cantum*
    Replaced by:
    Derivatives:

EXERCISE V.3 — LITERATURE AND VOCABULARY (Optional): Of the English scholars and authors of the late tenth century, the greatest was the abbot Aelfric of Eynsham, whose work reflects the spirit of the age. It was an age of mixed cultural and intellectual traditions: Germanic, Classical, and Christian. Perhaps the most charming of his works—which include homilies, lives of saints, interpretations of Biblical and Christian works, a glossary, a grammar, and numerous epistles—is a small work called *Colloquy*, a dialogue in Latin between a teacher and his pupils on everyday life in and around a monastic school. Since Latin was the language of learning, students were discouraged from using the vernacular, but they needed to learn how to talk about the common things around them in Latin. The *Colloquy* was written to meet this pedagogical need. It gained an added importance from the fact that it was glossed in Old English (or Anglo-Saxon) by an anonymous monk shortly after it was written. The translation, written above the Latin text, is the only piece of sustained dialogue in Old English. The little text, consisting of questions and answers between the master and a series of workers (plowman, shepherd, fisherman, merchant, cook, baker, hunter, and smith)—the roles to be taken by the students in the class—gives us a witty glance at life in the tenth century. In the Old English version, the *Colloquy* contains about three dozen words from Latin or Greek, including a number of fish listed by the fisherman and some items of trade mentioned by the merchant. For these exercises, we will consider two of the Anglo-Saxon glosses, *ceaster* (city) and *kempa* (soldier).

a. CEASTER — In the dialogue, the master asks the fisherman where he sells his catch and the fisherman replies, A-S "on ceastre" (Latin *in civitate)*, "in the city." "And who buys them," asks the teacher, to which the fisherman answers, A-S "ceaser-wara" (Latin *cives*), "town-dwellers, citizens." *Ceaster* is one of our earliest loanwords from Latin. It comes from the Latin word *castra*, camp. Since the Romano-Britons built their towns around military camps, the word *ceaster* became the common word for city, fortified town. It survives in place names such as Chester and those ending in -chester, -caster, and -cester.

EXERCISE V.3A 1.— CASTRA: list several cities and towns in England and the United States or elsewhere ending in -chester, -caster, and -cester.

We no longer speak of the chester or ceaster, but have replaced this term with *city*, derived from Latin through French from the Latin *civitas* (base *civitat-*), the word that is glossed by *ceaster* in the A-S translation of the *Colloquy*. *Ceasterwara* glosses the Latin *cives*, citizens. Both Latin *civitas* and English *citizens* are derived from Latin *civis*.

EXERCISE V.3A 2— CIVES. Can you think of some other English words from *civ-*, the base of *civis*?

b. KEMPA — Another interesting word in the *Colloquy* is *kempa*, glossing the Latin *miles*, soldier. *Kempa* probably comes from Latin *campus*, field. *Kempa* has fallen out of use in English, replaced by SOLDIER which also ultimately comes from Latin (<Middle English *souldeur* < Old French *soudier, soldier* < *soulde*, pay < Latin *solidus nummus*, an ancient Roman coin, indicating that the term soldier was originally applied to those hired for pay, that is, mercenaries, also from Latin < *merces*, pay, wages).

EXERCISE V.3B — DERIVATIVES: Give English derivatives from:
    1. *merces*, pay, wages or *merx, merc-*, goods, wares
    2. *campus*, field
    3. *solidus*, "made of the same material throughout" (of a coin); solid

EXERCISE V. 4 — WORDS FROM LATIN CULTURE. The most important English prose from the ninth century is the writing of King Alfred. Much of his work is translation from Latin texts which, because of the subject matter introduces many words that are connected with Roman history into the English language. Words describing Roman cultural and political institutions have come into English at various periods.

A. EARLY BORROWINGS (the form used by Alfred is in brackets)
1. Caesar [casere] Modern: czar/tsar, Kaiser
2. centurion [centur]
3. consul [consul]
4. cohort [coorte]
5. legion [legie]
6. palace [palendse]
7. triumph [triumphan]
8. talent [talente]
9. dictator [tictator]
10. tunic [tunece]
11. noon [non] from *nona hora*, ninth hour

B. LATER BORROWINGS

1. forum	15. senate
2. auspices	16. salary
3. pagan	17. manumission
4. farce	18. sacrosanct
5. August	19. tribune
6. rostrum	20. augury
7. fanatic	21. sacrament
8. emancipate	22. applause
9. June	23. profane
10. paterfamilias	24. candidate
11. pontificate	25. Fascist
12. censor	26. municipal
13. succinct	27. July
14. capitol	

Choose two words from either list and find out what you can about the person, place, thing, institution (use the Oxford Classical Dictionary to start for persons, places, or institutions). Using the OED, answer these questions:
— When did the word come into English?
— Did it undergo reborrowing?
— Give an example of the word used in a sentence.
— Are there any other English words derived from it?
— Has its meaning changed?

EXERCISE V.5 REVIEW: Recognizing Related Words
Match words from the same Latin base.[1] Extra: Give meaning of the base.

A	B
1. forum	a. diabolical
2. bishop	b. castle
3. creed	c. reliquary
4. alb	d. credulous
5. cross	e. palatine
6. saint	f. diaconate
7. deacon	g. predicate
8. place	h. missal
9. offer	I. forensic
10. Mass	j. oleomargarine
11. relic	k. episcopal
12. wine	l. plaza
13. oil	m. album
14. Chester	n. sanctify
15. merchant	o. oblation
16. city	p. vintage
17. Palace	q. commercial
18. augury	r. civilian
19. devil	s. inauguration
20. capitol	t. chapter
21. preach	u. crucifixion

EXERCISE V. 6 — SCANDINAVIAN WORDS IN ENGLISH
Many Scandinavian words were adopted during the Old and Middle English periods
as a result of the Viking invasions of the eighth, ninth, and tenth centuries and
especially of the peaceful settlement of the Scandinavians and their association with
English folk in the eleventh and twelfth centuries. The earliest Scandinavian words
have to do primarily with the sea and the law, though later loanwords are more
general, including some of the most ordinary words, and do not imply the
introduction of new things or new ideas.

The Scandinavian dialects used by the invaders resembled the English dialects
of the time, especially in vocabulary, since all belonged to the Germanic branch.
Bilingualism or at least mutual intelligibility was common. For this reason the
Scandinavian influence was both great and largely imperceptible, since many of the
borrowed words did not feel foreign. Because many words in the two groups are
cognates and some even identical, it is sometimes difficult to know for certain
whether a particular word is a loanword or not. Sometimes the meaning of an
English word is changed under Scandinavian influence. Another indication of
borrowing is the spelling. The most noticeable variation is Scandinavian *sk-* for Old
English *sh-*: *skirt* (of Scandinavian origin) is thus a double for English *shirt*. Early

Scandinavian borrowings include sky, skill, skulk, skull, skin, score, scrape, scrap, and scare; some borrowed later (after the sixteenth century) are scud, scrag, scuffle, scrub, skit, skittles, skewer, and ski.

V.6 — SCANDINAVIAN WORDS: choose a word from the lists below and find out:
—What was its Scandinavian ancestor?
—What was its original meaning?
—When did it come into English?
—Did it already have cognates in English?
—Has its meaning changed?
a. Legal and quasi-legal terms:

law	wapentake	loan	wrong	crook
fellow	husband	husting	bond	crooked

b. Nautical terms:

haven   boatswain

c. Commonplace words:

they, their, them (developed under Scandinavian influence)

call	take	let	knife	loft	wing	band	score
egg	gape	get	skin	skill	leg	bait	sale
die	cast	root	bull	anger	booth	rag	want
hit	snare	boon	awe	thrall	meek		

give (replaced OE *yive*)

NOTE

1. Answers for V.5: 1–I; 2–k; 3–d; 4–m; 5–u; 6–n; 7–f; 8–l; 9–o; 10–h; 11–c; 12–p; 13–j; 14–b; 15–q; 16–r; 17–e; 18–s; 19–a; 20–t; 21–g.

SECTION ONE: HISTORY IN WORDS

CHAPTER SIX: THE NORMANS IN ENGLAND

1066 is commonly taken as the year in which Norman French influence began to be felt in England, but the groundwork for this influence was laid many decades earlier. As the English were not native to the British Isles, but Baltic Teutons, neither were the Normans native to France. Their very name tells us that they were Northmen or Scandinavians. They had invaded France around the year 900 and stayed to become French. Like the English who accepted Christianity, the religion of southern Europe, the Normans converted after they settled in their new home. Unlike their neighbors across the English Channel, the Normans did not retain their Germanic language, but readily adopted the Romance, Vulgar Latin of France. One other point of similarity between the Normans and the English is that once they both settled in their new homes, they resisted further incursions by the still southward pushing Scandinavians.

Close commercial and political ties had linked Normandy and England for some time. Their common struggle against raiding Vikings had drawn them into an on-again, off-again alliance. The Normans, however, were pursuing not only a defensive policy, protecting what was theirs, as were the English, but they were—in the Scandinavian fashion—expansionistic as well. The Normans needed elbow room, and so their younger sons went roaming, planting Norman rule as far afield as southern Italy, Sicily, and Palestine. In order to carry out this practice of keeping their French lands unhindered by Vikings and at the same time expand their federated empire, the Normans occasionally came to tacit agreement with the raiding Scandinavians not to oppose them. Occasionally the English suffered because of the loss of their ally.

Even after Emma, the sister of the Duke of Normandy, married King Aethelred of England, the alliance between the two countries was not guaranteed. And so when the Danes made a bold thrust into the heartland of England in 1013, the Normans did nothing more than offer refuge to the fleeing English royal family for the sake of their kinswoman, Queen Emma. This Danish invasion succeeded to a degree none of the earlier Scandinavian raids had done, and a Viking was placed on the throne of England. Canute (or Cnut) became king of both Denmark and England. His English policy, however, was one of reconciliation to the traditional families. He championed the cause of English Christianity, and brought a measure of stability to the island.

Once again the Normans managed to insinuate themselves into English history even after the island was lost to the Scandinavian invader. By this time Aethelred had died and his Norman widow was available for another marriage; once again she married the king of England, Canute the Dane. By her first marriage to the Anglo-Saxon king she was mother of an heir to the throne and by Canute she became mother to another, Hardicanute (or Harthacnut).

The course of English history nowhere becomes so confused and romantic as it does at this juncture. In the twice-married, twice Queen of England, we see the intersecting of the cross-currents which have affected the British Isles throughout history. The island is prisoner to its geographical location, caught on the north-south migratory routes of the Germanic tribes and situated on the outer path of the south-north road of Mediterranean cultural expansion. These northern and southern influences meet and merge in England. In the person of Emma these various strains are vividly embodied. As a Norman, she was by nationality Scandinavian. By culture she was Mediterranean. She spoke a language that was derived from the type of Latin spoken by the French legionnaires and farmers who settled in Gaul in the wake of Caesar's conquest. She was devoted to a religion that carried the stamp of its non-European origins. And as a Norman, Emma was a vigorous adherent of practical expansionism.

The marriage between Emma and the Anglo-Saxon Aethelred seemed to the English to give them a permanent claim on Normandy's support. In this, as we have seen, they were wrong. The Danish king Canute, it seems, married Emma with the idea that, as the widow of the former native king, she would impart to him and their heirs a degree of Anglo-Saxon legitimacy in the eyes of his English subjects. However wisely Canute had calculated the benefits of this marriage, Emma had other motives.

While Emma was back in England bearing and rearing a Scandinavian heir to the throne, her first son by Aethelred remained with his Norman kinsmen in France. As the years slipped by the English became acclimated to Danish rule and the new rulers were becoming acclimated to the island. The impression that the Danish rulers were being accepted was strengthened in 1035 when Canute died. In rapid succession two of his sons came to the throne of England, and each was in turn protected by English noblemen from threats launched by Aethelred's children who were taking the opportunity to regain their lost heritage. Emma's Danish son Hardicanute was eventually enthroned in England. By 1040 he felt secure enough to invite his half brother Edward to return to England. Within two years Edward succeeded to the throne, a relief to the English, since as Aethelred's son he represented the continuity of Anglo-Saxon rule.

Edward's thirty-year exile in France had left its mark on him. He brought back to England a Norman attitude to government and culture and showed preference to his Norman French acquaintances in making appointments to political and ecclesiastical posts. Edward was, in fact, so Norman in his preferments that he went so far as to name as heir to the English throne his cousin William, Duke of Normandy. The Anglo-Saxon nobles, however, did not take kindly to their king's French leanings since they had expected his restoration would mean a complete restoration of their rights as well. A civil war followed. The struggle failed to unseat Edward, but the nobles did succeed in forcing the king to submit to their will for the rest of his reign. During the last fourteen years of his life Edward acquired a reputation for piety, centering around his activities in building churches and monasteries which did not incite Anglo-Saxon mistrust. He came to be known as Edward the Confessor.

When he died in January 1066, Edward left no natural heir to the crown and the Anglo-Saxon nobles were not eager to see his chosen successor, the Duke of Normandy ascend to the throne. Harold son of Godwin, Duke of Wessex, the last Anglo-Saxon king of England, was crowned on January 6, 1066. Matters were unsettled. William's claim was a threat to the Anglo-Saxons. The same year there was a renewed Viking incursion. While King Harold was in the north trying to stave off the Norsemen, William the Norman earned his nickname, the Conqueror, by landing a force in the undefended south. When the harried English king hurried to fight him, William defeated him at the Battle of Hastings on the fourteenth of October. On Christmas day of 1066, less than a year after his cousin Edward's death, William the Conqueror was formally crowned king of England at Westminster Abbey.

When the Normans conquered England, they were met with a culture far more advanced than their own. Literacy and education was relatively common in England compared to Normandy. This is seen in the fact that the English kept numerous records of public and private doings, while written records of any kind were virtually unknown to the Norman French. Also the English were the first in Europe to find their daily language worthy of writing; other peoples wrote only in Latin.

The pen, however, in an open fight, is not mightier than the sword and so the literate English were conquered by the mostly illiterate Normans, both politically and for the time linguistically. Perhaps because William the Conqueror, shortly after his coronation, tried to learn English and failed, the Normans decided to retain their own language instead of adopting the language that they found on the island. Even in the face of the overwhelming military superiority of the French conquerors, who took complete control of the island, the *Anglo-Saxon Chronicle* was still being written in English nearly a hundred years after the Conquest. The upper classes of English society, nevertheless, came to speak French.

Within a scant generation of the Battle of Hastings, nearly all the leading personages of England were either French by birth or French speakers by preference. The adoption of the language of the Norman French invaders did not necessarily mean that the English also adopted their conquerors' anti-intellectual attitude toward literacy and culture. In the year 1140 a remarkable event occurred in the midlands of England, An event which is as notable in the history of ideas and culture as the Invasion had been in the annals of politics. In that year it is reported that the Lady Constance Fitz Gilbert of Lincolnshire had not only gone to the expense of paying one Mark in silver to have a vernacular poem on the life of Henry I copied out for herself, but that she also often read the poem in her room to herself. On the face of it, this may not seem too extraordinary, but this is the first recorded instance we know of in post-Roman Europe that popular literature written in the everyday tongue was purchased and read by an individual for pleasure. Within a quarter of a century of this momentous date there was in England a thriving trade in manuscripts of vernacular poetry which was fueled mostly by aristocratic ladies who sought light reading material.

At this time the vernacular language that the Anglo-Saxon aristocracy spoke and read was the French of the conqueror. An English writer[1] some two hundred years later, commenting on those times, tells us that wellborn children then were taught to "leve here oune longage" [leave their own language] for French from the time they were "yrokked in here cradel" [rocked in their cradle]. What was true of the aristocracy, who feared the politically dominant Normans and feared that they might seem ignorant if they could not speak French, was not true of the majority of Englishmen who continued to speak their native language.

Throughout the next two hundred fifty years or so Anglo-Saxon, now at the stage known as Middle English (from the late twelfth to late fifteenth century), was not only spoken by the masses of common men and women, but it was also written. Around 1205 Layamon of Worcestershire wrote a verse chronicle of English history (called *Brut*) of over 30,000 lines using fewer than fifty words borrowed from French. Still Anglo-Saxon could not resist for long the influence of the conquerors' language. Gradually not only bilingual Englishmen, but the lower classes who spoke only their native tongue began to assimilate a growing number of French words into their everyday speech. During this period the vocabulary of Anglo-Saxon changed and its grammar was affected, but English still managed to maintain a distinct identity. And many Englishmen began to view their native language with nationalistic pride.

In 1295 the Anglo-Norman king of England found himself at war with the king of France. He was not able to muster much enthusiasm for this particular war among his English subjects until he made the claim that his French adversary had threatened to utterly wipe out the English language in the event of his victory. This appeal to linguistic nationalism swung the vote.

At the beginning of the fourteenth century, French was still a compulsory subject in the grammar schools of England. But within two generations the tide rapidly changed. A schoolmaster named John Cornwell, it seems, was the first to experiment with a curriculum based on English rather than French. His reforms were carried further by one of his students, Richard Pencritch. Before long French was nearly unheard in the classrooms of English grammar schools. By 1362 a statute was decreed changing the official language of the law courts from French to English, because the former was "much unknown in the realm."

EXERCISES

EXERCISE VI.1 — DAILY LIFE: Read through all the sections A through J and choose projects in those that interest you.

A. THE RAW AND THE COOKED: In a famous passage from Sir Walter Scott's 1820 novel, *Ivanhoe*, Wamba, the jester, tells the pig-keeper, Gurth, that his herd will be converted into Normans before morning:

> "The swine turned Normans to my comfort!" quoth Gurth, "expound that to me Wamba, for my brain is too dull and my mind too vexed to read riddles."
>
> "Why, how call you those grunting brutes running about on four legs?" demanded Wamba.
>
> "Swine, fool—swine," said the herd; "every fool knows that."
>
> "And swine is good Saxon," said the jester, "but how call you the sow when she is flayed and drawn and quartered, and hung up by the heels like a traitor?"
>
> "Pork," answered the swineherd.
>
> "I am glad every fool knows that too," said Wamba, "and pork,[2] I think, is good Norman French. And so, when the brute lives and is in charge of a Saxon slave, she goes by her Saxon name, but becomes a Norman and is called pork when she is carried to the castlehall to feast among the nobles. . ."

And what of the other animals kept for the table? Anglo-Saxon on the hoof, but Norman on the platter:

> cow, oxen, kine turn into *beef*
> calf turns into *veal*
> deer become *venison*
> sheep become *mutton*
> fowl turn into *poultry*

Wamba concludes, "He is Saxon when he requires tendance, and takes a Norman name when he becomes a matter of enjoyment."

The social significance of the Norman Conquest is clearly seen in the language not only of domestic animals on the hoof and on the table, but in all aspects of life, from the kitchen to the court, from the boudoir to the battlefield. By the fifteenth century no form of business or pleasure could be talked about without the use of French words.

FOODS AND COOKING TERMS INFLUENCED BY FRENCH (eleventh to fifteenth centuries):

lentil	beef	mutton	veal	pork	bacon
venison	oyster	gravy	almond	mace	clove

sugar	ginger	onion	potage	gelatin	sauce
vinegar	oil	fig	spice	crepes	flour
grease	batter	suet	capon	mallard	date
saffron	raisin	paste	fruit	supper	dinner
bottle	banquet	table	feast	diet	plate
grape	blanche	boil	parboil	mince	fry[3]

Many additional words have entered English from French more recently; for example: casserole, croquette, meringue, ramekin, rissole, tureen, ragout, praline, liqueur, cuisine, aspic, hors d'oeuvre, café, gourmet, restaurant, menu, soufflé, purée, fondant, mousse, sauté. Look up some words from these lists and find their French origins and when they entered English.

VI. 1. B. — Two Recipes: In these recipes underline the words from French.

(1) A fifteenth century English recipe for crepes (at the time, called *cryspes*):

Take white of eyren, Milke, and fyne floure, and bete hit togidre, and drawe hit thorgh a streynour, so that hit be rennyng, and noght to stiff; and caste theer-to sugur and salt, And then take a chaffur[4] full of fressh grece boyling; and þen put thi honde in the batur and lete the bater ren thorgh thi fingers into þe chaffur; And when it is ren togidre in the chaffre, and is ynowe, take a Skymour, and take hit oute of the chaffur, and putte oute al the grece, And lete ren; And putte hit in a faire dissh, and cast sugur thereon ynow, and serue it forth.[5]

(2) A twentieth century recipe for pancakes. Notice how similar the two recipes are, except that English spelling and measurements have become more standardized and spoons are now recommended instead of fingers.

    1¼ cups all-purpose flour
    3 teaspoons baking powder
    1 teaspoon sugar
    ½ teaspoon salt
    1 egg, beaten
    1 cup milk
    2 tablespoons cooking oil.

Sift together flour, baking powder, sugar, and salt. Mix egg, milk, and oil; add to dry ingredients, stirring until the flour is moistened. The batter will be lumpy. Cook on a generously oiled hot griddle or skillet. Turn when the tops are bubbly. Serve with butter and maple syrup.

Project: Take a typical lunch or dinner menu and find out how many names of the dishes and their ingredients are from French.

VI. 1. C. — Gaudeamus igitur: besides the pleasures of the table, many of our daily delights are of French origin. All the words in the list below entered the English language within three centuries of the Norman Conquest.

joy	delight	ease	folly	park	ornament
parlor	music	tavern	lodge	revel	journey

sojourn	juggler	minstrel	dance	rubies	diamonds
chair	lamp	habit	attire	color	vestment
tryst	letter				

Projects: See if you can think of a native English synonym or a phrase with about the same meaning as each of these imported words. Which do you feel you could do without and which are necessary for a civilized and comfortable life. Write a story using all these words [optional].

VI. 1. D. — SINE QUA NON: We may be able to live without some of the luxuries in exercise C, but many words for things, actions, feelings which we could not conceive of doing without also came into our speech with the Normans. Try to think of native synonyms (words or phrases) for the following words. It may be difficult since the words from the classical tongues that entered through French are often the common ones:

air	rock	desert	beast	cave	gravel
river	flower	change	cry	delay	pass
fail	pay	sign	strive	catch	record (v.)
depart	disturb	place	age	manner	discipline
cellar	city	envy	silence	noise	perfection
country	figure	sponge	towel	cage	lesson
chapter	story	cause	merit	plenty	circumstance
glutton	feeble	jealous	fame		

VI. 1. E. — FAMILY TREE: only our closest kin are called by Anglo-Saxon terms: mother, father, son, daughter, child, brother, sister.[6] But aunt, uncle, niece, nephew, cousin are from French and ultimately from Latin. Even the grand- of grandparents and grandchildren is from French. In the thirteenth century *grandsire* and *grandame* (taken directly from French) were used, but were replaced in the fifteenth century by grandfather and grandmother, French-English hybrids. The element grand- (great, full-grown, grand) was later, illogically, extended to the words granddaughter, grandson, grandchildren, formations unknown in French, which uses *petite-fille*, *petit-fils*, *petits-enfants*, words that make more sense. Our in-laws, mother-in-law, father-in-law, and so forth are made up of English elements (with the Scandinavian law), but are direct translations of Old French compounds. The words sire and dame or dam, once terms of respect for one's parents are now used almost exclusively to refer to animals: Nyquist, American Pharaoh, California Chrome and Secretariat are said to have sire and dam, but not so the Secretary of State. In American slang dame has become a designation for one whom "there ain't nothin' like." In England, however, dame along with sir (of the same origin as sire < Latin *senior*, elder) has retained its respectful usage.

Project: choose one of your imported kin: find out how he or she came into English and from what French and Latin words. Or make up a family tree, giving a brief etymology of each relative. Find out where family, spouse, wife, and husband come from.

VI.1. F. — STRATA OF SOCIETY: many terms describing status in society came into English with the Norman Conquest as a result of the rapid and complete Normanizing of the ruling classes: William and his Normans held not only the throne and the administration of the realm, but had even dispossessed the important English landowners and replaced the native bishops and abbots with Frenchmen. The language of life and business for anybody with ambitions became French.

Words for status from French include master, servant, butler. Degrees of the English titled class from French: duke, marquis, viscount, baron. Count was not adopted because the (nearly) native earl came to have about the same meaning as the French *count*; but countess was borrowed for the earl's lady, in keeping with the French custom of giving the wife of a titled man a title as well. Knight (< Old English *cniht*) was also retained. The top ranks of the royal family, the king and queen, retained their native names, but their children's titles, the prince and princess are French in origin.

Words applying to royal power and court life are largely from French:

castle	crown	majesty	reign	scepter	throne
realm	state	power	royal	court	sovereign
empress	emperor				

Take one of these and trace it back to its beginning. All go back to Latin or Greek.

VI. 1. G. — WAR IS *L'ENFER*: *army* and *navy* and our military ranks are from French:

officer	private	corporal	sergeant	lieutenant
captain	major	colonel	general	commander
ensign	soldier	admiral (influenced by emir from Arabic)		

Many other terms relating to war and peace were also adopted at this time.

war	peace	battle	enemy	tower
assail	assault	arms	armor	tournament
archer	conquer	siege	victory	challenge
ensign	banner	pennon	standard	

(Note: *flag* is native)

Project: Choose one from either list and find its derivation. What was the original meaning? For example, lieutenant is from French *lieu tenant* < Latin *locum tenentem*, place holding. How does this meaning fit the actual duty of the officer? See if you can find other words from the same roots.

VI. 1. H. — PEOPLE, PROFESSIONS, WAYS OF LIFE : the French influence is found in all aspects of daily life and business. All these people are called by French titles:

minister	attorney	legate	nurse	friar	chancellor
squire	mason	mariner	porter	clerk	physician
host	hostage	virgin	harlot	felon	bachelor
marshal	page	rebel	parson	person	messenger

In the world of business we have these borrowings:

rich	market	rent	treasure	poor	(to) seal
robber	poverty	ransom	debt	purse	prosperity
relief	pay	heir	heritage	grant	adversity
coffer	bargain	profit	purchase	guile	extortion
merchandise					

Project: choose one of the words above and trace its history. Try to think of a native English word or phrase for the same thing.

VI. 1. I. — LAW AND ORDER: words from French having to do with the justice system include:

prison	justice	privilege	degree	judge	advocate
term	gibbet	charter	counsel	court	evidence
jury	assize	common	felony	govern	franchise
homage	crime	pardon	warrant	accuse	jurisdiction
penalty	plaintiff	plead	tenure	session	property
suit	summon	noble	senator	senate	constable
peer	parliament	mayor	official	defendant	

In the News of Record or Police Blotter of your school or local paper, find words relating to the legal system that came over with the Conqueror.

VI. 1. J. — FAITH AND MORALS: a very large number of words relating to religion are from French, among them:

service	abbot	religion	cardinal	sacrament	chaplain
miracle	mercy	prophet	baptism	pilgrim	procession
saint	chapel	grace	nativity	passion	evangelist
cell	sermon	disciple	archangel	patriarch	orison
clerk	grief	chalice	chasten	simony	confess
paten	pity	covet	charity	envious	trespass
bible	savior	trinity	penitence	advent	hermit
prelate	primate	angel	purgatory	nunnery	crucifix
image	tempt	abbey	assumption	collect	abstinence
purity	blame	preach	blaspheme	praise	parishioner
temptation					

Project: Go over the list and look up any that you do not know or that interest you.

Most are ultimately from Latin, though several are from Greek; abbot and abbey are from Aramaic. In a few instances the French influence is at second hand because the word had already been borrowed: for example, abbot replaced the earlier *abbod* and angel replaced the earlier *engel*.

VI. 2— DOUBLES

VI. 2. A. — FORMULAS: one result of the Norman Conquest has been the doubling of English vocabulary. Often the French word did not replace the native word, but lived side by side with it. In formal, legal and religious usage there are many expressions which show this tendency of keeping the native word, adopting a French word and using the two together in a formulaic phrase, as in:

last will and testament
to assemble and meet together
to pardon and forgive
to aid and abet[7]
by act and deed
to acknowledge and confess
safe and sound
we have erred and strayed
not dissemble nor cloak
pray and beseech
as many as are here present
all who profess and call themselves
from all the perils and dangers of this night
poor and needy
confirm and strengthen
flourish and abound
dearth and famine
scarcity and dearth

Project: choose one pair and find out:
—Which is French and which native?
—What is the origin and original meaning of each word?
—Try to find other words related to each of your words?
—Are there differences in meaning or usage between your two words?
—Use each in a sentence without the other and then try switching the words.
    Example: save and deliver — 1) Save the children. 2) Deliver us from evil.
    Switched: Deliver the children. Save us from evil.
—Which seems to you the more common word?

VI. 2. B.— OTHER DOUBLES: English has many other doubles, but in ordinary speech they are not usually used together. Go over the list: decide which word is more common. In Column III give some English derivatives of the Latin root of each word in column II.

I (native)	II (from Latin base)	III Derivatives
foe	enemy (in- + amic-)	Ex. inimical, enmity
friendly	amicable (amic-)	
begin	commence (com- + initi-)	
shut	close (claudere, -clud-/ clus-)	
wish	desire (desider-)	
sell	vend (vend-)	
tale	story (Greek *historia*)	
dread	terror (terr-)	
work	labor (labor-)	
meal	flour (flor-)	
writer	scribe (scrib-, script-)	
wedding	nuptials (nupt-, nub-)	
teachable	docile (doc-)	
twofold	double (duo)	
feeling	sentiment (sent(i)-)	
truly	verily (veri-)	
lawful	legal (leg-)	
bloom	flower (flor-)	
blessing	benediction (bene- + dic-/dict-)	
forerunner	precursor (pre- + curr-/curs-)	

VI. 2. c. — MATCH the French/Latin-derived word in column I with the native English word in column II that has the same meaning:[8]

I	II
1. felicity	a. feeder
2. provide	b. teaching
3. fraternity	c. freedom
4. illegality	d. manifold
5. script	e. lively
6. pastor	f. burdensome
7. verity	g. brotherhood
8. doctrine	h. heavenly
9. cordial	I. childish
10. multiple	j. writing
11. incredible	k. deathly
12. carnal	l. foretell
13. vital	m. behead
14. royal	n. hearty
15. regal	o. truthfulness
16. celestial	p. happiness
17. liberty	q. fiery

18. mortal	r. unbelievable
19. onerous	s. kingly (use twice)
20. puerile	t. foresee
21. predict	u. lawlessness
22. igneous	v. oversee
23. decapitate	w. fleshy
24. supervise	

VI.3. A — MORE DOUBLES: sometimes the native word remains the common word for the thing or action, but adjectives used to describe it are from French or Latin. For example:

Noun	Adjective(s)
life	lively or vital (< Latin *vita*, life)
death	deadly or mortal (< Latin *mors, mort-*, death)
birth	natal (< Latin *natus*, born)
moon	lunar (< Latin *luna*, moon)
sun	solar (< Latin *sol*, sun)
tail	caudal (< Latin *cauda*, tail)

Fill in the adjective in -al or -ar using the Latin base (underlined). Note: -ar is used if an *l* occurs in one of the two preceding syllables, as lunar, solar, and stellar (< *stella*, star)

English parts	Latin bases	Adjective
ex. eye	oculus	*ocular*
ear	auris	*aural*
mouth	os, or-	
nose	nasus	
tongue	lingua	
head	caput, capit-	
flesh	caro, carn-	
body	corpus, corpor-	
hand	manus	
foot	pes, ped-	
finger, toe	digitus	
tooth	dens, dent-	
lip	labium	
mind	mens, ment-	

Sometimes the noun and adjective are both from Latin, but they look and sound different because the noun was borrowed from French and the adjective directly from Latin. For example:

Noun	Adjective	Latin base
voice	vocal	vox, voc-

ray	radial	radius
judge	judicial	judex, judic-
beast	bestial	bestia
doubt	dubious	dubium
feast	festal	festum
nurse	nutritious	nutrire (> nutrix, nutric-)

VI. 3. B — VARIETIES OF FRENCH: a further complication is difference in dialect between Norman and Parisian French which results in another small series of doubles or twice-borrowed words. In this list, choose one pair and find:

—The Latin original

—The differences in meaning between the words in each pair

Norman	Parisian
hard c	ch
catch	chase
capital	chapter
cancel	chancel
cattle	chattel
w	gu (words are of Germanic origin through French)
wage	gage / gauge
warden	guardian
g	j
gaud (gaudy)	joy

EXERCISE VI. 4 — REBORROWINGS: the words in this list have been borrowed twice or more, once from French and directly from Latin or once from popular French and then from literary French. Such pairs usually differ in meaning, if only slightly. Choose two sets.

—Look up the origin of the words in each group and explain the differences in meaning.

—Use each word in a sentence.

1. abbreviate — abridge
2. aggravate — aggrieve
3. amicable — amiable
4. carnal — charnel
5. compute — count
6. fact — feat
7. defect — defeat
8. estimate — esteem
9. fragile — frail
10. ratio — ration — reason
11. pauper — poor
12. prosecute — pursue

13. respect — respite
14. pungent — poignant
15. quiet — coy
16. cohort — court
17. corona — crown
18. faction — fashion
19. gentile — genteel — gentle
20. invidious — envious
21. legal — leal — loyal
22. major — mayor
23. pallid — pale
24. piety — pity
25. senior — sire — sir
26. vocal — vowel
27. species — spice
28. tradition — treason
29. dignity — dainty
30. conception — conceit
31. hospital — hostel — hotel
32. potion — poison
33. penitence — penance
34. particle — parcel
35. redemption — ransom

NOTES

1. John Trevisa in his 1387 translation of Ranulf Higden's *Polychronicon*.

2. The root *porko- properly means "young pig" and has among its derivatives: PORCUPINE (porco- + spina, *thorn*), PORCELAIN (from its resemblance to a young sow's back), PORPOISE (porco + piscis, *fish*), AARDVARK (Dutch "earth-pig"), and the Old English FARROW (a litter of pigs). The English SWINE also has its Latin cognate in *sus*, pig, which is the origin of SOIL (*to dirty*) and its Greek cognate *hus*, the source of HYENA.

3. The puerile move to change the name of French fries to "freedom fries" in the US congressional dining room was a failure from the start, since *fry* itself comes from French.

4. *Chaffur*, a deep fryer < Old French *chaufer*, to heat.

5. Quoted from Mary S. Serjeantson. *A History of Foreign Words in English*. New York: Dutton, 1936 (Barnes & Noble, 1960), p. 150.

6. Even sister has been affected by Scandinavian: the modern *sister* is not directly descended from A-S *sweoster*, but Old Norse *syster*.

7. Both *aid* and *abet* are actually from French, but *abet* was borrowed from the Scandinavians. Also *save* and *deliver* and *flourish* and *abound* are ultimately from Latin.

8. Answers for VI. 2. C: 1–p; 2–20; 3–g; 4–u; 5–j; 6–a; 7–o; 8–b; 9–n; 10–d; 11–r; 12–w; 13–e; 14–s; 15–s; 16–h; 17–c; 18–k; 19–f; 20–1; 21–1; 22–q; 23–m; 24–v.

SECTION ONE: HISTORY IN WORDS

AFTERWORD: MODERN ENGLISH

With the fourteenth century begins a remarkable development in the English language. It is the time of the beginning of the Great Vowel Shift, when the English long vowels began to be pronounced with the tongue higher in the mouth, a change that differentiates the sound of Modern English from that of Middle English.[1] In the Middle English period the vowel sounds were very close to the standard European vowels. After the vowel shift, we now pronounce, for example, a long *a* as most European languages pronounce long *e* and a long *e* as they pronounce a long *i.* That the change in pronunciation was not accompanied by a change in spelling is a major cause of the present confusion in English spelling, in which the same letter represents different sounds and the same sound may be spelled by different letters, in short, a cacographical spelling system.[2] Also in the late fifteenth century came the introduction of printing. The printed book exercises a tyranny over the written language that the manuscript could never achieve. Literacy became more widespread as books proliferated. Little by little spelling became standardized, but not rationalized. Attempts have been made at reform, but without success. Still there is something to be said for retaining the historical spelling: it can help us see where words came from and this can help us understand not only their origins but their meanings.

In the previous chapters we have introduced the foreign influence on English. Although many of the borrowed words at all periods came from literature, most entered from the spoken tongues of the people with whom the English came in contact. During the English Renaissance (the sixteenth and first half of the seventeenth centuries) the growth of English vocabulary was enormous. Words were taken in right and left from Latin and Greek called—by those who opposed the wholesale borrowing from the classical tongues—INKHORN words. There was a conscious effort on the part of many writers and scholars to enlarge the vocabulary of English and to make their native tongue a means of communication to rival Latin. The spread of education had produced a literate but semi-Latinless public for whom translations and epitomes of Latin literature were made. Anyone familiar with the process of translation will recognize that it is natural to translate a word with a word like itself. Often the native equivalent does not occur at once or there is no native equivalent and rather than go through a long periphrasis, the translator simply Englishes the Latin word. The exuberance of some writers at times went too far and must have sounded like the bureaucratic, administrative, and academic jargon that rings so harsh and incomprehensible in unaccustomed ears. Many words (like *adminiculation, eximious, impetrate*) missed the mark and were dropped before they ever caught on. Others have become so popular that we can hardly imagine living without them: words like *maturity, education, affability*, and hundreds of others. If ever we begin to think of Latin as a dead language, it is a good exercise to try to write a paragraph without any words from Latin or to take a page from a newspaper or magazine and cross out the words from Latin: it will have more black marks than a CIA redaction. The size of its vocabulary is one of the most conspicuous features of English. It has made the language one of the most remarkable human inventions ever. Technical terms are invented daily, mostly from Latin and Greek. We can well rejoice in the xenophilic nature of English which accepts immigrant words readily and does not cast a snobbish or ethnocentric eye on them. Neologisms are courageously forged from elements of various heritage,[3] as we exercise the very human prerogative of naming things. In the chapters that follow we will consider in the main LEARNED WORDS of the kind that began to flood into English during the Renaissance. Some may smell of the inkpot, but the principles you will learn will make these concoctions easy to understand and will allow you to create your own with facility and felicity when the need arises.

REVIEW EXERCISE — Multiple Choice Questions[4]
1. Which is *not* an Italic language?
      a. Latin b. French c. Spanish d. Italian e. Greek f. Romanian
2. Which of these belongs to the Indo-European family?
      a. Estonian b. Turkish c. Persian d. Basque e. Korean f. Magyar
3. Which word is derived from a person's name?
      a. smithy b. burke c. sweater d. cartwright   e. fjord f. ford
4. Which language did not make a large contribution to Modern English?
      a. Latin b. Welsh c. French d. Anglo-Saxon
5. Underline the words that come from languages other than Latin:
      a. mugwump b. floccule c.uncle d. shibboleth e. scrupulosity f. bugaboo

ENDGAME: LOCATE THE ORIGIN OF THESE WORDS
This is best done as a group exercise: choose two or three, look them up and find out WHERE they come from. If you have a wall map, it would be fun to place a pin on each of the places in the list.

Example: MAGENTA—*A bright purplish red*. The name comes from a town in Italy, Magenta, where a bloody battle was fought just before the discovery of the dye.

copper	silk	antimacasser	bedlam
blarney	canter	calico	cambric
currant	damask	damson	lesbian
guinea	cologne	magnet	limerick
meander	milliner	sardonic	donnybrook
sybarite	peach	denim	[blue] jeans
wiener	hamburger	frankfurter	bologna
pilsner	bible	bunkum	cos (lettuce)
cheddar	Parmesan		

WORDS IN CONTEXT

When the *psionic* fire went out of her . . .
> Michael Chabon, *Telegraph Avenue*, 2012

psionic < psi (*psyche*) + [electr]onics; meaning: paranormal, telepathic.

. . .the wings had been lifeless films and struts of *chitin* . . .
> E. O. Wilson, *Anthill*, 2010

chitin < Greek *chiton*, a man's garment, tunic; meaning: the material of the exoskeleton of insects.

Ants, forced to be *pheremonal*, think only in taste and smell.
> E. O. Wilson, *Anthill*, 2010

pheremone < Greek *pherein*, carry + [hor]mone; meaning: chemical that triggers a social response.

VOCABULARY NOTE:

GUN: a portable firearm, such as a rifle or revolver; also a cannon.

From Middle English *gonne*, cannon, short for *Gunnilda*, a woman's name, applied to a siege engine, from Old Norse *Gunnhildr*. In the records of munitions at Windsor Castle for 1330 is this entry:

una magna balista de cornu quae vocatur Domina Gunilda.

[a large military machine of horn which is called the Lady Gunilda].

Appropriately to the derivative (though not to women given this name) the two parts of the name *gunnr* and *hildr* both mean war. *Gunnr* is from the I-E root *gwhen-, strike or kill. Other related words include: bane, gonfalon (< Italian for battle flag), defend (< Latin *defendere*, ward off), fence, and offend, and the *bahn* of *autobahn*.

NOTES

1. The period of Middle English is roughly from the late twelfth to the late fifteenth century; Early Modern English (also called the language of Shakespeare) lasted from the late fifteenth to the mid-seventeenth century.

2. The linguistic word puzzle, *what does* ghoti *spell?* is humorous evidence of this cacographical chaos. It spells FISH: *gh* as in *enough*; *o* as in *women*; *ti* as in *ignition*.

3. The jocular word *snowmageddon*, compounded from snow plus Armageddon, in 2009 to characterize a Canadian blizzard and popularized in the U.S. in 2010 for another major snow storm is a good example: snow is from Old English *snaw*; -mageddon is from Armageddon, the Biblical site of the final battle before the end of the world, from a Hebrew phrase meaning "the mountain region of Megiddo."

4. Answers: 1–e; 2–c; 3–b; 4–b; 5–a, d, f.

SECTION TWO: LATIN WORDS IN ENGLISH

CHAPTER ONE: VADE MECUM

So many Latin words have entered English, both the everyday word stock and the technical and scientific vocabularies of nearly every field, that even a brief introduction to Latin and how it works can be of immeasurable help in understanding and organizing the English lexicon. English and Latin share an Indo-European heritage, but are quite different in their grammars. Though an ability to understand human language and its structure may be innate to human beings, knowledge of grammatical terminology is not. To be able to talk about language we need a common vocabulary which, for better or worse, has been provided by our forebears. Most of our grammatical vocabulary is derived from Latin and much of it, in fact, ultimately, from Greek: not that the Latin terms are derived from Greek, but they are direct translations of Greek words and phrases. As off-putting as grammar and its jargon often seem, take a moment to compare this list selected from the Abbot Aelfric's coined Anglo-Saxon equivalents with the Latinate words they translate.

Aelfric's Coinage	Modern English Term (from Latin)
name	noun
word	verb
namen speliend	pronoun
betwuxaworpennys	interjection
dael nimend	participle
staefgefeg	syllable
clypiendlice	vowels
healfclypiendlice	semi-vowels
undertheodendlic	subjunctive

After NAME (noun < Latin *nomen*, name) and WORD (verb < Latin *verbum*, word) Aelfric's offerings are a mouthful to utter and feel more foreign than their Latin equivalents.

PARTS OF SPEECH

In speaking of grammar, traditionally we start with PARTS OF SPEECH (a translation of the Latin phrase *partes orationis*, which is itself a translation of the Greek expression *ta merē ta tēs phōnēs*). We usually divide speech into eight parts, though that number is not absolute:

English	Latin
noun	*nomen* (name)
verb	*verbum* (word)
adjective	*adjectivum* (something thrown, or added, to)
adverb	*adverbium* (thing beside the word/verb)
pronoun	*pronomen* (instead of a name/noun)
preposition	*praepositio* (a putting before, thing put before)
conjunction	*conjunctio* (a joining together)
interjection	*interjectio* (a throwing in between)

These PARTS OF SPEECH in the two languages correspond to a great degree. In a simple sentence we would probably use a noun to translate a noun and a verb to translate a verb. But the process is more than a mere word for word correspondence.

In an English sentence how do we determine what part of speech a given words is? It is not always easy to do. In general we go by the function of a word in relation to other words in the sentence. We ask, "What part does this word play in the sentence?" In Latin, on the other hand, not only function, but form (how the word looks) tells us what part of speech a word is. This is a major difference between the grammars of English and Latin.

Latin has a means, that English does not have to any great extent, to enable a reader or listener to determine the part of speech by the shape of the word: Latin has INFLECTIONS. It is what we call an INFLECTED language. What this means is that it changes the form of the word to show its relation to the other words in the sentence. How does English show these relations? Not, in general, by changing the form[1], but by the PLACEMENT of the words. Usually we can tell what a sentence means by its adherence to accepted word order. Not so in Latin. In Latin the order of words is much more flexible, because the form of a word tells what its relation is to other words.

In English, to take a simple, historical example, we would say:

Brutus killed Caesar.[2]

From the order of the words we know who did the deed and who had it done to him. And if we changed these words around we would get the grammatically correct but anti-historical utterance:

Caesar killed Brutus.

Or a jumble of words. There are, as common sense and the rules of permutations, show us, six possibilities for arranging the three words. The first two make sense, but only one is right. Two others could make sense if the right tone of voice is used, but are affectations:

Brutus Caesar killed.

Caesar, Brutus killed.

The last two might work as pretentiously contrived questions, but are closer to nonsense:

Killed Brutus Caesar?

Killed *Caesar* Brutus?

The words can be listed in any of these ways, but only the first says what we want it to say in an unaffected style. It is the only order acceptable for prose.

In Latin, to make the same statement, we also have three words:

Brutus: Brutus (in the nominative, used for the sbject)

interfecit: [he] killed

Caesarem: Caesar (in the accusative case: the case for the object)

The word *Brutus* in Latin tells us more than the name of the man. Because the ending *-us* is a NOMINATIVE ending, it says that Brutus is the subject of the sentence, the one who did the killing, the actor in the plot. The other noun (or name) in the sentence, *Caesarem*, can be only the object of the sentence, the victim of the plot, the one who received the action of the active verb *killed*. The ending *-em* tells us this. We can arrange the three words in any of the six possible orders without changing the relationship between the doer and the receiver of the action, the killer and victim in the grammatical drama of this sentence.

In Latin the most normal arrangement would be:

Brutus Caesarem interfecit.

subject—object—verb

Any of the other orders is possible and would not offend the ears of a Roman. The emphasis would be changed somewhat if we put the victim first and the killer last and interposed the action between them, but the GRAMMATICAL RELATIONSHIP WOULD REMAIN UNCHANGED, because *Brutus* is NOMINATIVE and, therefore, the subject of the verb; and *Caesarem* is ACCUSATIVE and the object.

Caesarem interfecit Brutus.

Brutus interfecit Caesarem.

Caesarem Brutus interfecit.

Interfecit Brutus Caesarem.

Interfecit Caesarem Brutus.

All are possible. All say the same thing.

1. Nouns

Nominative and accusative are the names of cases. CASE (< Latin *casus*, a falling, translated from the Greek equivalent *ptōsis*) tells the relation of nouns, adjectives, and pronouns to one another in the context of a sentence. The cases in Latin are:

NOMINATIVE (nom. < Latin *nomen, nomin-*, name): for the subject of the sentence and anything that agrees with the subject.

GENITIVE (gen. < Latin *genitum*, past participle of *gignere*, to beget, bear <

genus, gener-, birth, origin): the case of origin, that is, of direct dependence of one noun on another. One of the most common uses of the genitive is to show possession: for example, "Brutus' dagger": *sicca Bruti* (of Brutus); "Caesar's death": *mors Caesaris* (of Caesar).

DATIVE (dat. < Latin, *datum*, past participle of *dare*, to give): the case of giving, used for the indirect object, and other relationships implied by English *to* or *for*: for example, "a wound to Caesar": *vulnus Caesari*.

ACCUSATIVE (acc. < Latin *accusare, accusatum* < *causa*, cause): the case of the thing caused by the action of the verb, used for the direct object, the one that receives directly the action of the verb: "he killed Caesar": *necavit Caesarem*. The accusative is used for other relationships and, like the objective case in English, it is used with prepositions: *ad urbem*, to the city.

ABLATIVE (abl.< Latin *ab-*, away + *latum*, the past participle of *ferre*, to carry): the case of separation (for which we use the preposition *from*); also used for instrument (*with, by*) and location (*in, at, on*). For example, "It was done by Brutus" (*a Bruto*), "by Caesar" (*a Caesare*). He was killed with a sword (*gladio*). It is used with and without a preposition.

VOCATIVE (voc.< Latin *vocatum*, past participle of *vocare*, call < *vox, voc-*, voice): the case of calling or addressing someone directly: *et tu, Brute* ("even you, Brutus"); *ave, Caesar* ("hail, Caesar").

English is clearly capable of expressing the same relationships as Latin, but where Latin changes the endings of the nouns, English either puts the words in a certain word order (subject, verb, object) or uses prepositional phrases. The branch of grammar that deals with the way words are put together to form sentences and phrases is called SYNTAX (< Greek *sun-*, with, together + *tassein*, to arrange). The syntax of Latin is basically INFLECTIONAL: relationships are shown by different endings; that of English is POSITIONAL: relationships are shown by the placement of words in the sentence or phrase. An inflected language like Latin (or Greek) is also called, in linguistic jargon, SYNTHETIC (< Greek *sun-* + *tithenai*, to put); an essentially uninflected language like English (Turkish or Chinese) is called ANALYTIC (< Greek *ana-*, up, throughout + *luein*, to break) because it tends to use two or more words instead of a single inflected form: for example we break up into two or more words expressions like "to her", "with a sword", "they were going" for which Latin would use a single word (*ei, gladio, ibant*).

On the other hand, English still uses inflected forms of its personal pronouns (I, my, me; he, his, him; she, hers, her; they, their, them; we, our, us; you and it have shed their inflections, except for a possessive); and for the relative and interrogative pronouns (who, whose, whom). These must still go into their proper places.

Further Characteristics of Nouns

Besides CASE, nouns have NUMBER, which tells how many are involved: one

(SINGULAR) or more than one (PLURAL).[3] Latin has a variety of endings to show number and a separate ending for each of the cases in singular and plural. English shows the plural regularly by adding -s or -es to the singular. In a few words there is vowel gradation in the plural; that is, the stem vowel is changed, as in woman, women; man, men; mouse, mice; louse, lice; goose, geese. A few nouns show other changes, as child, children; ox, oxen. Some words are the same in singular and plural, as fish, moose.

In Latin, nouns have GENDER, whether or not we attach to them any kind of natural characteristics that would make gender identification automatic. In general, however, nouns referring to natural females are FEMININE; those referring to males are MASCULINE; but other nouns referring to things to which our minds attach no gender can be MASCULINE, FEMININE, or NEUTER. This is called GRAMMATICAL GENDER. Thus, a sword in Latin (*gladius*) is masculine; its sheath (*vagina*) is feminine; the wound it makes (*vulnus*) is neuter. A book (*liber*) is masculine; the quality of manliness (*virtus*) along with many other abstractions is feminine; the sea (*mare*) is neuter. In English we do not put up with such arbitrary regulations: only male people or animals are masculine: for them we substitute *he, his, him.* Only females are feminine and take *she, hers, her.* Everything else is called *it*, except for some vehicles, machines, whales, and disasters—until the naming of hurricane Bob—to which we imaginatively fix feminine personalities and pronouns, as in "she's a beaut" or "thar she blows." We use gender only when we believe or mean to say that something or someone is masculine or feminine. In the plural English pronouns make no gender distinctions, which has led to the growing tendency to use the gender-neutral *they* and, especially, *their* to refer to a singular noun.

Finally, nouns in Latin are said to belong to DECLENSIONS. A declension is simply a pattern of inflection according to which a group of nouns changes its endings for case and number. The classification of nouns by declension is a useful tool. Latin has five declensions, referred to by the ordinal numbers first through fifth. Except in a few very rare instances, each noun belongs to one declension and does not change to another. The cases have the same uses no matter what declension the noun belongs to. Examples of the declensions are given in Appendix I.[4] There are some variations, but these are the basic patterns and are more than sufficient for your study of English word formation.

How to Recognize Latin Nouns in Word Lists

When a noun is listed in the vocabulary of a Latin book or in a Latin dictionary, the nominative, genitive, and gender (m, f, n) are given. The genitive is included for two reasons:

1. To show the base, which is not always clear from the nominative.[5]
2. To show the declension or pattern the noun follows.

In this book, nouns will be given in the nominative; the base will be given if it is not clear in the nominative form. The gender will only be given if it affects the plural formation.

Examples:

amicus, amici, m., friend, belongs to the second declension which we see from *-us*, *-i* endings. The base is *amic-* (amici-).

rex, regis, m., king, belongs to the third declension which shows *-is* in the genitive. The base is *reg-* (regi-).

> Rule: the base of a noun is found by removing the case ending from the genitive singular. English derivatives usually come from the base. For example, from *rex, reg-*: regal, regalia, regicide. *-i-* is the most common combining or connecting vowel.

genus, generis, n., race, origin, kind, belongs to the third declension. The -us ending does not make this clear because it is also found in the nominative of both second and fourth declension nouns. The genitive not only shows the base (*gener-*) but makes the declension clear. In English we use the word *genus*, with plural *genera* in taxonomy, but most other derivatives are built on the base: for example, general, generous, degenerate.[6]

poeta, -ae, m., poet and *agricola, -ae*, m., farmer and a few others[7] belong to the first declension and are masculine, even though most first declension nouns are feminine. Membership in a declension does not necessarily determine gender.

Latin Noun Plurals

It is important to learn the plurals of the various declensions because sometimes (though by no means always) the Latin plural is the only correct form of the plural of a Latin noun that comes directly (that is, without any change) into English. Often an English plural with *-s* or *-es* exists alongside a Latin plural (for example: *antenna*, plural *antenna*s or *antenna*e). Sometimes the word uses the English plural in its everyday use and the Latin plural in a scientific sense.

> BASE: the part of a word that remains constant though the endings change. The *base* is used in the formation of most English derivatives and in the formation of the plural.

First Declension

    Nouns ending in -a, plural in -ae

        alumna [foster daughter], pl. *alumnae*

    Most nouns of the first declension are feminine. The base of a first declension noun is found by removing -a from the given (or nominative) form.

Second Declension

    Nouns ending in -us, plural in -i

        alumnus [foster son], pl. *alumni*

    Most nouns in -us are masculine. The base is found by removing -us from the nominative.[8]

Nouns ending in -um, plural in -a

datum [thing given], pl. *data*

All these nouns are neuter. The base is found by removing -um from the nominative.

Third Declension

Nouns of this type vary widely in the nominative (or subject form) and usually a second form, showing the base, must be learned.

appendix [f. an addition], base *appendic-*, plural *appendices* (or appendixes)

onus [n. burden], base *oner-*, plural *onera*

Plurals:

a) masculine and feminine, base + -es

index [forefinger, pointer], base *indic-*, pl. *indices* (or indexes)

cicatrix [scar > scar tissue], base *cicatric-*, pl. *cicatrices*

b) neuter, base + -a

genus [kind, birth], base *gener-*, pl. *genera*

corpus [body], base *corpor-*, pl. *corpora*

In the vocabularies, the bases and, where useful, also the genders of these nouns will be given.

Fourth Declension

Nouns end in -us (the few neuters end in -u); the Latin plural is spelled the same as the singular (the neuters in -ua), but the Latin plurals of these are not much used in English, except for formal scientific writing.

The base is found by removing -s or -us.

gradus [step] > gradual, grade: base gradu- or grad-

sensus [feeling] > sensual, sense: base sensu- or sens-

For masculines and feminines the nominative plural in Latin is the same as the singular.

hiatus [gap], pl. hiatuses (or *hiatus*)

plexus [network], pl. plexuses (or *plexus*)

nexus [bond, link, connection], pl. nexuses (or *nexus*)

apparatus [preparation, system, device], pl. apparatuses or *apparatus*

For neuters the Latin plural adds -a.

cornu [horn], pl. *cornua*

Fifth Declension

Nouns in -es; the plural is the same as the singular

species [appearance > kind], pl. *species*

series [row], pl. *series*

The base is found by removing -es.

Every noun has gender, but this need only be a concern in determining the plural of third declension nouns.

EXERCISES

EXERCISES I. 1 — LATIN PLURALS: form the plurals of the following. (Numbers in parentheses indicate declensions; neut. stands for neuter).
Examples:

> erratum (mistake, thing that has gone wrong, II) > pl. errata
>
> caries (dry rot, V) > pl. caries

1. datum (thing given, II)
2. memorandum (thing to be noted, II)
3. corpus, corpor-is (body, III neut.)
4. focus (hearth, II)
5. addendum (thing to be added, II)
6. formula (small form, I)
7. curriculum (place for running, II)
8. stadium (race-track, II)
9. index, indic-is (pointer, III m.)
10. medium (thing in the middle, II)
11. dictum (thing said, II)
12. antenna (yardarm, I)
13. axis, ax-is (pole, III m.)
14. basis, bas-is (base, III f.)
15. gladiolus (little sword, II)
16. locus (place, II)
17. Magus (wise man, II)
18. nucleus (little nut, II)
19. ovum (egg, II)
20. nebula (mist, I)
21. series (sequence, V)
22. opus, oper-is (III neut.)
23. excursus (raid, running out, IV)
24. salmonella (I) (New Latin < Daniel E. Salmon)
25. talus (ankle, heel, II)
26. sternum (< Greek *sternon*, breastbone, II)
27. primordium (beginning, II)
28. genu (knee, IV neut.)
29. carpus (wrist, II)
30. rostrum (beak > pl. orators' platform, II)
31. erratum (thing that has gone wrong, II)
32. nidus (nest, II)
33. sinus (curve, hollow, IV)
34. quercus (oak, IV f.)
35. species (appearance, V)

2. Adjectives

In Latin adjectives have the same characteristics as nouns: they belong to declensions and have case, number, and gender. The major difference between adjectives and nouns is that gender is not inherent to adjectives, as it is to nouns. In Latin, adjectives differ from nouns in that they change gender according to the gender of the noun that they qualify. Otherwise, in form, they are for the most part like nouns. The largest class of adjectives shows -*us* (masculine), -*a* (feminine), -*um* (neuter) in the nominative singular and belongs to the first (for feminine) and second (for masculine and neuter) declensions:

> *altus, alta, altum* (high, deep)

The base is found by removing -us/-a/-um.[9]

There are also adjectives in the third declension. Most are of two-terminations: one for masculine and feminine (-*is*), the other for neuter (-*e*). There are some single-termination adjectives, using the same form in the nominative singular for all genders; for these the base will be given:

> *omnis, omne* (all): base omni-
>
> *sapiens* (wise): base sapient-

Adjectives have comparative and superlative degrees, comparable to English -er (more) and -est (most). In Latin, the regular formation is base + -*ior* (m., f.) and -*ius* (n.) for the comparative; -*issimus, -a, -um* (with variations) for the superlative. *Junior* (younger) and *senior* (older) are examples of comparatives from Latin. Superlatives are most commonly seen in Italian musical terms ending in -*issimo*, like *fortissimo* (very loud < Latin *fortissimus*, strongest). The comparatives and superlatives that have been used to form the most English words are the irregularly formed ones. These have to be learned as separate vocabulary entries.
For example:

> *magnus*, large, great > magnum, magnify, magnitude
>
> *maior, maius*, larger, greater > major, majority
>
> *maximus*, largest, greatest > maximum, max out, to the max, maximalist

EXERCISES

EXERCISE I. 2 — LATIN ADJECTIVES AND NOUNS IN WELL-KNOWN PHRASES: choose five or six and pick the correct form of the adjective to agree with the noun (in gender, number, and case) in each expression. Give the meaning of each of your chosen expressions. Hints are given. (Consult Appendix I if necessary.)

1. *res* (f.) _____   *adjudicatus   adjudicata   adjudicatum*
   (*res*, "matter at law")
2. *Pater* (m.) _____   *noster   nostra   nostrum*
3. _____ *opus* (neut.)   *magnus   magna   magnum*
4. _____ *ego* (m.[10])   *alter   altera   alterum*
5. _____ *fide* (f. abl.)   *bonus   bonā   bonum*
6. _____ *bonum* (neut., adj. used as a noun)   *communis   commune*

7. *ceteris* (n. pl. abl.)   *pares*   *pari*   *paribus*
   ("other things being equal")
8. *Deo* _____ (abl.)   *volens*   *volente*
9. *fraus* _____ (f. nom.)   *pius*   *pia*   *pium*
   ("a pious deception")
10. *in* _____ *res* (f. acc. pl.)   *medius*   *medias*   *medios*
11. *in* _____ *personā* (f. abl.)   *propriae*   *propriā*   *proprio*
12. _____ *verba* (neut. pl.)   *ipsissimus*   *ipsissimum*   *ipsissima*
13. _____ *facto* (neut. abl.)   *ipso*   *ipsa*   *ipsum*
14. *loco* _____ (m. abl.)   *citatus*   *citato*   *citatum*
15. _____ *Charta* (f.)   *Magnus*   *Magna*   *Magnum*
16. _____ *cum laude* (f. abl.)   *summo*   *summā*   *summis*
17. _____ *homo* (m. nom. sg.)   *novus*   *novi*   *novum*
(used of one who gains distinction on his own rather than through family influence)
18. _____ *facie* (f. abl. sg.)   *primus*   *primo*   *primā*
19. _____ *avis* (f.)   *rarus*   *rara*   *rarum*
20. _____ *generis* (neut. gen.) *suum*   *suo*   *sui*
21. *terra* _____ (f.)   *firmus*   *firmae*   *firma*
22. *corpus* _____ (neut.)   *luteus*   *lutea*   *luteum*

3. Adverbs

Adverbs are used to qualify verbs, adjectives, or other adverbs. Even in Latin they are not inflected. A few Latin adverbs come directly into English, some as adverbs, others as nouns or adjectives.

Adverb	Meaning of Latin word
alibi	elsewhere
alias	otherwise
interim	meanwhile
item	likewise
tandem	at length
verbatim	word for word
gratis	for free
extra	beyond
passim	everywhere, throughout

EXERCISES

Exercise I. 3 — LATIN ADVERBS
Choose three or four of the adverbs above. Tell what parts of speech they are in English and use each in a sentence or phrase.

4. Pronouns

Pronouns stand for nouns and so are declined according to case, number, and gender. In Latin, as in English, pronouns fall into several categories:

Personal: I (*ego*); we (*nos*); you (*tu, vos*), etc.

Reflexive: self—herself, himself, themselves (*sui*)

Relative: who, which, that (*qui, quae, quod*; with some forms in *cui-*)

Interrogative: who, what? (*quis, quid*)

Intensive: -self (*ipse*)

Demonstrative: this, that (*hic, haec, hoc; is, ea, id; ille, illa, illud*)

Indefinite: someone, something (*aliquis, aliquid* and many others in Latin)

Some English Words Derived from Latin Pronouns

ego, super-ego, id: the Freudian terms for parts of the psyche.

suicide: self-slaughter

quiddity: what-ness: that which distinguishes a thing from everything else.

quidnunc: what now?: a busybody or gossip

EXERCISES

EXERCISE I.4 — LATIN PRONOUNS IN USEFUL EXPRESSIONS: many common phrases use Latin pronouns, for example:

1. ad hoc   "to/for this"
2. ipse dixit; ipsa dixit   "he himself said it"; "she herself said it"
3. quid pro quo   "what for what"
4. status quo   "state at which"
5. alter ego   "another I"
6. ipso facto   "by the very fact / by the fact itself"
7. per se   "through itself" (see also ampersand, *and* per se *and*)
8. sui generis   "of its own kind"
9. sine qua non   "without which, not"
10. pax vobiscum   "peace be with you"
11. cui bono   "for whose good?"
12. inter nos   "among us / ourselves"
13. post hoc, ergo propter hoc   "after this, therefore because of this"
14. Q. E. D. (*quod erat demonstrandum*) "which was to be demonstrated"
15. Te Deum laudamus   "we praise you, God"
16. terminus ante quem   "limit before which" [also, terminus post quem]
17. i.e. (id est)   "that is"
18. q.v. (quod vide)   "which see"
19. me judice   "with me as judge" (IMHO)
20. vade mecum   "go with me" (one's constant companion)
21. locus in quo   "the place in which"[11]

Choose three or four of these expressions. Identify the pronouns by type (personal, relative, etc.). Use each phrase in a sentence.

5. Prepositions

Latin prepositions are used with the accusative and ablative cases and, in general, further define the meaning of the case with which they are used. Their influence on English is primarily as prefixes added to verb, adjective, and noun bases.

Examples of prepositions:

Latin	With (case)	Meaning	Meaning as prefix	Derivatives
a, ab, abs	ablative	from	off, away	avert, abduct, abstruse
e, ex	ablative	out of	out, completely	evert, exact
per	accusative	through	through, thoroughly	perfect

EXERCISES

EXERCISE I. 5 — LATIN PREPOSITIONAL PHRASES: although the Latin prepositions are most important to our study in their role as prefixes, their force as prepositions can be seen in these common Latin expressions:

1. ab initio   "from the beginning"
2. ad infinitum   "to the endless" (i.e., "without end")
3. ad litteram   "to the letter"
4. ad rem   "to the matter"
5. cum laude   "with praise" (magna cum laude, summa cum laude)
6. cum grano salis   "with a grain of salt"
7. de facto   "from the thing done"
8. e pluribus unum   "from more/many, one"
9. ex tempore   "from the time"
10. in absentia   "in absence"
11. in extremis   "at the last" ("at death's door," "in a dire situation")
12. inter nos   "between/among ourselves"
13. per annum   "through the year" ("for each year")
14. per se   "through itself"
15. pro tempore   "for the time"
16. sine qua non   "without which not"
17. de profundis   "from the depths"
18. in toto   "on the whole"
19. sub judice   "under the judge" ("not yet decided")
20. sub rosa   "under the rose" ("in confidence")
21. a priori   "from the former" (deductive)
22. a posteriori   "from the subsequent" (inductive, empirical)

Read through the list. The definitions are literal. Choose two or three and explain what they mean; use each in a sentence.

Example: *sub rosa*, literally, "under the rose"; meaning: "in secret." The expression comes from the practice of hanging a rose over a meeting as a symbol of secrecy, from the legend that Cupid once gave Harpocrates a rose to make sure he kept the secrets of Venus.

6. Interjections and Conjunctions

Except for *et*, and, these have had little effect on English vocabulary.

etc.	et cetera
et al.	et alii (m. or m. and f.), et aliae (f.), et alia (n.)
et tu, Brute	"you, too, Brutus" Caesar's last words in Shakespeare's *Julius Caesar*
ecce homo	"behold the man" (used as a title of paintings, from John 19.15 in the New Testament)
O tempora! O mores!	"Oh, these times! Oh, the customs!" Cicero and, later, Ted Cruz.
vae victis	"woe to the defeated"

7. Verbs

The VERB, as its name in Latin (*verbum*, word) implies, is the WORD of the sentence and is often saved to the end. The verb is the one word that is most necessary to produce a grammatical sentence. A verb alone can make a complete and grammatical sentence, as "Stop!" "Go!" "Help!"

An adequate definition of verb is yet to be devised. Often we say that a verb is the part of speech that expresses action, existence, or occurrence. This is a definition according to function and meaning. A formal definition (which does not quite cover all English verbs) can also be concocted: a verb is that part of speech which undergoes certain changes in form:

-s for the third person singular — work: he/she/it works; sing: sings

-ing for present participle and gerund — working; singing

-ed or other change for past tense — worked; sang

-ed or other change for past participle — have worked; have sung

At most, then, the regular English verb has five different forms. The verb "to be" has more, but some verbs have only two forms or even one (that is, only one change or none at all), and yet, we still call them verbs. These are such words as *may/might*; *can/could*; *will/would*; *shall/should*; and *must*. These are AUXILIARY (or helping) verbs, often called MODAL (< Latin *modus*, manner) AUXILIARIES because they express the mood or attitude of the speaker or writer toward the reality of the verb's action.

In Latin, VERB is easier to define. In form, the Latin verb differs from its English counterpart in a very important aspect: the Latin verb is highly inflected, in a multiplicity of forms that give more information than the few English inflections. First, most of the forms contain their own subject,[12] that is, endings vary according to person and number. In English we have to use two words to say "I see," "you see," "he/she/it/ Mr. Magoo sees," etc. , a pronoun (or noun) and a verb. In Latin *video*, *vides*, *videt* are sufficient and the pronoun is omitted except for contrast or special emphasis. Of course, if a Latin writer or speaker wants to make the subject more specific than the generic "he/she/it" or "they" a subject is added; *Caesar videt*, "Caesar sees," *Romani vident*, "the Romans see." In English the verb form *see* is not sufficient because it can be anything (except third person singular) from first person singular or plural (*I see, we see*) to third person plural (*they see*) to an infinitive (*able to see, must see*) to an imperative (*see!*). In Latin a new form of the verb is needed for each of these, respectively *video, videmus* (*I see, we see*), *vident* (*they see*), *vidēre* (*to see*), *vide* (singular imperative, *see*), *videte* (plural imperative, [*y'all*] *see*).

The forms with personal endings are called FINITE forms (< *finis* end, boundary, limit) because they are defined or limited to one grammatical number and one person. Opposed to finite forms are INFINITIVES, so called because they are not limited either by person or number. Infinitives can be used as nouns, as in "to err is human" (*errare est humanum*)[13] and they can be used for any person and number (from *possum vidēre*, "I can see" to *possunt vidēre*, "they can see") without changing form.

Other characteristics of verbs include tense, voice and mood. TENSE tells the time of the action, occurrence, or existence. Latin has six tenses, all of which are represented by different forms of the verb: present, imperfect, future, perfect, pluperfect, future perfect. English has many more, but, except for the simple present and simple past, they are represented by compound (or, periphrastic) tenses, using participles or infinitives with various auxiliary verbs.

Examples:

	Latin	English
Present	duco; ducit	I lead, am leading; he/she leads, is leading, etc.
Imperfect	ducebam	I was leading, I used to lead, I kept leading
Future	ducam	I will/shall lead, I am going to lead
Perfect	duxi	I led, I have led
Pluperfect	duxeram	I had led
Future Perfect	duxero	I shall/will have led

Although this does not exhaust the possibilities of the English system of compound tenses, it should give an idea of the enormous flexibility of English for producing a great number of verbal times with a very limited supply of different forms. Notice how few forms of the verb "lead" are needed in English (only four); in Latin, however, the six forms of the tenses in the first person singular (listed above) need to be multiplied by six for the other persons and number. We have yet to glance at the passive voice, the subjunctive and imperative moods, the infinitives, and participles. But all the parts of the English verb have already been laid out: all we have to do to form the other voice and moods is change the auxiliaries.

VOICE tells the relationship of the subject to the action of the verb. In the ACTIVE voice, the subject performs the action: she/he *leads*. In the PASSIVE (< Latin *passus*, participle of *pati*, to suffer, experience), the subject is acted upon, she/he experiences, or in grammatical jargon suffers the action of the verb: he/she *is led*.

The distinction can be vital: in our earlier example, turned into the passive, "Caesar was killed by Brutus."[14] Caesar, though now the grammatical subject of the passive verb is still the one to end up dead. For each of the tenses given above, Latin has a separate form of the verb (except that in the perfect system, compound tenses are used: the perfect passive participle with forms of the Latin verb *esse*, to be). English forms all the tenses of the passive with forms of the verb *be* and the past participle.

	Latin	English
Present	ducor	I am led, I am being led
Imperfect	ducebar	I was being led, I used to be led, I kept being led
Future	ducar	I will/shall be led, I am going to be led
Perfect	ductus/a sum	I was led, I have been led
Pluperfect	ductus/a eram	I had been led
Future Perfect	ductus/a ero	I will/shall have been led

MOOD tells the attitude of the writer or speaker to the action: is it a fact, a supposition, a hope, a possibility, a command? In Latin the three moods are INDICATIVE (< Latin *indicare*, point out), which is used for stating facts, for talking about reality, for asking questions about reality[15]; SUBJUNCTIVE (< Latin *sub*, under + *junctum* < *jungere*, join), which is used for a variety of less than factual attitudes, such as purpose or intention, result or consequence, some conditions, possibilities, hopes, and fears; and IMPERATIVE (< Latin *imperare*, to command), which gives an order. Latin, predictably, has different forms for the different moods, and English, equally predictably, uses the same forms of the verb, but a variety of auxiliaries for the subjunctive. For the imperative, English uses the simplest form of the verb alone, without a subject (*you* is understood: go, stop; eat, drink, and be merry). The auxiliaries that show mood, called MODALS, express all the varieties that the different Latin forms and grammatical structures do.

Finally there are the VERBALS: participles, infinitives, and gerunds. A PARTICIPLE is a verbal adjective; INFINITIVES and GERUNDS are verbal nouns. Latin participles are especially important for the study of English vocabulary, because so many of them have entered our language. As a verbal advective, a PARTICIPLE (< Latin *particeps* < *pars*, *part-*, part + *capere*, take, therefore a *part-taker* or sharer, a translation of Greek *metochē*) shares the characteristics of adjectives and verbs. As an adjective it has case, number, and gender, and is declined to agree with its noun; as a verb it is derived from the verb base, has tense and voice, and can take an object. Gerunds look like participles, but are used as nouns.

PRINCIPAL PARTS: Latin verbs have four principal parts which give all the forms necessary to conjugate the verb in full, if you know all the appropriate endings. The principal parts are:
   1. The first person singular, present active indicative: *amo*, I love; *video*, I see;

duco, I lead; *audio*, I hear.

2. The present active infinitive: *amare*, to love; *vidēre*, to see; *ducere*, to lead; *audire*, to hear.

3. The first person singular, perfect active indicative: *amavi*, I loved; *vidi*, I saw; *duxi*, I led; *audivi*, I heard.

4. The perfect passive participle in the neuter singular: *amatum*, loved/having been loved; *visum*, seen; *ductum*, led; *auditum*, heard.

For English word formation, the important parts are 2 and 4, the present infinitive and the perfect passive participle (*PPP*). Others will be given only in special circumstances.

CONJUGATIONS: Verbs are divided into conjugations, which —like declensions of nouns— indicate the patterns the verb forms follow. There are four conjugations of regular verbs in Latin, recognizable by the stem vowel in the present infinitive.

1. First conjugation, or -a-conjugation: the infinitive ends in *-are*.

   amo, amare, amavi, amatum *love*: nearly all verbs of the first conjugation follow this pattern.

2. Second conjugation, or -ē- conjugation: the infinitive ends in *-ēre*.

   video, vidēre, vidi, visum *see*

   teneo, tenēre, tenui, tentum *hold*

3. Third conjugation: the infinitive ends in *-ere*.

   duco, ducere, duxi, ductum *lead*

   mitto, mittere, misi, missum *send*

A second type has -io in the first principal part. This -i- is usually retained in English words that come from the present base.

   capio, capere, cepi, captum *take*

4. Fourth conjugation or -i- conjugation: the infinitive ends in *-ire*.

   audio, audire, audivi, auditum *hear*

   venio, venire, veni, ventum *come*

DEPONENT VERBS: Verbs that have no active forms, but are conjugated only in the passive are called DEPONENTS. They usually have active meanings. They may belong to any conjugation.

1. conor, conari, conatum *try*

2. fateor, fatēri, fassum *acknowledge*

3. nascor, nasci,[16] natum *be born*

   3 -i- patior, pati, passum *suffer*

4. experior, experiri, expertum *experience*

EXERCISES

EXERCISE I.6 — LATIN VERBS: many Latin verbs have been very productive of English words. For example, a partial listing of derivatives of duco, ducere/ductum includes:

> adduce, educe, induce, produce, seduce, reduce, conduce; induct, abduct, duct, aqueduct, viaduct, ductile, conduct, induction, abduction, seduction, reduction, inductive, conducive, traduce, introduce, introduction

Choose one of these verbs and try to think of ten English derivatives from it (The example gives some useful prefixes and suffixes that you can use.):

a. *mittere, missum,* send: bases mitt-/mit and miss-

b. *portare,* carry: bases port-, portat-

c. *venire, ventum,* come: bases veni-, vent-

d. *vidēre, visum,* see: bases vide-, vis-

EXERCISE I.7—LATIN PARTS OF SPEECH: the words in this list are unusual: they have entered English with their Latin inflectional endings intact. Choose two and try to find out:

a. What is the literal meaning of the Latin word?

b. What part of speech is it in Latin?

c. What is the meaning of the English word?

d. What part of speech is it in English?

e. Find some uses of it in English.

f. Note any peculiarities of your word. When did it come into English? Does it come from a specific work?

g. Is it a common word? Did you know it before?

1. via	2. placebo	3. quorum	4. imprimatur
5. introit	6. nostrum	7. specie	8. ignoramus
9. propaganda	10. exit; exeunt	11. rebus	12. fiat
13. recto	14. caveat	15. posse	16. numero
17. vim	18. innuendo	19. recipe	20. omnibus
21. credo	22. verso	23. deficit	24. habitat
25. proviso	26. affidavit	27. interest	28. tenet
29. veto	30. floruit	31. memento	32. limbo
33. requiem	34. caret	35. mandamus	36. variorum
37. habeas corpus			

ENDGAME

Guess which words are from Latin:[17]

state	constitution	cheer	felicity	cook	culinary
nurse	nutrition	charm	incantation	add	subtract
poor	pauper	joy	gaudy	damn	condemn
boil	fail	face	infallible	faith	integrity
course	clear	doubt	cursive	clarity	indubitably
false	veracity	fierce	feast	school	imprecate
pray	pain	penalty	ebullient	festive	semiferal
chance	cadence	force	fortitude		

CHECKLIST FOR CHAPTER ONE: WHAT YOU SHOULD KNOW

1. The parts of speech; characteristics of nous and verbs

2. Latin Plurals

I	-a	-ae
II	-us	-i
	-um	-a
III	various	-es (masculine and feminine)
		-a (neuter)
IV	-us	-us
V	-es	-es

3. Finding base: remove the ending that is peculiar to the declension:
    I -a
    II -us/-um
    III learn special form
    IV -us/-s
    V -es

REVIEW OF PLURALS—PREVIEW OF VOCABULARY

Form the plurals of these nouns from the vocabulary of Chapter Two:
1. *caput*, base: capit- (neut.), head (as in *per* _____)
2. *corpus*, base: corpor-, body
3. *focus*, hearth
4. *genus*, base, gener- (neut.), kind
5. *littera*, letter (as in _____ *humaniores*, another name for the humanities or Classics)
6. *locus*, place
7. *opus*, base: oper- (neut.), work
8. *species*, sight, kind
9. *terminus*, end, limit
10. *terra*, land

NOTES

1. English does have some inflections, primarily in verbs and pronouns.

2. On the Ides of March, 44 B.C.E., a group of dissident republicans (in the ancient sense, advocates of the restoration and revitalization of the Roman Republic) attacked and killed the dictator Julius Caesar in the Senate chamber. They were acting in the ancient tradition of TYRANNICIDE (a Greco-Latin formation < Greek *tyrannos*, tyrant + Latin -CIDE < *caedere*, to kill) by which, among others, the Athenians Harmodius and Aristogeiton won undying glory (even though they killed the wrong man). The founder of the Roman Republic, Lucius Junius Brutus, moreover, by ridding the state of its last king, Tarquin the Proud, both achieved fame and became the eponymous hero of the month June. Among the conspirators against Caesar (eponymous hero, by the way, of the month July, earlier called Quintilis), who numbered about sixty, was one Marcus Junius Brutus, a descendant of the original republican regicide. This latter hater of one man rule was a close friend to Caesar. For such disloyalty he is placed by Dante in the lowest circle of Hell with only Judas Iscariot below him. But Shakespeare, through the mouth of Marc Antony, went so far as to say of him, after his demise in the play, *Julius Caesar*, "This was the noblest Roman of them all." Through Shakespeare's retelling, this incident has added much to our language, for example "et tu, Brute" (in the ancient source, Caesar speaks to Brutus in Greek, gasping "*Kai su, teknon*," "even you, my child"); "beware the Ides of March"; "it was Greek to me"; "friends, Romans, countrymen"; "the fault, dear Brutus, is not in our stars, but in ourselves"; "yon Cassius has a lean and hungry look"; "ambition should be made of sterner stuff."

3. Greek has a third number, the DUAL for only two, but by the Classical period it was already going out of use.

4. Adjectives follow the patterns for the first three declensions, except that there are some variations in the third declension.

5. In fact the accusative singular is the form that most often carried over into the Romance languages and from there into English. If a word has passed through one of the Romance languages before entering English, dictionaries will often use the accusative to explain its etymology.

6. Genesis, gene, genetic, genome, genocide are based on the Greek cognate *genos*; genitive, progenitor come from the cognate Latin verb *gignere, genitum*, to beget, bear.

7. Among the masculine nouns of the first declension are *nauta* sailor, *incola* inhabitant, *accola* neighbor, *auriga* charioteer, *scriba* scribe, and various killers: *regicida, fratricida, sororicida* (killers of a king, brother, or sister), and *scurra*, buffoon (the origin of scurrilous) as well as some names like Caligula, Caracalla, Catilina, and some borrowings fom Greek.

8. A few nouns of the second declension and adjectives with masculine in -er require the listing of a second form to show the base because in some the -er is retained, but in others the -e- is dropped.
    ager [field], base *agr*- [cf. agriculture, agrarian]
    pulcher [beautiful, handsome], base *pulchr*- [cf. pulchritude, pulchritudinous]
    puer [boy, child], base *puer*- [cf. puerile]
    liber [free], base *liber*- [cf. liberal, liberty]

9. There are also adjectives of the -er type, for example: *pulcher, pulchra, pulchrum,* beautiful, handsome, base *pulchr-* > pulchritude, pulchritudinous; *liber,libera, liberum,* free, base *liber-* > liberty, liberal; *noster, nostra, nostrum,* our, base *nostr-* > nostrum (a patent medicine, "*our own* formula")

10. *Ego* can be feminine, but in the expression it is taken as masculine.

11. From *Rumpole of the Bailey,* RUMPOLE (speaking of the scene of the murder): It's what we lawyers call the *locus in quo.* REPLY: Really? How camp of you. We actors call it the dressing room.

12. Exceptions are infinitives, participles, and gerunds which are verbal nouns and adjectives.

13. This use is equivalent to the use of gerunds, as in "swimming is fun."

14. In informal English we sometimes use "get/got" to form the passive: "Who got killed?" "Caesar got stabbed." "I used to get beaten up every day on my way to school." "We got stung by hornets."

15. The facts do not have to be true. One can lie in the indicative.

16. Note that the passive infinitive of the third conjugation does not follow the pattern of the others with the stem vowel + -ri, but has only -i- as the ending.

17. Hint: if there are any you think are not from Latin, look them up for a surprise.

SECTION TWO: LATIN
A. Latin Nouns and Adjectives

Chapter Two: Direct Entries & Simple Changes

A: Direct Entries

Many Latin nouns and adjectives have come directly into English, or, in spite of certain historical changes, have ended up in English looking exactly like their Latin originals.

Examples of direct entries: NOUNS

> *actor, actoris,* m. a doer > actor
>
> *delirium, delirii,* n. a going off track (In Latin this is a agricultural term < *lira,* furrow > *delirare* to go out of the furrow > to be off one's track.) > delirium (cf. English expressions "off one's rocker"; "off one's trolley")
>
> *omen, ominis,* n. a sign of the future (note that the base is *omin-* and so derivatives will show -i-, as ominous, abominate) > omen

Some words have gone through changes but have come around to the same spellings as their Latin originals. These will be treated as direct entries in the exercises. Examples:

> *labor, laboris,* m., work, accusative *laborem* > O.F. *labor/labour* (Modern French *labeur*) > English *labor/labour.* Note that the American spelling of words in -or is identical to the Latin, while the British -our takes the Old French spelling. The accusative case is commonly the form from which the Romance languages derive nouns. This can be seen more clearly in the Italian form, *labore* > labor
>
> *orator, oratoris,* m., speaker, accusative *oratorem* > O.F. *orateur* > Anglo-French *oratour,* relatinized to orator

Examples of direct entries: ADJECTIVES

> *bonus, bona, bonum,* good: the masculine form *bonus* has become an English noun meaning "a good thing", in this case "an extra dividend or payment."

The English noun *bonus* is a made-up word, invented by students or office-boys as a joke. If scholars had coined it, the neuter form, *bonum*, would have been used, since in Latin the masculine *bonus* means "a good man."

albus, alba, album, white: here the neuter form of the adjective comes into English as a noun. *Album* was used in Latin as a noun, too, meaning a white or blank tablet for lists of dates or names of officials. Samuel Johnson in his famous dictionary of 1755 defines *album* as "a book in which foreigners have long been accustomed to insert the autographs of celebrated people."

similis, simile, like: simile, "a likeness" or "comparison," was also used as a noun in Latin: the use of neuter adjectives as abstract nouns is very common in Latin, evidence of the Roman preference for the concrete. For example, *bona* (neuter plural) means "good things, goods"; *mala* means "bad things, evils." *Simile*, literally "a thing like" is now used as a technical term in literary studies for "a figure of speech in which an explicit comparison is made between two essentially unlike things, by the use of *like* or *as*."

Examples of similes:

> O my Luve's like a red, red rose
> That's newly sprung in June;
> O my Luve's like the melodie
> That's sweetly play'd in tune.   Robert Burns

> Love is like the measles; we all have to go through it.
>   Jerome K. Jerome (from the time before the MMR vaccination)

Among the direct entries from Latin are both common and unusual words. The words in the next exercises are found in both English and Latin Dictionaries.

EXERCISES

EXERCISE IIA. 1—LATIN/ENGLISH WORDS (Recommended for group work.)
—Go over the list and check off the words that are familiar to you and jot down a synonym or a brief definition.
— Choose two or three of the unfamiliar words, noting if the word has gone through any change in meaning in its passage from Latin to English.
—Choose two or three of the words marked with an asterisk (*) even if you know their meanings to find their origins.

Meaning in Latin—Meaning in English   Comments

1. vapor
2. honor
3. color
4. odor

5. *murmur
6. *minister
7. rumor
8. acumen
9. furor
10. *abecedarium
11. *aegis
12. *animal
13. animus
14. ardor
15. *senator
16. appendix
17. arbiter
18. locus
19. lector
20. libido
21. magisterium
22. monitor
23. mores (pl. of *mos*, *mor-*)
24. onus
25. opus
26. *doctor
27. opprobrium
28. dolor
29. *error
30. exemplar
31. facetiae
32. *fasces
33. *formula
34. *fungus
35. genus
36. *horror
37. *index
38. *cancer
39. cantor
40. *cervix
41. *circus
42. clamor
43. compendium
44. corpus
45. *crux
46. vector
47. *tutor

48. virago
49. terminus
50. dementia

EXERCISE IIA. 2—WORDS WITH CHANGED MEANINGS: Choose three or four. Tell how each word has changed. Has it become more specialized or more generalized.

1. area
2. campus
3. camera
4. arena
5. corona
6. focus
7. fulcrum
8. humus
9. imago
10. integer
11. nausea
12. rabies
13. radius
14. ratio
15. Africa
16. Asia
17. farina
18. liquor
19. virus

EXERCISE IIA.3—METAPHORS: These words have changed their applications, as *delirium* in Latin originally applied to agriculture, but now refers to a mental condition. Choose two or three and find out what they were applied to in Latin and how they are used now:

1. cirrus
2. pastor
3. candor
4. columbarium
5. incunabulum
6. nucleus
7. persona
8. prevaricator
9. rostrum
10. larva
11. calculus
12. codex
13. genius

14. placenta

EXERCISE IIA.4—NOUN OR ADJECTIVE: using the glossary of Latin words in the back of the book, tell what part of speech each is in Latin and what part of speech it is in English; give the meaning in Latin and in English.

1. major (Lat. maior)
2. medium
3. sanctum (as in inner sanctum)
4. miser
5. quota
6. Sanctus
7. minor, minus
8. vacuum
9. exterior
10. quantum
11. pauper
12. animal
13. nostrum
14. senior

EXERCISE IIA.5—PRODUCTIVE BASES: choose three and try to find five derivatives of each.
Example: *albus, alba, album*, white > album, alb, albino, albumen, albedo, albite, daub, auburn (for several of these a dictionary was needed).

1. *animus*, spirit
2. *finis*, base: fin-/fini-, end
3. *similis*, like
4. *rex*, base: reg-, king
5. *opus*, base: oper- work
6. *locus*, place
7. *genus*, base: gener-, birth, kind
8. *species*, base: speci-, sight, appearance
9. *annus*, year
10. *domus*, combining base: domi-, home
11. *terra*, land

Begin learning these words and their meanings.

EXERCISE IIA.6—WORDS FROM ROMAN HISTORY AND CULTURE: check the words in this list that apply to modern institutions that you know of. Choose any two or three and find out what they meant to the Romans. Start with an English dictionary. If you get interested, look in the Oxford Classical Dictionary.

1. lictor   2. latifundia
3. toga   4. paterfamilias

5. lar (pl. lares)   6. plebe
7. forum   8. censor
9. dictator   10. atrium
11. consul   12. praetorium
13. procurator   14. curia
15. lustrum

EXERCISE IIA.7—LATIN WORDS IN ENGLISH LITERATURE: give meanings of italicized words.

1. And after "*Amor vincit omnia*" (_____ conquers all). Chaucer
2. Beyond the Atlantic things civil and things spiritual move in their separate spheres, without any need for an *arbiter* between them. Gladstone
3. The condition of true naming on the poet's part, is his resigning himself to the divine *aura* which breathes through forms. Emerson
4. Like a dismal *Clangor* heard from farre. Shakespeare
5. With this *exordium* . . . Nickleby took a newspaper from his pocket. Dickens
6. Those deserts whose *fervor*s scarce allowed a bird to live. Shelley
7. The *hiatus* in Phutatorius's breeches was sufficiently wide to receive the chesnut. Sterne
8. Apollonius . . . by some probable conjectures, found her out to be a serpent, a *Lamia*. Burton
9. The *progenitor*s of Birds and the *progenitor*s of Man at a very remote period were probably one. Drummond
10. Hovel piled upon hovel—*squalor* immortalized in undecaying tone. Hawthorne
11. They included all learning in the seven liberal arts; of which grammar, rhetoric, and dialectics formed what they called the *trivium*. Rankin
12. And crowne your heads with heavenly coronall,
     such as the Angels weare before Gods *tribunal*l. Spenser

QUISQUILIA—SOME AUGUST RELATIONS

Augur, in Latin, "a diviner, soothsayer, seer, one who predicted the future by interpreting the flights of birds or their songs, the lightning and other unusual occurrences." In English, as a noun, "a prophet or seer"; as a verb "to predict the future from signs and omens" or "to be an omen or sign of the future", as in "that augurs well." AUGUR is from the root of *augēre*, to increase: the bases of this verb are *aug-* [auge-] and *auct-* which produce such English words as augment, augmentative, augmentation, author (< Latin *auctor*), authority, authorize, auction, augend, augury, inaugurate, inaugural, Augustus (the "majestic, venerable, magnificent", a title first assumed by the emperor Octavius), august, the month August (named after the emperor Augustus), auxiliary (from *auxilium*, aid, increased troops). The I-E root of these words is *AUG- to increase. The native English cognate to Latin *augēre* is the Old English verb *eacan* from which we get the verb *eke* ("to strain to fill, to make a living with great effort") and the noun *nickname* (originally "an ekename", that is, "an added name"). In an extended form (*WEGS-, OE *weaxan*), the same root gives us *wax*, grow, used especially of the moon, which waxes and wanes, and of public speakers, who may occasionally wax eloquent. The Greek *auxein*, from the same root has given us several scientific derivatives: auxin (a plant hormone that affects growth); auxesis (an increase in the size of a cell without cell division); the suffix *-auxe* (enlargement), as in hepatauxe, "enlargement of the liver".

B: SIMPLE CHANGES

Many Latin words have come into English, showing very slight change. Most of these follow simple rules.

1. BASE ALONE — The Latin ending is often dropped, so that the base of the Latin word becomes the English word.
Examples:
Nouns:
    ars, art-, skill > art[1]
    verbum, word > verb
Adjectives:
    absurdus, unmusical, senseless > absurd
    grandis, large, tall, old > grand

2. BASE + SILENT -E: English often adds a silent -e at the end of the base; words ending in -o usually drop the -o and replace it with silent -e. Examples:
Nouns: *nodus*, knot > node
    magnitudo (base: *magnitudin-*), greatness, size > magnitude
Adjectives: *arcanus*, secret > arcane
    gravis, heavy, serious > grave

3. CHANGES IN THE ENDINGS: Latin endings are Englished.
A. Final *-ia, -ius, -ium* becomes -y; final *-tas* becomes -ty.
Final *-tia, -tius, -tium* and *-cia, -cium* become -cy or -ce; *-gium* becomes -ge.
Examples:
Nouns: *penuria*, poverty > penury
    pietas, devotion to duty > piety
    alimonium, nourishment > alimony
    collegium, association in office, guild > college
    gratia, thanks, favor > grace
    contumacia, obstinacy > contumacy
    silentium, stillness > silence
    provincia, province > province

Adjectives: *amatorius*, of love > amatory
    litterarius, of letters/reading and writing > literary
B.The -us ending becomes -ous.
Adjectives: *noxius*, harmful > noxious
    pius,[2] devoted to duty > pious
    anxius, troubled > anxious

4. ANYTHING CAN HAPPEN: Other, unpredictable changes sometimes take place. This is especially true of words that have come into English after enjoying a period of time in the French language.
Some examples:
    joy is from Latin *gaudia* (pl.of *gaudium*, delight, enjoyment). The Latin base
        shows up in the word *gaudy*
    author is from Latin *auctor* which is from the same root as auction < *auctum*,
        participle of *augēre*, to increase
    reason < Latin *ratio*, reason, proportion (> also ration, ratio, rational)
    larceny < Latin *latrocinium*, robbery, piracy
    couple < Latin *copula*, bond, rope

EXERCISE IIB.1—SIMPLE CHANGES: Choose four or five and answer the following questions:
1. What English word is derived from the Latin word?
2. Which rule does it follow? No change; base + silent -e; change of ending.
3. Is it a noun or an adjective? Are the English and Latin words the same part of speech?
4. The words marked with an asterisk have changed considerably in meaning. Give meaning of the English word.
Examples:
nullus, no, none > null — drops ending — adjective; now means "invalidated"
facilis, easy > facile — adds silent -e — adjective
tumor, swelling > tumor — no change — noun
custodia, care > custody — -ia becomes -y — noun
Note: Latin *ae* becomes *e* in English: *scaena* > scene (base + silent -e)
    1. *auctio*, base: *auction-*, act of increasing
    2. *dubius*, doubtful
    3. *extremus*, outermost
    4. *calumnia*, false accusation
    5. **egregius*, outstanding, out of the flock
    6. *aptus*, fitted to
    7. *aedificium*, building
    8. *fiduciarius* (to be held in trust < *fides*, trust, faith)
    9. *luridus*, yellow
    10. *justitia*, rightness, fairness

11. *amplitudo*, size, distinction, fulness
12. *antiquus*, old, ancient
13. *fanum*, temple
14. *docilis*, easily taught
15. *aequitas*, condition of being even
16. *agilis*, easily moved
17. *familia*, household
18. *mimus*, actor in a farce
19. *contumelia*, abuse, insult
20. *digitus*, finger
21. **immunis*, exempt from taxes
22. **seminarium*, a place for seeds, nursery
23. **sermo, sermon-*, talk, conversation
24. **stipendium*, tribute, penalty, income
25. **cliens, client-*, dependent
26. **suavis*, sweet
27. *benignus*, kind
28. **rota*, wheel
29. *silentium*, stillness
30. **paganus*, rural
31. **obesus*, eaten away
32. **profanus*, outside the temple (< *fanum*, temple)
33. *obscenus*, filthy, ominous
34. *integer*, whole, untouched

IIB. 2— A FEW LITERARY EXAMPLES: change the Latin word to its English form.
1. _____ should be made of sterner stuff.   Shakespeare
   ambitio, ambition-, a going around, canvassing for votes
2. Thus _____ does make cowards of us all.   Shakespeare
   conscientia, joint/shared knowledge
3. _____ indications of the better marriages she might have made shown
   athwart the awful gloom of her composure.   Dickens
   luridus, pale yellow, ghastly
4. The short _____ way in mathematiques will not do in metaphysiques.
   Berkeley
   jejunus, without food, fasting
5. To forgive is the most _____ pitch human nature can arrive at.
   Steele
   arduus, high, steep, difficult
6. Teachinge things which they ought not, because of filthy _____ .
   Tyndale
   lucrum, gain, profit
7. The oppressors wrong, the poore mans _____ .   Shakespeare

contumelia, abuse, insult, reproach

IIB. 3—ADDITIONAL PRACTICE (to show the variety of direct and nearly direct entries of Latin words): change to English spelling; mark noun (N) or adjective (A). Recommended as an oral exercise, with brief discussion of meanings of unfamiliar words. Note: Latin *ae* becomes *e* in English: *aequitas > equity* (N).

1. *abortio, abortion-*, miscarriage
2. *advocatus*, one called to another's aid
3. *caerimonia*, sacredness, sacred work
4. *gratia*, thanks, favor, charm, service
5. *divinus*, of deity, godly
6. *exemptus*, taken away
7. *inanis*, empty, vain
8. *indecorus*, unseemly, unbecoming
9. *arcus*, bow
10. *experientia*, practice, experiment
11. *devius*, out of the way
12. *cella*, storeroom
13. *adventus*, a coming to
14. *fortuitus*, casual, accidental
15. *dignitas* worthiness
16. *conscius*, knowing with
17. *gloria*, fame
18. *diffidentia*, mistrust
19. *luteus*, yellow
20. *utilis*, able to be used, useful
21. *juvenilis*, youthful
22. *modus*, manner
23. *mimus*, farcical
24. *merus*, pure, undiluted
25. *mutus*, speechless
26. *beneficium*, kindness
27. *frons, front-*, forehead
28. *artificium*, trade, handicraft, skill
29. *forma*, shape, beauty
30. *accentus*, signal, tone
31. *clementia*, mildness
32. *acerbus*, harsh to the taste, sharp, sour
33. *firmus*, strong, stable
34. *editio, edition-*, a giving out, publishing
35. *praemium*, reward
36. *audientia*, a hearing
37. *decens, decent-* (adj.), seemly, becoming

38. *alienus*, belonging to another
39. *aemulatio*, aemulation-, rivalry
40. *arrogantia*, haughtiness
41. *furtivus*, of/like a thief
42. *frigidus*, cold
43. *junctura*, a joining
44. *germanus*, genuine, born of the same parents
45. *fatum*, the thing said
46. *futurus*, about to be
47. *abstrusus*, pushed away, deep, reserved
48. *dirus*, fearful
49. *justus*, fair, lawful
50, *causa*, reason, purpose, case
51. *pius*, devoted to duty
52. *vividus*, lively
53. *norma*, capenter's square
54. *rudis*, unwrought, rough
55. *nasturtium*, cress (lit. "nose turner")
56. *polus*, end of an axis
57. *squalidus*, stiff with dirt
58. *aurura*, dawn
59. *pronus*, leaning forward
60. *farrago*, mixed fodder for cattle, mash
61. *primus*, first
62. *pyra*, funeral pile
63. *specimen*, that by which a thing is seen, mark, token, proof
64. *sordidus*, dirty
65. *index*, a pointer (Latin pl., *indices*)
66. *quartanus*, belonging to the fourth
67. *curator*, one who cares for
68. *prudentia*, a foreseeing
69. *vastus*, empty
70. *pallor*, paleness
71. *scaena*, stage
72. *osseus*, bony
73. *hiatus*, gap, opening
74. *ornatus*, fitted out
75. *rarus*, porous, thin
76. *cicada*, tree-cricket
77. *sensus*, feeling, perception
78. *potentia*, power, ability
79. *ruina*, downfall
80. *quadrivium*, the four ways

81. *viscera* (pl.), internal organs
82. *copia*, abundance, resources
83. *sonorus*, noisy
84. *octavus*, eighth
85. *patens, patent-*, lying open
86. *tribus*, a division of the people
87. *obsoletus*, worn out, out of use
88. *vertigo*, a turning around
89. *pictura*, a painting
90. *uxorius*, fond of one's wife, hen-pecked
91. *ulcus, ulcer-*, sore
92. *marsuppium*, pouch
93. *precursor*, forerunner
94. *usus*, employment, exercise
95. *opportunus*, fit, suitable
96. *fiscus*, money basket
97. *patronus*, protector
98. *noxius*, harmful
99. *popularis*, of the people
100. *caduceus*, a herald's staff (the winged staff with serpents carried by Hermes)

IIB. 4—UNPREDICTABLE CHANGES: in the English words listed below, the Latin base has been more or less obscured. Try to find another English word that more clearly shows the Latin base. Example: *able* from Latin *habilis* (manageable, handy) > habile, rehabilitate, *Homo habilis, femina habilis*

English	from Latin	Other derivative(s)
1. heir	*heres, hered-*, heir	
2. clear	*clarus*, bright, clear, famous	
3. debt	*debitum*, something owed	
4. governor	*gubernator*, pilot	
5. empire	*imperium*, supreme power	
6. judge	*judex, judic-*, judge	
7. lagoon	*lacuna*, hole, pit	
8. grain	*granum*, grain	
9. humble	*humilis*, lowly, on the ground	
10. mister, master	*magister, magistr-*, teacher	
11. merchant	*mercator*, tradesman	
12. poor	*pauper*, poor	
13. peace	*pax, pac-*, peace	
14. pencil	*penicillus*, little brush	
15. pound	*pondus*, ponder-, weight	
16. people	*populus*, the people	
17. saint	*sanctus*, holy	

18. tower	*turris*, tower
19. royal	*rex, reg-*, king > *regalis* kingly
20. brief	*brevis*, short
21. vow	*votum*, vow
22. beef	*bos, bov-*, cow, ox
23. isle	*insula*, island
24. court	*cohors, cohort-*, company of soldiers
25. uncle	*avunculus*, uncle
26. memoir	*memoria*, memory
27. pair	*paria* (neuter pl. of *par*), equal things, equals
28. deign	*dignus*, worthy
29. count	*computare*, reckon
30. flail	*fagellum*, whip
31. avenge	*vindicare*, lay claim
32. vain	*vanus*, empty
33. round	*rotundus*, wheel-shaped
34. poison	*potio, potion-*, drink
35. fount	*fons, font-*, spring, source
36. sound	*sonus*, noise
37. number	*numerus*, number
38. powder	*pulvis, pulver-*, dust
39. term	*terminus*, limit, end
40. tavern	*taberna*, shed, shop
41. cage, jail	*cavea*, hollow
42. journal	*diurnalis* (< *dies*, day), daily
43. chef,chief	*caput, capit-*, head
44. corps	*corpus, corpor-*, body
45. etude	*studium*, zeal
46. menu	*minutum*, a little thing, detail
47. naive	*nativus*, natural;
48. savant	*sapiens, sapient-*, wise
49. seance	*sedēre*, to sit
50. antic	*antiquus*, old, ancient
51. ensign	*insignis*, distinguished, marked

C—VOCABULARY

Study these lists. Learn Latin word and base (if different) and meaning. Fill in two English derivatives of each.

Adjectives

amplus	*large, spacious*	> ample, amplify, amplitude
antiquus	*old*	
bonus / bene [adv.]	*good / well*	
brevis	*short*	> brief

clarus	*bright, clear*	> clear
dignus	*worthy*	> deign
divus	*of a god*	> diva, divine
facilis	*easy*	
difficilis	*hard* < facilis	
humilis	*lowly, on the ground* (adj. < *humus*, see Chapter III)	
par	*equal*	
plenus	*full*	> plenum
primus	*first*	
sanctus	*holy*	
similis	*like*	
vacuus	*empty*	
verus	*true*	

Nouns

animus; anima[3]	*spirit, breath*	> pusillanimous, magnanimity
caput, capit- (neut.)	*head*	
causa	*cause, reason*	
corpus, corpor-	*body*	
domus [domes-][4]	*home, house*	
fatum	*the thing said, fate*	
finis	*end*	
focus	*hearth* > *fire*	
genus, gener- (neut.)	*race, kind, birth*	
gratia	*favor, thanks*	
gratus [adj.]	*grateful, thankful*	
labor, labor-	*work*	
littera	*letter*	
locus	*place*	
modus	*manner*	
onus, oner- (neut.)	*burden*	
opus, oper- (neut.)	*work*	
pax, pac-	*peace*	
populus	*people*	
rota	*wheel*	
species	*sight, appearance, kind*	
studium	*eagerness, zeal*	
terminus	*end, limit*	
terra	*earth, land*	
via	*way, road*	

EXERCISES FOR LEARNING THE VOCABULARY

EXERCISE IIc. 1—LATIN NOUN BASES: match the English derivative to the meaning of the Latin base word. Tell what the Latin base word is.

0. impervious _a_	a. way [via]
1. exterminate___	b. body
2. rotunda___	c. the thing said
3. a la mode___	d. thanks
4. pusillanimous___	e. eagerness
5. deviate___	f. kind
6. because___	g. appearance
7. corpuscle___	h. place
8. studious___	i. end: use twice
9. pay___	j. head
10. fatalism___	k. peace
11. specious___	l. burden
12. depopulate___	m. manner
13. lieutenant___	n. home
14. gratis___	o. the people
15. exonerate___	p. spirit
16. generic___	q. wheel
17. definitive___	r. reason
18. major-domo___	

EXERCISE IIc. 2—LATIN ADJECTIVE BASES: give the meaning of the Latin adjective from which each of these is derived:

1. verisimilitude [2 bases]
2. claret
3. antiquary
4. indignity
5. sanctuary
6. parity
7. primordium
8. breviary
9. amplitude
10. bon mot
11. benediction
12. facility
13. divination

EXERCISE IIc. 3—RELATIVES OR LOOK-ALIKES: which word does not belong? Choose a word in each group that does not share a common base with the others. Some of these are tricky. It would not be cheating to look up any unfamiliar words

in the dictionary (or check answers in note).[5]
1. very aver average verisimilitude
2. focus foyer curfew feud fuel
3. fin finial finance finocchio paraffin infinitesimal
4. ingrate gratin gracious gratuity grace gracious
5. domain indomitable dome domicile dominate doom don
6. diva devotee divine divination divinity
7. infradig deign condign digit
8. viable viaduct obvious deviate voyage convoy
9. humus human exhume posthumous humble humid humility
10. studious stucco study student studio
11. compare par parity umpire pair peer impair
12. prime prince primer primary prima facie primogeniture imprimatur
13. terrain Mediterranean deterrent terra firma terroir
14. vacuum evacuate vacuous vaccine
15. plenipotentiary plenum plane plenty replenish
16. vital viable vitiate vitamin
17. literal litter literate literature letter
18. casual causal because causation
19. rotiform rotor rotisserie orotund rotogravure rotunda
20. fuel feud bifocals foci
21. alliteration literatim literal litter
22. Santa Claus sanity saintly sanctimonious inner sanctum
23. simian resemble simile simultaneous
24. belligerent bonny bon mot belladonna belle
25. beau beatific beautiful beldam

EXERCISE IIc. 4 — QUICK REVIEW: for a review of Chapter Two try this quiz on some of the words from chapter 1:[6]
1. quantum a. large number b. life-style c. open excavation d. amount or specified portion
2. virago a. maiden b. manly c. heroic woman d. zodiac sign
3. inane a. become used to b. empty c. lifeless d. loving
4. lucre a. filth b. profit c. ill-gotten goods d. shine
5. carnal a. meat-eating b. obscene c. spiritual d. fleshly
6. invidious a. sightless b. offensive c. requesting participation d. treacherous
7. pusillanimous a. generous b. boyish c. mean-spirited d. kittenish
8. specious a. extraordinary b. deceptive c. concerning kind d. of caves
9. jejune a. youthful b. intercalary month c. insubstantial d. happy
10. uxorious a. charging excessive interest b. seizing the government without the consent of the senate c. hen-pecked d. extravagant

QUISQUILIA

Back-to-Back: some surprising relations

Latin *dorsum* means "back" and is used in English as an anatomical term for the back or any backlike part or organ. The adjective derived from it is dorsal, meaning "having to do with the back." The dorsal fin, for example, is the main fin on the back of fish and other marine mammals. A number of scientific and semi-scientific terms use *dorso-*, *dorsi-*, or *dors-* as a combining form, such as:

dorsad	toward the back
dorsibranchiate	having gills on the back
dorsicumbant	lying on the back
dorsiduct	carry towards the back
dorsifixed	fastened by the back
dorsiparous	hatching the young on the back
dorsocaudal	relating to back and tail
dorsoventral	extending from dorsal to ventral surface

The words in this list, being fashioned by scientists, are all predictable: their elements are recognizable because they are put together from Latin (or in one case Greek) word elements, keeping the whole of the base. Some other words derived from *dorsum* are not so easily recognizable:

endorse	to countersign (i.e., to sign on the back)
do-si-do	a square dance movement in which the partners circle each other back to back. From French *dos-a-dos*, back to back. A dos-a-dos is also a seat or carriage for seating two people back to back.
doss house	in British slang, a cheap sleeping house, where one lies down on one's back; a flop-house
dosser	a large pack basket or an ornamental hanging for the back of a chair (also called a dossal)
dorse	obsolete, but useful in acting: "to throw someone on his back"
dossier	a file of papers and documents on a particular person or subject, so named because of the label placed on the back
extrados, intrados	the upper (or outer) curve of an arch and the inner curve of an arch, respectively
reredos	the back of an altar or fireplace (from *ad retro dorsum*, "behind the back")

ENDGAME

Find the Malapropisms.

Mrs. Malaprop, a delightful creation of Richard Brinsley Sheridan, and now a household word (as in, "Mother is a veritable Mrs. Malaprop"), in scene after scene of *The Rivals* (1775) allows her love of language to get the better of her, as she tries to prevent her niece and ward, Lydia Languish, from throwing herself away on a mere Ensign. Find malapropisms in the quotations that follow. What is Mrs. M. saying and what does she mean?

1. But the point we would request of you is, that you promise to forget this fellow—to illiterate him, I say, quite from your memory.

2. Now don't attempt to extirpate yourself from the matter; you know I have proof controvertible of it.

3. Observe me, Sir Anthony, I would by no means wish a daughter of mine to be a progeny of learning; I don't think so much learning becomes a young woman; for instance, I would never let her meddle with Greek, or Hebrew, or algebra, or simony, or fluxions, or paradoxes or such inflammatory branches of learning—neither would it be necessary for her to handle your mathematical, astronomical, diabolical instruments. —But, Sir Anthony, I would send her, at nine years old, to a boarding school, in order to learn a little ingenuity and artifice. Then, sir, she should have a supercilious knowledge in accounts; and as she grew up, I would have her instructed in geometry, that she might know something of the contagious countries; —but above all, Sir Anthony, she should be mistress of orthodoxy, that she might not mis-spell and mis-pronounce so shamefully as girls usually do; and likewise that she might reprehend the true meaning of what she is saying. This, Sir Anthony, is what I would have a woman know; and there is not a superstitious article in it.

4. He is the very pine-apple of politness!

5. Long ago I laid positive conjunctions on her, never to think of the fellow again; I have since laid Sir Anthony's preposition before her; but I am sorry to say, she seems resolved to decline every particle that I enjoin her.

6. Oh! it gives me the hydrostatics to such a degree. I thought she had persisted from corresponding with him; but behold, this very day, I have intercepted another letter from the fellow; I believe I have it in my pocket.

7. There, sir, an attack on my parts of speech! was ever such a brute! Sure, if I reprehend any thing in this world it is the use of my oracular tongue, and a nice derangement of epitaphs!

8. No caparisons, miss, if you please. Caparisons don't become a young woman. No! Captain Absolute is indeed a fine gentleman . . . and has so much to say for himself: —in such good language, too! His physiognomy so grammatical! Then his presence so noble! I protest, when I saw him, I thought of what Hamlet says in the play: —"Hesperian curls—the front of Job himself!—an eye, like March to threaten at command! —A station like Harry Mercury, new. . ."[7] Something about kissing—on a hill—however, the similitude struck me directly.

CHECKLIST FOR CHAPTER TWO: WHAT YOU SHOULD KNOW

1. Simple changes
     a. no change
     b. base alone
     c. base + e
     d. -ia, -tas > -y,-ty
     e. -ti-, -ci- > -cy, -ce; -gi- > -ge, -gy
     f. -us > -ous
     g. ae > e
     h. various unpredictable changes
     Fill in an example for each of the rules above.
2. Learn Latin vocabulary
3. Practice any new English words in the lesson. It helps to use each new word in a sentence or phrase.

NOTES

1. See the common expression *ars gratia artis* ("art for art's sake"), the motto of MGM displayed below Leo, the roaring lion, and parodied as *ars gratia pecuniae* (*pecunia*, money); also *ars longa, vita brevis* ("art is long, life is short").

2. In Vergil's *Aeneid* (Book 1, line 377), Aeneas introduces himself, *sum pius Aeneas*, "I am Aeneas, a good man."

3. It is unusual for nouns to have both a masculine and a feminine form.

4. The base *domes-* occurs in some derivatives.

5. Answers for II C.3:1. average 2. feud 3. finocchio 4. gratin 5. doom 6. devotee 7. digit 8. viable 9. humid 10. stucco 11. impair 12. imprimatur 13. deterrent 14. vaccine 15. plane 16. vitiate 17. litter 18. casual 19. rotisserie 20. feud 21. litter 22. sanity 23. simian 24. belligerent 25. beatific

6. Answers for IIc. 4: 1-d; 2-c; 3-b; 4-b; 5-d; 6-b; 7-c; 8-b; 9-c; 10-c

7. The speech Mrs. Malaprop mangles so deliciously is from Shakespeare's *Hamlet* Act 3, scene 4, where the young prince considers a portrait of his dead father:
     Hyperion's curls, the front of Jove himself,
     An eye like Mars to threaten and command,
     A station like the herald Mercury
     New-lighted on a heaven-kissing hill—

SECTION TWO: LATIN
A. LATIN NOUNS AND ADJECTIVES

CHAPTER THREE: ADJECTIVE-FORMING SUFFIXES

Adjectives are used to give attributes of nouns. Most of the English and Latin adjectives in this chapter are formed from nouns; a few are built on adjective or adverb bases. In Latin, as in English, various endings are used to make nouns into adjectives. In English we use the suffixes *-y*, *-ly*, *-ish*[1] to form adjectives meaning "of, belonging to, having the nature of"; and the suffixes *-ful*, and *-some* to mean "like, having, tending to be, full of."

SOME ENGLISH AND LATIN NOUN > ADJECTIVE EXAMPLES

English (noun/adj.)	Latin
heart > hearty	*cor, cord*[i]- > cordialis >
world > worldly	*mundus* > mundanus >
boy > boyish	*puer, puer-* > puerilis >
law > lawful	*lex, leg-* > legalis >
burden > burdensome	*onus, oner-* > onerosus >

Notice that in Latin the suffix is added to the base of the noun. See if you can change the Latin adjectives in the list (above) to their English forms by using the rules you learned in Chapter Two. Note that *-osus* can become *-ose* or *-ous*.

Examples of English Adjective-Forming Suffixes, -y, -ish, -ly

NOUNS	ADJECTIVES
might	mighty
sky	skyey
girl	girlish
book	bookish
world	worldly
king	kingly

EXERCISES

EXERCISE III. 1: ENGLISH ADJECTIVES: form English adjectives from: mood, thirst, health, meal, noise, home, nose, clay; boy, ape, clown, fool, self, hell, ghoul, brute; beast, love, scholar, time, man, woman, day, night, year.

These suffixes (-Y, -ISH, -LY) are very productive for forming instant adjectives. Take a noun or even a phrase and add -y, -ish, or -ly and you have an adjective.[2]

Is the sauce too *garlicky*?

Don't be so *stand-offish*?

EXERCISE III.2: FIND ADJECTIVES: Can you think of ten more English adjectives using each of the native English suffixes -Y, -ISH, -LY?

A: LATIN ADJECTIVE-FORMING SUFFIXES

With meanings similar to -Y, -ISH, -LY: "of, having to do with, having the nature or character of, pertaining to, concerning":

Form in English	From Latin	Examples
-al	-alis	*manus, manu-* (hand) > manual
-ar	-aris	*luna* (moon) > lunar
-ary	-arius, -aris	*necesse* (unavoidable) > necessary
-arious	-arius	*grex, greg-* (flock) > gregarious
-il, ile	-ilis	*puer* (boy) > puerile
-an, ane	-anus	*mundus* (world) > mundane; *urbs, urb-* (city) > urban, urbane
-ine	-inus	*canis, can-* (dog) > canine
-ic,	-icus,	*civis, civ-* (citizen) > civic
-tic	-ticus	*luna* (moon) > lunatic; *fanum* (temple) > fanatic
-eous, -eal	-eus	*ignis, ign-* (fire) > igneous; *arbor* (tree) >arboreal
-aceous	-aceus	*sebum* (tallow, suet) > sebaceous
-aneous	-aneus	*miscellus* (mixed) > miscellaneous
-ernal, -ern	-ernus	*hibernus* (wintry, winter) > hibernal, cf., hest-ernal (< *hesternus*, yesterday's), hodiernal (< *hodie*, today); *modus* (manner) > modern
-urnal, -urn	-urnus	*dies*, base, *di-* (day) > diurnal, cf., nocturnal (< *nox, noct-*, night)
-nal	-nus	*mater, matr-* (mother) > maternal; cf. eternal
-ate	-atus	*deliciae* (pet, delight) > delicate

Notes on the Adjective-forming Suffixes:

-ar is a variant of *-al*: it is used when the letter *l* occurs in one of the last two

syllables of the base word [e.g. *popul-aris, sol-aris, lun-aris*].

The neuter plurals of adjectives in *-alis, -ilis,* and *-anus* are respectively *-alia, -ilia,* and *-ana.* These can be used as nouns meaning "things having to do with"; as, for example, *realia* (real or actual things, artifacts), *juvenilia* (the works of one's youth < *iuvenis,* a youth); *Americana* (a collection of things relating to American history and culture).

-arius:

> From Latin *-arius,* the masculine form, are derived nouns in -ary meaning "one who is concerned with, one who": *adversus* (turned against): adversary.

> From the neuter *-arium* come nouns in *-arium, -ary* meaning "thing/place of" or "thing/place for": *aqua* (water): aquarium; *avis* (bird): aviary; *apis* (bee): apiary

-anus sometimes becomes *-ain,* under French influence: *montanus* > mountain (see also, the adjective, montane); *certanus* > certain; *capitanus* > captain. Mean is from *medianus* which also produces median.

The English forms *-ernal/-ern; -urnal, -urn; -nal* from Latin suffixes in *-ernus, -urnus, -nus* may best be learned together as a group.

The adjective ending *-ate* should not be confused with the noun ending *-ate* ("office or function of" as in principate, rabbinate, emirate) which will be treated in the next chapter, nor with the verb forming suffix *-ate* ("to do, make, cause" as in invigilate, capitulate) which will be treated in the section on Latin verbs. If in doubt, think about what part of speech the word in question is. Some examples of words using *-ate* as an adjective-forming suffix are: delicate, Latinate, immaculate, confederate, desperate, immoderate, adequate.

Uses of -ARY reviewed:

> 1. *-ary,* adjective suffix derived from Latin *-aris* or *-arius,* meaning "of, having to do with" > cautionary, plenipotentiary

> 2. *-ary,* noun suffix derived from the masculine form of *-arius,* meaning "one who is concerned with" > voluptuary, dignitary, emissary, antiquary, votary, adversary.

> 3. *-ary,* noun suffix from the neuter *-arium,* meaning "place for" or, sometimes, "thing for" > apiary, mortuary, ossuary, sanctuary, penitentiary, reliquary, library, salary, diary, breviary, formicary, itinerary, vocabulary.

Boundary shows the neuter -ary ending, added to an originally Celtic base.

What about *quandary*? A good question. Probably "origin unknown" is the best that can be done, but Eric Partridge suggests more boldly the possibility of its being from Latin *quam dare* or *quantum dare,* "how to give?" or "how much to give?" respectively.

EXERCISES

EXERCISE III. A 1—VOCABULARY REVIEW WITH SUFFIXES: review the vocabulary of the previous lesson; divide the following English words into base and suffix; give the meaning of each part and the meaning of the whole or use it in a sentence or phrase. Example: general: base *gener-* [*genus*], kind: suffix -al [-alis], of, concerning; meaning: of [or belonging to] a kind

1. popular
2. corporal
3. corporeal
4. special
5. finial
6. modern
7. rotary
8. antiquary
9. modal
10. breviary
11. divine
12. sanctuary
13. similar
14. terminal
15. domestic
16. generic
17. animal
18. primary
19. primal
20. terrarium
21. final
22. terraqueous
23. literal
24. pinnate (*pinna*, feather)
25. vicarious (*vic-*, change, turn, alteration)
26. alar, alate (*ala*, wing)
27. herbaceous, herbal (*herba*, grass, herb)
28. sebaceous (*sebum*, tallow)
29. Cretaceous, cretaceous (*creta*, chalk)
30. farinaceous (*farina*, grain)
31. Quaternary, quaternary (*quaterni*, four each)
32. rostrate (*rostrum*[3], beak)
33. rosary (*rosa*, rose > *rosarium*, rose garden)
34. venal (*venum*, sale)
35. meretricious (*meretrix*, prostitute)
36. antiquarian (*antiquus*, old)

EXERCISE III. A 2.—ADJECTIVE FORMATION: form English adjectives from these Latin nouns or adjectives. Example: *aqua* > aqueous, aquatic
1. fatum

2. locus
3. similis
4. causa
5. tempus, tempor- (time)
6. humus (ground)
7. aquila (eagle)
8. equus (horse)
9. ancilla (maidservant)
10. arca (chest)
11. auxilium (help, aid)
12. bos, bov- (cow, bull)
13. ovis (sheep)
14. crux, cruci- (cross)
15. dorsum (back)
16. femina (woman)
17. flos, flor- (flower)
18. ferus (wild)
19. grex, greg- (flock, herd)
20. hostis (enemy)
21. insula (island)
22. limen, limen- (threshold)
23. os, or- (mouth)
24. puer (boy, child)
25. passer (sparrow)
26. inimicus (enemy)

EXERCISE III A 3.—ADJECTIVE DOUBLETS: give an adjective using Latin elements (base and suffix) that is etymologically synonymous with the adjective using English elements. Tell how (if at all) the two words differ in meaning or use.

Examples: handy and manual (*manu-*, hand)
      friendly and amiable, amicable (*amicus*, friend)

1. godly
2. watery (*aqua*)
3. bodily
4. homey, homely
5. hearty
6. lawful
7. spirited, having spirit
8. cloudy (*nebula*)
9. lively (*vita*)
10. fleshly (*caro*, *carn-*)
11. deathly (*mors*, *mort-*)
12. kingly (*rex*, *reg-*)

13. fiery (*ign-*)
14. brotherly (*frater*)
15. wifely (*uxori-*)

EXAMPLES OF ENGLISH ADJECTIVES USING -SOME[4] AND -FUL
What are the bases and meanings of these English words?

winsome	handsome
lithesome	toothsome
cuddlesome	lonesome
cumbersome	blithesome
frolicsome	loathsome
wholesome	burdensome
mournful	joyful
woeful	peaceful
beautiful	mindful
graceful	fruitful
playful	useful

B: MORE ADJECTIVE-FORMING SUFFIXES FROM LATIN

With meanings similar to English *-ful*, *-some*: "having, tending to be, full of":
-ose, -ous[5]   -osus   *copia* (abundance) > copious; *otium* (leisure) > otiose
-lent   -lentus   *vis* (force) > violent; *virus* (poison) > virulent
    This suffix may appear as -ilent, -olent, -ulent

Notes:
    The suffix *-ous* may come from either Latin *-us* (a simple adjective ending) or from *-osus* (the adjective suffix meaning "full of").

EXERCISES

EXERCISE III B 1— VOCABULARY REVIEW WITH SUFFIXES: divide into parts (base, suffix); give meaning of word.
1. onerous
2. corpulent
3. populous
4. gracious [ti > ci]
5. generous
6. specious
7. studious
8. otiose [*otium*, leisure]
9. famous [*fama*, talk, rumor]

10. insidious [*insidiae* pl., ambush, trap]
11. lacrimose [*lacrima*, tear]
12. invidious [*invidia*, envy, ill-will]
13. turbulent [*turba*, uproar, riot]
14. ramose [*ramus*, branch]
15. rugose [*ruga*, wrinkle]
16. fraudulent [*fraus, fraud-*, deceit]
17. opulent [*ops, op-* wealth]
18. glorious [*gloria*, fame, glory, praise]
19. succulent [*sucus*, juice]
20. jocose [*jocus*, jest]
21. purulent [*pus, pur-* pus]
22. callous [*callus*, hard skin]

EXERCISE III B 2— GENERAL QUESTIONS

1. What is the difference between specious and special?
2. Fulsome is often misused. What do you think it means? If you are not sure, look up it in your dictionary and use it in a sentence.
3. Try to find five more English words using the suffixes -some and -ful.
4. Find six words using -lent and six using -ose.

C: VOCABULARY

Learn the Latin words, bases and meanings and form two or more derivatives of each as in the example.

annus [after a prefix -*enn*-] *year* > annals, annual, perennial, A.D., anniversary, centennial, superannuated, sesquicentennial

aqua	*water*
caput, capit-	*head*
caro, carn-	*flesh*
civis, civ-	*citizen*
copia	*abundance, supplies*
dies, di-	*day*
funus, funer-	*death, rites for the dead*
ignis, ign-	*fire*
latus, later-	*side*
lex, leg-	*law*
manus, manu-	*hand*
mare, mar-	*sea*
mater, matr[i]-	*mother*
miles, milit-	*soldier*
mors, mort-	*death*
mortuus	*dead body*

mos, mor-	*custom, manner, mood*
murus	*wall*
navis, nav-	*ship*
necesse	*unavoidable*
nervus	*tendon*
nomen, nomin-	*name*
nox, noct-	*night*
numerus	*number*
oculus	*eye*
odium	*hatred*
ordo, ordin-	*rank, row*
os, oss-	*bone*
pater, patr[i]-	*father*
pes, ped-	*foot*
pestis, pest[i]-	*plague*
radius, radi-	*rod, ray, spoke of a wheel*
radix, radic-	*root*
ratio, ration-	*reason, reckoning*
rex, reg-	*king*
rus, rur-	*the country*
saeculum	*age, the times*
salus, salut-	*health, safety*
sanguis, sanguin-	*blood*
sol, sol-	*sun*
somnus	*sleep*
tempus, tempor-	*time*
urbs, urb-	*city*
verbum	*word*
vinum	*wine*
vir, vir-	*man, male*
virus	*poison*
vitium	*fault*
vox, voc-	*voice*

VOCABULARY NOTES

Some Words from TEMPUS (time, with the extended meanings of "due season" or "proper time"): temporal, temporary, contemporary, temporize, tempest, tempestuous (< *tempestas,* storm, weather, season), temper, temperate, temperature, temperament, temperance (< *temperare,* mingle in due proportion); tempera (a painting medium in which pigment is mixed with egg, etc.)

But NOT the other *temporal,* "of the temples (of the head)": which comes from the root *ten-,* "stretch" [cf. *tendere, tentum/tensum* in chapter 5].

And NOT *temple,* a place devoted to the worship or presence of a/the deity, which is from *templum*, a space marked off for observation, from a root meaning "cut". *Templar* and *contemplate* are also from *templum*. And NOT *template* < *templum*, a small piece of wood (part of a loom).

Some word-words from Latin VERBUM: verb, adverb, proverb, verbatim, verbal noun [cf. gerund, infinitive], verbalize, verbosity, verbiage, verve

EXERCISES

EXERCISE III. C 1.—VOCABULARY: fill in at least one English word for each new Latin word. If possible practice the material from the new chapter and the previous chapter in forming your derivatives (suffixes, prefixes, etc.).

Example: verbum > *verb, verbal, verbose* (using the new suffixes, as well as many others such as adverb, adverbial, proverb).

EXERCISE III. C 2.— FORMING WORDS: study the vocabulary; find words meaning:

Example: of the city > city is *urbs*, urb- "of" -an (from *-anus*)> urban

Note: the hard part is deciding which suffix to use. If you are unsure that your word is a word, check it in the dictionary.

1. fatherly
2. motherly
3. during the night
4. daily allowance for food (this is the ancient meaning) > place (or book) for keeping [records of] the day
5. sleepy [full of sleep]
6. full of flaws/faults
7. of/for the foot
8. many [full of numbers]
9. abundant [full of supplies]
10. affected by the moon
11. of the head
12. fleshly
13. yearly
14. of/on the side
15. of the sea
16. of soldiers
17. of ships
18. hateful
19. of/in ranks
20. full of plague
21. of the root
22. of rays
23. of the age/these times
24. of the voice

25. watery

EXERCISE III C 3.—LATIN ADJECTIVES: review the vocabulary of this and the previous lesson. Give Latin base word and its meaning. Change the Latin adjectives to their English equivalents.

Example: nemorosus < *nemus, nemor-*, grove > nemerose

1. morosus	2. somnolentus
3. maternus	4. onerosus
5. verbosus	6. spontaneus (*sponte*, of one's own accord)
7. externus (*exter*, outer)	8. osseous
9. vitiosus	10. ambitosus (*ambitio*, a going around)
11. ramosus (*ramus*, branch)	12. prodigiosus (*prodigium*, portent)
13. copiosus	14. flatulentus (*flatus*, a blowing)
15. funereus	16. callosus (*callum*, hard skin)
17. diurnus (< *dies*)	18. truculentus (*trux, truc-*, wild, rough)
19. nervosus	20. infernus (*infernus*, beneath)
21. paternus	22. vinolentus
23. jocosus (*iocus*, jest)	24. studiosus

EXERCISE III C. 3— DIVIDING INTO BASE AND PREFIX: take apart and give meaning of each part; give a synonym (a word or phrase with the same meaning) for each word.

Example: radical < *radix, radic-*, root + -al, of—meaning: from the root

1. onerous
2. diurnal
3. osseous
4. nominal
5. regal
6. igneous
7. majestic [*major/majus*]
8. temporal
9. verbal
10. verbose
11. dial
12. manual
13. mural
14. numeral
15. terrain [-ain from -enus = -anus]
16. salutary
17. temporary
18. mortuary
19. ordinary
20. vinolent

21. vinose
22. sanguinary
23. aquatic
24. virulent
25. urbane
26. terraqueous
27. aquamarine

EXERCISE III C. 4—PLACE OR THING FOR: form words meaning a place for:
Example: a place for books > library
>   water
>   earth
>   bones (os, use ossu- as base)
>   dead bodies
>   holy things
>   planets
>   herbs
>   the sun
>   dormice [*glis, glir-*]
>   bees [*apis, api-*]
>   beasts [*bestia*]
>   ants [*formica*]

Calvary is the "place of the skull" < *calva*, skull.
An estuary is a tidal river, a place subject to tides < *aestus*, tide.
What is treated at the Palouse Ocularium?
What is an abecedarium?

EXERCISE III C. 5—GENERAL QUESTIONS ON MEANINGS AND USAGE
1. Distinguish in meaning

aquatic	aqueous	
rural	rustic	
corporal	corporeal	corpulent
ordinal	cardinal [< *cardo, cardin-*, hinge]	
radial	radical	
moral	morose	morale
mortal	moral	
urban	urbane	
civil	civic	
temporary	temporal	
funerary	funereal	
sanguine	sanguinary	
viral	virulent	
virile	viral	

2. Which is a synonym for secular? religious temporal parochial sectarian

3. Which costs less, entrance *gratis* or *for a nominal fee?*

4. What is wrong with saying *free gratis?*

5. What do these words have in common, fane, fan, fanatic, profane?

6. Distinguish these: fane, feign, fain. What do you call words that sound alike but have different meanings?

EXERCISE III C. 6—WHICH DOES NOT BELONG?[6]

1. aqua sewer aquiline aqueduct

2. virulent viral virile virus

3. vice vital vituperate vitiate vicious

4. osmosis ossify ossuary osseous

5. capital chief precipitate cape capacity

6. collateral quadrilateral latitudinarian trilateral

7. manure manic manual maneuver legerdemain amanuensis

8. temporal template tempera tempest tempo

9. nomenclature binomial anomie misnomer cognomen nominate

10. verve adverb verbatim verbosity verity

EXERCISES FOR REVIEW

EXERCISE III C 7—FORMING LATIN ADJECTIVES: form Latin adjectives meaning "full of, having" using -osus or -lentus from these Latin nouns. Give meaning of Latin adjective and English form.

Examples: *ingenium*, native talent > *ingeniosus*, having/full of innate ability> ingenious

vis, vi-, force > *violentus*, given to force > violent

Add -osus > -ous, -ose

1. *fama*, fame

2. *sumptus, sumptu-*, expense

3. *victoria*, victory

4. *odium*, hatred

5. *injuria*, injury

6. *insidiae* (pl.), ambush, trap

7. *perfidia*, false faith

8. *lachryma (lacrima)*, tear

9. *numerus*, number

10. *contumelia*, insult, invective

Add *-lentus* > -lent

11. *ops, op- (opu-)*, means, resources, wealth

12. *fraus, fraud- (fraudu-)*, deceit

13. *pestis, pesti-*, plague

14. *virus, viru-*, poison

15. *turba* (*turbu-*), uproar

EXERCISE III C 8—DIVIDING WORDS: divide into base, suffix(es) and give meaning
of each part. Use each word in a sentence.
Example: sylvan (silvan): base *silva*, woods, forest + -anus "of, having to do with."
Pan was a sylvan god.
1. urbane
2. libertine < *libertus*, freedman
3. radial
4. pedal
5. venal < *venum*, sale
6. callous
7. otiose
8. radical
9. morose
10. insidious
11. corpulent
12. verbose
13. breviary
14. terminal
15. funereal
16. lunatic
17. marine
18. prodigal < *prodigus*, wasteful

EXERCISE III C 9—MATCHING MEANINGS
a. Match words from Latin with their native Enlish equivalent. In column C add
another English word from the Latin base of the word in column B.

	A	B	C
Ex.	1. bloody _h_	a. annual	anniversary, perennial
	2. wordy__	b. verbose	
	3. kingly__	c. somnolent	
	4. nightly__	d. regal	
	5. yearly__	e. odious	
	6. childish__	f. igneous	
	7. sleepy__	g. nasal	
	8. burdensome__	h. sanguine	
	9. hateful__	i. virile	
	10. fiery__	j. puerile	
	11. nosey__	k. onerous	
	12. manly__	l. nocturnal	

b. Match words from Latin with their native Enlish equivalent. In column C add another English word using the same Latin suffix as the word in column B.

Ex. 1. timely_e_   a. mundane   urbane, montane
     2. homey__   b. copious
     3. beastly__   c. aqueous
     4. worldly__   d. vicious
     5. watery__   e. temporary
     6. boney__   f. maternal
     7. fulsome__   g. lachrymose
     8. faulty__   h. domestic
     9. motherly__   i. osseous
    10. tearful__   j. opulent
    11. wealthy   k. corporeal
    12. bodily__   l. bestial

QUISQUILIA

Some interesting words from the new vocabulary
   dismal probably comes from *dies mali*, bad days
   pew is from *pes, ped-*, foot
   sangfroid from *sanguis + frigidus > froid* in French, cold blood
   rosemary from *mare* [+ *ros, ror-*, dew]

BOBBED WORDS: some words have lost large parts of themselves in their transition into English. For example:

MOB < Latin *mobile vulgus*, the fickle crowd

BUS < Latin *omnibus*, for all/everybody: *bus* is just the ending, the dative plural, indicating the relationship *for*

ANA: a collection or anthology, from the custom of calling a collection of verses or sayings by an author by that author's name with -*ana* attached (neuter plural of Latin suffix -*anus*, "of, belonging to"), as in Shakespeariana, Vergiliana and extended to include collectibles like Americana. Southey wrote that Boswell's *Life of Johnson* , "for its intrinsic worth, is the *Ana* of all *Anas*" (1834).

FAN: a devotee, an avid admirer, is short for fanatic < Latin *fanaticus*, of the temple (*fanum*); that is, inspired or maddened by a god.

BIB < Latin *bibere*, to drink

FENCE: short for defense < *defendere*, defend, protect

SCOUR < Middle Dutch *scuren* < Old French *escurer* < Late Latin *excurare*, to clean out < *ex-*, out + *curare* < *cura*, care

SCOUT < Latin *auscultare*, to listen

SPORT < Latin *disportare*, to carry [*portare*] oneself away from [*dis-*] that is, to amuse oneself

ENDGAME: RECOGNIZING NEW WORDS

1. A unicorn looks like a horse except that it has one [*un-*, *uni-*] horn [*cornu*]. Explain the meanings and parts of these words:
    unanimous
    unilateral
    cornea
    cornucopia

2. At the equinox day and night [*nox*, *nocti-*] are approximately equal [*aequus* > *equi-*, even] in length. Explain these words:
    equivocal
    equivoque: explain how this comes to mean a *pun* (-voque < *vox*)
    equilateral
    equanimity [-ity condition of being/having]
    equity
    equilibrium [*libra*, balance]
    equivalent [*valens*, *valent-*, being strong]
    equipollent [*pollens*, *pollent-*, being powerful]
    equal, equality, equalitarian [= egalitarian < French *egal* < Latin *aequalis*]
    Other *aequ-* words include equator, equipoise, equable, equation, equitable,
        equidistant, inequity, adequate,
    What is an adjective meaning "of or relating to the equinox"?
    These *aequi-* words must not be confused with words from *equus*, horse, which include equine, equerry, equestrian, equestrienne, equitation, Equuleus, Equisetum (the genus that includes the horsetails), and which is related to the Greek word *hippos* and perhaps to *kuon*, dog.

3. Amble comes from *ambulare*, go, walk. What do these mean?
    somnambulism
    noctambulism
    ambulatory
    funambulist [*funis*, rope]
    ambulacrum [*-acrum*, place for]
    preamble
    ambulance [< French hôpital ambulant, moving hospital]

4. What do these have to do with hand?

manumission	manuscript
manifest	mandate
manure	maneuver
legerdemain	emancipate
amanuensis	mortmain

WORDS IN CONTEXT

There were the legends of the past, spread like *vellum*[7] pages of scripture, and then there was the living dream of the past, the moments he carried, as real as the silver napkin ring in his *portmanteau*[8]—the smell of his father searing white wood for a canoe, or the taste of guava and wild meat during a feast.

Dominic Smith, *Bright and Distant Shores*, 2011

"What's my payment if I come back without a trader? A kick in my *corpulent* arse?"

Dominic Smith, *Bright and Distant Shores*, 2011

But the fug below had made him *qualmish* and he'd come above in search of fresh air.

Dominic Smith, *Bright and Distant Shores*, 2011

CHECKLIST FOR CHAPTER THREE: WHAT YOU SHOULD KNOW

1. Adjective forming suffixes from Latin. Special uses of -ary, -arium.
2. Vocabulary list
3. New English words

Suffixes:

Fill in this chart of suffixes: give meaning and an example. A few of the less common ones are filled in.

Ex. -al	of, having the nature of	*penal, autumnal, fatal, total*
-alia	things having to do with	*regalia*
-an, ane;		
-ana,	things having to do with	*Americana, Vergiliana, ana*
-ar		
-ary [adj.]		
-ary [noun, masc.]		
-ary [noun, neuter]		
-arious		
-arium		
-ate		
-eous, -eal, -ean		*Mediterranean*
-ernal, -ern		*co-eternal, modern*
-ic		
-il, -ile;		
-ilia,	things having to do with	*juvenilia*
-ine		
-lent		
-nal		*vernal, internal, fraternal*

-ose
-ous
-tic
-urnal, -urn   *nocturnal, taciturn*

NOTES

1. These correspond to German -lich, -ig, -haft, as in *Herz*, *herzlich* (cognate to heart), *Welt*, *weltlich* (cf. world),

2. -y and -ish are often used for describing colors: purplish, orangy-red. -y is frequently used for flavors and textures: peppery, oniony, creamy, runny, woody. -ish is used for fashions and pretensions: Queen Annish, Jet Settish, modish. -ish is also used for some adjectives for national names: English, Scottish, Flemish, Polish, Pictish.

3. *Rostrum*, a dais or speaker's platform, is named for the speakers' stand in the Forum of ancient Rome which was decorated with the prows or beaks of captured enemy ships.

4. The English suffix *-some*, meaning "like", is related etymologically to the Latin word *similis*.

5. *-ous* is used in Chemistry to indicate "having a valence lower than that in a comparable *-ic* compound." Compare *ferrous* and *ferric*.

6. Answers for III c. 6: 1. aquiline 2. virile 3. vital 4. osmosis 5. capacity 6. latitudinarian 7. manic 8. template 9. anomie 10. verity

7. *vellum*, parchment made of calfskin, kidskin, or lambskin < Latin *vitellus*, little calf.

8. *portmanteau*, a suitcase with two compartments < Latin (through French) *portare* carry + *mantellum*, cloak.

SECTION TWO: LATIN
A. LATIN NOUNS AND ADJECTIVES

CHAPTER FOUR: NOUN-FORMING SUFFIXES

PART A: SUFFIXES, ENGLISH AND LATIN

In English we have a number of suffixes used to convert adjectives into nouns that express the state or quality of being what is named by the adjective. Such nouns are called ABSTRACT NOUNS. The English suffix -*ness* (cognate to German -*nis*) is very productive for forming abstract nouns from adjectives and past participles:

    dark > darkness mindful > mindfulness contented > contentedness

-*ness* can be added to any adjective, whatever its origin: we can add it to adjectives derived from Latin as well as native English; it can be added to phrases, pronouns and adverbs as in completeness, togetherness, uptightness, get-atableness, up-to-dateness, otherworldliness, self-centeredness, awesomeness, bittersweetness, boneheadedness, easygoingness, interchangeableness, overindebtedness, and the exquisite *dislike-to-getting-up-in-the-morningness* of George Eliot. And in a more recent oblique coinage by Jacob Rubin in *The Poser* (2015): *off-to-the-sidedness.* —*ness* can even be used as a noun in its own right, as in:

    cheerfulness, kindliness, cleverness, and contentedness, and all the other good nesses
    .... Lowell, 1888

As useful as -*ness* is, English has several other abstract-noun-forming suffixes: -*ship*, -*dom*, and -*hood* (corresponding to German -*schaft*, -*tum*, and -*heit*).

Like -ness, -*ship* can be added to adjectives and past participles, but is mostly added to noun bases. It denotes the state or condition of being, and the office, position, or rank, art or functioning:

    hard > hardship   author > authorship   scholar > scholarship
    leader > leadership   king >kingship   steward > stewardship

Also such formations as penmanship, oneupsmanship, ecopreneurship (eco- + entrepreneur).

    The suffix -*dom*, once an independent noun meaning "putting, setting, position, statute" is now a living suffix used to form nouns expressing "condition, dignity, domain, realm" and is attached to nouns and adjectives:

    free > freedom   owl > owldom   wise > wisdom   bore > boredom

It is used for nonce-formations, in this case instant abstractions like pineappledom, B.A.dom, do-your-own-thingdom, fandom, Elvisdom, dudedom, memedom.

Like -dom, *-hood* started as a separate noun, meaning "person, personality, condition, sex, quality, rank," but was so freely combined with other words that it ceased to be a noun in its own right and is used as a suffix to denote condition or state:

    duckhood, childhood, likelihood, victimhood, zombiehood, personhood

    adminhood: rank of systems administrator (internet usage)

    kidulthood: condition of adults who participate in children's activities

EXERCISES

EXERCISE IVA.1—ENGLISH ABSTRACTS: Form seven English words using each of these suffixes:

    -hood

    -dom

    -ship

and twelve using:

    -ness

LATIN NOUN-FORMING SUFFIXES

A. With meanings, "the state of being, the quality or condition of being"

Form in English	From Latin	Examples
-ity/-ety/-ty[1]	-tas	*qualis* (of what kind) > quality
		varius (diverse) > variety
		difficilis (difficult) > difficulty
-y	-ia	*miser* (wretched): misery
-ce[2]	-(t)ia	*sapiens* (wise): sapience
-ice	-itia	*avarus* (greedy): avarice
-(i)tude	-(i)tudo	*magnus* (big): magnitude

                (base in -itudin- as in multitudinous[3], latitudinal)

-mony	-monia/monium	*acer*, acr- (sharp): acrimony

B. With various meanings

-y	-ium	*augur* (soothsayer): augury

"act, office, place, or condition of"

-ate	-atus	*pontifex* (priest): pontificate

"office, function of"; cf. directorate, episcopate, consulate, emirate, diaconate, caliphate

-ine	-ina	*discipulus* (pupil): discipline

"act, office, art, condition of"; cf. medicine, famine

C. Diminutive suffixes: these add the meaning "small" to nouns. Both the English and Latin forms are in common use in technical terminology. The most important diminutive suffixes from Latin are:

-ule, -le	-ulus/a/um	*granum* (grain): granule
		forma (shape): formula
		scrupus (sharp stone): scruple
-ole	-olus/a/um	*gladius* (sword): gladiolus
-cule, -cle	-culus/a/um	*pars*, part- (part): particle
		homo, homin- (man): homunculus[4]
-el,-il	-illus, ellus/a/um	*cerebrum* (brain): cerebellum
-leus/a/um	-leus/a/um	*nux*, nuc- (nut): nucleus

For more examples of diminutives, see exercises below.

Note on Noun-forming suffixes

Remember that *-ium* added to a base ending in *c-*, *t-*, or *g-* will undergo the changes to -ce/cy, -ge described in Chapter 2.

EXERCISES

EXERCISE IVA. 2.—REVIEW THE VOCABULARY of previous lessons and try to take apart and define these words:

Example: animosity < *anim-*, mind, spirit + *-os-*, full of + *-ity*, condition of being "condition of being full of spirit": animosity is used in a negative sense, as is *animus* in English, "a spirit of hostility"
 1. causality
 2. corpulence
 3. fatality
 4. gratitude
 5. magnanimity
 6. annuity (< *annuus*, yearly)
 7. city (from Latin *civitas* < *civis*, citizen)
 8. matrimony
 9. patrimony
10. morality
11. pestilence
12. divinity
13. domesticity
14. generosity
15. radicle
16. corpuscle
17. module

18. capsule (*capsa*, box)
19. gladiolus (*gladius*, sword)
20. grace, gracious

EXERCISE IVA. 3— PRACTICE WITH SUFFIXES: Form words meaning:
1. shortness
2. brightness
3. worthiness
4. office of the first place holder (*princeps, princip-*)
5. likeness
6. largeness
7. wordiness
8. unavoidableness
9. lawfulness
10. fatherhood
11. lowliness
12. a small open space [*area*, open space]
13. condition of being full of small sharp stones [*scrupus*, sharp stone]
14. a small papyrus leaf [*scheda*, papyrus leaf]
15. a small knife [*scalper* use as base *scalp-*, knife]
16. condition of having an end
17. fullness
18. condition of being of the people

EXERCISE IVA. 4 —TWO NEW SUFFIXES: take apart the words in the list:
-ism, *action, state, condition, usage, doctrine, belief in/of*
-ist, *one concerned with, skilled in, an adherent of*
1. secularism
2. rationalist
3. militarist
4. vocalism
5. nominalism
6. legalistic
7. radicalism
8. oculist
9. specialist
10. generalist
11. finalist
12. localism
Find a word meaning (optional exercise):
1. a man or woman concerned with the people
2. the doctrine of betterment, i.e., that human activity makes things better [*melior*, better]

3. one concerned with [things] related to the head
4. doctrine concerned with the thing said
5. one skilled in that which has to do with the voice

EXERCISE IVA. 5—DISTINGUISH
    1. paternity from patrimony
    2. maternity from matrimony
    3. faculty from facility

PART B: VOCABULARY

Learn the Latin bases and meanings and form two or more derivatives of each using one of the new suffixes: as in the examples.

acer, acr-	*sharp, bitter* >	acrimony
aequus (equ[i]-)	*even, equal* > equal, equity, equanimity	
aevum	*age* >	longevity, primeval, coeval
altus	*high, deep*	
aptus	*fitted to* (often shows *-ept-* after a prefix)	
auris, aur-	*ear*	
beatus	*happy, blessed*	
cavus	*hollow*	
cella	*storeroom*	
fatuus	*silly, foolish*	
forma	*shape*	
fortis	*strong, brave*	
granum	*grain*	
gravis	*heavy, serious*	
heres, hered-	*heir*	
hostis, host-	*enemy*	
humus	*the ground, soil*	
humanus	*human*	
humilis	*lowly*	
jocus	*jest*	
latus-a-um	*wide*	
latus, later-	*side*	
levis	*light* (not heavy or serious)	
liber, liber-	*free*	
longus	*long*	
magnus	*big, great*	
major, majus (majes-)	*bigger, greater, older*	
maximus	*biggest, greatest, oldest*	
malus	*bad*	

pejor; pessimus	*worse; worst*
minor, minus (mines-)	*smaller, younger, less*
minimus	*smallest, least*
miser	*wretched, unhappy*
moles, mole-	*heap, mass*
mus, mur-	*mouse*
nux, nuc-	*nut*
pars, part-	*part*
pauci (pl. adj.)	*few*
pius	*devoted to duty*
posterus	*coming after*
proprius	*one's own*
pulcher, pulchri-	*handsome, beautiful*
qualis	*of what kind*
quantus	*how much*
sanus	*sound, healthy*
satis	*enough*
senex, sen-	*old (man)*
servus	*slave*
socius	*comrade, ally*
testis	*witness*
unus	*one*
varius	*speckled, changing*
vicus	*quarter, section of a city* > vicinity

Vocabulary Notes

GRAVIS produces *grave* (adj. meaning "weighty, heavy, serious"), *gravid, gravity, gravitational, aggravate, aggrieve, grievous, grieve, gravimetric* (concerned with the measurement of weight), the musical term *grave* (solemnly), the legal term *gravamen* (the part of the charge that weighs most heavily against the accused); but NOT *grave* (noun, a place for burial in the ground) and not *grave*, engrave or carve, as in *graven images*; nor *gravy* which comes from *granum* (grain > sauce flavored or thickened with grain or flour).

ACER is from the root AK- meaning sharp and is related to the native English expression "to egg on" and to the Latin word *acus*, needle > *acute, acumen, acupuncture*; and to *acere* > acid and *acerbus* > *acerb, acerbic, exacerbate*. From *acer* come *acrid, acrimonious, acrimony, acerate, eager,* and *vinegar*. The Greek words *akros*, topmost (> acrobat, acrophobia, acronym), *akme*, point (> acme and acne), and *oxus* (oxy-) are from the same root.

BONUS (vocabulary chapter 1) gives us *bonus, bonanza, bonbon, bonny, boon, bon mot* (a good word or witticism), *bonhomie* (good nature, affable disposition), *debonair* ("of good air" i.e., suave, jaunty). The adverb is *bene*> benison, benefactor, benediction, benign, benevolent, benefit. Can you think of additional words using *bene*? Its opposite is *male*. Can you form opposites of some of the *bene*-words? *bellus* is the diminutive of *bonus* > belle, beau, belladonna, beldam, embellish, beauty, beautiful, *Beaux Arts*.

MINUS is the source of minus, minor, minister, minuscule, minuet, minute, minutiae, mince, menu, diminish and diminutive and the prefix *mis-*. The Latin word *nimis* is from the same root as *minus*; with the negative prefix, *ni-*, it means "too much" and is the origin of the English word *nimiety*. See if you can find *nimiety* in your dictionary; if not, look in a bigger dictionary.

There are three HOSTS in English: host (1) from *hospes*; host (2) from *hostis*; and host (3) from *hostia*. Find out how each is used and which ones (if any) are related etymologically.

From *hospes, hospit-* (see exercises in chapter 1), literally "master of strangers" come *host* (1), hostess, hospice, hostel, hospital, inhospitable, hospitality, Hospitaller, hotel, hostler (or ostler, a stableman at an inn). The Germanic word *guest* is a cognate to *hospes*.

EXERCISES

EXERCISE IVB. 1— NEW SUFFIXES (using new vocabulary).
a. Take apart and define parts: Ex. cellulose < *cella*, storeroom + *-ul-*, small + *-ose*, full of
1. multitudinous
2. acrimony
3. altitude
4. aptitude
5. auricle
6. beatitude
7. fatuity
8. fortitude
9. granular
10. gravity
11. hereditary
12. hostility
13. humanitarian
14. latitudinarian
15. liberality
16. malicious
17. misery
18. molecule
19. muscular
20. particularity
21. piety
22. nucleolus
23. posterity
24. pulchritudinous
25. senate
26. uniformity
27. testimonial

28. satiety
29. cavity
30. service

b. Distinguish in meaning between:
1. property and propriety
2. social and societal
3. nucleus and nucleolus
4. service and servitude
5. libertinism and liberalism
6. quality and quantity
7. proper and proprietary

c. Give English spelling and meaning of:
1. triumviratus (*trium*, of three)
2. pontificatus (*pontifex*, high priest)
3. tribunatus (*tribunus*, tribune)
4. senatus (*senex, sen-*, old man)
5. auspicium (bird watching < *avis*)

EXERCISE IVB. 2— FORM WORDS MEANING:
1. tending to/full of sharpness
2. a small shape
3. a small grain
4. human-ness
5. wideness
6. lightness
7. longness
8. largeness
9. freedom
10. wickedness
11. condition of being older/bigger
12. condition of being younger/fewer
13. wretchedness
14. concerning a small heap
15. concerning a small mouse
16. a small nut
17. a small part
18. condition of being few
19. devoted to duty
20. condition of being beautiful
21. comradeship
22. condition of being like an old man

23. state of being sound/healthy
24. state of being a slave
25. act of being a witness
26. oneness
27. oneness of mind
28. changingness
29. of a small ear
30. condition of being concerned with shape

EXERCISE IV B. 3— MORE DIMINUTIVES:
a. Take apart and define:
1. cellulose (*cella*, a storeroom; cf. cell, cellar)
2. cerebellum (*cerebrum*, brain; cf. cerebral, cerebrate)
3. clavicle (*clavis*, key; cf. enclave, clavichord)
4. globular (*globus*, globe)
5. reticle (*rete*, net)
6. meticulous (*metus*, fear)
7. scrupulosity (*scrupus*, stone)
8. libellous (*liber* book > *libellus*, small book)
9. castle (< *castellum* < *castra*, fortified camp)
10. codicil (*codex*, tree trunk, book)
11. corolla (< *corona*, crown)
b. Form diminutives of:
1. *calx*, calc-, pebble
2. *forma*, shape
3. *artus*, joint
4. *alveus*, hollow
5. *cutis*, skin
6. *pes, ped-*, foot
7. *minus*
8. *majus*
9. *hamus*, hook
10. *venter, ventr-*, stomach (cf. ventriloquist < *loqui* speak)
11. *granum*
12. *nux, nuc-*
13. *moles*, mass, heap
14. *gladius*, sword

EXERCISE IV B. 4— RECOGNIZING BASES: Give meaning of base word and an additional word from each Latin base:
Examples: coeval, base -*ev*-, from *aevum*, age—other words from base: longevity, primeval, medieval
ineptitude, base -*ept*-, from *aptus*, fitted to—other words: apt, aptitude, adapt,

adept, inept

In this exercise concentrate on recognizing the base; prefixes and some suffixes will be treated later.

1. exacerbate
2. beatific
3. excavation
4. infatuation
5. reformation
6. ingrain
7. gravitational
8. inherit
9. exhumation
10. posthumous
11. jocund
12. alleviate
13. pejoration
14. majesty
15. minister
16. commiserate
17. appropriate
18. dissatisfaction
19. variegated
20. musculature
21. mayoralty
22. preposterous

EXERCISE IV B. 5— RELATIVES OR LOOK-ALIKES: which word in each group does not belong (i.e., does not share a Latin base with the others)?[5]

1. longevity evil coeval medieval
2. aural oracle auricle binaural
3. cavern cavea caveat cavity excavate
4. fortitude fortify aqua fortis fortuitous comfort
5. granite granule ingrain grandiose granary
6. gravity graveyard gravitational grievous
7. heretic inherit heredity hereditary heir
8. latitudinarian lateral unilateral bilateral
9. liberty illiberal libertine library
10. magic mayor majuscule majesty
11. muscle murine musculature mural
12. propraetor appropriate proper propriety

EXERCISES FOR PRACTICE AND REVIEW

EXERCISE IV B. 6—FINDING BASES: give Latin base word and meaning; define compound; change to English spelling. Example: *facilitas* < *facilis*, easy, doable; meaning: "easiness"; facility

1. gravitas
2. patrimonium
3. maternitas
4. vinolentia
5. unanimitas
6. turbulentia (< *turba*, uproar)
7. pestilentia
8. militia
9. latitudo
10. urbanitas
11. humanitas
12. justitia
13. necessitas
14. majestas
15. satietas
16. vicinitas (< *vicus*, section of a town or village > *vicinus*, neighbor)
17. paucitas
18. miseria
19. avaritia (< *avarus*, greedy)
20. altitudo
21. proprietas
22. acrimonium
23. sanctimonium
24. magnitudo
25. claritas
26. beatitudo
27. levitas
28. pietas
29. malitia
30. lassitudo (< *lassus*, weary,tired)

EXERCISE IV B. 7— WORD FORMATION: for each adjective or noun in the list, form an abstract noun in -ty, -mony, -ice, -ce, -tude, or -y. Example: *sanctus*, holy > sanctity, sanctitude, sanctimony. If you are unsure that your creation is a real word, it is not cheating to check in the dictionary or on the internet. Fill in the meaning of the adjective (or noun) if it is not given.

1. varius
2. testis

3. sollicitus (anxious, concerned)
4. efficax, efficac- (accomplishing)
5. pulcher
6. longus
7. parcus (sparing—the English word uses *parsi-* as the base)
8. comis (courteous, friendly)
9. controversus (turned against)
10. fortis
11. heres, hered-
12. debilis (weak)
13. unus
14. qualis
15. mendax, mendac- (lying)
16. posterus
17. universus (all together)
18. dignus
19. asper (harsh, rough)
20. quantus
21. quietus (at rest)
22. celeber, celebri- (crowded, honored)
23. amoenus (pleasant; note -oe- > English -e-)
24. animosus
25. alacer, alacri- (eager, quick)
26. felix, felic- (happy)
27. gratus
28. liber (adj.)
29. brevis
30. clarus
31. deus
32. divinus
33. facilis
34. par
35. mater, matr-

EXERCISE IV B. 8— MEANINGS: match the words in column A with words in column B that have about the same meanings. In column C give a word from the same Latin base as the word in column A (as in item 1).
Some new Vocabulary for this exercise:

asper	*harsh, bitter, rough*
avarus	*greedy*
fecundus	*fertile*
mendax, mendac-	*lying*
turpis	*base, shameful*

A	B	C
1. solitude _f_	a. greediness	solo, solitary, solipsism
2. liberty __	b. mannerliness	
3. avarice__	c. righteousness	
4. mendacity__	d. wickedness	
5. modesty__	e. shortness	
6. turpitude__	f. aloneness	
7. justice__	g. wretchedness	
8. misery__	h. highness	
9. altitude __	i. falsehood	
10. brevity__	j. freedom	
11. asperity__	k. fruitfulness	
12. fecundity__	l. hardship	

EXERCISE IV B. 9— MATCHING BASE-NOUNS— Find the Latin base of the two words in each pair. Choose two or three and look up the second word of the pair to see how it changed.

Example: lassitude, alas < *lassus*, tired; alas < Old French *a las, helas* "ah [I am] weary"

1. piety, pity
2. propriety, property
3. sanctity, saint
4. majesty, mayor,
5. clarity, clear
6. beatitude, beauty
7. acrimony, eager
8. aptitude, attitude
9. hostility, host

EXERCISE IV B. 10— USING THE NEW FORMATIONS: use each of these in a sentence:

1. posterity
2. debility (< *debilis*, weak)
3. sanctimony, sanctity
4. pulchritude
5. acrimony
6. comity (< *comis*, courteous)
7. quality
8. quantity
9. quiddity (< *quid*, what?)
10. amenity (< *amoenus*, pleasant)

EXERCISE IV B. 11— NOUNS TO ADJECTIVES: using adjective-forming suffixes from the previous lesson, form adjectives from these nouns. Example: acrimony >

acrimonious

1. pulchritude	7. longitude
2. society	8. heredity
3. parsimony	9. malice
4. propriety	10. avarice
5. variety	11. sanctimony
6. majesty	12. latitude

CHAPTER FOUR: SUMMARY AND CHECK LIST

1. Noun-forming suffixes from Latin: -ty, -y, -ice, -tude (base, -tudin-), mony, -ate, -ine

Diminutive suffixes from Latin: -ulus/ule; -olus/ole; -culus/cule; -cle; -ellus/el, il; -leus

Know meanings and be able to form at least one word using each suffix. For review form an adjective related to each noun in your list of examples. For example: malice, adj. malicious; pulchritude, adj. pulchritudinous; piety, adj. pious.

2. Learn new vocabulary.

ENDGAME: ARTHUR'S HOMONYM GAME[6]

Find two or more words that sound the same to fit the definitions in each line. For example: to pretend, gladly, a temple (feign, fain, fane)

1. laurel, body of water, to howl, reddish brown horse, projecting window, and an Ottoman governor
2. run away (from) a pest
3. a fern, to stop, and to rupture
4. expectorated, a petty quarrel, oysters do it
5. female deer, bread in the making and the long green
6. to bend, a branch
7. discoursed, part of a wheel
8. more daring (with) a large rock
9. a four base hit, the father of poetry
10. agreeable, metamorphic rock
11. abase, grounds of a mansion
12. a narrow gorge, to make dirty
13. superlatively bad, sausage
14. build up, tear down

Words that are written the same but mean different things (whether or not they are pronounced the same) are called *homographs*. Words that sound the same but have opposite meanings are called *enantionyms*.

NOTES

1. Usually -i- precedes the suffix -ty; -ety is used if the base ends in -i- (as *sobrius* > sobriety); sometimes there is no connecting vowel (as *liber* > liberty). The suffixes -ty (< -tas) and -y (< -ia) are sometimes added to noun bases as society < *societas* < *socius*, comrade, ally and victory < *victoria* < *victor*, conqueror.

2. The suffix -ce results from -*ia* being added to a base in *t* (for example corpulent is the adjective, corpulence is the noun < *corpulentia*).

3. Macbeth: "No, this my hand will rather the *multitudinous* seas incarnadine, making the green one red," Shakespeare, *Macbeth*, Act 2, scene 2.

4. The *u* of hom*u*nculus can be explained by the assonance of the vowel sounds (to make them sound better and easier to pronounce).

5. Answers to IV B. 5: 1. evil 2. oracle 3. caveat 4. fortuitous 5. grandiose 6. graveyard 7. heretic 8. latitudinarian 9. library 10. magic 11. mural 12. propraetor

6. Answers: 1. bay, Bey 2. flee, flea 3. brake, break 4. spat 5. doe, dough 6. bow, bough 7. spoke 8. bolder, boulder 9. homer, Homer 10. nice, gneiss 11. demean, demesne 12. defile 13. worst, wurst 14. raise, raze

SECTION TWO: LATIN
A. LATIN NOUNS AND ADJECTIVES

INTERLUDE 1
REVIEW OF LATIN NOUNS & ADJECTIVES: CHAPTERS ONE TO FOUR

A. DERIVATIVES 1—from each of the following form a) one simple or direct entry; b) one adjective; and c) one noun. Give meaning of Latin word. Be able to define each English derivative. Example: *corpus, corpor-* (body): a) corpus, corpse, corps; b) corporal, corporeal, corpulent; c) corpulence, corpuscle

1. animus
2. species
3. gratia
4. modus
5. genus
6. fatum
7. forma
8. heres, hered-
9. aqua
10. primus

B. DERIVATIVES 2—from each of the following form one noun and one adjective. Give meaning of the Latin word. Example: *focus* (hearth): noun, focus (also curfew, fuel); adjective, focal.

1. plenus
2. finis
3. locus
4. onus
5. populus
6. amplus
7. rota
8. studium

9. terminus
10. antiquus
11. clarus
12. divus
13. facilis
14. humilis
15. par
16. sanctus
17. similis
18. annus
19. aqua
20. civis
21. dies
22. funus, funer-
23. mater, matri-
24. miles, milit-
25. mors, mort-
26. mos, mor-
27. navis
28. necesse
29. nervus
30. odium
31. ratio, ration-
32. tempus, tempor-
33. vox, voc-
34. verbum
35. vir
36. virus
37. vitium
38. acer, acr-
39. aptus
40. granum
41. gravis
42. hostis
43. humanus
44. liber, liber-
45. malus
46. miser
47. nux, nuc-
48. pius
49. sanus
50. senex, sen-
51. socius

52. servus
53. varius

C. WORD ELEMENTS—give meaning of each base word and define each compound.
Example: scrupulosity < *scrupus*, sharp stone + *-ul-* small + *-os-* full of + *-ity*
condition of being; meaning: "the condition of being beset by petty qualms."
 1. laborious
 2. breviary
 3. dignity
 4. verity
 5. capital
 6. carnal
 7. fanatic
 8. copious
 9. unilateral
10. igneous
11. quality
12. satiety
13. jocular
14. manual
15. mural
16. nominal
17. nocturnal
18. numerous
19. ocular
20. ordinary
21. osseous
22. patrimony
23. pedal
24. testimony
25. pestilence
26. radial
27. radical
28. regal
29. secular
30. salutary
31. solar
32. somnolent
33. urbane
34. terrarium
35. altitudinal
36. vacuous
37. beatitude

38. fatuous
39. fortitude
40. latitude
41. levity
42. longitude
43. magnanimity
44. minority
45. molecular
46. muscular
47. particular
48. posterity
49. pulchritudinous
50. plenitude

D. IDENTIFYING BASES—what noun, adjective, or adverb does each come from:
Examples: latitudinarian < *latus* (adj.), wide; multilateralism < *latus, later-* (noun),
side.
1. incarnation
2. bonbon
3. evacuate
4. benefit
5. eradicate
6. irradiate
7. impediment
8. coordinate
9. consanguinity
10. somnambulism
11. suburb
12. vintner
13. infatuate
14. obliterate
15. excavate

E. SINGULAR OR PLURAL—tell which number each is, singular or plural, and change
to the opposite number.
Example: *data*—plural; the singular is *datum*

1. media	2. focus
3. genera	4. formula
5. agendum	6. memoranda
7. series	8. loci
9. alumnae	10. corpora
11. species	12. opus

F. SUFFIXES (Optional)—match suffixes with similar meanings[1]

____tude (3)	a. ary (use three times)	
____tic (6)	b. lent	c. cule
____ose (1)	d. el	e. al
____arium (1)	f. ule	g. ine (use twice)
____ist (1)	h. ic	i. mony
____cle (4)	j. ane	k. ity
	l. ice	m. ile n. leus

G. MEANINGS OF BASES—match with meaning of base word:

_x_0. particular	a. sinew	n. fat
___1. musculature	b. foolish	o. country
___2. rusticate	c. heart	p. center
___3. nucleolus	d. death	q. smaller
___4. minority	e. wide	r. side
___5. pejorative	f. mouse	s. swear
___6. fatuity	g. young	t. thing said
___7. fatalism	h. voice	u. like
___8. immortal	i. obese	v. wall
___9. morality	j. strong	w. nut
__10. latitude	k. custom	x. part
__11. verisimilitude (2)	l. worse	y. even
__12. equivocate (2)	m. disease	z. true

H. GENERAL VOCABULARY—know meanings of:

1. puerile	11. invidious
2. onerous	12. incarnation
3. farrago	13. secular
4. virago	14. sanguine
5. crux	15. amanuensis
6. obtuse	16. pulchritude
7. mansuetude	17. proprietary
8. plenipotentiary	18. libertine
9. orotund	19. coeval
10. pusillanimous	20. jejune

I. VOCABULARY—MULTIPLE CHOICE[2]

1. A *little ear* is: a. an earwig b. eerie c. an auricle d. an oracle e. aural
2. Another word for *heartiness* is: a. cordial b. coronary c.cordiality d. cardiac
3. *Radical* and *eradicate* come from the same Latin noun meaning: a. rub out b. pull up c. root d. ray e. radish
4. *Onus*, *onerous*, and *exonerate* come from the Latin word meaning: a. burden b. honor c. reward d. responsibility e. work

5. A *small net* (or grid) is: a. rectilinear b. a reticle c. reticent d. reticulendothelial

6. A *rara avis* is: a. a rent-a-car agency that tries harder b. an uncommon fowl c. an extinct bee d. an undercooked turkey

7. A synonym for *felicity* is: a. beatitude b. pulchritude c. gladsome d. opulence

8. *Egregious* and *gregarious* are from a Latin noun meaning: a. greeting b. flock c. birth or family d. Hellenic

9. A *finial* would most likely be found: a. at an Irish wake b. on the back of a fish c. at the top a lampshade d. on the production line of a flax factory e. in Helsinki

10. *Sanguine* and *sanguinary* are from a Latin word meaning: a. bloody b. cheerfulness c. red   d. death e. blood

11. A *corpuscle* is a. a division of the army b. the body of a pecadillo c. a small body d. a muscle in the heart

12. Which word is not from Latin *virus*: a. virology b. virility c. viral d. virulent

13. *Nominal* and *noun* come from Latin *nomen* meaning a. phenomena b. absence of males c. an omen d. a name c. a part of speech

14. A word meaning the opposite of *opulence* is: a perjury b. pecuniosity c. penury d. infelicity

15. *lucre* and *lucrative* come from a Latin word meaning: a. profit b. money c. usury d. filth e. embezzlement

16. Which of these shows a change in spelling from its Latin original: a. omen b. via c. aquarium d. amenity e. album f. simile

17. A *fatuous* person: a. should exercise more b. is silly c. is a bit corpulent d. speaks in tongues

18. A person who displays *comity*: a. brings down the house with amusing anecdotes b. is an agreeable companion c. seems to be in a deep sleep d. is never late to a party

19. A *bilingual* parrot: a. speaks with forked tongue b. knows Latin, Greek, and Hebrew c. speaks in two languages d. eats twice aday

20. A *millennium* is a. a period of one thousand years b. the last milestone c. the end of the world d. a place to buy hats e. a chiliast's dream come true

21. An *ingenuous* answer is a. suggested by one's protective spirit b. clever and whimsical c. cute and cutting d. frank and forthright e. inutterably stupid

22. A *bona fide* agreement is a. signed and sealed b. in good faith c. dead and buried d. concerned with an osseous pet

23. What is the meaning of *sinecure*: a. absolution from sin b. an incurable illness c. a wicked curate d. without care?

24. *Major, mayor, majuscule* are derived from the Latin word meaning: a. progeny b. leader c. bigger d. ancestors

25. A *lacuna* in the text: a. can be read only with the help of a magnifying glass. b. is black c. is blank d. is wet

26. *Linguini* is a type of pasta shaped like a. tongues b. worms c. tubes d. butterflies e. shells

27. To *rusticate* is: a. remove rust b. become rusty c. put on rouge d. live in the country e. bring back to life

28. A *mortuary* is a. an urn b. a tool for grinding c. a place where corpses are prepared for burial d. a pigeon-hole for storing document

29. *Gladiators*: a. fight willingly for their freedom b. die saluting c. engage in combat with swords d. are eaten by lions e. wear clear cellophane

30. *Co-evals*: a. exist at the same time b. are wicked together c. evolved from the same parents d. are etermal

31. A *magnum opus* might be: a. Clint Eastwood's handgun b. an author's masterpiece c. a very large bottle of Champagne d. a graduation honor

32. *et al.* means: a. you too, Alvin b. proof that a person was elsewhere c. for the sake of example d. and the others

33. *Focal* and *curfew* are from the Latin word meaning a. center b. fire alarm c. threshing floor d. hearth

34. *Quota*, *bonus*, *simile*, *miser*, and *album* are: a. English adjectives derived from Latin nouns. b. feminine adjective forms c. English nouns derived from Latin adjectives with gender endings unchanged d. words made up by university students

35. An example of a *sesquipedalian* word is: a. yard-stick b. foot-pad c. centipede d. a size 14 shoe e. floccinaucinihilpilification

DOUBLES TO CONSIDER

acrimony—sharpness	altitude—highness	sociology—folklore
turpitude—wickedness	odium—hatred	amicable—friendly
nuptials—wedding	felicity—happiness	sorority—sisterhood
igneous—fiery	verity—truth	jejune—hungry
sentiment—feeling	science—knowledge	sapience—wisdom
carnal—fleshy	confirm—strengthen	err—stray
supervise—oversee	desperate—hopeless	

WORDS IN CONTEXT

Do not, as some ungracious pastors do,
Show me the steep and thorny way to heaven,
Whiles, like a puffed and reckless *libertine*,
Himself the primrose path of dalliance treads,
And recks not his own rede.
    Shakespeare, *Hamlet*, Act 1, scene 3.

VOCABULARY: CHAPTERS TWO TO FOUR

A	acer, acr-	*sharp, bitter*
	aequus (equ[i]-)	*even, equal*
	aevum	*age*
	altus	*high, deep*
	amplus	*large, spacious*

	animus; anima	*spirit, breath*
	antiquus	*old*
	aptus	*fitted to*
	aqua	*water*
	auris, aur-	*ear*
B	beatus	*happy, blessed*
	bonus / bene	*good / well*
	brevis	*short*
C	caput, capit- (neuter)	*head*
	caro, carn-	*flesh*
	causa cause,	*reason*
	cavus	*hollow*
	cella	*storeroom*
	civis, civ-	*citizen*
	clarus	*bright, clear*
	copia	*abundance, supplies*
	corpus, corpor- (neuter)	*body*
D	dies, di-	*day*
	difficilis	*hard < facilis*
	dignus	*worthy*
	divus	*of a god*
	domus [domes-]	*home, house*
F	facilis	*easy*
	fatum	*the thing said, fate*
	fatuus	*silly, foolish*
	finis	*end*
	focus	*hearth > fire*
	forma	*shape*
	fortis	*strong, brave*
	funus, funer-	*death, rites for the dead*
G	genus, gener- (neuter)	*race, kind, birth*
	granum	*grain*
	gratia	*favor, thanks*
	gratus	*grateful, thankful*
	gravis	*heavy, serious*
H	heres, hered-	*heir*
	hostis, host-	*enemy*
	humanus	*human (< humus)*
	humilis	*lowly, on the ground (< humus)*
	humus	*the ground, soil*
I	ignis, ign-	*fire*
J	jocus	*jest*
L	labor, labor-	*work*

	latus-a-um	*wide*
	latus, later-	*side*
	levis	*light* (not heavy and not serious)
	lex, leg-	*law*
	liber, liber-	*free*
	liber, libr-	*book*
	littera	*letter*
	locus	*place*
	longus	*long*
M	magnus	*big, great*
	major, majus (majes-)	*bigger, greater, older*
	malus	*bad, worse, worst*
	manus, manu-	*hand*
	mare, mar-	*sea*
	mater, matr[i]-	*mother*
	maximus	*biggest, greatest. oldest*
	miles, milit-	*soldier*
	minor, minus (mines-)	*smaller, younger, less*
	minimus	*smallest, least*
	miser	*wretched, unhappy*
	modus	*manner*
	moles, mole-	*heap, mass*
	mors, mort-	*death*
	mortuus	*dead body*
	mos, mor-	*custom, manner, mood*
	murus	*wall*
	mus, mur-	*mouse*
N	navis, nav-	*ship*
	necesse	*unavoidable*
	nervus	*tendon*
	nomen, nomin-	*name*
	nox, noct-	*night*
	numerus	*number*
	nux, nuc-	*nut*
O	oculus	*eye*
	odium	*hatred*
	onus, oner- (neuter)	*burden*
	opus, oper- (neuter)	*work*
	ordo, ordin-	*rank, row*
	os, oss-	*bone*
P	par	*equal*
	pars, part-	*part*
	pater, patr[i]-	*father*

	pauci (pl. adj.)	*few*
	pax, pac-	*peace*
	pejor	*worse*
	pes, ped-	*foot*
	pessimus	*worst*
	pestis, pest[i]-	*plague*
	pius	*devoted to duty*
	plenus	*full*
	populus	*people*
	posterus	*coming after*
	primus	*first*
	proprius	*one's own*
	pulcher, pulchri-	*handsome, beautiful*
Q	qualis	*of what kind*
	quantus	*how much*
R	radius, radi-	*rod, ray, spoke of a wheel*
	radix, radic-	*root*
	ratio, ration-	*reason, reckoning*
	rex, reg-	*king*
	rota	*wheel*
	rus, rur-	*the country*
S	saeculum	*age, the times*
	salus, salut-	*health, safety*
	sanctus	*holy*
	sanguis, sanguin-	*blood*
	sanus	*sound, healthy*
	satis	*enough*
	senex, sen-	*old (man)*
	servus	*slave*
	similis	*like*
	socius	*comrade, ally*
	sol, sol-	*sun*
	somnus	*sleep*
	species	*sight, appearance, kind*
	studium	*eagerness, zeal*
T	tempus, tempor-	*time*
	terminus	*end, limit*
	terra	*earth, land*
	testis	*witness*
U	unus	*one*
	urbs, urb-	*city*
V	vacuus	*empty*
	varius	*speckled, changing*

verbum	*word*
verus	*true*
via	*way, road*
vicus	*quarter, section of a city* > vicinity
vinum	*wine*
vir, vir-	*man, male*
virus	*poison*
vitium	*fault*
vox, voc-	*voice*

REVIEW OF SUFFIXES FROM CHAPTERS THREE AND FOUR

Fill in this chart of suffixes: give meaning and an example; tell what part of speech each forms:

	Meaning	Examples
-al (3); -alia (3, review)		
-an, ane (3); -ana (3, review)		
-ar (3)		
-ary [adj.] (3)		
-ary [noun, masc.] (3)		
-ary [noun, neuter] (3)		
-arious (3)		
-arium (3)		
-ate [adj.] (3)		
-ate [noun] (4)		
-cle (4)		clavicle, particle, reticle
-culus, -cule (4)		
-ellus, -el (4)		cerebellum, scalpel
-eous, -eal, -ean (3)		
-ernal, -ern (3)		co-eternal, modern
-ety (4) see -ty		variety
-ic (3)		
-ice (4)		
-il, -ile (3); -ilia (3, review)		
-illus, -il (4)		bacillus, codicil
-ine [adj.] (3)		
-ine [noun] (4)		
-ism (4)		
-ist (4)		
-(i)tude (4) = -tude		
-ity (4) see -ety, -ty		quiddity
-lent (3); -lence (4) = -lent- + -ia "condition of being full of"		
-leus (4)		nucleus

-mony (4)	
-nal (3)	
-olus, -ole (4)	nucleolus, areole
-ose (3)	
-ous (1) < -us	
-ous (3) < -osus	
-tic (3)	
-tude, base; -tudin- (4)	
-ty (4) [see -ity, -ety]	faculty
-ulus, -ule (4)	calculus, formula, granule
-urnal, -urn (3)	nocturnal, taciturn
-y (4)	

Choose one suffix and give 10 to 20 words using it and see if you can find any special usages of your suffix: Example: *-ine* (adjective-forming suffix) is commonly used for animal names.

bos, bov-, cow, bull > bovine; *cervus*, deer > cervine; *ovis*, sheep > ovine

canis, dog	
felis, cat	_____
asinus, ass, donkey	_____
ursa, bear	_____
columba, dove	_____
aquila, eagle	_____
lupus, wolf	_____
equus, horse	_____
passer, sparrow	_____
mus, mur-, mouse	_____
vulpes, vulp-, fox	_____
corvus, raven, crow	_____

QUISQUILIA

One of the odder word sites on the internet is the Dictionary of Obscure Sorrows: http://www.dictionaryofobscuresorrows.com/ which includes words like *lachesism*, *exulansis*, and *Altschmerz*.

NOTES

1. Answers to Exercise F Suffixes: -tude: i, k, l; -tic: a, e, g, h, j, m; -ose: b; -arium: a; -ist: a; -cle: c, d, f, n.

2. Answers to Exercise I vocabulary: 1. c ; 2. c; 3. c; 4. a; 5. b; 6. b; 7. a; 8. b; 9. c; 10. e; 11. c; 12. a; 13 .d; 14. e; 15. a; 16. d; 17. b; 18. b; 19. c; 20. a; 21. d; 22. b; 23. d; 24. c; 25. c; 26. a; 27. d; 28. c; 29. c; 30. a; 31. b; 32 .d; 33. d; 34. c; 35. e.

SECTION TWO: LATIN
B. LATIN VERBS

CHAPTER FIVE: LATIN VERBS BECOME ENGLISH

A. FORMS OF THE LATIN VERB

Verbs are the most fertile source of Latin words in English. The Latin verb has many forms which show PERSON, NUMBER, TENSE, VOICE, and MOOD. For more explanation see the supplement to this chapter and the exercise "parsing Latin verbs." Of these numerous forms two are most important for the formation of English words. Only these two forms, therefore, need be learned for most verbs.[1]

On the other hand there are some verbs for which you need to learn only one form, either because the first or second form does not exist or because it is not productive of English words. ("Unproductive" bases will be enclosed in square brackets.) In a few cases additional forms which are variations of the two bases (showing vowel reduction) should also be studied. There are also a few special variations that show French influence (as -CEIVE < *capere* and -CLAIM < *clamare*) which should be noticed as well. These special forms are indicated in the vocabulary lists and are easy to learn if you think of examples of each.

The two forms to be learned are the PRESENT INFINITIVE and the PERFECT PASSIVE PARTICIPLE (in the neuter nominative singular). This latter form will be abbreviated *ppp*.

INFINITIVES	bases	PARTICIPLES	bases
I portare (to carry)	port(a)	portatum (carried)	portat-
II docēre (to teach)	doc(ē)	doctum (taught)	doct-
III ducere (to lead)	duc(e)	ductum (led)	duct-
IIIi capere (to take)	capi(e)	captum (taken)	capt-
IV sentire (to feel)	sent(i)	sensum (felt)	sens-

All the *ppp* forms end in *-um* (because the neuter form is given). To find the base remove *-um*. The infinitives (except for deponents which end in *-ri* or *-i* and a few irregulars, like *esse, posse*) end in a vowel + *re*. The base is found by removing the vowel and -*re*. In some compounds the vowel is retained. Certain verbs of the third conjugation (III) have *i* as part of the stem (IIIi, above). For these the additional form -*io* will be given. All verbs in -*ire* also have *i* as part of the stem in the present.

Verbs are divided into conjugations according to the vowel before -*re*: -*are*, first conjugation (I); -*ēre*, second conjugation (II); -*ere*, third conjugation (III); -*ire*, fourth conjugation (IV). CONJUGATIONS are patterns of changes in the present system of Latin verbs (that is, present, imperfect, or continuous past, and future) for which the forms depend upon the stem vowel.

There is a type of verbs called deponents which end in -*ri* or -*i* in the present infinitive. For example, *mirari* (to wonder); *sequi* (to follow): simply remove the vowel and -*ri* or the -*i* to find the base. These are the forms of the *passive* infinitive: deponents are verbs which appear only in passive forms.

The verbs ending in -*are* (almost) always have their *ppp* in -*atum*; some, but not all, in -*ire* also retain the -*i*- in the *ppp*.

First conjugation:

    portare—portatum, *carry*
    dare—datum, *give*
    stare—statum, *stand*

Fourth conjugation:

    audire—auditum, *hear*
    munire—munitum, *fortify*

but

    sentire—sensum, *feel*
    venire—ventum, *come*

Most verbs add -*tum* directly to the last consonant of the base.

    capere—captum, *take*
    facere—factum, *do/make*
    canere—cantum, *sing*
    dicere—dictum, *say/tell*

If the present base ends in a *g* or *b* assimilation takes place before -*tum*. The *g* changes to *c* and the *b* to *p* to make them easier to pronounce before -*tum*.

    legere—lectum (for leg-tum), *gather/choose/read*
    agere—actum (for ag-tum), *do*
    scribere—scriptum (for scrib-tum), *write*

A dental sound (*d*, *t*) at the end of the base usually causes a change to -*sum* in the *ppp*. In these instances the dental is dropped.

    mittere—missum, *send/let go*
    videre—visum, *see*
    cadere—casum, *fall*
    cedere—cessum, *go/yield*

Those verbs that retain the stem vowel in the *ppp* are not affected by this rule, as, for example, *audire—auditum* and *portare—portatum*.

There are also many irregularly formed *ppp*s which need to be learned separately. For example:

    pellere—pulsum, *push*
    premere—pressum, *squeeze*
    ferre—latum, *bear/carry*
    emere—emptum, *buy/take*
    torquēre—tortum, *twist*

EXERCISES

EXERCISE II. 5A 1—PRACTICE EXERCISES: Form the *ppp* (in -tum or -sum) for each of the following present infinitives. In *this* exercise all *-are* verbs have *-atum* and all *-ire* verbs have *-itum*. Others do not retain the vowel. Begin learning the vocabulary for 1–15. Try to think of at least one English word from each base.

Examples: errare (go astray): *ppp* erratum > err, errata
    ludere (play): *ppp* lusum (note: dental stem) > allude, illusion

1. audire (hear)
2. clamare (shout)
3. vertere (turn)
4. tenēre (hold, keep)
5. facere (make, do)
6. cadere (fall)
7. caedere (cut, kill)
8. jacere (throw)
9. ire (go, present base *-i* as in *transient*)
10. dicere (say)
11. stare (stand)
12. rogare (ask)
13. canere (sing)
14. regere (guide, rule)
15. specere (look at)
16. jungere (join, derivatives from the present base show *jug-*)
17. tegere (cover; from present base, *integument*)
18. texere (weave; Eng. words from this verb are from the *ppp*)
19. tingere (dip)
20. tondēre (shear, clip, shave; find a word from the *ppp*)
21. ludere (play)
22. pendere (hang, weigh)
23. prehendere (seize, grasp)
24. amare (love)
25. ducere (lead)

26. capere (take, seize)
27. parare (get, get ready)
28. vidēre (see)
29. augēre (increase)
30. fari (speak)

EXERCISE II.5A 2. IRREGULAR *PPP*—match present with *ppp* and try to think of an
English word from the *ppp*.

Ex. 1. monēre (warn)	gestum 3 derivatives: gestate, digest, gesture
2. sumere (take up)	tortum __
3. gerere (carry on, wage)	quaesitum __
4. ponere (put)	victum __
5. rumpere (burst)	solutum __
6. torquēre (twist)	venditum __ > vendition
7. vincere (win, conquer)	cursum __
8. pellere (push)	cretum __
9. solvere (loosen)	conditum __
10. vendere (sell)	monitum __
11. cernere (sift)	emptum __
12. condere (store, build)	positum __
13. currere (run)	ruptum __
14. emere (buy, take)	sectum __
15. trahere (drag, draw)	pulsum __
16. secare (cut)	sumptum __
17. quaerere (ask)	tractum __

B. MAKING LATIN VERBS INTO ENGLISH WORDS

Latin verbs come into English as verbs, nouns, and adjectives in the following ways:
1. Base alone
    present base: errare > err (verb)
    ppp base: auditum (hear) > audit (verb, noun)
2. Base + silent -e
    present base: eludere (cheat) > elude (verb)
    ppp base: reversum (turned back) > reverse (noun, adjective, verb)
3. A double consonant at the end of the Latin present base is usually reduced to a
single consonant in the English word.
    impellere (push on) > impel (verb)
    remittere (send back) > remit (verb)
    incurrere (run against/into) > incur (verb)
But the double consonant often reappears when suffixes are added:
    repellent (pushing back)
    admittance (act of letting go to)

occurrence (result of running toward)

4. Unpredictable changes may take place (especially under French influence).

cantare > chant

retinēre > retain

decipere > deceive

clamare > claim

fallere > fail

capere > captare > chase

perire > perish

reparare > repair

jacere > jactare > jet

remanēre > remain

secutum (*ppp* of *sequi*) > suit, suite

attingere > attain

visum (*ppp* of *vidēre*) > view

English verbs from the present bases of capere (-cipere), tenēre (-tinēre), clamare show respectively -ceive, -tain, -claim. But suffixed derivatives will usually show the Latin base:

receive, recipient (but conceive, inconceivable)

contain, continent; pertain, pertinent

claim, clamor (but claimant)

EXERCISES

EXERCISE II.5 B. 1— SIMPLE DERIVATIVES: give a simple (i.e. do not add any additional prefixes or suffixes) English derivative of each; tell what part(s) of speech the derivative is; describe the change; and tell whether the Latin form is present infinitive or *ppp*.

Example: *decipere* > deceive, a verb with irregular change influenced by French; it comes from the present base.

repulsum > repulse, a verb from the *ppp* base + silent -e.

1. actum (done)
2. parare (make ready)
3. erodere (gnaw out)
4. sensum (felt)
5. pressum (squeezed)
6. solvere (loosen)
7. clamare (shout)
8. recipere (take back)
9. addictum (sentenced to)
10. tendere (stretch, aim at)
11. cedere (yield, go)
12. datum (given)

13. factum (done)
14. pulsum (pushed)
15. cantum (sung)
16. raptum (snatched)
17. cultum (tilled, honored)
18. textum (woven)
19. vexare (shake)
20. habitum (had, held)

EXERCISE II.5 B. 2— SIMPLE CHANGES: Form English verbs from the following Latin verbs. Tell what type of change takes place. Examples: *revertere* > revert: present base alone; *reversum* > reverse: *ppp* base + silent -e; *clamare* > claim: irregular change. Do not add suffixes or additional prefixes (several of these verbs have prefixes; they will be treated in the next chapter).
1. vendere, venditum (sell)
2. laborare, laboratum (work)
3. declarare, declaratum (express, make known)
4. eludere, elusum (cheat, frustrate)
5. parare, paratum (get ready, prepare)
6. premere, pressum (squeeze)
7. curare, curatum (take care of)
8. errare, erratum (go astray)
9. servire, servitum (be a slave to)
10. edere, editum (give out, put forth, publish)
11. recipere, receptum (take back)
12. accipere, acceptum (take to)
13. deferre, delatum (carry away, bring to, submit)
14. impellere, impulsum (drive on, push, urge on)
15. cedere, cessum (go, yield)
16. impedire, impeditum (hinder, get in the way, be underfoot < *pes, ped-*, foot)
17. impingere, impactum (dash against)
18. evocare, evocatum (call out)

EXERCISE II.5 B. 3— FILL IN FOR REVIEW: look over the Latin verbs in Exercise 5b. 2 and fill in the blank.
1. A vending machine _____ things.
2. To collaborate is to _____ together.
3. A declarative sentence _____ a statement.
4. An elusive gladiator tends to _____ his or her opponent's blows.
5. Paring certain fruits and vegetables is a way of _____ them.
6. Suppression is the act of _____ under (sub-).
7. Curative measures _____ the situation.
8. Erroneous answers _____ .

9. Acclamation is the act of _____ (to).
10. An editor is one who _____ .
11. Acceptance is the act of _____ to oneself.
12. Deference is _____ to another person's feelings or will.
13. An impulse _____ one on.
14. The antecedent generally _____ before (ante-) the relative pronoun.
15. An impediment _____ you.
16. An evocation of memories _____ them out (e-/ex-).

EXERCISE II.5 B. 4—FOR EXTRA PRACTICE (optional): Sometimes the direct derivatives from *ppp* bases are adjectives or nouns since the participle is, in fact, a verbal adjective. Give the most direct English derivative from the *ppp* base. Mark verb (v.), adjective (adj.), and noun (n.). Some may be more than one part of speech. Example: 1. abstrahere, abstractum (drag away) > abstract adj. (also v. and n.)
2. abstrudere, abstrusum (conceal)
3. abrumpere, abruptum (break off)
4. abominari, abominatum (curse)
5. aboriri, abortum (miscarry)
6. accipere, acceptum (take, receive)
7. acuere, acutum (sharpen)
8. affligere, afflictum (dash against)
9. affigere, affixum (fasten to)
10. afficere, affectum (influence)
11. adducere, addictum (award to)
12. insecare, insectum (cut in)
13. eximere, exemptum (take up)
14. exhaurire, exhaustum (drain off)
15. delēre, deletum (destroy)
16. devovere, devotum (vow, dedicate)
17. erodere, erosum (gnaw away)
18. finire, finitum (limit, end)
19. fallere, falsum (cheat, deceive)
20. tendere, tensum (stretch)

C. VERBS FROM NOUNS (DENOMINATIVES)

Verbs are formed from nouns usually by adding the -are/-atum endings (i.e., first conjugation endings) to the noun base. These most often come into English with the suffix -ate (from the *ppp* base), with the meaning "to use, to cause, to make." Examples:

> *os, or-* (mouth) > orare, oratum (to use the mouth: pray, speak) > orate
> *donum* (gift) > donare (to make a gift) > donate
> *alienus* (belonging to another) > alienate

Sometimes the suffix -ite is used.

ignis (fire) > ignite

Sometimes no suffix is added in the English word:

vestis (clothes) > vest (divest, invest)

salus, salut- (health) > salute

flamma (flame) > inflame

EXERCISES

EXERCISES II. 5C. 1— FORM DENOMINATIVES: Form English verbs from these Latin nouns, adjectives, adverbs:

Example: satis (enough) > satiate, satisfy (-fy < facere)

1. locus
2. alienus (belonging to another)
3. insula (island; also > isolate, through Italian)
4. opus, oper-
5. radius
6. liber
7. nomen, nomin-
8. genus, gener-
9. populus
10. ordo, ordin-
11. rota
12. miles, milit-
13. terminus
14. tabula (table)
15. humilis
16. vitium
17. decimus (tenth)
18. fluctus (wave)
19. germen, germin- (sprout)
20. lacer (mangled)
21. stimulus (goad)
22. frustra (in vain)
23. gradus, gradu- (step)
24. dominus (master < *domus*)
25. rusticus (adjective < *rus, rur-*)

EXERCISES II. 5C. 2— FIND BASES: Tell what Latin noun or adjective each of these English verbs comes from. Example: domesticate < *domus*, home

1. facilitate
2. necessitate
3. marinate

4. allocate (prefix al- < ad-, to)
5. exalt (prefix ex-, out)
6. adapt (prefix ad-)
7. impede (prefix in-, in)
8. cerebrate
9. equivocate (*equi-* < *aequus*, even, equal)
10. divest, invest (< *vestis*, clothes) (prefixes di- < dis, in different directions; in-)
11. expedite (prefix ex-)
12. dislocate (prefix dis-)
13. enervate (prefix e-, ex-)
14. inoculate (prefix in-)
15. exonerate (prefix ex-)
16. elongate (prefix e-, ex-)
17. pejorate
18. satiate

PART D. VOCABULARY

Learn both bases. Try to give an English word from each base. *These verbs undergo vowel reduction, explained below. The forms in parentheses show the result of vowel reduction.

* agere, actum (-ig-) *do, drive, lead* > agile, actor
* cadere, casum (-cid-) *fall*
* caedere, caesum (-cid-, -cis-) *cut, kill*
* capere [-io], captum (-cipi-, -cept-) *take, seize*; -ceive
cedere, cessum *go, yield*; -ceed/-cede
clamare, clamatum *shout*; -claim
* claudere, clausum (-clud-, -clus-) *close*; -close
* dare, datum (-d-, -dit-) *give*
ducere, ductum *lead*
errare, erratum *go astray*
* facere [-io], factum (-fici-, -fect-) *do, make*; -fy
ferre (fer-), latum *bear, carry*
ire, itum *go* (present base i-; *ppp* base it-)
* jacere [-io], jactum (-ject-) *throw*
      jacēre [< jacere] *lie* [no *ppp*]
mittere, missum *send, let go*
parare, paratum *get, get ready*
pellere, pulsum *push*
premere, pressum *squeeze*
[rumpere], ruptum *break, burst* (derivatives are from the *ppp*.)
scribere, scriptum *write*
sentire, sensum *feel*

solvere, solutum *loosen, undo*
* tenēre, tentum (-tin-, -tent-) *hold, keep*; -tain
vendere, venditum *sell*
venire, ventum *come*
vertere, versum *turn*
vocare, vocatum *call, use the vox*
vorare, [voratum] *devour, eat*

Suffixes from verbs:

   -cide *killer, killing of* (from caedere) > homicide, pesticide
   -fer, -ferous *bearer, bearing* (from ferre) > conifer, aquifer; coniferous
   -vore, -vorous *eater, eating* (from vorare) > herbivore, omnivorous
   -fy (from facere) *do, cause, make* > exemplify, quantify

EXERCISES

EXERCISE 5D.1—USING NEW VOCABULARY: fill in the blanks (numbers refer to prefixes)

1. To accede is to _____ to. (ac- < *ad* to)
2. An agent is one who (-ent, one who) _____ .
3. To exclaim is to _____ out. (*ex*- out)
4. To seduce is to _____ aside (*se*- apart, aside)
5. transfer, _____ across (*trans*- across)
6. prepare, _____ ahead (*pre*- before)
7. permit, _____ through (*per*- through, thoroughly)
8. dissolve, _____ (*dis*- in different directions)
9. Errata are things that have _____ .
10. suppress, _____ under (sup- < *sub* under)
11. transcribe _____ _____ (*trans*-, see 5, above)
12. insensate, not _____ (*in*-2, not)
13. vend, _____
14. revert, _____ back (*re*- again, back)
15. evoke, _____ _____ (*e*- = *ex*-, see 3)
16. irrupt, _____ in, into (*in*-1, in, into)
17. convene, _____ together (*co*-, *con*-, *com*- with, together)
18. contain, _____ _____
19. expel, _____ _____ (3)
20. reject, _____ _____ (14)
21. transitory, tending to _____ _____ (5)
22. data are things _____ . What is the singular of data?
23. accident, something that _____ _____ someone (1)
24. incision, the result of _____ _____ (*in*-1, 16)
25. deception, the act of _____ _____ (*de*- down, badly)

26. confection, the result of _____ _____ (17)
27. occlude _____ _____ (oc- < *ob* against, thoroughly)
Notice changes in the stem vowel in 23-27. Can you figure out which verbs these are from? For further explanation see below (VOWEL REDUCTION).

VOWEL REDUCTION

It is common when a prefix is added that certain vowels change to a reduced or weakened form. When a prefix is added:
1. an a or e before a single consonant becomes i
   tenant: cont*i*nent
   c*a*dence: inc*i*dence
2. an a before two consonants becomes e
   f*a*ct: inf*e*ct
3. ae becomes i
   c*ae*sura: inc*i*se
4. au becomes u
   cl*au*se: recl*u*sive
Which verbs in the vocabulary show vowel reduction?
Examples of vowel reduction from the previous exercise:
   accident: base -*cid*- from cadere
   incision: base -*cis*- from caesum, *ppp* of caedere
   deception: base -*cept*- from captum, *ppp* of capere
   confection: base -*fect*- from factum, *ppp* of facere
   occlude: base -*clud*- from claudere

A few common prefixes are used in the previous exercise. Study these as a preview for the next exercises. They will be treated in more detail in Chapter Six.

ad-, ac-	*to*
con-, com-, co-	*with, together*
de-	*down*
ex-, e-	*out*
in-, ir- [1]	*in, into*
in-, ir- [2]	*not, un-*
per-	*through*
re-	*back, again*
se-	*apart, aside*
sub-, sup-	*under*
trans	*across*

Vowel reduction takes place in compounds formed from some noun, adjective, and adverb bases too.
   castus,-a,-um, pure, chaste: in+castus > incestus > incest

ars, art-, skill: in+art- > inert
annus, year: through the years > perennial
aptus, fitted: not fit > inept

EXERCISES

EXERCISE 5D.2—VOWEL REDUCTION :
The verbs in this lesson showing vowel reduction are:
agere, (actum)
cadere, (casum)
caedere, caesum
capere, captum
claudere, clausum
dare, datum
facere, factum
(jacere), jactum
tenēre, (tentum)

Give the reduced forms of each of these; check in the vocabulary list if you are uncertain. The forms in parentheses in this list do not show vowel reduction in their English derivatives. Give an English derivative of each reduced base. E.g., capere, captum: -cip(i)-, -cept- > incipient, receptacle

EXERCISE 5D.3—RECOGNIZING VOWEL REDUCTION:
a) Explain the vowel changes, identify base verb, define prefix; ignore suffixes (for the time being).
Example: intransigent: -ig- reduced verb base of agere
prefixes: in, not; trans, across (-ent = -ing)
 1. pertinent (-ent = -ing)
 2. addition (-ion = act, result of)
 3. receptacle (-cle = thing for)
 4. dejected
 5. exclusive (-ive = tending to)
 6. incipient
 7. perfect
 8. conclude
 9. efficient (ef- < ex before an f)
10. seclusion
11. recidivism
12. trajectory (tra = trans; -ory tending to or place or thing for)
b). Change to the correct spellings
 1. exagency
 2. infaction
 3. inclausive

4. adjactive
5. occadent
6. excaesion
7. percaption
8. addational
9. incontenent
10. interjaction
11. incapient
12. edation

EXERCISE 5D.4—MEANINGS: Match with the meaning of the base word of each derivative.

1. deactivate __	a. write
2. secession __	b. undo
3. errata __	c. carry
4. oblation __	d. go
5. reclamation __	e. squeeze
6. deductive __	f. feel
7. missionary __	g. get
8. impressive __	h. sell
9. reparations __	i. lead
10. postscript __	j. do/drive
11. insentient __	k. shout
12. dissolute __	l. turn
13. vendition __	m. call
14. conversion __	n. send
15. invocation __	o. wander

EXERCISE 5D.5—UNUSUAL CHANGES: these words have undergone changes that make the base unrecognizable. Choose two or three and find out how they got that way.

1. squat < cogere < co- + agere
2. essay < exigere < ex- + agere
3. ancestor < cedere
4. duchess < ducere
5. Mass < mittere
6. print < premere
7. shrive < scribere
8. serif < scribere
9. scent < sentire
10. prose < provertere
11. suzerain < sub- + vertere
12. vouch < vocare

EXERCISE 5D.6—REVIEW OF VOCABULARY (OPTIONAL)
a) Match with meaning of the base verb:

1. devour	a. take
2. appertain	b. write
3. dissolute	c. push
4. rescript	d. do, make
5. transition	e. eat
6. perfect	f. fall
7. dispel	g. go
8. reclaim	h. hold
9. atavicide	i. yield, go
10. process	j. shout
11. occasional	k. kill, cut
12. incipient	l. loosen

b) Match with a derivative from the other base of the same verb; tell meaning of the Latin verb:

1. agile	a. admittance
2. conduct	b. compel
3. crucifer	c. scripture
4. ambient	d. convenient
5. mission	e. reduce
6. impulse	f. vertical
7. imprimatur	g. oblation
8. scribal	h. transitive
9. sensual	i. sentimental
10. aversion	j. actor
11. evoke	k. pressure
12. eventual	l. avocation

c) Tell what each is bearing:

crucifer, aquifer, baccifer, conifer, vociferous professors, carboniferous deposits?

What does each kill:

fratricide, herbicide, pesticide, genocide, homocide, matricide, sororicide, patricide, parricide, deicide, regicide, tyrannicide, insecticide, fungicide, infanticide, vermicide? Add ten more -cides.

What does each eat:

carnivore, omnivore, herbivore, avivore, apivore, insectivore? Add five more -vores.

VOCABULARY NOTES

Words from *parare/paratum*: pare, prepare, preparation, repair, reparative, reparation, apparatus, apparel, separate, sever, disparate; parry, parade, parasol, parachute; also related are words from Latin *imperare*, (command < lit., "prepare against") > imperative, imperial, empire, emperor. NOT related is *compare* < *par*, equal.

Words from *jacere/jactum*: abject, adjective, conjecture, deject, disject, eject, ejecta (matter thrown out as from an erupting volcano), inject, interjection, objective, project, reject, trajectory, subject, jactation (boasting), jactitation (false boast), joist, ejaculate, gist. NOT *javelin*, from a Celtic root, nor *jacket*, from the name Jacques.

QUISQUILIA—THE JOYS OF SESQUIPEDALIA

The WORD for today is: floccinaucinihilipilification:
"The act of making something worthless" as in "I loved him for nothing so much as his *floccinaucinihilipilification* of money." (1741, cited in *OED*)

> *floccus*, a tuft of wool > floccose ("full of or containing tufts of wool") and flocculus (a small tuft of wool) > flocculent (resembling a tuft of wool) and flocculate (to gather into tufts of wool).
>
> *nauci* is related to *nugae*, trifles, trivial things > nugacious, nugatory, nugilogue (trivial talk, small talk), nugigerulous ("carrying toys" as would be an attribute of Santa Claus on Christmas Eve), but *not* nougat which comes from *nux, nuc-*, nut.
>
> *nihil*, nothing > nil, null, nihilism, nihilist, nihility, annihilate.
>
> *pilus*, hair > piliferous ("hirsute"), depilatory, plush, caterpillar ("hairy cat"), pileus ("cap") and by a connection that remains obscure, possibly *pillage*.
>
> *-fication*, act of making < *facere*, to make

CHAPTER FIVE: SUMMARY AND CHECK LIST

1. The two bases of the Latin verb from
   a. present infinitive (ends in -re; deponents in -ri, -i)
   b. the *ppp* (perfect passive participle) (ends in -um)
2. Know how to recognize the four conjugations by stem vowel in form a (the present infinitive)
   I   -are
   II -ēre
   III -ere (III-i -ere)
   IV -ire
3. Know how to form the *ppp* from the present base; learn all irregular *ppp*s.
4. Ways of forming English words from Latin verbs:
   a. base alone
   b. base + silent -e

c. various irregular changes: remember especially -ceive from capere; -tain from tenēre; -claim from clamare.
5. To make verbs from noun bases, usually add -ate to the noun base.
6. Always learn both bases of new verbs.
7. Vowel reduction takes place after a prefix:

a, e > i before one consonant

a > e before two (or more) consonants

ae > i

au > u

ENDGAME

Parsing Latin Verbs:

For the most part only the present and *ppp* bases of Latin verbs are needed to form English derivatives. There are a few words that come from Latin with their conjugational endings intact. Choose two or three and identify the verb forms (as in number 1): this information should be in your dictionary.

1. fiat, *a command or decree*, comes from the present subjunctive of *fio* (passive of *facio*), third person singular and means literally "let it be done".
2. placebo (literally, "I will please")
3. vide (common as the abbreviation v.)
4. ignoramus
5. caveat (cf. *caveat emptor*)
6. recipe (cf. R_x)
7. habitat (from the opening of descriptions of animals or plants, "it dwells")
8. deficit
9. veto
10. imprimatur
11. floruit
12. tenet
13. memento
14. caret (^), "there is lacking"
15. mandamus
16. habeas corpus
17. exit (cf. *exeunt omnes*)
18. scire facias
19. venire (as in "change of venire")

APPENDIX TO CHAPTER FIVE—LATIN AND ENGLISH VERBS

The English verb system is a marvel of simplicity and subtlety. To appreciate this, you need only compare it to the verb system of an inflected language like Latin. The Latin verb system is a marvel too, but of a different kind. Latin has six tenses. The tenses in English are harder to count, but there are many more than six. The

Latin verb has scores of forms: it changes to show *person* (I, you, he/she/it, we, they) and *number* (I/we, she/they) and *tense* (present, various pasts, future) and *mood* (indicative, subjunctive, imperative, plus infinitives and participles) and *voice* (active and passive). To express all these changes English uses very few forms, no more than five (with the exception of the verb *to be* which has eight forms). Latin changes the the form of the verb to show the changes; English changes the words that accompany the verb (pronouns, auxiliaries), but the same combinations can go with any verb and our memories are not over-taxed.

Take, for example, a regular and an irregular verb and put them through their paces, WORK and DO:

How many *different* forms does each have?

work: work, works, working, worked

do: do, does, doing, did, done

How many uses does each of these forms have?

WORK is used for

1. the present: I work, we work

2. the infinitive: [to] work

3. the imperative: work harder!

4. after many modal and temporal auxiliaries: you must work, you may, might, will, shall, should, would, can, could work, you do or don't work.

WORKS is used for present third person singular: he, she, it works; Aspasia works, Perses works, the computer works.

WORKING is the present participle, used:

1. as an adjective (a participle is a verbal adjective): working men and women; a working draft

2. for progressive tenses (progressive tenses look at the action or activity as going on, i.e. in progress) in the active voice: I am working, we were working, she has been working, they will have been working, etc.

3. as a gerund (a gerund is a verbal noun which has the same form as the participle in English): by working hard we make progress; working under pressure may work for some people.

WORKED is used both as simple past and as past participle:

1. simple past: we worked

2. past participle:

a. active perfect tenses: we have worked, they had worked, you will have worked

b. the passive system: it is worked, we are being over-worked, this land has not been worked for years.

c. as passive participle: an over-worked expression

DO is an irregular verb (of very wide and idiomatic application) and shows a fifth form (or fourth change): do, does, doing, did, done. These forms are used in similar ways to those of work:

DO: we do our homework every week night; do it over.

DOES: she does her lessons.

DOING: we were doing it; when doing well we are happy; doing good deeds is its own reward.

DID: George did it.

DONE: we have done it; it was done before we knew it; it is the done thing.

Besides these uses as an ordinary verb, do has a number of special uses:

–in questions: do you say so? (the tense form of *do* shows the tense of the question; *did* you say that?)

–in negatives: I do not understand.

–for emphasis: I do try. I do think you could work a little harder.

–as a pro-verb (to stand for another verb and avoid repetition): Perses works hard and so do I.

Compare this simple and elegant verb system to that of Latin. The Latin verb has the virtue of being more precise and (sometimes) less ambiguous. Instead of using pronouns, the Latin verb changes its endings to show person. Instead of piling up auxiliaries, the Latin verb has temporal and modal suffixes to which personal endings are added.

The changes in form show person, number, tense, voice, mood.

PERSON tells what the subject is.

NUMBER tells how many (one or more than one).

TENSE refers to the time of the action and to its aspect: is the action going on or completed?

VOICE tells the relationship of the subject to the action of the verb (the subject does the action of an active verb; in the passive the action is done to the subject): Martha bit her hotdog (Active). George was bitten by a mad dog (Passive).

MOOD tells the attitude of the speaker or writer to the reality of the action (indicative for statements, questions; subjunctive for possibilities, purposes, hopes, fears, and the like).

For these changes, English combines its pronouns and its auxiliaries and Latin changes the endings of the verb. For example:

PERSON: the word for *do* in "I do" differs from "you do": *facio* (I do), *facis* (you do)

NUMBER: the *do* of "I do" differs from that of "we do": *facio* (I do) *facimus* (we do)

TENSE: "I am doing": *facio*; "I was doing": *faciebam*

VOICE: "he/she/it does": *facit*; "it is being done": *fit*

"he/she/it did": *fecit*; "it was done": *factum est*

MOOD: "he does [it]": *facit*; "let him do [it]": *faciat*

"it is being done": *fit*; "let it be done": *fiat*

WORDS IN CONTEXT

That he knew I wasn't ready to come home yet, that if I didn't stay to see some of the fight I would forever be filled with the echoes of regret and the *ague* of *remorse*.
                    Laird Hunt, *Neverhome*, 2014

The events of the long day and now this strange *colloquy* had done their work and I had got settled down, alongside the Akron boys and Lord's horse, into my own froggy snores.
                    Laird Hunt, *Neverhome*, 2014

He was growing into a man inside a dark chamber, a *camera obscura* fashioned by worn curtain fabric and August light.
                    Dominic Smith, *The Mercury Visions of Louis Daguerre*, 2006

NOTE

1. There are a few exceptions: certain -i-stem verbs for which the presence of an -i- in the stem would be ambiguous without a third form: these will be marked [-io] in the vocabulary lists and designated IIIi in the charts.

SECTION TWO: LATIN
B. Latin Verbs

Chapter Six: Prefixes

A. Latin & English Prefixes

The most common Latin prefixes are derived from prepositions. They are added most frequently to verb bases, but also to the bases of nouns and adjectives. English has native prefixes of a similar kind, but they are no longer as productive as those from Latin.

Native word	Compare to derivative from Latin
onrush	incursion
uphold	sustain
overturn	subvert
withstanding	constant
bygone	preterite
backslide	relapse
outcome	event
foreknowledge	prescience
afterword	postscript
underwrite	subscribe
foreword	preface

There are some prefixes which are not derived from prepositions.

English un- corresponds to Latin in- [2]:

unfeeling	insentient

English all, as prefix all-, al- corresponds to Latin *omni-*:

almighty	omnipotent
all-knowing	omniscient

Before working with the prefixes two linguistic phenomena are worth considering:

1. VOWEL REDUCTION (or weakening) See chapter 5 for examples.

2. ASSIMILATION (< base, *simil-*, like) is the act of making one thing like (*ad-*,

to) another; that is, sometimes a consonant at the end of a prefix changes so that it will be easier to pronounce before the first consonant of the base word. For example:

ad-, to, becomes ac- before c; as- before s

   ad-cede > accede; ad-similation > assimilation

com- becomes cor- before r

   com-rupt > corrupt

After ex- an initial s is dropped in English

   ex-spect > expect; ex-stirpate (< *stirps*, trunk and roots) > extirpate

The variations are listed with the prefixes.

PREFIXES FROM LATIN

Learn these prefixes from Latin. An asterisk (*) marks the most productive.

* 1. *ab-, a-, abs-* away from, off, badly: the usual form is *ab-*; *a-* is used before m, p, v; *abs-* before c, t.

   Examples: abrupt (broken off < *rumpere, ruptum,* break), avert (turn away < *vertere,* turn), abstract (drawn away < *trahere, tractum,* drag, draw)

* 2. *ad-* to, toward, against, intensely: *ad-* appears also as *ac-* (before c, q), *af-, ag-, al-, an-, ap-, ar-, as-, at-,* and *a-* (before sc, sp, st, gn).]

   Examples: advent (a coming towards < *venire, ventum* come), accurate (attended to < *curare* < *cura,* care), annotate (add notes to < *notare* < *nota,* mark),   assent (feel to, agree < *sentire,* feel), aspect (a looking at, view < *specere* look)

3. *ambi-* around, about, on both sides; amb- before vowels.

   Examples: ambiguous (going around, uncertain < agere, -ig-), ambidextrous (right-handed on both sides < *dexter,* right-handed)

* 4. *ante-* before, in front of, ahead of

   Example: antecede (go before < *cedere,* go)

* 5. *circum-* around

   Examples: circumcise (cut around < *caedere, caesum,* cut), circumflex ([something] bent around < *flectere, flexum,* bend)

6. *cis-* on this side of

   Examples: cisalpine (on this side of the Alps), cislunar (on this side of the moon < *luna,* moon), cisgender (having a gender identity that conforms with the gender assigned at birth)

* 7. *com-* with, together, very: com- before b, p, m; > *cor-* before r; *col-* before l; *co-* before h, gn and usually before vowels; con- before all other consonants (from preposition, *cum,* as in *cum laude, cum grano salis*)

   Examples: colloquium (a speaking together < *loqui,* speak), corrode (gnaw thoroughly < *rodere,* gnaw), cohere (stick together < *haerēre,* cling, stick), combine (put two things together < *bini,* two by two)

* 8. *de-* down from, off, utterly; this prefix may imply removal or cessation and it may give a bad (or negative) sense to the word.

Examples: devolve (roll down < *volvere*, roll), deformed (ill/badly formed < *forma*, shape), defoliate (remove the leaves < *folium*, leaf), destroy (build down < *struere*, pile up)

* 9. *dis-* apart, in different directions, at intervals; it can also have a negative force. > *di-* before voiced consonants; *dif-* before f; sometimes > *de-*, under French influence: depart, defy

Examples: differ (bear/carry apart < *ferre*, bring), dispel (push in different directions < *pellere*, push), discursive (tending to run in different directions < *currere, cursum*, run)

* 10. *ex-, e-* out from, out of, off, away, away from, thoroughly > *ef-* before f

Examples: event (outcome < *venire, ventum*, come), effect (make thoroughly < *facere, factum*, do, make), extol (raise out < *tollere*, raise), expect (look out, await *spectare*, look)

11. *extra-* (variant, *extro-*) outside, beyond; used mostly with noun bases

Example: extraordinary (beyond the rank < *ordo, ordin-*, rank). Most English words using extra- are non-classical formations like extraterrestrial (< *terra*, earth)

* 12. *in-*(1) in, into, on, toward, against > *il-* before l; *im-* before b, m, p; *ir-* before r; sometimes *en-* under French influence: endue < *induere*, put on.

Examples: incise (cut into < *caedere, caesum*, cut), impel (push on < *pellere*, push), infringe (break in < *frangere*, break)

* 13. *in-*(2) not, lacking, without > *i-* before gn; other changes as in *in-*(1): used mostly with adjective and adverb bases; sometimes with nouns.

Examples: illegal (unlawful < *lex, leg-*, law), ignoble (not noble < *nobilis*, known, noted)

14. *infra-* below, beneath, inferior to, after, later

Example: infrared

* 15. *inter-* among, between, at intervals, mutually, each other > *intel-* before l.

Examples: intercept (take between < *capere, captum*, take), intercede (go between < *cedere*, go), intellect (a choosing between < *legere, lectum*, gather, choose)

16. *intra-* in, within, inside of

Example: intramural (within the walls < *mura*, wall)

17. *intro-* in, into, inward

Example: introduce (lead into < *ducere*, lead)

18. *juxta-* near, beside

Example: juxtapose (put beside < *ponere, positum*, place, put)

* 19. *ob-* toward, against, across, in the way of, opposite to, down, for, out of, intensely > *o-* before m; *oc-* before c; *of-* before f; *op-* before p.

Examples: oblong (long across < *longus*, long), offer (bring for < *ferre*, carry, bring), obdurate (hardened against < *durus*, hard)

* 20. *per-* through, by, thoroughly, away, badly, to the bad > *pel-* before l.
　　Examples: permeate (pass through < *meare, go, pass*), perfidy (bad faith < *fides*, faith), pellucid (thoroughly clear/bright < *lux, luc-*, light)

* 21. *post-*　behind, after
　　Examples: postpone (put after < *ponere, put*), postnatal (after birth < *nasci, natum*, be born)

* 22. *pre-* (< Latin *prae-*) before, in advance, in front of, headfirst, at the end
　　Examples: precede (go before < *cedere*, go), pretend (spread in front, give as an excuse < *tendere*, stretch)

23. *preter-* (< Latin *praeter*) past, beyond
　　Examples: preterite (gone past < *ire, itum*, go), preternatural (beyond what is natural < *natura*, nature), preterpostmodernism (movement that is past the postmodernist period)

* 24. *pro-* forth, for, forward, publicly, instead of; before vowels > *prod-*
　　Examples: proclaim (shout publicly/forth < *clamare*, shout), proceed (go forward < *cedere*, go), prodigal (wasteful < *prodigere*, squander < pro- + *agere*)

* 25. *re-* back, again, against, behind; can have both intensive and negative force; > *red-* before vowels
　　Examples: repel (push back < *pellere*, push), record (bring back to mind < *cor, cord-*, heart), redeem (buy back <*emere*, buy)

26. *retro-* backwards, behind
　　Example: retrogressive (tending to step/move backwards < *gradi*, step)

* 27. *se-* aside, apart, away; > *sed-* before vowels
　　Examples: secure (away from/free from care < *cura*, care), seduce (lead apart < *ducere*, lead)

28. *sine-* without
　　Example: sinecure (without [the] care [of souls] < *cura*, care)

* 29. *sub-* under, inferior, secondary, less than, in place of, secretly > *suc-* before c; *suf-* before f; *sug-* before g; *sum-* before m; *sup-* before p; *sur-* before r; sometimes *sus-* before c, p, t.
　　Example: subtract (draw from under < *trahere*, drag, draw), suspend (hang down < *pendere*, hang)

30. *subter-* beneath, secretly
　　Example: subterfuge (evasion, fleeing in secret < *fugere*, flee)

* 31. *super-* over, above, excessively, beyond; > *sur-* under French influence: surtax, surcharge, surrealism.
　　Example: superimpose (put over/on top < *ponere, positum*, put)

32. *supra-* above, over, greater than, preceding
　　Example: suprarenal (above the kidney < *renes*, kidneys)

* 33. *trans-* across, over, beyond, through, very > *tran-* before s; sometimes appears as *tra-*
　　Examples: transport (carry across/over <*portare*, carry), transgress (step across < *gradi*, step), transcribe (write across < *scribere*, write), traduce (lead over <

ducere, lead)

SOME OBSERVATIONS ON PER-

per- is used literally to mean "through" as in *pervade, permeate, impervious.*

From "through" to "through and through" or "thoroughly" is an easy step: *perfect, pellucid, perceive.*

"Through to the end" is another nearly imperceptible gradation as in: *permanent, persist, perpetual.*

"Through to the core and so to the bad" requires a little more imagination, as in words such as *perfidious, pervert, perverse, perish.*

per is also used as a separate word in certain expressions:

    per diem, per annum, per cent, per capita: "for each"

    per bearer: "by means of"

    as *per instructions*: "according to"

EXERCISES

EXERCISE 6 A. 1— PRACTICE ASSIMILATING * Practice vowel reduction on these.
Example: ob-cur > occur

1. ad-similation	2. in-pel
3. sub-fer	4. ex-rupt
5. com-vert	6. trans-scribe
7. ab-cess	8. ad-claim
9. ex-fact*	10. com-tain
11. ad-capt*	12. ad-sent
13. ab-tract	14. ad-quisitive
15. com-loquy	

EXERCISE 6 A. 2 —USING PREFIXES: Find 5 words using each new prefix marked with an asterisk (*); choose one and find twenty words using it. Try to find subtleties of meaning for your prefix.
Example: *ob-* becomes oc-, op-, of-, o- (before *m*). The basic meaning is *to, toward,* but it also shows the meaning *against, in opposition to* (that is "to or toward in a *hostile* or *negative sense*"). It can also show the slight shades of meaning suggested by "opposite to", "for", "in a certain direction (down, over, in back of, out of, away)" and it can show intensified action. A special meaning of ob- in botany is "in inverse shape".

    —*to/toward*: offer, obvert, obey, object, oblation, oblige, obligate, obnoxious, observe, obverse, obviate, occur, office, officious, opportune ("toward the harbor" < *portus*), obsequious, obsequies

    — *opposite to/before*: obsess, obstetrics (< *obstetrix* midwife < "she who stands next to"), oblate (spheroid < "carried to")

—*against/in opposition to*: opprobrium, obloquy, offend, offensive, opponent, oppose, opposite, obstacle, obtrude, obstruct, oppugn (fight against > "call into question"), oppress, oppressive, obstreperous, obtund, obtuse

—*for*: obsecrate (beg for something)

—*of various directions*: *down*: obituary, occasion, occident; *over*: obtect, obscure; *in back of*: occiput (in back of the head); *out of/away*: obliterate, omit, omission, obsolete

—*intensified action*: obtain, occlude, obfuscate, oblong, occupy, obdurate

—*inverse shape*: obcordate, obovate, oblanceolate

—*others*: oblivion, obturate, occult

EXERCISE 6A. 3— PUTTING TOGETHER VERBS AND PREFIXES: find words meaning (using verbs from previous lesson):

1. go (yield) back
2. shout forth
3. lead into
4. bear toward/against
5. send under
6. get ready in advance
7. write under
8. feel differently
9. call out
10. turn to the bad
11. lead apart
12. come together again
13. hold/keep through
14. give to
15. push out
16. throw in between
17. close in
18. thoroughly done/made
19. close off
20. come around

EXERCISE 6A. 4—(1) TAKE APART AND DEFINE PARTS: and find (1) one additional word using the same prefix and (2) one word using the same verb base.

Example: *omit*: o- (from *ob-*) off + *mit* < present base of *mittere* let go; other words: 1. obfuscate 2. intermittent.

1. transmit
2. collate
3. suppress
4. compare
5. declaim
6. proscribe
7. resent
8. resolve
9. provoke
10. diverse
11. consensus
12. secede
13. advent
14. transient

15. abstain
16. interrupt
17. abject
18. excise
19. precept
20. preclude
21. defect
22. abrupt
23. intervene
24. circumscribe
25. antecede
26. intercept
27. postscript
28. supercede
29. object
30. oppress
31. dismiss
32.-35. commit, admit, remit, submit

(2) Take apart and define these words which use noun bases:
Example: juxtamarine < *juxta* beside + *mare* sea + *-ine* of. Meaning: "beside the sea"
1. devious
2. obvious
3. impervious
4. supernumerary
5. ineptitude (< *aptus*)
6. circumlunar
7. extraterrestrial
8. subterranean
9. immure (*murus*, wall)
10. intravenous (*vena*, vein)
11. adept
12. perennial
13. cismontane (< *mons, mont-*, mountain)
14. posthumous
15. inert (*ars, art-*, skill)
16. intramolecular
17. antepenult (< *paene*, almost + *ultimus*, last)
18. perfidious (< *fides*, faith)
19. interregnum (< *regnum*, kingship)
20. concord (*cor, cord-*, heart)

EXERCISE 6A. 5— PRODUCTIVE VERBS WITH PREFIXES: using the new prefixes, make up ten words from each of these verbs:

> Example: venire, ventum > advent, convent, invent, convene, reconvene, convenient, inconvenience, subvention, prevent, eventual, intervene, circumvent, supervene, contravene (also by various routes: avenue, parvenu, adventure, souvenir, provenance).

1. ducere, ductum
2. facere, factum
3. cedere, cessum
4. tenere, tentum
5. capere, captum
6. mittere, missum
7. legere, lectum (collect, gather, choose, read)
8. currere, cursum (run)
9. tendere, tensum/tentum (stretch)
10. pellere, pulsum

B. VOCABULARY

Learn these verbs; fill in a derivative for each base

canere, cantum	*sing*	> canorous, canticle
cernere, cretum	*sift*	
condere, conditum	*build, store, hide*	
currere, cursum	*run*	
dicere, dictum	*say, speak*	
emere, emptum	*buy, procure* (from pres. base *redeem*)	
flectere, flexum	*bend*	
fundere, fusum	*pour*	
gerere, gestum	*carry, wage*	
haerere, -haesum	*cling, stick*	
legere, lectum	*collect, gather, choose, read*	
ludere, lusum	*play*	
pendere, pensum	*hang, weigh*	
petere, petitum	*aim at, seek*	
ponere, positum	*put, place*	
portare, portatum	*carry*	
prehendere, prehensum	*seize*	
quaerere, quaesitum (-quirere, -quisitum)	*seek, ask*	
rogare, rogatum	*ask*	
scandere (-scendere, -scensum)	*climb*	
secare, sectum	*cut*	
servare, servatum	*save*	
sistere, statum	*set, stand*	

stare, statum	*stand*
sumere, sumptum	*take (up)*
tendere, tentum/tensum	*stretch, spread, aim*
trahere, tractum	*draw, drag* > subtrahend, subtract, intractable
uti, usum	*use*
vadere, -vasum	*go, make one's way*
vincere, victum	*conquer, win*
vivere, victum	*live*

VOCABULARY NOTE

Words from *canere/cantum*: canorous (tuneful), cant (monotonous, whining, hypocritical speech; jargon), recant (renounce a position), cantilate (chant in a monotone), chant (through French), Carmen, charm, carmina, cantata, cantabile (lyrical), canticle (a nonmetrical chant based on a Biblical text), canzone (a style of verse), accent, incentive (what sets the tune), incantation, descant (ornamental melody), and precentor (a choir master).

Pitfalls: students over the years have asked about a number of other words with *can-* in them: NOT these:

canary < *canis* dog [find out why]

canon < Greek *kanōn* rule, rod

decant, canteen, cantina < *canthus* rim of a vessel

EXERCISES

EXERCISE 6B. 1— NEW VERBS AND PREFIXES: take apart and define each; give at least one other English word from the same Latin verb.

Example: *survive*: sur- (from *super* beyond] + *vivere* live; other words: convivial, revive, vivacious, vivid, victuals

1. abscond
2. edict
3. recondite
4. exempt
5. infuse
6. append
7. appetite
8. composite
9. desist
10. contend
11. interdict
12. perpetual
13. peremptory
14. impetus

15. compendium (-ium, a thing)
16. discern
17. incline (*clinare*, lean, bend)
18. deflect
19. transport
20. cohere
21. apprehend
22. surrogate
23. perquisite
24. recant
25. ascend
26. convivial
27. insect
28. pervade
29. assume
30. observe
31. intersect
32. contract
33. abuse
34. evict
35. intellect
36. abrogate
37. arrogate
38. derogate
39. interrogate
40. acquire

VOCABULARY NOTE

portare (to carry), *porta* (door), *portus* (harbor) are all related, the idea of passage being common to them all. From *porta* > portal, porter, porch, portico, portcullis; from *portus* > port, importune, opportune. English cognates include *ferry, ford, fare; fjord* is also related, as is Greek *poros* which gives us *pore, emporium, aporia* ("dilemma, situation without a crossing"), *aporetic* ("in doubt, at a loss, inconclusive").

EXERCISE 6B. 2—REVIEW VERBS AND PREFIXES: make up words meaning:
1. speak against (against: *contra, in*)
2. poured forth
3. play to
4. hang under
5. seek with
6. put after

7. stand out
8. stretch before/in front
9. stand to
10. sing back
11. sifted apart
12. take (up) to
13. bend down
14. stick to
15. seize together
16. sought back in advance
17. climb down with
18. of living together
19. use thoroughly
20. make one's way away/out
21. choose apart
22. use away (badly)
23. sought out
24. drag out, drag down, drag/draw together
25. live beyond

INTERLUDE

Prefix scramble: unscramble each to spell a prefix; the underscored letters spell a word.

X̱UTJA CR̲UMIC RANTS̲ TRINE̲ P̲URES F̲IRAN NE̲AT SCI̲

– – – – – – – –

Prefix drill:

Match with meaning and give a word using each prefix:

per-	1. around
ob-	2. to, toward
ab-	3. beyond
trans-	4. after
circum-	5. across
post-	6. under, up from under
preter-	7. through
sub-	8. over
super-/sur-	9. away from
ad-	10. to, against, for

EXERCISE 6B. 3— DENOMINATIVES USING PREFIXES: take apart, define each part.
Note: -*ion* "act, result of"; -*ive* "tending to"
1. evacuate
2. assimilate

3. exaggerate (*agger*, mound, built-up mass)
4. exacerbate
5. obliterate (*littera*, letter)
6. accumulate (*cumulus*, heap)
7. reiterate (*iterum*, again)
8. excoriate (*corium*, hide, skin)
9. transliterate
10. incarcerate (*carcer*, prison)
11. excavate
12. eradicate
13. irradiate
14. exonerate
15. infatuate
16. cooperate
17. incorporate
18. enunciate (*nuntius*, message)
19. investigate (*vestigium*, footprint, trace)
20. corrugate (*ruga*, wrinkle)
21. exculpate (*culpa*, fault)
22. depreciate (*pretium*, price)
23. deprecate (*prex, prec-*, prayer)
24. decapitate
25. concatenation (*catena*, chain)
26. exaltation (*altus*, high)
27. superannuated
28. adaptation
29. inaugurate (*augur*, increaser, seer)
30. abbreviate (*brevis*, short)
31. incarnation (*caro, carn-*, flesh)
32. indentation (*dens, dent-*, tooth)
33. predominate (*dominus*, master < *domus*)
34. inflammation (*flamma*, flame)
35. counterreformation (counter < *contra*)
36. elaborate (*labor*, work)
37. regenerate
38. degenerate
39. collaborate
40. alleviate (*levis*, light)
41. corroborate (*robor*, strength)
42. illuminate (*lumen, lumin-*, light)
43. eliminate (*limen, limin-*, threshhold)
44. alliterate
45. inoculate (*oculus*, eye, bud)

46. annihilate (*nihil*, nothing)
47. denominative
48. innovate (*novus*, new)
49. insinuate (*sinus*, wave, fold)

QUISQUILIA: SOME LATIN EXPRESSIONS USING PREPOSITIONS[1]

ab incunabulis from the cradle (What is an *incunabula*?)
ab ovo from the egg (Can you give three other derivatives of *ovum*, egg?)
ab imo pectore from the bottom of the heart
ad libitum at one's pleasure (Usually heard in the abbreviated form, ad lib.)
ad astra per aspera to the stars through hardships
ante bellum before the war (Give two additional derivatives of *bellum*.)
cum grano salis with a grain of salt(English salary comes from Latin *sal*, salt; see if you can find out why.)
Dominus vobiscum The Lord be with you (What does *A.D.* stand for? What does *pax vobiscum* mean?)
de gustibus non est disputandum there's no arguing about tastes (Can you think of another word from Latin *gustus*?)
de minimis non curat lex the law is not concerned about minutiae
de mortuis nil nisi bonum of the dead [say] nothing but good
deus ex machina the god from the machine (Translation of Greek *theos apo mēchanēs*.)
ex cathedra from the seat [of authority]
ex oriente lux light from the East
in vino veritas in wine, truth
mens sana in corpore sano a sound mind in a sound body
inter nos among ourselves
inter arma silent leges among arms, the laws are silent
ex post facto from after the fact
post equitem sedet atra cura behind the horseman sits black care
post hoc ergo propter hoc after this, therefore because of this
pro bono publico for the public good
palma non sine pulvere the palm [is] not without dust (effort); no prize without struggle (cf. "no pain, no gain")
sub rosa under the rose (i.e., in private)
sub specie aeternitatis under the sight of eternity

Look up any of these useful phrases you do not know:

ad hoc	*ad rem*	*de facto*	*de jure*	*per diem*
sine die	*pro bono*	*ex officio*	*inter alia*	*sine qua non*
in absentia				

CHECKLIST FOR CHAPTER SIX

1. Assimilation: the change in a final consonant of a prefix for ease in pronunciation before the first consonant of the base word. Make a list of all prefixes that assimilate and give one example of each change.

For example: a, ab, abs: averse, abominate, abduct, abstruse, abscess

ad, ac, af, ag, al, an, ap, ar, as, at, a: adversary, acquire, accumulate, affirm, aggressor, alleviate, annunciation, approve, arrive, assent, attend, ascribe

2. Learn all prefixes. Make a list of all prefixes which can be used to mean *very*. Make a list of all prefixes that can mean *not* or can be used in any negative sense.

3. Learn both bases of all new verbs. Think of a derivative to associate with each base.

REVIEW EXERCISE 6B. 1—VOCABULARY BUILDING: it is best to know the meanings of words and not just their parts. Test yourself by taking this quiz on meanings of some of the words that have used the elements from chapters five and six.[2]

1. *recondite* a. seasoned b. rebuilt c. highly recommended d. obscure

2. *trajectory* a. target b. path of a moving object c. opening in a door for cross-ventilation d. throwing away

3. *incarnation* condition of being a. deified b. in the flesh c. spiritual d. be-flowered

4. *sinecure* a. dog's tail b. apathy c. office without work d. absolution

5. *factotum* a. bit of information b. plant manager c. a do-all d. manmade cult object

6. *compendium* a. heavy tome b. those who hang together c. a summary d. a place or instrument for weighing

7. *interdiction* a. entreaty for another b. a conversation c. ban d. interruption of a speech

8. *peremptory* a. sold out b. thoroughly empty c. urgent d. not long lasting

9. *recant* a. sing over and over b. retract a position c. an ornamental melody d. to pour back into the bottle

REVIEW EXERCISE 6B. 2—PREFIX TORTURE[3]

1. Which of these can mean "very" or "thoroughly": per, ob, ad, com, ex,super, de?

2. Which of these prefixes can mean "not" or "to the bad" or in general take a negative sense: per, in, dis, ab, de, re, sine?

WORDS IN CONTEXT

Women are soft, milde, pittifull, and flexible;
Thou, sterne, *obdurate*, flintie, rough, *remorselesse*.

Shakespeare, *Henry VI, part 3*, Act 1, scene 3

They have joined the most *obdurate consonants* without one *intervening* vowel.
    Jonathan Swift, *A Proposal for Correcting, Improving and Ascertaining the English Tongue*,1712

Do not *affect* little shifts and *subterfuges* to avoid the force of an argument.
    Isaac Watts, *The Improvement of the Mind*, 1741

Many of the best institutions moulder into *sinecures.*
    Patrick Colquhoun, *A Treatise on the Commerce and Police of the River Thames,* 1800

He shall do this or else I do *recant* the pardon that I late *pronounced* here.
    Shakespeare, *Merchant of Venice*, Act 4, scene 1

No, of course not; what with all her children, and what with making war and making peace, and giving balls and *proroguing* Parliaments, and the Government always changing, she has not much time for visiting, poor thing!
    Emily Eden, *The Semi-Attached Couple & the Semi-Detached House,*1860

We are always doing, says he, something for *Posterity*, but I would fain see *Posterity* do something for us.
    Joseph Addison and Richard Steele, *The Spectator*, 1711–12

ENDGAME—SOME INTERESTING COMPOUNDS

Choose two or three and find out what each is combined from:

factotum	facsimile	amanuensis	accord
alarm	arrive	annoy	biscuit
cauliflower	accost	combine	apparel
conclave	convey	dismal	mischief
precocious	recalcitrant		

NOTES

1. A useful website for Latin phrases is
http://en.wikipedia.org/wiki/List_of_Latin_phrases_%28A%29

2. Answers to vocabulary quiz, 6B1: 1. D 2. B 3. B 4. C 5. C 6. C 7. C 8. C 9. B

3. Answers to prefix questions, 6B2: 1. all of these; 2. all of these

SECTION TWO: LATIN
B. Latin Verbs

Interlude 2
Review of Latin Verbs and Prefixes— Chapters Five to Six

A. Vocabulary of Verbs and Prefixes
Using prefixes, give ten words from each of the following (try to include at least one word from each base). Example: *vertere, versum* (turn) avert, averse, adverse, invert, inverse, pervert, perverse, revert, reversion, convert, conversation, subvert, subversive, obverse, divert, traverse, transverse, extroverted, introvert. Give meaning of the Latin verb.

  capere, captum
  cedere, cessum
  mittere, missum
  pellere, pulsum
  scribere, scriptum
  currere, cursum
  ludere, lusum
  trahere, tractum [pres. > subtrahend]
  sistere, stat- (-stit-)
  legere, lectum
  ducere, ductum
Using as many prefixes as you can, give five words from each:
  haerēre, haesum
  sumere, sumptum
  rogare, rogatum
  clamare, clamatum
  (gerere), gestum (use *ppp* base)
  (dicere), dictum (use *ppp* base)
  portare, portatum
  emere, emptum (pres. redeem)

fundere, fusum
tendere, tensum/tentum

B. PREFIXES— Chose one of the prefixes listed in Chapter Six and give its meaning and ten words using it; practice the assimilated forms, if any.

Example: ad- *to* adverse, affect, accept, advent, accede, adhere, attend, assist, addict, admission, attract, adduce, arrogant, acclaim

C.—RECOGNIZING STEM VARIATIONS:

1) Match words on the left with the other word from the ***present*** stem of the same verb and fill in the meaning of the verb. Example: 1– h transient – perish (ire) *go*

1. __ transient	a. proficient (use twice)
2. __ agent	b. convenient
3. __ cadence	c. abstain
4. __ capacity (2 ans.)	d. exceed
5. __ reify	e. deciduous
6. __ face	f. continent
7. __ tenant (2 ans.)	g. conceive
8. __ secede	h. perish (ire)
9. __ venue	i. incipient
	j. exigency

2) Match with another word from the *ppp* of the same verb and give meaning of the verb. Example: 1– h fact – effect (*do, make*)

1. __ fact	a. edition
2. __ caesura	b. receptacle
3. __ captivate	c. excise
4. __ jactitation	d. accent
5. __ disclose	e. injection
6. __ data	f. inclusive
7. __ canticle	g. occasion
8. __ case	h. effect

3) Match the word on the left from the present base to a word from the *ppp* of the same verb and give meaning of the verb.

Example: 1. component—h. posture (*put*)

1. __ component	a. accept
2. __ suffer	b. hesitate
3. __ repel	c. abuse
4. __ utile	d. recant
5. __ coherent	e. compulsive
6. __ canorous	f. excrete
7. __ belligerent	g. collate
8. __ discern	h. posture
9. __ convenient	i. incisive

10. __ imprimatur	j. digest
11. __ deceive	k. eventual
12. __ recidivism	l. casual
13. __ suicide	m. repressive

D. MAKE UP WORDS MEANING[1]:

Examples: *make very* (= out) *bitter*: ex-acerb-ate; *bring back*: refer, relate

1. drag out
2. throw down
3. come around
4. write under
5. send across
6. close out
7. seize between
8. thrown away/off
9. shout publicly
10. hold together
11. push in different directions
12. loosen back/again
13. hide away
14. stick in
15. stretch in front of
16. play together
17. drag under
18. live beyond
19. make one's way through
20. choose apart
21. turn inward

E. PRACTICE VOWEL REDUCTION AND ASSIMILATION

1) VOWEL REDUCTION: change to proper English spellings; give meaning of prefix and base verb

1. ad-jactive
2. de-facient
3. circum-caesion
4. ex-clausive
5. re-capient
6. re-captacle
7. con-tenent
8. ex-caption
9. con-jacture
10. ef-fact
11. ef-facient

12. abs-tenent
13. in-caesive
14. de-captive
15. in-jaction
16. per-caption
17. af-fact
18. de-fact
19. in-faction
20. ac-cadent

2) ASSIMILATION: change to proper English spelling; give meaning of prefix and base verb/noun
   1. ad-gravate
   2. ambi-ition
   3. com-venient
   4. dis-ferent
   5. com-lect
   6. ex-sist
   7. ex-fect
   8. con-laborate
   9. ad-finity
   10. ob-cur
   11. sub-fer
   12. in-moderate

F. MORE REVIEW
1) Take apart and give meaning of English word:
Example: retain < re- + -tain < *tenēre*: hold, keep back
   1. abstain
   2. convent
   3. exclude
   4. add (hint: < *dare*)
   5. deceive
   6. contain
   7. abject
   8. expel
   9. exit
   10. affect
   11. effect
   12. disrupt
   13. excise
   14. except
   15. conceive
   16. confection (*-ion*, act, result of)

17. adit (meaning: "entrance to a mine")
18. coitus (hint < *ire, itum*)
19. eject
20. corrupt
21. advent
22. exact
23. access
24. acclaim
25. educe
26. dismiss
27. dissent
28. conscript
29. dissolute
30. averse

2) Form words meaning[2]:
  1. feel together
  2. outcome
  3. come together
  4. break out
  5. throw out
  6. send out
  7. yield to
  8. turn away
  9. write around
  10. come around
  11. cut down
  12. lead together
  13. lead down (use both bases)
  14. lead to
  15. feel toward
  16. squeeze out
  17. taken out
  18. cut out
  19. take to
  20. give out
  21. close in
  22. bring in
  23. turn to the bad
  24. write down
  25. loosen away
  26. send/let go to
  27. squeeze against
  28. go out

29. thoroughly made
30. take between
31. push in different directions
32. push on
33. break in between
34. cut together (adj.)
35. fall in together
36. something said (spoken) out
37. roll in
38. throw against
39. hold (-tain) through to
40. hold off from
41. put to (adj.)
42. put against (adj.)
43. put down
44. put after
45. pour in
46. stretch out
47. stand with
48. stand out
49. stand off/down
50. stand through
51. hang (on) to
52. hang down
53. speak between
54. play out
55. play together
56. play to
57. (something) played between
58. (something) played after
59. (something) played before
60. hide away
61. bought off/out
62. sing back
63. sifted apart
64. sift apart
65. run against
66. run back
67. bend down/away
68. carry (wage) under
69. stick to
70. carry across
71. seize together

72. ask down
73. bring/come back to life
74. make one's way through
75. make one's way in
76. cut between
77. stick together
78. use through and through
79. choose apart
80. take up again

VOCABULARY—VERBS FOR CHAPTERS 5 AND 6

Give words from each base. Test each other for meanings.

agere, actum (-ig-)	*do, drive, lead* > agile, actor
cadere, casum (-cid-, -cas-)	*fall*
caedere, caesum (-cid-, -cis-)	*cut, kill*
canere, cantum	*sing* > canorous, canticle
capere (-io), captum (-cipi-, -cept-)	*take, seize* -ceive
cedere, cessum	*go, yield* (-ceed/-cede)
cernere, cretum	*sift*
clamare, clamatum	*shout* -claim
claudere, clausum (-clud-, -clus-)	*close* -close
condere, conditum	*build, store, hide*
currere, cursum	*run*
dare, datum (-d-, -dit-)	*give*
dicere, dictum	*say, speak*
ducere, ductum	*lead*
emere, emptum	*buy, procure* (from pres. base *redeem*)
errare, erratum	*go astray*
facere (-io), factum (-fici-, -fect-)	*do, make* -fy
ferre (fer-), latum	*bear, carry*
flectere, flexum	*bend*
fundere, fusum	*pour*
gerere, gestum	*carry, wage*
haerēre, -haesum	*cling, stick*
ire, itum	*go* (present base i-; *ppp* base it-)
jacere (-io), jactum (-ject-)	*throw*
jacēre (< jacere)	*lie* [no *ppp*]
legere, lectum	*collect, gather, choose, read*
ludere, lusum	*play*
mittere, missum	*send, let go*
parare, paratum	*get, get ready*
pellere, pulsum	*push*
pendere, pensum	*hang, weigh*

petere, petitum	*aim at, seek*
ponere, positum	*put, place*
portare, portatum	*carry*
prehendere, prehensum	*seize*
premere, pressum	*squeeze*
quaerere, quaesitum (-quir-/-quisit-)	*seek, ask*
rogare, rogatum	*ask*
[rumpere], ruptum	*break, burst* (derivatives are from the *ppp.*)
scandere (-scendere, -scensum)	*climb*
scribere, scriptum	*write*
secare, sectum	*cut*
sentire, sensum	*feel*
servare, servatum	*save*
sistere, statum	*set, stand*
solvere, solutum	*loosen, undo*
stare, statum	*stand*
sumere, sumptum	*take (up)*
tendere, tentum/tensum	*stretch, spread, aim*
tenēre, tentum (-tin-, -tent-)	*hold, keep* -tain
trahere, tractum	*draw, drag* > subtrahend, subtract, intractable
uti, usum	*use*
vadere, -vasum	*go, make one's way*
vendere, venditum	*sell*
venire, ventum	*come*
vertere, versum	*turn*
vincere, victum	*conquer, win*
vivere, victum	*live*
vocare, vocatum	*call, use the* vox
vorare, [voratum]	*devour, eat*

QUISQUILIA

Some Latin Abbreviations Using Verb Forms
1. *cf.*—imperative of *conferre*: compare
2. *et seq.*—*et sequens* (singular) *et seqq.*—*et sequentia* (plural): and the following
3. *i.e.*—*id est*: that is
4. *loc. cit.*—*in loco citato*: in the place cited
5. *N.B.*—*nota bene*: note well
6. *ob.*—*obiit*: he/she died
7. *op. cit.*—*in opere citato*: in the work cited
8. *P.S.*—*post scriptum*: written afterward
9. *q. v.*—*quod vide*: which see (used to direct the reader to the work referred to)
10. ℞—*recipe*: take (imperative of recipere)

11. *R. I. P.*—*requiescat in pace*: may he/she rest in peace
12. *v.*—*vide*: see (imperative of *vidēre*)
13. *viz.*—*videlicit* (*vidēre licet*): it is permitted to see, to wit, namely
14. *sc.*—*scilicet* (*scire licet*): it is permitted to know, that is, "you may understand"
Some abbreviations without verbs:
15. *et al.*—*et alii/et aliae/et alia* (different forms indicate the different genders, masculine, feminine, neuter, respectively), and others
16. *ibid.*—*ibidem*, in the same place
17. *id.*—*idem* the same
18. *e. g.*—*exempli gratia*, for example
19. *etc.*—*et cetera*, and the others, and so forth
20. Not abbreviations, but useful:
   passim, here and there, throughout
   sic, thus (for pointing out that you recognize an error in a citation you make to another's work)

ENDGAME

Which of these are from Latin?[3]

litmus	caucus	bunkum	doldrums
catalpa	buckram	totem	

NOTES

1. Answers for Exercise D. 1. extract 2. deject 3. circumvent 4. subscribe 5. transmit 6. exclude 7. intercept 8. abject 9. proclaim 10. contain 11. dispel 12. resolve 13. abscond 14. inhere 15. pretend 16. collude 17. subtract 18. survive 19. pervade 20. select 21. introvert

2. Answers for Review F. 2)— 1. consent 2. event 3. convene 4. erupt 5.eject 6. emit 7. accede 8. avert 9. circumscribe 10. circumvent 11. decide 12. conduce, conduct 13. conduce, conduct 14. adduce 15. assent 16. express 17. except 18. excise 19. accept 20. edit 21. include 22. infer 23. pervert 24. describe 25. absolve 26. admit 27. oppress 28. exit 29. perfect 30. intercept 31. dispel 32. impel 33. interrupt 34. concise 35. coincide 36. edict 37. involve 38. object 39. appertain 40. abstain 41. apposite 42. opposite 43. depose, also depone 44. postpone 45. infuse 46. extend 47. consist 48. exist 49. desist 50. persist 51. append 52. depend 53. interdict 54. elude 55. collude 56. allude 57. interlude 58. postlude 59. prelude 60. abscond 61. exempt 62. recant 63. discrete, discreet 64. discern 65. occur 66. recur 67. deflect 68. suggest 69. adhere 70. transfer, transport 71. comprehend 72. derogate 73. revive 74. pervade 75. invade 76. intersect 77. cohere 78. peruse 79. select 80. resume

3. Prepare to be surprised: *litmus* is from Old Norse meaning "dye moss"; *caucus* is from Algonquin for "counselor"; *bunkum* < Buncombe County, NC; *doldrums* < dull + tantrum; *catalpa* < Creek "head with wings", referring to the shape of the flowers; *buckram*, a coarse cotton fabric < Bukhara in Uzbekistan; *totem* < Ojibwa "my family mark".

SECTION TWO: LATIN
B. LATIN VERBS

CHAPTER SEVEN: SUFFIXES WITH THE PRESENT BASE OF LATIN VERBS

There are many suffixes added to verb bases to form nouns, adjectives and other verbs. Some are added to the *present* base and others to the *ppp* base. A few are used with both bases. This chapter will treat those added to the present base. Before beginning the new material, review the verbs from previous chapters, paying special attention to the present bases.

A. NOUN-FORMING SUFFIXES

-or [Latin -or] "condition of being"
> *rigēre*, be stiff > rigor: condition of being stiff

-ium, -y [Latin -ium] "act of, something connected with the act of" (-cium > -ce; -gium > -ge) *colloqui*, speak together > colloquium, colloquy: the act of speaking together

-ion [Latin -io, -ion-] "act or result of" (also added to *ppp* base)
> *legere*, collect > legion: result of gathering [troops]

-men [Latin -men, -min-] "result" or "means of"
> *regere*, guide, control > regimen: means of controlling

-ment [Latin -mentum] "result" or "means of an act"
> *impedire*, hinder > impediment: means of hindering

-bulum, -ble [Latin -bulum, -bula] "means, instrument, place/thing for"
> *stare* stand > stable: place for standing

-culum, -cle [Latin -culum] "means, place for, thing for"
> *currere*, run > curriculum: place for running

Suffixes in Use
Additional words using the suffixes: try to add to these lists.

    -OR — valor, squalor, tenor, ardor, terror, horror, furor, error, fervor, favor, vigor, liquor, tremor, clamor, stupor, candor. It is important to distinguish this suffix from -or added to the *ppp* base which means "one who/that which." (This will usually show up as -tor or -sor.)

-IUM, -Y (-ce, -ge: see Chapter 2, part B: -cium/gium > -ce/ge) — study, college, auspice, colloquium, colloquy, soliloquy, query, augury, compendium, convivial (< *convivium*, party + -al), tedium, effluvium, obloquy, refuge, benefice. Try not to confuse this suffix with -y from -*ia* added to noun bases.

-ION — option (< *optare*, choose, wish for), suspicion, opinion, region, legion, condition (< *condicio* "speaking together, agreement" < dicere). -*ion* is also added to the *ppp* base.

-MEN — regimen (also regime < French), specimen, foramen (hole < *forare*, to bore), liquamen (a sauce used in Roman cuisine); also stamen (< sta-), putamen (< *putare*, to prune)

-MENT — regiment, tenement, condiment, aliment (alimentary), augment, document, ferment, foment, fragment, argument, figment (< *fingere*), torment (< *torquēre*), discernment, firmament, sentiment, testament, monument, sediment, instrument, pigment (< *pingere*).

-BULUM, -BLE — fable (and fabulous), stable, infundibulum (funnel < *fundere*, pour), incunabula (pl. "swaddling clothes"). Be extra careful not to confuse this suffix which means "thing for or place for" with the adjective suffix -ble (<-bilis) which means "able" or "able to be".

-CULUM, -CLE — curriculum, miracle (miraculous), spectacle (< spectare, the frequentative of specere, see chapter 7; spectacular), vehicle (vehicular), obstacle, oracle (oracular), receptacle, tentacle (< *tentare* < *temptare*, feel, touch, test > tentative). Notice that adjectives formed from nouns using this suffix return to the -*cul*- form (as in spectacular, miraculous). Try not to confuse this suffix added to verb bases with the diminutive suffix (-cul-, -cle) added to noun bases; -*crum* is also found, as in the Latin word *sepulcrum* > English sepulchre (< *sepelire*, bury).

EXERCISES

EXERCISE 7A 1—PRACTICE USING SUFFIXES: Take apart and define parts
Example: presentiment—*pre*, before *senti*, feel[ing] *ment*, means of
1. error
2. vocabulary
3. condiment (< *condire*, to season, related to *condere*)
4. comportment
5. segment [seg- = sec-: assimilation before *m*]
6. tenement
7. inducement

8. discernment
9. clamorous
10. cement [< caed-ment]
11. tenor
12. compendium
13. argument [*arguere*, make clear]
14. vehicle [*vehere*, convey]
15. monument [*monēre*, warn]
16. option [*optare*, wish]
17. fervor, ferment [*fervēre*, boil]
18. miracle [*mirari*, wonder at]
19. foment [*fovēre*, warm]
20. experiment [*experiri*, try, test]
21. sepulchre [< *sepulcrum* < *sepelire*, bury]
22. ardor [*ardēre*, burn]
23. vigor [*vigēre* thrive]
24. nutriment [*nutrire*, nourish]
25. postponement

B. VOCABULARY I

An asterisk (*) marks the verbs that are most productive of English derivatives.
Find at least two words from each Latin verb; one word from each base for those
having two bases. (Note that many intransitive verbs, like *candēre* and *lucēre*, have
no *ppp*.) For those marked with the asterisk, find four or more words.

* alere, altum	*grow, nourish* > coalesce, alimentary, alimony; exalt
* augēre, auctum	*increase* > augment, augur, inaugurate, auction, auctioneer
candēre	*shine, be white*
* creare, creatum	*create*
* docēre, doctum	*teach*
fervēre	*boil*
* frangere (frag-), fractum	*break*
horrēre	*shudder, stand stiff*
liquēre	*be fluid, be clear*
* loqui, locutum	*speak*
lucēre	*shine, be light*
* rapere, raptum	*snatch*
* regere, rectum	*move in a straight line, guide, direct, rule*
solēre, solitum	*become accustomed* > obsolescent, obsolete
* specere/spicere, spectum	*look at*
studēre	*be diligent, be eager, study*
terrēre	*frighten*
timēre	*fear*
tremere	*quake, tremble*

* valēre   *be well, be strong   Valē*, pl. *valēte*, means "goodbye" as in
                            valedictorian.

VOCABULARY NOTES

ALERE/ALTUM, grow, nourish, is related to English *old, elder, alderman*. The *ppp altum* is none other than your familar *altus*, tall, i.e., full grown. Words from it include exalt, enhance, haughty, hautboy (oboe) and the various *alti/alto-* words, an alto, referring originally to a high male voice. From the present base come aliment, alimentary, alible, alimony, coalesce, alumnus/a, altricial, alma mater, adult, adolescent. It is also related to the Latin word *proles* offspring > prolific, proletarian (originally a Roman citizen of the lowest economic class whose contribution to the state was said to consist in producing citizen children).

AUGĒRE/AUCTUM, increase, is related to English *eke* (as in "to eke out a living") and *nickname* (an *eke*, or added, name). Besides words like augment, augmentative, auction, and auctioneeer, some of the less immediately obvious derivatives are augur, inaugurate, august, and Augustus (really a title of respect rather like "Majesty"), author and its two adjectives authorial and auctorial.

EXERCISES

EXERCISE 7B. 1— USING NEW VOCABULARY AND SUFFIXES: Take apart and define parts; give one additional derivative for each verb:

1. augment
2. candor
3. document
4. fragmentary
5. humorous
6. liquor
7. obloquy
8. regimen
9. specimen
10. studious
11. terror
12. timorous
13. tremor
14. valorous
15. colloquium
16. fervor
17. alimentary
18. soliloquy (*solus*, alone)
19. tedium (*taedere*, be weary)
20. auspice (au < *avis*, bird + *spicere*)
21. emolument (*emolere* lit. "to grind out" > a miller's fee for grinding grain); another word from the verbal root is *molar*.

22. acumen (< *acuere*, sharpen)
23. liniment (< *linere*, smear)
24. suspicion
25. caloric (< *calēre*, be warm)

C. Noun- and Adjective-forming Suffixes

1) Adjectives and Nouns from present participles and gerundives/gerunds
Participles
   -nt [Latin -ns, -nt-] "-ing"
   -nce, -ncy [Latin -ntia] "state or condition of _____ing"
   I *portare* > important, bringing in > importance
   II *tenēre* (-tin-) > continent, holding together > continence
   III *vertere* > inadvertent, not turning to > inadvertence
   IIIi *facere* (-fici-) > efficient, making thoroughly > efficiency
   IV *sentire* > sentient, feeling > sentience
Although many of the English derivatives retain the Latin stem vowel before -nt, others, especially those showing French influence have -ant, regardless of the Latin stem vowel. This is especially common if the English word is a noun: the suffix -nt is also used to form nouns meaning "one/a person who is _____ing" or "something _____ing".
   tenant, one holding [< *tenēre*]
   pendant, something hanging [< *pendere*]; but cf. pendent, adj., hanging, as in "pendent nests"
Gerundives/Gerunds[1]
   -nd, -ndum [pl. -nda] "that which must be ____ / thing to be ____ "
      augend, thing to be increased [< *augēre*]
      agendum, thing to be done, that which must be done
      agenda, things to be done; a list of things to be done (used with a singular verb) [*agere*]
   -ous may be added to form adjectives from the forms in -nd
      tremendous, of something to be quaked at [< *tremere*]

Exercises

EXERCISE 7C. 1—USING THE PARTICIPIAL SUFFIXES: go through the vocabulary lists of verbs in this and earlier chapters and try to find a word using one or more of the participial suffixes from each present base. It might help to work in groups. For example:
   agere > agent, agency; exigent, exigency, agenda
   cadere > cadent, cadence; incident, incidence, accident, accidence
   capere > incipient, recipient
   cedere > antecedent, precedent; incessant (from frequentative,[2] *cessare*)

clamare > claimant
ducere > adducent
facere > efficient, proficiency
ferre > afferent, efferent, reference, interference
ire > ambient, ambience, transient; also itinerant, errant

Note: -ENT, -ANT words that come directly from Latin show the ending typical of the conjugation to which the Latin verb belongs. -*are* verbs show -ant, as in important (< portare). Verbs in long or short -ere show -ent, as in adjacent (< jacēre), intermittent (< mittere). Those from -i-stems of the third conjugation and from -ire verbs show -ient as in efficient, incipient; convenient, sentient, audience. Unfortunately Latin is not always the key to correct spelling because many words have entered English through French and so the spelling is affected not only by the pen but by the tongue. Many words from Latin participles that should end in -ent actually show -ant, because the present participle in French shows -ant regardless of the conjugation. This is especially true of the participles that become nouns rather than adjectives, as in the first three examples.

confidant, confidante (n)	confident (adj)
tenant	continent
pendant	interdependent
repentant	penitent
valiant	prevalent
mordant (adj., n.)	mordent (n)
propellant	repellent

EXERCISE 7C. 2—FORMING WORDS USING THE NEW SUFFIXES:
Review prefixes and verb bases. In this exercise, -ing should become -nt; state of -ing should be either -nce or -ncy; thing to be is -nd or -ndum; things to be is -nda.
Example: "shining/showing light across" > *translucent* ; "state of shining across" > *translucence* or *translucency*
1. not leading/driving across (meaning "uncompromising")
2. state of not leading across
3. one ruling
4. state, condition of ruling
5. hanging down
6. state of hanging down
7. standing together
8. state of standing together
9. falling on
10. state of falling on
11. making thoroughly [out]
12. condition of making thoroughly
13. going before

14. act of going before
15. one doing/driving
16. condition of doing/driving
17. feeling
18. condition of feeling
19. loosening
20. condition of loosening
21. thing to be drawn (dragged) under
22. thing to be added
23. thing to be divided
24. thing to be reduced (*minuere*)
25. things to be corrected (*corrigere*)
26. things to be done
27. thing to be noted (memorare)
28. things to be added
29. one doing
30. condition of holding together

MORE VOCABULARY NOTES

FRANGERE (frag-)/FRACTUM, break (cognate to English *break*) – fragment, infringe, infrangible, irrefragable, frangible, fragile, ossifrage, saxifrage, frail, frailty, refrain, Fraktur (a style of German letters), fraction, fracture, anfractuous ("full of twists and turns"), fractious ("troublesome, cranky"), refract, infraction, diffraction, and fracas.

LOQUI/LOCUTUM, speak – loquacious, loquacity, colloquial, colloquy, soliloquy, ventriloquist (*venter*, belly), eloquent, magniloquent, grandiloquent, locution, allocution, elocution, circumlocution, interlocutor, prolocutor.

EXERCISE 7C. 3—MORE PRACTICE WITH NEW SUFFIXES: Take apart and define parts:
1. student
2. intermittent
3. accident
4. repellent
5. incipient
6. claimant
7. docent
8. deference
9. important
10. cadence
11. experience [*experiri*, try, test]
12. valiant
13. inference
14. attendance
15. tendency

16. incontinence
17. interdependence
18. recipient
19. prevalent
20. consistent

2) Other Adjective-forming Suffixes Added to the Present Base
   -id [Latin -idus] "tending to"
       squalid [< *squalēre*, be filthy]: tending to be filthy
   -ile [Latin -ilis] "able to be"
       docile [*docēre*, teach]: able to be taught
   -ble [Latin -bilis] "able to be"
       arable [< *arare*, plow]: able to be plowed
   -acious [Latin -ax, -ac-] "tending to"
       audacious [< *audēre*, dare]: tending to dare
   -ulous [Latin -ulus] "tending to"
       credulous [<*credere*, believe]: tending to believe
   -uous [Latin -uus] "tending to"
       innocuous [< *nocēre*, harm]: tending not to harm

EXERCISES

EXERCISE 7C. 4—NEW SUFFIXES: define each word, use in a sentence; give noun form of those marked with an asterisk (*).
Examples: *tumid (< *tumēre*, swell): "swollen, bulging". My tummy is tumid after Thanksgiving dinner. Noun: tumor. *capacious: "tending to hold, able to contain a lot, roomy". The new recycling bin is more capacious than the old one. Noun: capacity.
1. * candid
2. * valid
3. *facile
4. *docile
5. *audacious
6. pellucid
7. rapacious
8. tenacious
9. *humid (< *humēre*, be moist)
10. *rapid
11. conspicuous
12. feracious
13. incredulous
14. incredible
15. invalid

16. placid (< *placēre*, please, be agreeable)
17. *languid (< *languēre*, be weary, droop)
18. *sensible
19. fallible (< *fallere*, deceive, fail, be mistaken)
20. *rancid (<*rancēre*, stink)
21. *timid
22. fragile (< *frangere*)
23. tenacity
24. tremor (*tremere*, quake, quiver)
25. tepid (*tepēre* be lukewarm)
26. fallacious (< *fallere*, deceive, fail, be mistaken)
27. *rigid (< *rigēre*, be stiff)
28. tremulous (< *tremere*, quake, quiver)
29. *rancid (< *rancēre*, stink)
30. querulous (< *queri*, complain)
31. continuous
32. bibulous (< *bibere*, drink)
33. perspicuous
34. perspicacious
35. promiscuous (< *miscēre*, mix)
36. voluble (< *volvere*, roll)
37. pugnacious (< *pugnare* < *pugna*, fight)
38. insoluble (< *solvere*)
39. arable (< *arare*, plow)
40. garrulous (< *garrire*, chatter)

EXERCISE 7C. 4—RELATIONS OF THE NEW SUFFIXES: For each of these verbs give
1) a noun meaning "condition of being"; 2) an adjective derived from it meaning "of
or pertaining to the condition of being"; 3) an adjective meaning "tending to be";
4) a noun derived from it meaning "condition of tending to be." Example: *rigēre* (be
stiff): 1) rigor; 2) rigorous; 3) rigid; 4) rigidity
1. humēre (be damp)
2. timēre (fear)
3. valēre
4. stupēre (be stunned)
5. languēre (be weary, droop)
6. rancēre (stink)
7. tumēre (swell)
8. squalēre (be matted with filth)
9. fervēre (boil)
10. torpēre (be stiff or numb)

EXERCISE 7C. 5— CHART OF SUFFIXES: make a chart, like the one done earlier for noun-forming suffixes. 1) For the suffixes -nt, -nce/ncy give 10-20 English derivatives and 2) for -nd and the adjective suffixes listed above, give 5-10 English derivatives. You may include words using the new vocabulary given below.
Examples:
-id "tending to" > gravid, livid, timid, tumid, valid, stupid, languid, rancid, torpid, tepid
-nd/-ndum "thing to be" > addend, minuend, subtrahend, dividend, legend, multiplicand, agenda, memorandum, corrigendum, referendum

D. VOCABULARY II

Fill in derivatives of each base.

* audire, auditum	*hear* > audience, auditorium	
esse, futurum	*be* (*futurum* is the future participle) essence, futuristic	
fari, fatum	*speak* (present base: *fa-*)	
fidere	*trust, rely on*	
fluere, fluxum	*flow*	
jacēre	*lie* (derived from *jacere*, throw)	
* manēre, mansum	*remain*	
migrare, migratum	*move, change one's place of living*	
mordēre, morsum	*bite*	
* nasci, natum	*be born*	
oriri, ortum	*rise*	
paenitēre	*repent*	
placēre, [placitum]	*please, be agreeable*	
posse (pot-)	*be able*	
salire (-silire), saltum	*leap, jump*	
scire, [scitum]	*know*	
sedēre, sessum	*sit*	
* sequi, secutum	*follow*	
stringere, strictum	*draw tight*	
* tangere (-ting-), tactum	*touch*	
* vidēre, visum	*see*	
PREFIX: omni-	*all*	

EXERCISES

EXERCISE 7 D. 1)—PRODUCTIVE VERBS: Find ten English words from each of the verbs marked with an asterisk (*) in the vocabulary list above.
Examples:
   nasci, natum: nascent, renascence, Renaissance, natal, nation, native, pre-natal, nature, agnate, adnate, innate, cognate, naive (originally gnasci,

related to *genus, gignere*, bear, beget.)

audire, auditum: audiometer, audiophile, audiovisual, audible, audile, inaudible, audient, audience, obey, audit, audition, auditor, auditory, auditorium, sub-audition, *oyez* (a Norman French imperative used three times to introduce the opening of a session at court), *oyer and terminer* (a hearing or trial, from Norman French, "to hear and determine").

1. manēre/mansum
2. sequi/secutum
3. tangere/tactum
4. vidēre/visum

VOCABULARY NOTES: INTERESTING WORDS FROM THE VOCABULARY

ESSE: essence, essential, quintessence, entity, absent, present, represent, interest, proud (< *prodesse*, be beneficial); the toast PROSIT (or prost) "to your health", literally "may it be to your benefit."

SCIRE: science, pseudoscience, nescience, nescient (*ne-*, a negative prefix), conscious, conscience, unconscious, plebiscite (from the *ppp*).

FARI, FATUM: fable, affable, effable, ineffable, infant, infancy, infantry, infantile, infanticide, infanta, infante (the daughter and son, other than the heir apparent, of a Spanish or Portuguese king); from a suffixed form of the same root come fame, famous, infamy, infamous. *Fari* is cognate to Greek *phanai* and to the Germanic *banns, banal*.

EXERCISE 7 D. 2)—PRACTICE WITH SUFFIXES: make up words meaning:
1. thing to be increased
2. tending to be shining white
3. able to be taught
4. breakable
5. tending to be moist (*humēre*, to be moist)
6. talkative (tending to talk; hint: use *loqui*)
7. tending to be seen through
8. tending to be afraid
9. tending to quiver (*tremere*)
10. tending to be strong
11. able to be heard
12. one not speaking
13. trusting with
14. flowing
15. lying under
16. remaining through
17. one moving out
18. biting
19. being born
20. rising

21. repenting
22. being thoroughly (= "together") pleased
23. leaping
24. state of knowing
25. being able
26. jumping back

EXERCISE 7 D. 3)—PRACTICE WITH NEW VERBS & SUFFIXES: Take apart and define each part
 1. adjacent
 2. audience
 3. essence
 4. affable
 5. diffident
 6. confluence
 7. immanent
 8. renascence
 9. impotent
10. nescience (*ne-*, not)
11. consequence
12. sedentary
13. astringent
14. evident
15. tangent
16. contingent
17. audile
18. conspicuous
19. continuous
20. tenacious
21. audacious
22. invalid
23. rapacity
24. loquacity
25. eloquent
26. current
27. arrogant
28. subtrahend
29. vivid
30. vivacious
31. belligerent
32. illegible
33. eligible
34. capacious

35. capacity
36. subjacent
37. efficacious
38. competent
39. subsistence
40. extant
41. consistency
42. deficient
43. convenience
44. horrendous
45. tremendous
46. infancy
47. inaudible
48. inconsequential
49. essential
50. existential

EXERCISE 7 D. 4)—REVIEW OF NEW SUFFIXES: make up three or more words using each of the new suffixes; give meaning and tell what part of speech each forms. Be sure to add the suffixes to the present base. Add any interesting information you find.

   Example: -nd- (including -ndous, -ndum)

      -nd, -ndum (pl. -nda), "that which must be"; forms nouns

      -ndous "of that which must be"; forms adjectives

Words using the suffix -nd-

agenda	horrendous	memorandum	addendum	corrigendum
tremendous	reprimand	nuntiandum	baptizand	multiplicand
dividend	crescendo	subtrahend	minuend	stupendous
legend	referendum	gerund	reverend	innuendo
propaganda	confirmand	addend	viand [< vivenda]	

Expressions:

   modus operandi (M.O.)

   modus vivendi (less trite than *lifestyle*)

   Q. E. D. *quod erat demonstrandum*

Note: Not to be confused with -nd- that is part of the base of the verb, as *pendere* > compendium; *tendere*> pretend.

EXERCISE 7 D. 5)—SUFFIXES WITH NEW VERBS: Define each of these or use in a sentence.

1. bibulous (*bibere*, drink)
2. ardent (*ardēre*, burn)
3. caloric (*calēre*, be warm)
4. liniment (*linere*, smear)

5. lividity (*livēre*, be black and blue)
6. rancorous (*rancēre*, stink)
7. stupor (*stupēre*, be stunned)
8. torpid (*torpēre*, be numb)
9. querulous (*queri*, complain)
10. promiscuity (*miscēre*, mix)
11. garrulousness, garrulity (*garrire*, chatter)

E. VERB-FORMING SUFFIXES

1) INCHOATIVES are verbs formed from other verbs with the meaning "begin to".
  -sc- (Latin -scere) added to present base "begin to"
    alere, grow > coalesce "begin to grow together"
    florēre , to flower > efflorescent "beginning to flower out"
    creare , form, create > *crescere* begin to be formed > increase > crescent
      "beginning to increase"
    -*scent*, "beginning to"
  The suffix -sc- sometimes becomes -*ish* in English as in finish, abolish.
  Some other words showing the Latin inchoative suffix: nascent, renascence,
    reminisce, convalesce, convalescent, incandescence, fluorescent, excres-
    cence, obsolescence, adolescent.
2) Other verbal suffixes
  -fy "to make" < -ficare < *facere* forms verbs
  -fic "making" forms adjectives
    deify "make into a god" < *deus*
    beatific "making blessed" < *beatus*
  -igate "to drive, to cause to be" < *agere*
    navigate "drive a ship"

EXERCISE 7 E. 1)—USING -FY: Take apart and define parts; give one additional word
using the noun/adjective base of each. Example: 8. sanctify < *sanctus*, holy + -*fy*, to
make > saint, sanctity, sanctimony, sanctum sanctorum, inner sanctum, sanctuary,
sacrosanct, sanctitude, corposant, sanction, Sanctus
  1. unify
  2. clarify
  3. amplify
  4. dignify
  5. beatify
  6. modify
  7. mortify
  8. sanctify
  9. satisfy

10. qualify
11. quantify
12. specify
13. ossify
14. gratify
15. fortify
16. Make up or find ten additional words using the suffixes -fy and/or -fic.

EXERCISE 7 E. 2)—USING THE VERB-FORMING SUFFIXES: Take apart and define:
1. circumnavigate
2. castigate (< *castus*, pure, chaste)
3. variegate
4. fumigate (< *fumus*, smoke)
5. excrescence
6. obsolescence
7. convalesce
8. incandescence
9. coalescent
10. fluorescent
11. fustigate (< *fustis*, stick, cudgel)
12. litigate (cf. litigious < *litigium*, dispute < *lis, lit-*, dispute, lawsuit)

EXERCISE 7 E. 3)—REVIEW EXERCISE: make up words meaning. This is recommended as a participatory exercise in class.[3]
1. able to be used
2. going across
3. means of sifting in different directions
4. placing together
5. asking to [oneself]
6. means of seasoning (< *condire*, related to *condere*, store)
7. running back
8. things to be done
9. to make clear
10. taking on
11. condition of not feeling
12. concerned with climbing across
13. following under
14. knowing all
15. [thing] touching
16. condition of knowing with
17. sticking together
18. thing to be read
19. [thing] cutting

20. causing to stand [= setting] together
21. standing out
22. lively [tending to live]
23. biting
24. condition of being born again
25. able to be spoken to [easy to talk to]
26. falling down
27. being strong in front
28. beginning to be strong together
29. [one] climbing down
30. pushing back
31. condition of jumping back
32. condition of lying upon <*cumbere*, to lie
33. condition of lying hidden <*latēre*, to lie hidden
34. make cheap < *vilis*, cheap, worthless
35. being wakeful < *vigilare*, be wakeful
36. condition of being wanting < *delinquere*, be wanting
37. from *humēre*, be wet/moist:
    a. condition of being moist
    b. pertaining to the condition of being moist
    c. tending to be moist
    d. condition of tending to be moist
38. from *squalēre*, to be stiff/clotted: form words as in 37a-d
39. from *tumēre*, to be swollen: form words as in 37-38
40. act of looking at from underneath
41. of the means of building in (*struere*, build, pile up)
42. a thing for standing against (*ob-*)
43. the result of making will (*testari*, *testatum*, "make a will" < *testis*, witness)
44. of living together
45. tending to hold together
46. tending to devour

CHAPTER SIX: CHECKLIST

1. Suffixes added to the present base
a. Noun-forming
> -or
> -ium, -y
> -ion
> -men
> -ment
> -bulum, -ble
> -culum, -cle

b. Participial suffixes
-nt
-nce, -ncy
-nd, -ndous
c. Adjective-forming
-id
-ile
-ble
-acious
-ulous
-uous
d. Verbal suffixes
-sc- [-esce, -isce]
-fy, -fic, -fication
-igate

Fill in meaning and at least one example of each suffix used in a word.

2. Vocabulary: learn all new words, concentrating on those marked with an asterisk (*). Fill in a derivative of each base given for each verb.

HUMOR from Latin *humor* < *humēre*, to be moist: In ancient and medieval physiology, one of the four "cardinal humors" which by their proportions determined a person's disposition both mental and physical.

BLOOD—sanguine [< Latin *sanguis*]: ruddy in complexion and optimistic or rosy in temperament

PHLEGM—phlegmatic [< Greek *phlegein*, to burn]: sluggish in temperament

CHOLER—choleric (or bilious) [< Greek *chole*, bile]: yellowish in coloring, angry in disposition

MELANCHOLIA—melancholic [< Greek *melan-* black + *chole*]—dark and gloomy

From these the meaning travels to mental disposition or mood and then to a particular inclination or whim and then more specifically to the quality that excites amusement or jocularity and the ability to express it to arrive at our own usage in the expression, "sense of humor."

VERB GAME

Which does not belong[4] (i.e. which does not share a Latin verb with the others)?

1. agent	intransigent	agenda	age	agile
2. captor	capacious	incipient	decapitate	
3. pare	parachute	parallel	preparation	
4. audacious	auditorium	inaudible	obey	
5. data	date	addenda	editorial	ditto
6. duchess	aqueduct	induction	deuce	
7. repel	pell-mell	impulsive	pulse	

8. clam	clamor	exclamation	claimant
9. captain	receive	incipient	conception
10. omit	emission	miss	remittance
11. fail	infallible	fall	fallacious

NOTES

1. Gerunds are verbal nouns; gerundives are peculiar Latin forms that use the same stem as the gerund, but are adjectives and are also called the future passive participle.

2. See Section Two, Chapter 8 for frequentatives.

3. Answers for Exercise 7 E 3: 1. utile; 2. transient; 3. discernment; 4. component; 5. arrogant; 6. condiment; 7. recurrent; 8. agenda; 9. clarify; 10. incipient; 11. insentience, nescience; 12. transcendent; 13. subsequent; 14. omniscient; 15. tangent; 16. conscience; 17. coherent; 18. legend; 19. secant; 20. consistent; 21. existent, extant; 22. vivid; vivacious; 23. mordant; 24. renascence, Renaissance; 25. affable; 26. decadent; 27. prevalent; 28. convalescent; 29. descendant; 30. repellent; 31. resiliency; 32. incumbency; 33. latency; 34. vilify; 35. vigilant; 36. delinquency; 37 a. humor, b. humorous, c. humid, d. humidity; 38. squalor, squalorous, squalid, squalidity; 39. tumor, tumorous, tumid, tumidity; 40. suspicion; 41. instrumental; 42. obstacle; 43. testament; 44. convivial; 45. continent; 46. voracious

4. Answers for Verb Game: 1. age; 2. decapitate; 3. parallel; 4. audacious; 5. ditto; 6. deuce; 7. pell-mell; 8. clam; 9. captain; 10. miss; 11. fall

SECTION TWO: LATIN
B. LATIN VERBS

CHAPTER EIGHT: THE PERFECT PASSIVE PARTICIPIAL BASE OF LATIN VERBS, SUFFIXES

A. FORMING ENGLISH WORDS FROM THE *PPP* BASE

1) Simple Changes: The *ppp* bases of Latin verbs are used to form many English words: adjectives, nouns, and verbs. Often the base alone is used or the base plus silent -e.

Examples:

donare, donatum, give > donate (verb)

rumpere, ruptum, break + ab- > abrupt (adjective)

dicere, dictum, say, speak > dictum (something said with authority, pl. *dicta*) and + e- > edict (nouns)

EXERCISES

EXERCISE 8A.1). 1—REVIEW OF *PPP* BASES: Give the meaning of the Latin base verb, the meaning of the prefix and a brief definition of or synonym for the English derivative or use it in a sentence. Tell what part(s) of speech the English word is.

Example: redact < *agere/actum* do, drive + *re-/red-* again, back; meaning in English, "edit, revise"; verb. Sentence: The report was heavily redacted.

1. precise
2. composite
3. oblate
4. subject
5. errata
6. abrupt
7. apposite

8. cognate
9. erose
10. discrete
11. irresolute
12. exquisite
13. intense
14. transcript
15. interdict
16. separate
17. reject
18. recondite
19. emigrate
20. remorse
21. process
22. prosecute
23. subtract
24. prefect
25. exempt
26. prerequisite
27. adverse
28. profuse
29. finite (< *finire*, to limit < *finis*)
30. indefinite
31. circumvent
32. reconstruct (*struere/structum*, build)
33. circumspect
34. discredit (*credere/creditum*, believe)
35. collapse (*labi/lapsum*, slip)
36. transgress (*gradi/gressum*, step)
37. diffuse
38. recluse

EXERCISE 8A.1). 2—MORE VERBS: make up one or more word(s) from the *ppp* base of each of these; add prefixes but do not be concerned about suffixes (yet):

Example: *jacere/jactum* (-ject), throw > reject, project, deject, abject, *disjecta membra* (scattered parts).

1. movēre/motum (move)
2. jungere/junctum (join)
3. pingere/pictum (prick, paint)
4. torquēre/tortum (twist)
5. tangere/tactum
6. oriri/ortum (rise)
7. sequi/secutum

8. vidēre/visum
9. fluere/fluxum (flow)
10. regere/rectum
11. facere/factum (-fect)
12. rogare/rogatum

2) Noun-forming suffixes added to *ppp* base

-or [Latin -or] "one who, that which"

narrator < *narrare/narratum*, to tell: one who tells

sector < *secare/sectum*, to cut: that which cuts

-ion [Latin -io, -ion-] "an act; the state or result of an act"

vision: the state of seeing

distortion: the result of twisting in different directions"

-ure [Latin -ura] "the act or result of

fracture: the result of breaking

pressure: the act of squeezing

-us [Latin -us, 4th decl.] "an act or the result of an act"

This suffix is often difficult to recognize because many words using it show simply the base or the base with silent -e added and so they look as if they come directly from the *ppp* base. Many words using this suffix will show a -u- in the stem if a second suffix is added and this will help you recognize the suffix.

sense: act/result of feeling (< *sensus*); sensual: concerned with the act of feeling

case: result of falling (< *casus*); casual: connected with the act or result of falling

process: a going forth (< *cessus*); processual: connected with going forth

There are some direct entries using the suffix -us, for example: status, prospectus, conspectus, census, consensus, plexus, nexus, apparatus. (For these words the Latin plural looks the same as the singular.)

Knowing this suffix will help you explain the presence of a -u- in such words as *factual, visual, eventual, actual, consensual.*

eventual: e/vent/u/al—out/come/result of/concerned with

EXERCISES

EXERCISE 8A.2). 1—PRACTICE WITH NEW SUFFIXES: using vocabulary words from previous chapters and the new suffixes, take apart and define each part:

1. oblation
2. actor
3. detractor
4. recessional
5. sensuality

6. verse
7. equivocation
8. scriptural
9. manumission ("the act of freeing": literally, _____)
10. interdiction
11. exemption
12. stature
13. tension
14. discretion
15. precursor
16. profession (< *fatēri, -fessum*, acknowledge)
17. gesture
18. lecture
19. auction
20. circumspection
21. audition
22. stricture
23. nature
24. restriction
25. intermission
26. circumlocution
27. contractual
28. interlocutor
29. excursion
30. resolution
31. collaboration
32. evacuation (*vacuus*)
33. recreational
34. decapitation (*caput, capit-*)
35. incarnational (*caro, carn-*)
36. cooperation (*opus, oper-*)
37. perturbation (*turba*, crowd, dis*turb*ance)
38. innovation (*novus*, new)
39. regeneration (*genus, gener-*)
40. annihilation (*nihil*, nothing)
41. raptor
42. constrictor
43. adventure
44. usury < *usura* < uti/usum
45. vendition
46. occlusion
47. subvention

EXERCISE 8A.2). 2—MAKE UP WORDS MEANING:

1. act of going (use the verb meaning "go/yield") between
2. act of buying back
3. result of taking to (oneself)
4. one who wins
5. one who teaches
6. result of breaking
7. result of snatching
8. act of moving rapidly in
9. act of sitting
10. result of seeing again
11. one who follows out
12. result of putting next to

EXERCISE 8A.). 3—MORE PRACTICE: Make up one agent [one who, that which] and one abstract [act, state, condition of being] from the *ppp* base of each of these verbs. Use prefixes if you want to. Remember vowel reduction.

Example: *cedere/cessum*—agent: intercessor, processor; abstract: intercession, process, recession

1. capere/captum
2. facere/factum
3. agere/actum
4. trahere/tractum
5. quaerere/quaesitum
6. sequi/secutum
7. loqui/locutum
8. audire/auditum
9. ducere/ductum
10. currere/cursum
11. legere/lectum
12. creare/creatum
13. rapere/raptum
14. petere/petitum
15. vincere/victum
16. rogare/rogatum

EXERCISE 8A.2). 4—REVIEW OF PRESENT BASE: Review noun-forming suffixes added to present base and make up one noun using each base

Example: *loqui/locutum* present: eloquence; *ppp*: circumlocution

1. frangere (frag-, -fring-)/fractum
2. regere/rectum
3. specere/spectum
4. legere/lectum

5. tendere/tentum, tensum
6. currere/cursum

3a) Adjective-forming Suffixes Added to *ppp* Base

-ile [Latin -ilis] "able to (be), related to"; as noun, "thing or something that can be"

> ductile: able to be drawn, led
> missile: (something) that can be sent
> tactile: related to touch

-ible [Latin -ibilis] "able to be"

> comprehensible: able to be understood
> plausible (< *plaudere/plausum*, clap, approve): able to be approved, deserving applause
> ostensible: able to be stretched in front (and so, "seeming, represented to be")

-ory, -orious, -orial [Latin -orius] "pertaining to, tending to"

> auditory: pertaining to/concerned with hearing
> censorious: tending to estimate

-orium (sometimes -ory) is the neuter of *-orius*, "thing or place for"

> auditorium: place for hearing
> laboratory: place for working
> crematorium: place for burning < *cremare*, incinerate
> observatory: place for looking at

-ive [Latin -ivus] "tending to"

> active: tending to do
> jussive: (< *jubēre/jussum*, command) tending to command
> ostensive: tending to stretch in front (and so, "seeming")

3b) Frequentatives

FREQUENTATIVES are verbs formed from verbs. They express constant, repeated, or intensified action. Frequentatives are usually formed from the *ppp* base, by adding first conjugation endings; that is, add *-are*, *-atum* to the *ppp* base. Sometimes *-itare*, *-itatum* is added instead. They are usually to be recognized by the presence of *-at-* or *-itat-* on a *ppp* base; sometimes by the presence of an *-a-* that otherwise does not seem to belong.

> gestate <*gerere/gestum*, carry: "to carry constantly"
> hesitate <*haerere/haesum*, stick: "to keep sticking"

EXERCISES

EXERCISE 8A.3). 1— USING THE ADJECTIVE-FORMING SUFFIXES :
Take apart; give meaning of verb stem, define suffix.
1. reactive

2. native
3. concessive
4. exclamatory
5. migratory
6. ductile
7. productive
8. relative
9. submissive
10. preparatory
11. proscriptive
12. sensible
13. evocative
14. redemptive
15. contradictory (*contra-*, against)
16. elusive
17. positive
18. prehensile
19. inquisitive
20. derogatory
21. evasive
22. corrective
23. tactile
24. consecutive
25. executive
26. recidivism (< *cadere*: note -ive added to the present base)
27. conducive (v. # 26, note)
28. sensory
29. peremptory
30. preemptive
31. incomprehensible
32. comprehensive
33. laudatory (*laudare*, praise)
34. presumptive
35. presumptuous (note -*uous* added to *ppp* base)
36. extensile
37. disjunctive
38. perfectible
39. imperceptible
40. expressive

EXERCISE 8A.3) 2—Make up words meaning
1. tending to lead/draw in
2. tending to weigh

3. tending to run
4. tending to save in advance

EXERCISE 8A.3) 3— FREQUENTATIVES: Identify verb, give meaning of compound
1. incantation
2. visitation
3. cessation
4. gestation
5. dictate
6. agitate (note frequentative ending added to present base)
7. jactitation
8. conversation
9. pulsate
10. expectation
11. spectator
12. sensation
13. habitation
14. tractate < *tractatus*, a handling < *tractare*, to draw effortfully (also: > treat, treatise; *protractare* > portray, portrait)

EXERCISE 8A.3). 4— VERB-FORMING SUFFIXES: Tell which are frequentatives, which are inchoatives, and which are denominatives; identify the base of each and give its meaning. Give meaning of the whole compound. Examples:

> *denominative*: is a denominative < base: *nomen, nomin-*, name; meaning: "tending to be made from nouns/names"
> *inchoative*: also a denominative < base: *choum/cohum* "a strap attaching the yoke to the plow" i.e. something used for the first step; meaning: tending to make a beginning
> *gestate*: is a frequentative < *gerere/gestum*, carry

1. incandescent
2. dictation
3. animate
4. elaborate
5. agitation
6. alienate
7. convalesce
8. crescent
9. hesitation
10. peroration (*orare* < *os, or-*, mouth)
11. obliterate
12. obsolescence
13. pulsating
14. finish

15. intractable
16. preventative
17. perish (< *ire*, go)
18. osculation (< *os*, mouth)

B VOCABULARY

An asterisk (*) marks the most productive. Fill in derivatives of each base, except for those in square brackets. The form in parentheses is more commonly used in words from the present base.

aperire, apertum	*open*	> aperient, aperture, apéritif, overt, overture
censere, censum	*assess, rate, estimate*	
* colere, cultum	*till, honor, dwell, worship*	
* credere, creditum	*believe*	
-fendere, -fensum	*strike, hurt*	
[findere], fissum	*split*	
fingere (fig-), fictum	*form*	
fugere, fugitum	*flee*	
fungi, functum	*perform*	
* gradi (-gred-), gressum	*step, walk*	
* habēre, habitum (-hibit-)	*have, hold*	
imitari, imitatum	*copy*	
* jungere, junctum	*join*	
labi, lapsum	*slip*	
* monēre, monitum	*warn*	
* movēre, motum	*move*	
mutare, mutatum	*change*	
* pati, passum	*suffer*	
pingere (pig-), pictum	*mark by incision, tatoo, paint*	
pungere, punctum	*prick, sting*	
[rēri], ratum	*think*	
stinguere, stinctum	*quench*	
struere, structum	*pile up, build*	
tegere, tectum	*cover*	
[texere], textum	*weave, build*	
tingere, tinctum	*dip*	
[tondere], tonsum	*shear, clip, shave*	
* torquēre (tor-), tortum	*twist*	
[vellere], vulsum	*pluck, pull*	
vexare, vexatum	*shake*	
[vovēre], votum	*vow, promise*	

VOCABULARY NOTES

colere/cultum > colony, colonial, cult, cultus, cultivate, culture, cultural, incult, cultigen, but *not* uncouth (from a root meaning "known" and so, "unknown, strange") and *not* colonel (a diminutive of *columna* "a column [of troops])" and *not* occult (from a root meaning "to hide").

habēre/habitum > habile (handy), able, *homo habilis, femina habilis,* habiliment ("clothes"), habilitate ("to supply with the means to do something"), rehabilitate, habit, habitable, habituate, habitue, habitual, habitat (literally "it lives" used at the beginning of descriptions of animals and plants), inhabit, inhabitant, inhibit, inhibition.

movēre/motum, move > move, movement, movie, movable, mobile, automobile, immobile, mob (< *mobile vulgus* "the fickle crowd"), moment, momentum, motor, motif, motive, motion, commotion, emote, emotion, promote, promotion, demote, remote, remove, *mosso* (a musical term meaning "with animation"); but NOT motto (from *muttum,* to grunt, which also yields *mot juste, bon mot,* and is related to the native word mutter, and to Greek *muein* > mystery, myopia); and NOT mote ("a speck of dust" which is of Old English origin).

jungere/junctum, join is from *jugum,* yoke, ridge, which is a cognate of English *yoke* and Greek *zugon.* From *jungere* come: join, enjoin, adjoin, subjoin, conjoin, conjugal, junction, adjunct, juncture, injunction, conjunction, joint, junta; from *jugum* > jugular, conjugate, subjugate.

torquēre/tortum > torque, torment, torsion, tort (something twisted > a legal wrong), contort, retort, extort, distort, torture, tortuous, nasturtium (so named because its pungent odor twists the nose), torch (made of twisted straw), cognate with *queer* and *thwart,* but NOT *torso,* "the trunk" which comes from *thyrsus,* the Bacchic revelers' staff (a word of unknown origin).

monēre/monitum > monitor, monitory, monition, admonition, admonish, premonition, monument, monster (< *monstrum* "a prodigy, warning"), monstrous, muster, demonstrate, monstrance, summon (< *sub-* + *monēre* "warn secretly").

censēre/censum > censure, censor, censorious, census, and recension (a critical revision of a text).

EXERCISES

EXERCISE 8B. 1— AGENT AND ABSTRACT NOUNS: using new vocabulary and new suffixes form one agent [in *-or*] and one abstract [in *-ion* or *-ure*] from each of the following. Use prefixes if you want or need them.

Example: *movēre/motum:* agent: motor; abstracts: motion, promotion, commotion, demotion, emotion

1. monēre
2. censēre
3. imitari
4. struere
5. tegere
6. gradi

EXERCISE 8B. 2—NOUN AND ADJECTIVE SUFFIXES: fill in *ppp* and make up one noun in *-ion* or *-ure* and one adjective in *-ive*, *-ile* or *-ory*. You may use prefixes.
Example: *movēre/motum*: noun motion; adjectives motive, emotive
1. jungere
2. monēre
3. vellere
4. tegere
5. stinguere
6. findere
7. fungi
8. gradi
9. rumpere
10. pellere
11. agere
12. capere
13. fundere
14. ponere
15. dicere
16. emere
17. specere
18. tendere
19. sequi
20. ducere
21. pati

EXERCISE 8B. 3—PREFIXES, VERBS, SYFFIXES: Make up words meaning:
1. act of twisting out
2. act of warning in advance
3. result of joining together
4. tending to pile down
5. result of painting
6. tending to flee
7. one who estimates
8. tending to walk to (or against)
9. result of having continuously
10. tending to perform through
11. tending to believe (use present base)
12. not able to be believed (use present base)

EXERCISE 8B. 4— REVIEW OF NEW VERBS: take apart and define
1. defunct
2. habile
3. aperture

4. censorious
5. credulous
6. credible
7. fictile
8. figment
9. labile
10. tincture
11. depictive
12. offensive
13. fissure
14. dereliction (*linquere, lictum*, leave)
15. culture
16. puncture
17. compunction
18. junction
19. disjunctive
20. destruction
21. constructive
22. restructure
23. votive
24. devotion
25. tonsure
26. commotion
27. protective
28. detector
29. revulsion
30. comprehensive
31. comprehensible
32. fissile
33. extrasensory perception

EXERCISE 8B. 5— REVIEW OF ADJECTIVE-FORMING SUFFIXES: make up one adjective each from the present base and the *ppp* base.
Example: *sequi/secutum* present: sequacious, subsequent; *ppp* consecutive
1. legere/lectum
2. agere/actum
3. facere/factum
4. sentire/sensum
5. loqui/locutum
6. cedere/cessum
7. venire/ventum
8. gradi/gressum
9. capere/captum

10. petere/petitum
11. nasci/natum
12. stringere/strictum
13. tangere/tactum
14. vidēre/visum
15. fari/fatum
16. pati/passum

EXERCISE 8B. 6— REVIEW OF NOUN SUFFIXES: make up one noun from each base
Example: *agere* present: agenda, agility, exigency; *ppp*: actor, action, activity, redaction

1. torquēre/tortum (present combining base: *tor-*)
2. tendere/tensum,tentum
3. stare/statum
4. vidēre/visum
5. loqui/locutum
6. pingere/pictum (pres. combining base: *pig-*)
7. augēre/auctum
8. sentire/sensum
9. currere/cursum
10. capere/captum
11. trahere/tractum
12. mittere/missum
13. legere/lectum
14. mutare/mutatum
15. pati/passum

CHAPTER EIGHT: CHECK LIST

1. Suffixes added to *ppp* base: Fill in meanings and examples
   Noun-forming suffixes
      -or
      -ion
      -ure
      -(t)us/-(s)us
   Adjective-forming suffixes
      -ile
      -ible
      -orious, -ory, -orial
      -ive
   Verb forming suffix: Frequentative
      -at-, -it-
2. Vocabulary

Extra: Explain these words (origins and meanings):

censorship, census
cultivated
creed
graduate
habitat
enjoin
movie
money
construe
textual/textural
retort

WORD GAME: ADD A LETTER[1]

Example: w o r d   w o r l d   clues: verbum, the cosmos

1. _ _ _ _ _ _   to establish as true   _ _ _ _ _ _ _ to write poetry
2. _ _ _ _ _   a sign of the zodiac   _ _ _ _ _ _   a heroic or domineering woman
3. _ _ _ _   dare or resist   _ _ _ _ _   to turn into a god
4. _ _ _ _   volcanic rock   _ _ _ _ _   insect stage
5. _ _ _ _ _   express happiness   _ _ _ _ _ _   likeness
6. _ _ _ _ _ _ plump   _ _ _ _ _ _ _   magniloquent
7. _ _ _ _ _   ethical   _ _ _ _ _ _ deadly
8. _ _ _ _   genuine   _ _ _ _ _   kingly   _ _ _ _ _ _   entertain
9. _ _ _ _ _ _ _   a small joint   _ _ _ _ _ _ _ _ a small piece
10. _ _ _ _   meat of calf   _ _ _ _ _   for sale
11. _ _ _ _ _   a press of people   _ _ _ _ _ _   boasted
12. _ _ _ _ _ did one's sums   _ _ _ _ _ _   confused
13. _ _ _ _ _   have fun   _ _ _ _ _ _   make manifest
14. _ _ _ _ _   respond   _ _ _ _ _ _   edit
15. _ _ _ _ _ _ _   freeing   _ _ _ _ _ _ _ _   enigmatic
16. _ _ _ _ _ _   used to   _ _ _ _ _ _ _   hurt
17. _ _ _ _ _ _ _ _   charged with a crime   _ _ _ _ _ _ _ _ _   pointed out

NOTE

1.Answers: 1. verify, versify 2. virgo, virago 3. defy, deify 4. lava, larva 5. smile, simile 6. rotund, orotund 7. moral, mortal 8. real, regal, regale 9. article, particle 10. veal, venal 11. crowd, crowed 12. added, addled 13. revel, reveal 14. react, redact 15. ridding, riddling 16. inured, injured 17. indicted, indicated

SECTION TWO: LATIN
B. LATIN VERBS

INTERLUDE 3:
REVIEW OF LATIN VERBS, PREFIXES, AND SUFFIXES

A. Suffixes: fill in meaning, tell which base(s) is (are) used with each, give an example:

Noun-forming suffixes
    -ion [pres. base]
        [ppp]
    -or [pres. base]
    -or [ppp] -(t)or -(t)rix (feminine) *aviatrix, creatrix*
    -ble
    -cle
    -cide [added to noun-base]
    -nce, -ncy
    -nd
    -men
    -ment
    -ium, -y
    -ure
    -(t)us/-(s)us
    -nd
    -vore [added to noun bases]

Adjective-forming suffixes
    -acious
    -id
    -ble
    -fic [added to adj., noun bases]
    -ile
    -ive

-ndous
-nt
-orious, -ory, -orial
-ulous
-uous
-vorous
Verb-forming suffixes
    -ate [to noun bases]
    -ate [to *ppp* bases]
    -sc-
    -fy
    -igate

B. Prefixes: review prefixes, concentrating on basic meanings.
An asterisk (*) marks the most productive. Fill in meanings and some derivatives.
    * 1. ab-, a-, abs-
    * 2. ad- > ac- (before *c*, *q*), af-, ag-, al-, an-, ap-, ar-, as-, at-, and a- (before *sc*, *sp*, *st*, *gn*).]
    3. ambi-
    * 4. ante-
    * 5. circum
    6. cis-
    * 7. com- com- before *b*, *p*, *m*; > cor- before *r*; col- before *l*; co- before *h*, *gn* and usually before vowels; con- before all other consonants.
    * 8. de-
    * 9. dis- > di- before voiced consonants; dif- before *f*; sometimes > de- under French influence:
    * 10. ex-, e- > ef- before *f*
    11. extra- (variant, extro-)
    * 12. in-(1) *in* > il- before *l*; im- before *b*, *m*, *p*; ir- before *r*; sometimes en- under French influence.
    * 13. in-(2) *not* > i before *gn*; other changes as in-(1): used mostly with adjective and adverb bases; sometimes with nouns.
    * 14. inter- > intel- before *l*.
    15. infra-
    16. intra-
    17. intro-
    18. juxta-
    * 19. ob- > o- before *m*; oc- before *c*; of- before *f*; op- before *p*.
    * 20. per- > pel- before *l*.
    * 21. post-
    * 22. pre- (< Latin prae-)
    23. preter- (< Latin praeter) past, beyond

* 24. pro-
* 25. re- > red- before vowels
26. retro-
* 27. se- > sed- before vowels
28. sine-
* 29. sub- > suc- before *c*; suf- before *f*; sug- before *g*; sum- before *m*; sup- before *p*; sur- before *r*; sometimes sus- before *c, p, t*.
30. subter-
* 31. super- > sur- under French influence
32. supra-
* 33. trans- > tran- before *s*, sometimes > tra-

List all prefixes that can mean:

    a. not, un-
    b. very, thoroughly

C. Productive Verbs

1) Most productive verbs: fill in meanings of all; give ten derivatives of each; choose one and find thirty derivatives

    1. agere/actum
    2. capere/captum
    3. ducere/ductum
    4. dicere/dictum
    5. gerere/gestum
    6. facere/factum
    7. cedere/cessum
    8. mittere/missum
    9. venire/ventum
    10. tenēre/tentum
    11. legere/lectum
    12. vertere/versum
    13. stare/statum
    14. regere/rectum
    15. vidēre/visum
    16. portare/portatum
    17. ferre/latum
    18. ponere/positum
    19. specere/spectum
    20. tendere/tentum, tensum

2) Choose one and answer these questions:
1. What are the two bases?
2. Is this an -i-stem?
3. Does this verb show vowel reduction?

4. Does it have any unusual forms in English?
5. List thirty derivatives (if possible fifty).
6. Optional: find words from your verb, showing unusual changes.

Example: capere/captum take, seize
    1. cap(i)-/capt-
    2. yes, it is an -i-stem.
    3. yes, -cipi-, -cept-
    4. yes, it has forms in -ceive
    5. capacious captor caption captive captivate captivity capacity deceive deceit incapacitate deception deceptive conceive concept incipient inception inceptive capture perceive conceivable precept preceptor except exception inconceivable conception accept capable incapable contraception conceptual intercept receive recipient imperceptible acceptance reception receptive recapture contraceptive receptacle principal principle participle participial misconception participate participatory acceptable susceptible anticipate perception perceptive exceptional
    6. some unusual derivatives: prince purchase cable caitiff capstan catch emancipate chase conceit occupy recipe recuperate

3) Other important verbs: give meanings and four derivatives
    1. alere/altum
    2. audire/auditum
    3. augēre/auctum
    4. cadere/casum
    5. caedere/caesum
    6. cernere/cretum
    7. claudere/clausum
    8. colere/cultum
    9. currere/cursum
    10. dare/datum
    11. emere/emptum
    12. fingere (fig-)/fictum
    13. fari/fatum
    14. frangere (frag-)/fractum
    15. fundere/fusum
    16. fungi/functum
    17. haerēre/-haesum, haesitare [freq.]
    18. ire/itum
    19. jacere (& jacēre)/jactum
    20. jungere (jug-)/junctum
    21. loqui/locutum
    22. manēre/mansum
    23. migrare/migratum

24. monēre/monitum
25. movēre/motum
26. mutare/mutatum
27. nasci/natum
28. pati/passum
29. pellere/pulsum
30. pendere/pensum
31. petere/petitum
32. ponere/positum
33. prehendere/prehensum
34. premere/pressum (from present base: *imprimatur*)
35. quaerere/quaesitum
36. rapere/raptum
37. scandere/scansum
38. scire [scitum] (from *ppp: plebiscite*)
39. sedēre/sessum
40. sentire/sensum
41. sequi/secutum
42. solvere/solutum
43. struere/structum
44. sumere/sumptum
45. tangere/tactum
46. torquēre (tor-)/tortum
47. trahere/tractum (from present base: *subtrahend*)
48. uti/usum
49. vivere/victum (from *ppp: victuals*)
50. volvere/volutum

4) Take apart and define parts. Example: utile: ut- *use* [pres of *uti/usum*], -ile *able to be*

1. defunct
2. habile
3. aperture
4. censorious
5. credulous
6. credible
7. fictile
8. figment
9. labile
10. tincture
11. depictive
12. offensive
13. fissure

14. dereliction [*linquere, lictum*, leave]
15. culture
16. puncture
17. compunction
18. junction
19. disjunctive
20. destruction
21. constructive
22. restructure
23. votive
24. devotion
25. tonsure
26. commotion
27. protective
28. detector
29. revulsion
30. comprehensive

D. Additional Review
1) Practice Assimilation— change to proper English spellings:
    1. ad-glutinative
    2. com-nive
    3. ad-grieve
    4. ambi-ition
    5. com-rode
    6. com-venient
    7. ad-stringent
    8. ex-fervescent
    9. dis-ferent
    10. com-lect
    11. ex-sist
    12. ex-fect
    13. con-laborate
    14. ad-finity
    15. sub-ference
    16. trans-scription
    17. re-emption
    18. se-ition (ire, itum)
    19. sub-press
    20. inter-lectual
    21. ex-stant

2) Vowel reduction

The major verbs that show vowel reduction when a prefix is added are:
    agere, actum (-ig-)
    cadere, casum (-cid-, -cas-)
    caedere, caesum (-cid-, -cis-)
    canere, cantum (-cent-)
    capere (-io), captum (-cipi-, -cept-) -ceive
    claudere, clausum (-clud-, -clus-) -close
    dare, datum (-dit-)
    facere (-io), factum (-fici-, -fect-) -fy
    frangere, fractum (frag-, -fring-)
    gradi (-gred-), gressum
    habēre, habitum (-hibit-)
    jacere (-io), jactum (-ject-)
    quaerere, quaesitum (-quirere, -quisitum)
    rapere, raptum (-rip-, -rept-)
    salire (-silire), saltum
    scandere (-scendere, -scensum)
    tangere (-ting-, -tig-), tactum
    tenēre, tentum (-tin-, -tent-) -tain

a. Practice Vowel Reduction b. Tell what verb each of these comes from:
    1. pertenent >
    2. resaliency >
    3. contangent >
    4. ascand >
    5. inquaesition >
    6. inhabition >
    7. ingradient >
    8. conjacture >
    9. disaffacted >
    10. incantive >
    11. contracaptive >
    12. percapient >
    13. exagency >
    14. accadental >
    15. exclausionary >
    16. ineffaciency >
    17. indecaesive >
    18. accant >
    19. recaptacle >
    20. surraptitious > (sur- < sub; "secretly")

E. List twenty or more new words you have learned in Part Two, Chapters 5–8.

VOCABULARY VERBS 5–8

Practice parts and meanings. Test each other. Learn one derivative for each base.

A   agere, actum (-ig-) *do, drive, lead*
     alere, altum *grow, nourish*
     aperire, apertum *open*
     audire, auditum *hear*
     augēre, auctum *increase*

C   cadere, casum (-cid-, -cas-) *fall*
     caedere, caesum (-cid-, -cis-) *cut, kill*
     candēre *shine, be white*
     canere, cantum (-cent-) *sing*
     capere (-io), captum (-cipi-, -cept-; -ceive) *take, seize*
     cedere, cessum (-ceed/-cede) *go, yield*
     censere, censum *assess, rate, estimate*
     cernere, cretum *sift*
     clamare, clamatum (-claim) *shout*
     claudere, clausum (-clud-, -clus-; -close) *close*
     colere, cultum *till, honor, dwell, worship*
     condere, conditum *build, store, hide*
     creare, creatum *create*
     credere, creditum *believe*
     currere, cursum *run*

D   dare, datum (-d-, -dit-) *give*
     dicere, dictum *say, speak*
     docēre, doctum *teach*
     ducere, ductum *lead*

E   emere, emptum *buy, procure* (from pres. base *redeem*)
     errare, erratum *go astray*
     esse, futurum *be* (*futurum* is the future participle) essence, futuristic

F   facere (-io), factum (-fici-, -fect-; -fy) *do, make*
     fari, fatum *speak* (present base: *fa-*)
     -fendere, -fensum *strike, hurt*
     ferre (fer-), latum *bear, carry*
     fervēre *boil*
     fidere *trust, rely on*
     findere, fissum *split*
     fingere (fig-), fictum *form*
     flectere, flexum *bend*
     fluere, fluxum *flow*
     frangere (frag-), fractum *break*
     fugere, fugitum *flee*
     fundere, fusum *pour*

fungi, functum *perform*

G   gerere, gestum *carry, wage*
    gradi (-gred-), gressum *step, walk*

H   habēre, habitum (-hibit-) *have, hold*
    haerēre, -haesum (-her-, -hes-) *cling, stick*
    horrēre *shudder, stand stiff*

I   imitari, imitatum *copy*
    ire, itum (present base i-; ppp base it-) *go*

J   jacere (< jacere) *lie* no ppp
    jacere (-io), jactum (-ject-) *throw*
    jacēre *lie* (derived from *jacere*, throw)
    jungere, junctum *join*

L   labi, lapsum *slip*
    legere, lectum *collect, gather, choose, read*
    liquēre *be fluid, be clear*
    loqui, locutum *speak*
    lucēre *shine, be light*
    ludere, lusum *play*

M   manēre, mansum *remain*
    migrare, migratum *move, change one's place of living*
    mittere, missum *send, let go*
    monēre, monitum *warn*
    mordēre, morsum *bite*
    movēre, motum *move*
    mutare, mutatum *change*

N   nasci, natum *be born*

O   oriri, ortum *rise*

P   paenitēre *repent*
    parare, paratum *get, get ready*
    pati, passum *suffer*
    pellere, pulsum *push*
    pendere, pensum *hang, weigh*
    petere, petitum *aim at, seek*
    pingere (pig-), pictum *mark by incision, tatoo, paint*
    placēre, [placitum] *please, be agreeable*
    ponere, positum *put, place*
    portare, portatum *carry*
    posse (pot-) *be able*
    prehendere, prehensum *seize*
    premere, pressum *squeeze*
    pungere, punctum *prick, sting*

Q   quaerere, quaesitum (-quirere, -quisitum) *seek, ask*

R   rapere, raptum (-rip-, -rept-) *snatch*

regere, rectum *move in a straight line, guide, direct, rule*
rēri, ratum *think*
rogare, rogatum *ask*
rumpere, ruptum *break, burst* (derivatives are from the *ppp.*)

S   salire (-silire), saltum *leap, jump*
scandere (-scendere, -scensum) *climb*
scire, [scitum] *know*
scribere, scriptum *write*
secare, sectum *cut*
sedēre, sessum *sit*
sentire, sensum *feel*
sequi, secutum *follow*
servare, servatum *save*
sistere, statum *set, stand*
solēre, solitum *become accustomed*
solvere, solutum *loosen, undo*
specere/spicere, spectum *look at*
stare, statum *stand*
stinguere, stinctum *quench*
stringere, strictum *draw tight*
struere, structum *pile up, build*
studēre *be diligent, be eager, study*
sumere, sumptum *take (up)*

T   tangere (-ting-), tactum *touch*
tegere, tectum *cover*
tendere, tentum/tensum *stretch, spread, aim*
tenere, tentum (-tin-, -tent-; -tain) *hold, keep*
terrēre *frighten*
texere, textum *weave, build*
timēre *fear*
tingere, tinctum *dip*
tondere, tonsum *shear, clip, shave*
torquēre (tor-), tortum *twist*
trahere, tractum *draw, drag*
tremere *quake, tremble*

U   uti, usum *use*
V   vadere, -vasum *go, make one's way*
valēre *be well, be strong*
vellere, vulsum *pluck, pull*
vendere, venditum *sell*
venire, ventum *come*
vertere, versum *turn*
vexare, vexatum *shake*

vidēre, visum *see*
vincere, victum *conquer, win*
vivere, victum *live*
vocare, vocatum *call, use the* vox, voc- (*voice*)
vorare, voratum *devour, eat*
vovere, votum *vow, promise*

ENDGAME: SURPRISES[1]

Match the Latin Verb with the English word derived from it. Answers are below.

1. mob ___	a. habēre (2 answers)
2. monster ___	b. pungere (3 answers)
3. pinto ___	c. pingere (2 answers)
4. junta___	d. gradi
5. point___	e. tingere
6. motif ___	f. fugere
7. summon___	g. texere
8. pun ___	h. credere
9. pimento___	i. aperire
10. arraign___	j. movēre (2 answers)
11. truss___	k. monēre (2 answers)
12. counterpane___	l. vovere
13. nastrutium ___	m. rēri
14. svelte___	n. jungere
15. devout___	o. fingere (2 answers)
16. aperitif ___	p. vellere
17. miscreant___	q. torquēre (2 answers)
18. tissue___	
19. effigy___	
20. feverfew___	
21. able___	
22. feign___	
23. stain___	
24. avoirdupois___	
25. degree ___	

NOTE

1. Answers: 1–j; 2–k; 3–c; 4–n; 5–b; 6–j; 7–k; 8–b; 9–c; 10–m; 11–q; 12–b; 13–q; 14–p; 15–l; 16–i; 17–h; 18–g; 19–o; 20–f; 21–a; 22–o; 23–e; 24–a; 25–d.

SECTION THREE: GREEK WORDS IN ENGLISH

CHAPTER NINE: GREEK WORDS—SIMPLE CHANGES

Greek, like Latin, is an inflected language. The explanations of cases, declensions, verbs, conjugations, principal parts, and so forth, need not be repeated here. Greek nouns and adjectives belong to three declensions with the third (or consonant declension, which has many variations) often showing a change in the nominative so that a second combining form (or base) will be given. The Greek verb is even more complex than its Latin counterpart, often showing vowel changes (vowel gradation) in its various tenses. The important variations in the stem which are used in English derivatives will be given with each verb (Chapter 14).

Since Greek is written in a different alphabet than Latin and English, before Greek words can be borrowed they must first be TRANSLITERATED, that is, changed from one alphabet into the other. It is traditional to change Greek words into Latin, to make them conform to Latin spelling conventions. There is, however, no entirely consistent method of transliteration (especially of Greek names) universally followed by writers of English, so that, for example, the name *Aeschylus* (Latin spelling) will sometimes be seen as *Aischulos* or even *Aiskhulos*, depending on the taste of the writer or editor. Many writers on classical Greek literature, history, or culture prefer the spelling that is closest to the original Greek in sound and appearance and so choose to write the name of the "father of tragedy" in one of the latter two forms.

The Greek words in these chapters will be given in the Roman alphabet in the transliteration closest to the Greek original (as in the second example, *Aischulos*). At the end of this chapter the supplement will give some explanations and exercises on the Greek alphabet and using the Greek dictionary.

Greek also has a definite article which in a Greek lexicon (dictionary, book of words) is given with nouns to indicate gender. The expression *hoi polloi*, "the many, the masses" uses the definite article (in the masculine nominative plural) with the adjective *polloi* (also in the masculine nominative plural[1]) from *polus, pollē, polu*, much, many, which also produces many technical or learned words in *poly-* such as polyhedron, polysyllabic, polygraph, polychrome, polyglot, polygon, polysyndeton, polypody. Sticklers object to using "the" with *hoi polloi*, because *hoi* already means "the." Still we often hear the expression "the *hoi polloi*" and might only bother to raise an eyebrow at the dismisive snobbishness of the term.[2]

A. GREEK INTO ENGLISH

Some Noun and Adjective Endings
Adjectives: If there are three terminations they are for 1) masculine, 2) feminine, and 3) neuter; two terminations are 1) masculine/feminine and 2) neuter.

Typical Adjective Endings:
   2nd–1st declension: -os, -ē, -on; -os, -a, -on; 2nd declension: -os, -on
   3rd declension: -ōn, -on; -ēs, -es
   3rd–1st declension: -us, -eia, -u; -ōn, -ousa, -on

Some typical noun endings are, by gender:
   Feminine: -a, -ē, -(s)is (with many variations in the third declension)
   Masculine: -os, -as, -(t)ēs, -eus, -tēr, -tōr (with variations in the third declension)
   Neuter: -on, -ma (base -mat-), -os (in the third declension, like the -us neuters in Latin, *corpus* and *genus*, for example. Greek *genos* corresponds to Latin *genus*.)
Note: eta (long *e*) = ē; omega (long *o*) = ō

TRANSLITERATION OF GREEK WORDS

1. Rules for making Greek words conform to Latin orthographical and morphological conventions (i.e., rules of spelling and grammar):
   k > c
       krisis > crisis
       But ch, kh represent the Greek letter *chi* (which resembles an X: cf. *chiastic*, forming an X): ch, kh > ch
   u > y (except in diphthongs: au, eu > au, eu; ou > u)
       hupo > hypo (cf. Lat. *sub*: I-E *s* often becomes *h* in Greek)
       huper > hyper (cf. Lat. *super*)
   ai > ae > e [Latin *ae* usually becomes English *e* except in proper nouns]
       Aischulos > Aeschylus
       ainigma > enigma
   ei > e or i
       eironeia > irony (-eia > -y, see below)
       Iphigeneia > Iphigenia (or Iphigeneia)
       Medeia > Medea
   oi > oe > e or i

Oidipous > Oedipus
oiko- > oeco- > eco- (*house*)
koino- > coeno-, ceno- (*common*)
Delphoi > Delphi
ou > u
plouto- > pluto- (*wealth*)
Thoukudides > Thucydides

2. Some of the changes in common noun endings:

Endings are frequently dropped as in derivatives from Latin, but when they are retained it is often in a corresponding Latin form.

-os > -us (second declension ending, masc/fem.)
-on > -um (second declension, neuter)
-ōn sometimes > -o (third declension)
-ē sometimes > -a (first declension)
-eia > -ia (often > -y in English)

Other details of transliteration will be treated in the supplement to this chapter. In proper names the Latin spelling is commonly retained, especially for well-known persons. For less famous individuals either the Latin spelling or an approximation of the Greek (with many variations) may be used. For example, Platon is almost universally spelled Plato in English (but cf. Italian *Platone*, French *Platon*, Spanish *Platon* and the adjective *Platonic*). Another Greek name is variously spelled Euclid when referring to the famous geometer and Euclides or Eukleides when referring to other persons of that name.

EXERCISES

EXERCISE 9A. 1—TRANSLITERATION: Change into Latin spellings and give an English derivative.

Example: *etumologia*, Latin *etymologia*, English etymology (remember that Latin -ia > English -y). Be sure you know what the word ETYMOLOGY means and do not confuse it with the equally fascinating *entomology* (the study of insects).

1. krisis
2. ainigma
3. daimōn
4. dunamis
5. koronē
6. eikōn (image)
7. Mousa (one of nine goddesses of the arts)
8. phoinix
9. phainomena (plural of *phainomenon*, thing seen)
10. papuros
11. psuchē

12. thēsauros (treasure)
13. kalux (pod, cup of a flower)
14. gumnasion
15. gunē, base: gunaiko- (woman)
16. martur (witness)
17. diskos
18. daktulos (digit, finger)
19. hupnos (sleep)
20. polus (many)
21. perimetron
22. peiratēs (brigand < "one who attempts")
23. paralusis (undoing, disabling)
24. sumpatheia (fellow feeling)

VOCABULARY NOTES

Mousa > Muse. Other words from this root are: museum (originally, a shrine of the Muses), music, musicology, museology, and mosaic. To *muse* (ponder over) is not related but comes from *muser* "to sniff around" from Medieval Latin *musum* (snout). *Amuse* is from *muser* with the prefix *ad-* added. *Muzzle* is from *musellum*, a diminutive of *musum*.

krisis is from the verb *krinein*, to judge, to separate (related to Latin *scribere* and *cernere*), and gives us: crisis, epicrisis, critique, criterion (a means of judging, pl. criteria), critic, critical, criticism, hypocrisy, hypocrite, endocrine, exocrine, apocrine, eccrine (excreting externally, as sweat glands), hematocrit (which separates the particulate matter of the blood, *hema, hemato-*, from the plasma).

EXERCISE 9 A. 2 1)—SOME PLACE NAMES. Try to transliterate these into common English spellings. Look up any you do not recognize.
1. Thermopulai (site of a famous battle[3])
2. Aiguptos
3. Surakousai (major city in Sicily)
4. Delphoi
5. Kithairon (mountain near Thebes, famous in song and story)
6. Athenai (the names of Greek cities sometimes are in the plural and end in -s in English)
7. Thebai
8. Lakedaimon
9. Kos

2) PROPER NAMES: transliterate and briefly identify any ten:
1. Kleopatra
2. Sokratēs
3. Thoukudidēs
4. Elektra

5. Kleio (a *Mousa*)
6. Aischulos
7. Alkibiadēs
8. Periklēs
9. Apollōn
10. Bakchos
11. Kalliope (another *Mousa*)
12. Alkaios
13. Sapphō
14. Thaleia (a *Mousa*)
15. Klutaimnestra
16. Hupatia
17. Alkestis
18. Korinna
19. Epikouros
20. Iokastē
21. Oidipous
22. Sophoklēs
23. Hesiodos
24. Homeros
25. Hippokratēs
26. Kritōn (a good friend of Sokratēs)
27. Athēnē
28. Kroisos
29. Aineias
30. Helenē
31. Apasia
32. Hupatia

Choose one or two of the personal names and look up the person in the Oxford Classical Dictionary. Jot down the vital statistics and significance.

CHANGING GREEK WORDS INTO ENGLISH

Greek words come into English in the same ways Latin words do.
1. No change (except in alphabet)
    hubris: violence, excessive arrogance > hubris, hybris
    agapē: love > agape
    ēchō: sound > echo (see if you can find the story of the nymph Echo and her love for Narcissus)
2. The base alone becomes the English word
    dicastēs: member of the jury, judge, > dicast
    humnos: song > hymn
    puxis: boxwood, box > pyx

    diaita: way of living > diet
3. The base + silent *-e*
    thumos: an aromatic herb > thyme; *thumos*, anger, spirit > thymus
    proselutos: one who comes to a place > proselyte
    sphaira: a ball > sphere
4. Changes of endings
    -ia > -y   *etumologia* > etymology
    -eia > -ia > -y   *politeia* > polity
    -tia > -cy   *demokratia* > democracy
5. Irregular changes
    hora, time > hour
    schole, leisure > school
    turannos, king > tyrant
    eleemosunē, mercy, pity > alms (cf. eleemosynary)

EXERCISES

EXERCISE 9A. 3—SOME OTHER IRREGULAR CHANGES: See if you can think of another English word from each of these[4]:
1. paidagogos > *pedant* and _____
2. parabolē > *parlor, Parliament,* and _____
3. archaios > *archive* and _____
4. choros > *choir* and _____
5. aēr > *air, aria* and _____
6. theos > *enthusiasm* and _____
7. nomos (> nomisma) > *numismatics* and _____

EXERCISE 9A. 4—SIMPLE CHANGES: change these to English words. First review the lists of common endings and the list of ways in which Greek words become English. Some will be unfamiliar. Examples:
    axioma (that which is thought worthy) > axiom (base alone)
    kosmopolites (a citizen of the world/cosmos) > cosmopolite (base + silent
      -e)
    aoidē (song) > ode (various, irregular changes take place)
1. thēma (something set, placed)
2. anathēma (something set up)
3. ergon (work)
4. skēnē (tent)
5. kuklos (circle)
6. Akademeia (Plato's school)
7. theatron (place for viewing)
8. sukophantēs (informer)
9. agora (marketplace)

10. angelos (messenger)
11. biblion (book)
12. diakonos (servant, attendant) (cf. diaconate)
13. eironeia (affected ignorance)
14. historia (inquiry)
15. lura (stringed instrument)
16. pompē (a sending > a solemn procession)
17. aiōn (age)
18. tupos (mark)
19. ekleipsis (a leaving out)
20. thronos (armchair)
21. drakōn (serpent: > both a constellation and a common, but fantastical, word)
22. paronomasia (play on words or pun)
23. oinopolēs (wine seller)
24. kinetikos (setting in motion)
25. analogia (proportion)
26. androgunos (man-woman)
27. atomos (uncut, indivisible)
28. epitheton (something added)
29. hilaros (cheerful)
30. paraklētos (summoned to one's aid)
31. hupokritēs (actor)
32. genealogia (tracing of a lineage)
33. Lukeion (a gymnasium at Athens where Aristotle lectured)
34. lukanthropos (a werewolf)
35. asteroeides (starlike)
36. tragoidia (a dramatic genre, sometimes interpreted as "goat song")
37. Ōkeanos (a son of Ouranos and Gē, god of the river encircling the earth)
38. gumnasion (place for exercising < *gumnos*, naked)

B. Vocabulary

aēr	*air*
angelos	*messenger*
anthrōpos	*human being*
astēr, astr-	*star*
axios	*worthy*
biblion	*book*
bios	*life (bio-* and as the ending of a word *-be* as in microbe)
chrōma, chromat-	*color*
daimōn	*spirit, divinity*
eikōn	*image, likeness*
ergon	*work*
ēthos	*custom*

hōra	*time, hour*
kosmos	*order, universe, adornment*
kuklos	*circle*
logos	*word, reason* -logy "science, theory, or study of"
metron	*measure* ; -meter "instrument for measuring"; -metry "measure-ment of"
mimos	*imitator*
philos	*beloved, dear, loving*; philo- "love of"; -phile "lover of"
phonē	*voice*
phōs, phot-	*light*
scholē	*leisure*
sophos	*wise*
theos	*god*
tupos	*mark*

EXERCISES

EXERCISE 9B. 1— DERIVATIVES: Give two or more English derivatives of each of the new vocabulary words.

Examples:

> *ergon* > erg, energy, synergy, ergophobia, ergometer, allergy, demiurge, dramaturgical, liturgy, liturgics, georgic, metallurgy, synergism, surgery, thaumaturgy, ergograph, exergue

> *biblion* > Bible, bibliography, bibliolater, bibliophile, biblioklept, gymnobiblist, biblical, bibliophobe, bibliomania, bibliomancy, bibliopole, bibliotics, bibliotheca (a collection or catalogue of books, cf. French, *bibliotheque*, library). *Biblion* is, in origin, a diminutive of *bublos*, papyrus scroll (or book), so named from the Phoenician port of *Bublos* through which Egyptian papyrus was exported to Greece.

Vocabulary Notes

angelos, messenger > angel, angelic, Angelus, angelology, angelica (an aromatic herb used in medicines and liqueurs), archangel, exangelos (the messenger from the house in a Greek tragedy), evangel (*ev-* = *eu-*, well, good), evangelist, televangelist. *Angelos* is of obscure origin.

anthrōpos, human being (also of obscure origin) > anthropomorphic, anthropocentric, misanthropy, philanthropic, lycanthropy, anthropopathism (the attribution of human feelings to nonhuman things), anthropometry, anthropophage, theanthropic, anthropoid, anthropogenesis, paleoanthropology.

EXERCISE 9B. 2— IDENTIFY BASE WORDS. Choose four and use them in sentences.
Example: bibliophile < *biblio-*, book + *-phile*, lover of: A bibliophile often is met in the library or at an independent bookstore.

1. anthropology
2. chromatotype
3. ergometry
4. aerophile
5. cosmometry
6. philosophy
7. theosophy
8. ethology
9. phonology
10. philology
11. photophile
12. astrology

EXERCISE 9B. 3— MORE DERIVATIVES: Study the vocabulary list; read the definitions of these words; give meaning of base and another word using it:

aeropause, _____ + *pauein* (stop): the region of the atmosphere above which planes cannot fly

anthropic, _____ + ic (of, pertaining to): relating to the era of human life on earth

saprobe, *sapro-* (rotten) + _____ : an organism that is nourished on non-living or decaying organic matter

chromonema (pl. chromonemata), _____ + *nema* (thread): the threadlike core of a chromosome

horary, _____ + the Latin suffix -ary: lasting an hour, occurring once an hour

philander, _____ + *aner, andr-* (man). In Greek *philandros* means "loving men" or "fond of masculine habits" or "fond of one's husband." From the use of the name Philander as a traditional literary lover, however, the word has come to mean "to engage in casual love affairs."

scholia (singular, scholion, Latin *scholium*), _____ + the diminutive suffix: lecture notes, explanatory notes or commentary

phenotype, *pheno-* (< *phainesthai*, appear, seem) + _____ : the observable appearance of an organism as determined by genetics and environment

Distinguish between: archetype and prototype.

CHECK LIST FOR CHAPTER NINE

1. Transliteration: give Roman spellings of: k u ai ei ou oi -os -on -eia
2. Simple changes: list the "rules."
3. Review vocabulary.

SUPPLEMENT TO CHAPTER NINE: THE GREEK ALPHABET

Greek character	Name	Transliteration	Pronunciation
Upper/lower case			
Αα	alpha	a	short: cup; long: father
Ββ	beta	b	b
Γγ	gamma	g, ng	hard, go; ng before g/k/ch
Δδ	delta	d	d
Εε	epsilon	e	short e: bet
Ζζ	zeta	z	sd: wisdom
Ηη	eta	ē	long e: ate
Θθ	theta	th	thing [or t-h]
Ιι	iota	i	short: tin; long: teen
Κκ	kappa	k, c	k
Λλ	lambda	l	l
Μμ	mu	m	m
Νν	nu	n	n
Ξξ	xi	x	ks, x
Οο	omicron	o	short o: pot
Ππ	pi	p	p
Ρρ	rho	r, rh	trilled r
Σσ, ς	sigma	s	s
Ττ	tau	t	t
Υυ	upsilon	y, u	French u
Φφ	phi	ph	phone [or p-h]
Χχ	chi	ch	loch [or c-h]
Ψψ	psi	ps	ps
Ωω	omega	ō	long o: go

The symbol ' is not transliterated, but ' stands for the letter h.
Diphthongs:

αι	> ai, ae, e
αυ	> au
ευ	> ei, e, i
οι	> oi, oe, e, i
ου	> u, ou
ηυ	> eu

EXERCISE 9C.1— GREEK ALPHABET

1). Transliterate into the Roman alphabet and give one English derivative:

1. ἄγγελος   γγ > ng
2. ἀστήρ
3. ἄξιος

4. βιβλίον
5. χρῶμα
6. δαίμων
7. ἔργον
8. ἦθος
9. ὥρα
10. κόσμος
11. κύκλος
12. μέτρον
13. φωνή
14. σχολή
15. τύπος
16. εἰκών

2) Put these into Greek:
1. Aspasia
2. Sapphō
3. Xanthippē
4. Antigonē
5. Ēlectra (first e is long)
6. Thēseus
7. Artemis
8. Astyanax
9. Alkēstis
10. Iphigeneia

3) Transliterate these; choose five and identify them.
1. Κλυταιμνῆστρα
2. Κασσάνδρα
3. Μηδεία
4. Ἕκτωρ
5. Ἀνδρομάχη
6. Ὅμηρος
7. Ἥρα
8. Ἀχιλλεύς
9. Ἱππόλυτος
10. Φαίδρα

4) Put into Greek letters: ē = η; ō = ω
1. chronos (time)
2. philos (loving, dear)
3. gunē (woman)
4. anēr (man)

5. anthrōpos (human being)
6. dēmos (the people)
7. dendron (tree)
8. hēlios (the sun)
9. lithos (stone)
10. xenos (stranger)
11. theos (a god, God)
12. zōon (living thing, animal)
13. bios (life)
14. mētēr (mother)
15. metron (measure)
16. ploutos (wealth)
17. sōma (body)
18. psuchē (soul)
19. logos (word, reason)
20. rhopalon (club) [cf. rhopalic]
21. hulē (wood, material)

Optional: Look up one of these words in a Classical Greek lexicon. The breathing mark [h sound] does not affect alphabetical order (i.e. look up hulē under u, upsilon).

CLIOMETRICS

The use of statistical analysis and data processing in the study of history. From Clio, the Muse of History + metrics (science of measurement). The Muses were not originally "Muses of this or that", but were beautiful singers who accompanied Apollo's lyre and sang for the gods and inspired mortals. Later they were given attributes and particular subjects:

Clio, the Muse of History

Calliope, the Muse of Epic Poetry

Erato, the Muse of lyric and mime

Euterpe, the Muse of lyric and music

Melpomene, the Muse of tragedy

Polyhymnia, the Muse of sacred music and song

Terpsichore, the Muse of choral song and dance

Thalia, the Muse of comedy

Urania, the Muse of astronomy

Hesiod writes (*Theogony*, 75–9):

These things the Muses sang, who have their homes on Olympus,

nine daughtres born of mighty Zeus:

Clio, Euterpe, Thalia, and Melpomene,

Terpsichore, Erato, Polymnia, Urania,

and Calliope: she is the greatest of them all.

WORD GAME: LETTER HUNT

Find the names of Greek or Roman letters in these words or phrases:

alphabet	abecedarium
iotacism	chiasmus
rhotacism	gamma rays
zed	delta [as Mississippi delta]
jot	lambda point
sigmoid flexure	tau cross
alpha and omega	betatron
lambda particle	alphanumeric
Phi Beta Kappa	asigmatic
rhotacism	lambdoidal (suture)
xi particle	chiasmatypy
chiastolite	

What is Y called in French?
What is the formula for the circumference of a circle? For the area of a circle?
What other Greek letters are used in mathematics and physics?

WORDS IN CONTEXT

Nor shall this peace sleep with her; but as when
The bird of wonder dies, the maiden *phoenix,*
Her ashes new-create another heir
As great in admiration as herself.
    Shakespeare, *Henry VIII,* Act 5, scene 5

Clap an extinquisher on your *irony,* if you are unhappily blessed with a vein of it.
    Charles Lamb, *Essays of Elia,* 1823

His locked, letter'd, braw brass collar
Shew'd him the gentleman and *scholar.*
    Robert Burns, "The Twa Dogs," 1786

The few rolls of *papyrus* which the ancients deemed a notable collection of books.
    Edward Bulwer-Lytton, *The Last Days of Pompeii,* 1834

What the energetic *pleonasm* of our ancestors called "a false lie."
    1860, cited in *OED*

Tobacco, divine, rare, superexcellent tobacco, which goes far beyond all their *panaceas*, potable gold, and philosopher's stones, a sovereign remedy to all diseases. But as it is commonly abused by most men . . . 'tis a plague, a mischief . . . hellish, devilish and damned tobacco, the ruin and overthrow of body and soul.

> Robert Burton, *Anatomy of Melancholy*, 1621

NOTES

1. Masculine is used for common (that is, either or both masculine and feminine) gender in Greek as in Latin.

2. *Hoi polloi* is sometimes confused with *hoity-toity* which means "snobbish, pompous, uppity" but the two are nearly opposites.

3. *Stranger, bring this news to the Lakedaimonians: here we lie, obedient to their words.* Simonides, Greek lyric poet of 6th–5th c. B.C.E.

4. Sample answers: 1. pedagogue, pedagogical; 2. parabola, parable; 3. archaic, archaism, archaeology; 4. chorus, choral, chorea, Terpsichore; 5. aerophage, aerobic, anaerobic, aerodynamics, aerometry, aerology; 6. theology, monotheism, polytheism, theosophy, theurgic, theist, henatheism, atheism, apotheosis, theocratic, pantheism, theodicy, theomorphism, theomachy; 7. nomad, economy, autonomy, astronomy, bionomics, binomial, agronomy, gastronomic, ergonomy, metronome.

SECTION THREE: GREEK

CHAPTER TEN: COMPOUNDS FROM TWO NOUN BASES

A. COMPOUNDS FROM TWO BASES

Ancient Greek is rich in compound words. The extensive vocabulary of Greek is one of its characteristic features and has given rise to the expession, "the Greeks had a word for it." And often they did.

Many derivatives from Greek are formed from two noun bases. In such compounds one element usually depends on the other in a genitive or adjectival relationship.

　　misology　　hatred of reason
　　skiaphobia　　fear of shadows
　　archbishop　　first [highest ranking] bishop

The compounds from two bases—whether two nouns, a noun and adjective, or a noun and verb— are the easiest Greek formations for a student of word origins to understand and use. Because Greek itself is so fond of compounding and the methods of forming compounds are already set in Greek, many modern terms, especially technical words, for things and concepts that the ancients did not know, are formed on the analogy of Greek practice.

The most common connecting vowel in such compounds is -o-; but -a- is sometimes used in compounds having a first declension noun as the first element. Nouns of the third declension sometimes retain their own stem vowel but often drop it and add -o-.

Study this list of combining forms commonly used as elements in compounds. Most are derived from nouns, though some are verbal. An asterisk (*) marks the most productive.

* philo-, phil- before a vowel (< Greek, *philos*, loving, dear), "love of"
　　philology, love of *logos*
　　* -phile, "one loving" > bibliophile, lover of books
　　-philous, -philic, "tending to love, having an affinity for, thriving in" > heliophil-

ous (adapted to intense sunlight), acidophilic (thriving in acid)

-philia, "love of, tendency toward, preference for, abnormal attraction to" >
necrophilia (*necro-*, dead body)

-philiac, "one abnormally attracted to" > necrophiliac

* miso- (< Greek, *misos*, hatred), "hate/hatred of"

misology, hatred of *logos*

misocapnist, one who hates smoke

* -meter (< Greek, *metron*, measure), "an instrument for measuring, a measure"

thermometer, an instrument for measuring heat

perimeter, the circumference or measure around

-metry, "the measurement of, science of measuring"

telemetry, measurement from a distance

* -phone (< Greek, *phonē*, voice), "sound, sound emitting device"

telephone, device for emitting sound from far away

-latry (< Greek, *latreia*, service for pay) "worship of"

idolatry, worship of idols

-later "worshiper of" > heliolater, sun worshiper

-latrous, "tending to worship" > chrematolatrous, tending to worship money

*-logy (< Greek *logos*, word), "discourse, speech, the science/theory/study of"

anthropology, the study of mankind; deontology, the study of duties; axiology,
the study of value judgments

*-phobia (< Greek *phobos*, fear), "fear of"

agoraphobia fear of the marketplace/open places

-phobe, "one who fears" > skiaphobe one who fears shadows

*-nomy (< Greek *nomos*, law, custom, usage), "systematized knowledge of, laws
concerning" > astronomy, systematized study of the stars

*-scope (< Greek *skopein*, to look at), instrument for observing

telescope, instrument for observing from afar

-gony, -geny (< Greek *goneia*, generation < *gonos*, offspring, seed), "production
of" > cosmogony, production/creation of the universe

orogeny, the generation of mountains

-genesis (< Greek, *genesis*, birth, origin), "generation, birth"

parthenogenesis, virgin birth

* -onym (< Greek *onoma*, name), "name"

pseudonym, false name; paronyms, words derived from the same root

heteronyms, words spelled the same, but with different meanings and pronunciation: row, row; bow, bow; lead, lead; sow, sow

eponym, a person (real or fictitious) believed to be the source of the name of
a place or thing

-mancy (< Greek *manteia*, prophecy), "telling the future by"

necromancy, divination by means of dead bodies/ghosts

rabdomancy, divining with a rod

-mancer, "one who divines" > pyromancer (< *pur*, fire)

-cracy (< Greek *kratia*, strength, power), "government by"
    democracy, government by the people
-iatry (< Greek *iatreia*, healing), "medical treatment"
    psychiatry, medical treatment of soul/mind
        -iatrist, -iatrician, "physician who treats" > podiatrist, foot doctor
            pediatrician, doctor who treats children
* -graphy (< Greek *graphein*, to write), "a method of writing; a descriptive science"
    iconography, method of drawing images
    geography, descriptive science of the earth
        -graph, "means of writing/drawing; something drawn/written"
        -graphic, "having to do with method of writing/descriptive science"
        -grapher, "one who writes about a field; one who uses a specific means of
            writing or drawing" > monograph; telegraphic; geographer
* -archy (< Greek *archē*, rule, beginning), "government, rule"
    monarchy, rule by one
    arch-, "chief, first" > archbishop
* -mania (< Greek *mania*, madness), "madness, exaggerated craving"
    bibliomania, excessive craving for books
        -maniac, "one displaying such an excessive craving" > pyromaniac

EXERCISES

EXERCISE 10A. 1—CONSTRUCTING WORDS USING TWO BASES: Using the new
combining elements and the vocabulary from the previous chapter (or words given
with the exercises below), make up words meaning:
    Note: The most common connecting vowel for Greek words is -o-.
1. one who fears books
2. systematized knowledge of work
3. study of marks
4. drawing of images
5. instrument to measure rings
6. worship of air
7. instrument for looking at the hour (of birth)
8. divination by stars
9. rule by imitators
10. the production of colors
11. excessive craving for voices
12. instrument for looking at a mask of Bacchus swinging from a tree (use the base
    oscillo- from Latin *oscillum*, small face/mouth)
13. worshiper of books or a book
14. measurement of the earth (*ge, geo-*)
15. one who loves to imitate
16. writing of marks

17. one who fears leisure
18. study of the universe
19. instrument for examining images
20. hate of work

Using the new combining forms and the vocabulary from chapter nine, make up four or more additional definitions and words:

21.
22.
23.
24.

EXERCISE 10 A. 2—DEFINING WORDS USING TWO BASES: what do these mean?

1. ethology
2. astrology
3. astronomy
4. bibliography
5. ergophobia
6. cosmology
7. typography
8. chromatometer
9. axiology
10. mimomania
11. cyclophobia
12. metrophile
13. iconolatry
14. angelography
15. ergomania
16. demonocracy
17. misobiblist
18. misologist
19. misanthrope
20. philanthropist
21. mimeograph
22. cosmography
23. ergonomy
24. chromatography
25. astrogenesis

EXERCISE 10A. 3a— –LOGIES: make up fifty -logies: if you run out use the glossary. Know what the subject of each -logy is.

Need some help? Perhaps there are some here you did not think of:

  agriology, the study of primitive cultures

  agrobiology, the study of plant and animal growth as related to soil

agrostology, the study of grass
doxology, a saying of glory
enology (oenology < *oinos*, wine)), the study of wine
psephology, the study of votes (*psephos*, pebble)
necrology, a word about the dead (i.e., obituary)
lexicology, the study of the making of dictionaries
rhyparology, the study of filth
thanatology, the study of death
palaeoanthropology, the study of ancient humans
papyrology, the study of papyrus documents
phenomenology, the study of things seen
epistemology, the study of knowing
ethology, the study of animal behavior
kinesiology, the study of human body movement
gerontology, the study of aging

EXERCISE 10A. 3b Optional exercise: what do these fear? (Answers below.)
1. triskaidekaphobe
2. skiaphobe
3. scotophobe
4. nyctophobe
5. hypnophobe
6. trichophobe
7. demophobe
8. demonophobe
9. cynophobe
10. capnophobe
11. pyrophobe
12. photophobe
13. heliophobe
14. xylophobe
15. dendrophobe
16. anthophobe
17. anthropophobe
18. agoraphobe
19. necrophobe
20. ornithophobe
21. ichthyophobe
22. arachnophobe
23. zoophobe
24. xenophobe
25. pyrotechnophobe
26. iatrophobe

27. gynecophobe
28. androphobe
29. phobophobe
30. pantophobe

Answers: 1. the number 13; 2. shadows; 3. darkness; 4. nighttime; 5. sleep; 6. hair; 7. the people; 8. demons; 9. dogs; 10. smoke; 11. fire; 12. light; 13. the sun; 14. wood; 15. trees ;16. flowers; 17. people; 18. the marketplace, crowds, or open spaces; 19. dead bodies; 20. birds; 21. fish; 22. spiders; 23. animals; 24. strangers, foreigners; 25. fireworks; 26. doctors; 27. women; 28. men; 29. fear itself; 30. everything.

Some words from the *Grandiloquent Dictionary* by Russell Rocke:

philotheoparoptesism (< *philo- theo- par(a)-* + *optan*, roast *paroptan*, to half roast), "to roast slowly for the love of God" said of heretics and others who have won the displeasure of the hierarchy.

osseocarnisanguineoviscericartilaginonervomedullary, without doubt a sesquipedalian, used to describe (in some detail) the structure of the human body, "made up of bone, flesh, blood, internal organs, cartilage, nerves and marrow." Translated into Greek elements, it becomes the comparatively streamlined, but still polysyllabic, *osteosarcohematenterochondroneuromyelic*.

dystopia, a place as bad as *utopia* is good, a word made up for humorous effect, as if utopia had been coined from *eu-* (good) instead of *ou-* (not, no) + *topos* (place).

B. Vocabulary

An asterisk (*) indicates the most productive. Fill in derivatives.

* algos [-algia]	*pain* > analgesic, nostalgia
anemos	*wind* > anemone, anemophore
[cognate to Latin, *animus/anima* breath, spirit]	
anēr, andr-	*man (male)*
atmos	*steam, vapor*
* chronos	*time*
dēmos	*the people*
dendron	*tree*
ethnos	*nation, people*
gamos	*marriage, sexual union*
* gē [geo-]	*earth*
glōssa/glōtta	*tongue, language*
* gunē, gunaik-	*woman*
haima, haimat- [hem-/hemat-]	*blood*
hēlios	*the sun*
histos	*web, tissue*
* hudōr, hydro-	*water*

* ichthus	*fish*
karpos	*fruit*
kephalē	*head*
* lithos	*stone*
lukos	*wolf*
* mētēr, metro-	*mother*
* morphē	*shape, form*
muthos	*speech, story*
naus	*ship* -naut *sailor*
nekros	*corpse*
nephos/nephalē	*cloud*
* oikos [eco-]	*house, environment*
ornis, ornitho-	*bird*
oros	*mountain*
osteon	*bone*
* pais, paid- [ped-]	*child*
* patēr, patro-	*father*
* pathos	*suffering, experience* -pathy *illness*
petra	*rock*
phōs, photo-	*light*
* polis	*city, city-state*
pous, pod-	*foot*
* psychē	*soul, breath, life*
pur [pyro-]	*fire*
* soma, somato-	*body*
stethos	*chest*
stichos	*line, verse*
taphos	*tomb*
tekton [-tect]	*carpenter, builder*
* technē	*art, skill*
telos [teleo-]	*end*
therapon/theraps	*attendant* therapeia *treatment*
topos	*place*
xenos	*foreigner, stranger*
* zōon	*animal, living thing*

Some additional words with some of their derivatives for use in the exercises:

aitia [etio-]	*cause* > etiology, etiological, etiologist
hupsos	*height* > hypsometer, hypsography
kruos [cryo-]	*frost* > cryotherapy, cryogenics
martur	*witness* > martyr, protomartyr, martyrology
ploutos	*wealth* > plutocrat, plutocracy, plutology
rhiza	*root* > rhizoid, rhizome, rhizopus, rhizogenic

skia	*shadow* > skiaphobe, skiagraphy, squirrel
tokos	*birth* > Theotokos, tocology
xulon	*wood* > xylophone, xylem, xylography, xylose

EXERCISES

EXERCISE 10B. 1: Make up or find two or more words using each of the new vocabulary words, five for those marked with an asterisk (*). Examples:

soma, base: *somat-*, body > chromosome, idiochromosome, schistosome, microsome, somatic, psychosomatic, somatopsychic, somatology, somatogenic (arising within the body), somatotype (physique), somatoplasm (the protoplasm of a body cell)

lithos, stone > lithoid, lithic, lithology, lithography, lithosphere (the earth's rocky crust), Neolithic, Palaeolithic, Mesolithic (Miolithic), monolith, nephrolithectomy, xenolith (foreign stone, that is, a rock foreign to the igneous mass in which it is found), lithiasis (production of bodily stones), litharge (silver stone), lithium (Li), lithophyte (a plant that grows on rocky surfaces), lithotrity and lithotripsy (stone crushing as a surgical procedure); the combining element *-lite* comes from *lithos*, as in phonolite (clinkstone, so named because it clinks when hit), chrysolite (gold stone, also called olivene)

xenos, strange, stranger > xenon (Xe), xenia (hospitality, used in botany with reference to hybrid plants), xenogenesis (supposed generation of offspring unlike the parents), xenogamy (cross-pollination), xenolith, xenophobe, xenophobia, euxenite (good to strangers, used of a mineral containing many strange elements), pyroxene (stranger to fire, of a foreign substance in igneous rock), xenoglossy (the speaking of a foreign language by a person in a trance), Euxine (the Greek name for the Black Sea)

taphos, funeral rites, grave > epitaph (inscription on a gravestone, unlike epithets, epitaphs are unlikely to be hurled), cenotaph (< *kenos*, empty), taphonomy (the study of what happens to bones after death)

EXERCISE 10B. 2—COMPOUNDS

1) Choose 15. Take apart and define or use in a sentence; a good exercise for group work:

1. etiology
2. neuralgia [*neuron*, nerve]
3. anemometer
4. anthropomorphic
5. androgyny
6. atmometer
7. biography
8. dendrochronology
9. ethnocentric

10. misogamy
11. geometrical
12. glossalgia
13. gyniatric
14. demophobia
15. hemophilia
16. heliograph
17. histopathology
18. hydromancy
19. ichthyornis
20. carpomania
21. hydrocephalous
22. cryoscope
23. lithograph
24. martyrology
25. metropolis
26. geomorphology
27. mythomania
28. cosmonaut
29. necropolis
30. economy
31. ornithocracy
32. orogeny
33. nephelolater
34. osteopath
35. pediatry
36. patriarch
37. psychopath
38. petroglyph [*gluphein*, carve]
39. photography
40. plutonomy
41. cosmopolis
42. podiatry
43. psychosomatic
44. rhizomorph
45. pyromancy
46. skiagraphy
47. chromosome
48. stethoscope
49. technocrat
50. stichomythia
51. teleological
52. theocracy

53. cryotherapy
54. Theotokos (*tokos*, birth, birth-giver)
55. topolatry
56. xylography
57. xenophile
58. zoogeography
59. xenoglossy
60. gynecocracy

2) Make up words meaning:
1. one who hates human beings
2. wolf-man [werewolf]
3. government by wealth
4. animal lover
5. wood-voice
6. line measurement
7. light-writing
8. one who fears shadows
9. government by the people
10. study of fish
11. study of the house/environment
12. treatment by the sun
13. worship of steam
14. fear of strangers
15. instrument for measuring time

EXERCISE 10B. 3—REVIEW: Give five or more derivatives from each of the following
1. bios
2. zōon
3. gē
4. psuchē
5. polis
6. sōma
7. ichthus
8. chronos

    Still looking for *-logies*? Perhaps these will help:
        chaology (the study of primal chaos)
        dactylology (communication with sign language)
        ctetology (the study of acquired characteristics)
        agnoiology (the study of ignorance)
        neonatology (the study of newborns)

scatology (the study of excrement or of obscenity)

EXERCISE 10B. 4—IDENTIFYING BASES: give meaning of base word(s); look up any that interest you.
Example: oread, base *oros*, mountain [oread, mountain nymph]
1. anemone
2. gamete
3. philodendron
4. hematoma
5. glossalalia [*lalia*, talk, chatter]
6. gynaeceum
7. helium
8. morpheme
9. ecumenical [< oikos]
10. patriot
11. phosphate
12. petroleum
13. pedagogue
14. empyreal
15. enthusiasm [en + theos]
16. hydra
17. teleost
Optional: Guess what bases these are hiding (answers below):
18. pew
19. squirrel
20. licorice
21. parsley
22. diocese
23. parish
24. talisman
[Answers: 18. *pod-*, foot 19. *skia*, shadow + *ouros*, tail 20. *gluko-*, sweet + *riza*, root   21. *petra*, rock 22-23 *oikos*, house 24. *telos*, end]

EXERCISE 10B. 5— MISCELLANEOUS
1) Give examples of:
1. an etiological myth or story
2. anthropomorphism
3. a gloss
4. a patronymic
5. a matronymic
6. a plutomaniac
7. a megalopolis
8. stichomythia (Hint: it means line by line dialogue in a play)

2) What are these concerned with?
1. onomastics
2. aeronomy
3. chromatogenesis
4. scopophiliac
5. seismography
6. ecesis (*oikesis*)

CHECKLIST FOT CHAPTER NINE

1. Common compounding nouns
2. New Vocabulary

Test yourself with this review. Give meaning of bases and combining elements and give another word using each. Examples:

1. *astromancy* from the base *aster*, star > asterisk, aster, asteroid, astronomy, astrology, catasterism, diaster, disaster + *-mancy*, foretelling the future by means of > necromancy, pyromancy, rhabdomancy, nephalomancy, cephalomancy, bibliomancy, stichomancy, oneiromancy (with dreams), chiromancy (= palmistry), podomancy

2. *xenogenesis* < *xenos*, foreigner, stranger > xenophile, xenogeography + *-genesis*, birth, generation, origin of > orogenesis (mountains = orogeny), biogenesis, anthropogenesis, frontogenesis (development of a weather front, < frons, front-, brow, forehead), cosmogenesis, asterogenesis, pyrogenesis, pathogenesis, paragenesis

_____ 1. astromancy _____
_____ 2. xenogenesis _____
_____ 3. misanthrope _____
_____ 4. philodendron _____
_____ 5. photometry _____
_____ 6. stethoscope _____
_____ 7. histology _____
_____ 8. mythomaniac _____
_____ 9. ichthyometer _____
_____ 10. cosmonaut _____
_____ 11. patriarchy _____
_____ 12. metronym _____
_____ 13. xylography _____
_____ 14. theogony _____
_____ 15. aerolatry _____
_____ 16. taphonomy _____
_____ 17. gynecophobe _____
_____ 18. podiatry _____

_____ 19. theocracy _____
_____ 20. lithographer _____

Some words from *arche/archein*: archaic, archaism, archaeology, archaeopteryx, Archeozoic, Archean, archbishop, archiepiscopate, archdeacon, archidiaconate, archpriest, archdiocese, archimage (cf. Magi), archduchess, archduke, archfiend, archdevil, exarch, archipelago, architect, architrave, archives, autarchy, menarche, archon, matriarch, patriarchate, archetypical, archenteron

---

WORDS FROM GREEK MYTHOLOGY AND CULTURE

1. Explain why:
The House of Atreus is not a good name for a family-style restaurant.
Leda and the Swan, *Europa and the Bull*, *Pasiphae's Pet* are not proper titles for children's books about people and animals.
The *Oresteia* might not be well-received on Mothers' Day.
Aulis may not be the ideal spot for a father/daughter reunion.
Perseus (in John Barth's *Chimera*) is credited with founding and filling the first sculpture museum.
Cronus had gastralgia on his youngest son's birthday.
An aircraft named Icarus does not inspire confidence.

2. What are these:
Trojan Horse
The Judgment of Paris
The Wrath of Achilles
The Labors of Heracles
Penelope's Web
The Seven against Thebes
Philoctetes' Cave
The Sirens' Song
The Sphinx's Riddle
Achilles' Heel
A Procrustean Bed
Amazonomachy
Batrachomyomachy
Nephelococcygia

3. IN SEARCH OF. . . Find twelve Olympian Gods in this puzzle:
Hint: The gods in question are: Aphrodite, Apollo, Ares, Artemis, Athena, Demeter, Dionysus, Hephaestus, Hera, Hermes, Poseidon, Zeus.

```
O R E H N O E H T N A P Z E G
A L M A H E P H A E S T U S O
P O S I E D E E P R A E E E H
H E U Z R R N R P O T Z S R C
R E T E M E D A O S H E P A R
O L P E A P O L L O E U M H A
D O S O N I E D O P N S I I E
I B A A L A S A T N A A N A S
T H E M E S U S Y N O I D R D
E X N O D I E S O P G D R A S
```

The Greeks had a word
for getting relief from debt:
it's *seisachtheia*.
[σεισάχθεια: *seis-*, shake, see seismic; *achthos*, burden; *-eia*, act of]

SECTION THREE: GREEK

CHAPTER ELEVEN: GREEK ADJECTIVES USED IN ENGLISH

A. VOCABULARY

Study these Greek adjectives. They are mostly used as first elements in compounds. Concentrate on those marked with an asterisk (*). The usual combining forms are given in brackets.

akros [acro-]	*topmost*	
* allos [allo-]	*other*	
aristos [aristo-]	*best*	
* autos [auto-]	*self*	
axios [axio-]	*worthy*	
barus [bary-, bari-, baro-]	*heavy* -*bar* a unit of pressure	
bathus [bathy-, batho-]	*deep*	
brachus [brachy-]	*short*	
etumos [etymo-]	*true*	
eurus [eury-]	*wide*	
gumnos [gymno-]	*naked*	
* heteros [hetero-]	*other, one of two*	
hieros [hiero-]	*holy*	
* holos [holo-]	*whole*	
homos [homo-]	*one and the same*	
homoios [homeo-, homoio-]	*like*	
hugros [hygro-]	*wet, moist*	
* idios [idio-]	*one's own, peculiar*	
* isos [iso-]	*equal*	
* kainos [ceno-, caeno-; -cene]	*new*	
kakos [caco-]	*bad, ugly*	
kalos [kal-, calo-, calli-]	*beautiful*	
kenos [ken-, ceno-]	*empty*	

koinos [ceno-, coeno-; -cene]   *common*
* makros [macro-]   *long*
* megas, megal- [mega-, megalo-; -megaly]   *big*
* mikros [micro-]   *small*
* monos [mono-]   *alone, only, single*
murios [myrio-]   *countless, 10,000*
* neos [neo-]   *new*
oligos [oligo-]   *few*
orthos [ortho-]   *straight*
oxus [oxy-]   *sharp*
* palaios [paleo-, palaeo-]   *old*
* pas, pant- [pan-, panto-]   *all*
platus [platy-]   *wide, broad*
* polus [poly-]   *much, many*
      pleion [plio-, pleo-]   *more, greater*
      pleistos [pleisto-, plisto-]   *most, greatest*
* protos [proto-]   *first*
* pseudes [pseudo-]   *false*
stenos [steno-]   *narrow*
stereos [stereo-]   *solid, firm*
* tele [tele-]   *far away* (an adverb)
thermos [thermo-]   *warm, hot*
trachus [trach-, trachy-]   *rugged, harsh*
xeros [xero-]   *dry*

EXERCISES

EXERCISE 11A 1— USING THE ADJECTIVE BASES: Form words meaning:
1. fear of high places [i.e., topmost things]
2. other writing [a signature made by one person for another]
3. rule by the "best"
4. self-law [i.e., the quality of being self-governing]
5. instrument for measuring weight [pressure]
6. deep rock
7. short headed [use suffix -*ic*]
8. truth of words
9. priestly [holy] government
10. whole writing
11. peculiar worship
12. of equal time [meaning, "equal in duration"]
13. recent birth or generation
14. naked seed [seed = *sperma*]
15. of other shape

16. of the same kind
17. instrument for measuring humidity
18. peculiar worship
19. ugly sound
20. new word usage [usage = *-ism*]
21. empty tomb
22. large o [o = *o*]
23. small universe
24. single rule [government by one]
25. government by a few
26. straight writing
27. sharp tone [tone = *tonos*]
28. study of old life
29. all-imitator
30. [one speaking] many tongues
31. first witness
32. false name
33. love of wisdom
34. dry writing
35. beautiful writing

EXERCISE 11A 2— VOCABULARY PRACTICE: give opposites of:
Example: calligraphic, opposite: cacographic
 1. heterodoxy [*dox-*, opinion]
 2. microcosm
 3. allogamy
 4. cacophony
 5. allopathy
 6. homogeneous
 7. polyphone
 8. monochrome
 9. misology
10. calligraphy
11. omicron
12. paleocene

EXERCISE 11A 3—MORE PRACTICE WITH ADJECTIVES: define parts; Choose 10 and give meaning of the whole word or use it in a sentence.
 1. acromegaly
 2. acropolis
 3. allogamy
 4. autoecious
 5. isobar

6. bathymetry
7. etymography
8. eurybathic
9. brachylogy
10. gymnobiblism
11. heterology
12. hieroglyph [*gluphein*, carve]
13. Holocene
14. homeopathy
15. hygroscope
16. idiolatry
17. isotope
18. pleistocene
19. kaleidoscope [*eidos*, form, what is seen]
20. caceconomy
21. cenobiarch
22. megalomania
23. omicron [*o* = o]
24. macron
25. monologue
26. myriapod
27. oligocene
28. orthoepy [*epos*, word]
29. paleontology [-*ont*-, being]
30. pantheon
31. platypus [*pous, pod*-, foot]
32. polyphone
33. prototype
34. gymnosophist
35. theosophy
36. stenography
37. stereophonic
38. stereoscope
39. isotherme
40. trachea
41. xerophil
42. telemetry
43. polychromatic
44. gymnophilia
45. holograph
46. isosceles [< *skelos*, leg]
47. pliocene
48. megalomorph

49. monoecious [< *oikos*]
50. orthoscope

EXERCISE 11A 4 —PRODUCTIVE ADJECTIVE BASES: Make up or find five words using each of these:
1. autos
2. protos
3. megas
4. micros
5. macros
6. monos
7. polus
8. pseudes
9. tele
10. palaios
11. neos
12. allos
Examples:
pas (all) [bases pan-, panto-]: pantomime, panacea, pantheon, pancreas, panoply, panegyric, pangenesis, pandemic, pandect, pandaemonium, panorama, pantograph, pantothenic acid [from *pantothen*, from all sides: -*then* adv. suffix], Pan-American, Pan-Hellenic

heteros (other, different): heteronym, heteromorphous, heterogeneous, heterogamy, heterosexual, heterodox, heterophyllous (*phulla*, leaves), heterophyte, heteroplasty, heterotrophic, heterosporous, heterochromatic (variegated)
heterodyne: having alternating currents
heteroecious: living on different hosts (of parasites)
heterogenous: originating outside the body
heterography: inconsistent system of spelling
heterogynous: having two different types of female
heterology: lack of correspondence
heteronomous: subject to external laws (not autonomous)
heterosis: increased strength through cross-breeding

isos (equal): isobar, isosceles, isotherm, isotone, isotope, isomorphism, isogram, isochromatic, isomer, isochronal, isoclinal, isodynamic, isogamete, isopoda, isometric, isogon (-*gon*, angle); isogloss (a boundary marking the area in which a given linguistic feature is present); isohel: a line connecting areas with equal sunlight

platus (wide): platy (a fish), platyhelminth (a flatworm), platyrrhine (having a broad nose), platypus, plateau, plate, platen, platform, platitude, platinum, plaice, plane tree (< *platanos*), and, through *plateia* (feminine of *platus*, with *hodos* "road, way, street" understood), place, plaza, piazza.

EXERCISE 11A 5.—REVIEW VOCABULARY: find two or more words using each new adjective. Some examples:

1. To help you distinguish *kainos, kenos, koinos*:

   kainos, new > Cenozoic, Holocene, Pleistocene, Pliocene, Miocene, Oligocene, Eocene, Paleocene, cenogenesis, kainite. Cognate to *recent* from Latin.

   kenos, empty > cenotaph, kenosis

   koinos, common > Koine, cenobium, cenobite, cenobiarch, epicene, coenocyte, coenurus. Cognate to Latin *cum* (with; cf. prefix *com-*)

2. Other examples:

   akros > acrophobia, acronym, acrobat, acrocarpous (bearing fruit on top), acrodont (having rootless teeth that are fused to the jaw), acrogen (a plant in which all growth is from the tip of the stem, as a fern), acromegaly (enlargement of the extremities), acropolis, acrostic (< *stichos*, line).

   hieros > hieroglyphic, hieratic, hierarchy (a body of people classified by rank, the clergy by ranks), hierocracy (government by the clergy), hierology (sacred literature), hierogram (a sacred symbol), hierodule (a temple slave), hierophant (one who officiates at the revelation of sacred things to initiates)

   idios > idiot, idiom, idiomorphic, idiopathy, idiosyncrasy, idiolect. idioplasm not to be confused with *ideo-* which indicates "idea, form" (ideology, ideogram, ideologue)

   stenos > stenographer, stenophagous, stenothermal

   stereos > stereo, stereophonic, stereobate (a solid base), stereochemistry, stereochromy, stereogram (a solid diagram or picture), stereotype, stereoscope, microstereoscopic, steroid, cholesterol, ergosterol, stereopticon

EXERCISE 11A 6—WORD-WORDS: Give examples of:

Example: *acronyms*: POSSLQ[1] (Person of Opposite Sex Sharing Living Quarters, coined by the United States Census Bureau); PESFA (Palouse Empire Science Fiction Association); RADAR (RAdio Detecting And Ranging); WASP (White Anglo-Saxon Protestant or Women Airforce Service Pilots); NOAA (National Oceanic & Atmospheric Administration); NATO (North Atlantic Treaty Organization); MADD (Mothers Against Drunk Driving; FOMO (Fear Of Missing Out).

1. heteronyms
2. allegory (allo- + *agoreuein*, speak publicly < *agora*, public space, marketplace)
3. oxymoron (*oxy-* + *moros*, foolish)[2]
4. cacoepy
5. cacography
6. brachylogy
7. homographs
8. homonyms
9. homophones

10. pseudonym
11. heterography

New nouns used in the exercises

chthon *earth*
dike *justice*
epos *word*
kolla *glue*
kreas *flesh, meat*
meros *part*
moros *fool*
odous, odont- *tooth*
sarx, sark- *flesh*
skelos *leg*
sperma, spermat- *seed*
tonos *tone, accent*

Use each of these word elements in an English word. If you cannot think of any, here are some hints:

– chthonic, autochthonous, allocthon
– dicast, dicastery, Eurydice, theodicy, syndic
– epic, cacoepy, orthoepy
– colloid, collotype, protocol
– pancreas, creosote
– isomer, polymer, meropia, allomerism
– moron, oxymoron
– conodont, orthodontia
– sarcophagus, sarcoma
– isosceles, triskelion (not skeleton < *skeletos*, dried up)
– gymnosperm, spermatazoa
– atonal, tonic, oxytone, monotonous

VOCABULARY NOTE

brachus, short, is cognate to the Latin *brevis*. Words in *brachy-*, such as brachylogy, brachycephalic, brachydactylic, brachyuran, brachypterous, are derived from it. From the comparative comes *brachion*, "the upper arm" < "shorter" (as opposed to the longer forearm) and such words as brachiopod, brachiosaur ("arm foot" and "arm lizard" respectively), brachial, brachiate. The superlative is *brachistos* > brachistochrone ("the shortest time").

EXERCISE 11A 7— INTERESTING WORDS USING NEW VOCABULARY: choose 3 or 4 and find their origins and meanings:

1. elixir
2. sophomore
3. autarky
4. Jerome

5. hoi polloi
6. pancreas
7. panacea
8. minster [as in Westminster]
9. autacoid
10. Eurydice
11. idiot
12. place
13. panoply
14. panegyric
15. protocol
16. cholesterol
17. phylloxera
18. xerox
19. barium
20. coenurus (*oura*, tail)
21. autochthonous
22. cacoepy
23. oxymoron (a sharp piece of foolishness, *e.g.*, old news, lowly pomp, modern classic)
24. coenosarc
25. etymon
26. pseudepigrapha
27. autopsy [*opsis* sight]
28. gymnosophist

CHECK LIST FOR CHAPTER TEN

1. Greek adjectives: review; use each in a word
2. New words in lesson: learn interesting ones and use them in sentences.

B. GREEK & LATIN NUMBERS

	Greek	Latin
half	hemi-	semi-, sesqui- (one half more)
one	hen-, en-	unus
first	proto-	primus
single	mono-	solus, unicus
two	di-, dy-	duo
second	deutero-	secundus
in two	dicho-	
double	diplo-	duplex
three	tri-	tres, tria

four	tetra-	quattuor, quadri-
five	pente-	quinque, quint-
six	hex-	sex, sext-
seven	hepta-	septem
eight	okto-	octo
nine	ennea-	novem, nonus (ninth)
ten	deka-, deca-	decem
twenty	icos-	viginti, vicen-, viges-
hundred	hecato-	centum
thousand	chili-, chilo-, kilo-	mille
number	arithmo-	numerus
angle	-gonia, -gon	
plane [seat]	-hedron	
line	-gram	linea
many	poly-	multus
few	oligo-	pauci
and, plus	kai	et, -que

EXERCISES

EXERCISE 11B 1—GREEK NUMBERS: tell how many:

triskaidekaphobia	dodecahedron
hexapolis	hemisphere
diplopia	chiliast
pentagon	ennead
triglyph	hemistich
monograph	kilometer
hexagram	Pentateuch
trilogy	distich
triptych	oligarchy
pentathlon	octohedron
decalogue	hecatomb
dichotomy	hexameter
tetrarchy	Deuteronomy
protagonist	deuteragonist
tritagonist	diplomat

Some interesting words derived from Greek numbers: diploma, hectare, enosis, dimity, hendiadys, hyphen, trapezoid, Pentecost, tetra, trivet

EXERCISE 11B 2—HOW MANY YEARS?
    vicennial
    centenary
    sesquicentennial

millennium
biennial
decennial (decade is from Greek)
quinqennium
quincentenary
quinceañera (*quince*, Spanish, fifteen < *quindecim*, Latin, fifteen)
quadrennial
nonagenarian (< *nonaginta*, ninety)

NUMBERS GAME: ORDINAL/CARDINAL IN GREEK & LATIN
Match cardinals with ordinals of the same rank and language:

1. Proto-Geometric   a. quinquennium
2. Deuteronomy   b. sexpartite
3. tritagonist   c. biceps
4. primogeniture   d. enotic
5. second-guess   e. trilateral
6. tertiary   f. December
7. quartan fever   g. quadrivium
8. quintessential   h. duopsony
9. sextant   i. unitarian
10. decimal   j. triarchy

CADRE, a small well-trained group from which a larger organization can be built, is from Latin *quadrum*, a square > Italian *quadro*, a frame. QUARRY, a pit from which stone is excavated is also from Latin *quadrum*. QUARANTINE, a period of confinement, is from Italian *quaranta*, forty < Latin *quadraginta,* forty.

ACADEMY

With *the*: the academic community, higher education, a society of artists and/or scholars. A secondary, college-preparatory, or military school; an institution ranked between a college or university and a school.

The Academy: Plato's school, the followers of Plato, or their philosophy. From Greek *Akademeia* (Akademia), a gymnasium near Athens where Plato and his associates talked, later divided into the old, middle and newer Academy. The place was named after the obscure Attic hero *Akademus*.

"Groves of Academe" comes to us from the Roman poet Horace:

inter silvas Academi quaerere verum, Epistles 2.2.45.

John Robinson, *Archaeologia Graeca* (1807):

The Academy . . . was a large enclosure of ground which was once the property of a citizen of Athens named Academus. Some however say that it received its name from an ancient hero. [OED]

WORDS IN CONTEXT

> . . . *Philologists* who chase
> A panting syllable through time and space,
> Start it at home, and hunt it in the dark,
> To Gaul, to Greece, and into Noah's ark.
>   William Cowper, "Retirement," 1782

Histories make men wise; *poets*, witty; the *mathematics*, subtle; natural *philosophy*, deep, moral, grave; *logic* and *rhetoric* able to contend.
        Francis Bacon, *Essays*, 1625

Hardy became a sort of village *atheist* brooding and blaspheming over the village *idiot*.
        G. K. Chesterton, *The Victorian Age in Literature*, 1913

NOTES

1. A hint about how to pronounce POSSLQ as a word is given in this rhymed couplet by Charles Osgood from his poem "My POSSLQ": "There's nothing that I wouldn't do / If you would be my POSSLQ."

2. For some seriously funny lists of oxymorons (or oxymora) see:
        http://www.oxymoronlist.com/ and http://literarydevices.net/oxymoron/

SECTION THREE: GREEK

CHAPTER TWELVE: GREEK SUFFIXES

A. NOUN- AND ADJECTIVE-FORMING SUFFIXES

-ic, -tic "pertaining to, having to do with"
> *ethnic*, having to do with a people or nation
> *cosmetic*, having to do with beautification

-ac used instead of -*ic* if an -*i* immediately precedes: "pertaining to, having to do with"
> *cardiac*, having to do with the heart

-ics [Greek, -*ika*, neut. pl.], "things having to do with" > "art, science, study of" [usually used with a singular verb]
> *acoustics*, study of sounds (used with a singular verb); things that are heard, the effect of sound in a place (with a plural verb in the second sense)
> *physics*, study of nature [< *phy-*, grow]

-ical < -*ic* + -*al* (from Latin): "pertaining to, having the nature of"
> *political*, pertaining to citizens/having to do with the relationship of citizens to the state (*polis*)

-oid, "resembling, like, shaped"
> *android*, [thing that is] man-shaped; *thyroid*, door-shaped (< *thura*)
> *factoid*, (< Latin *factum*, thing done) originally, a "fact-like, but inaccurate or untrue, item, presented by the media as a fact that is accepted as fact" has come to have the additional meaning of "a small, but interesting piece of information" from its use with this meaning by CNN Headline News. A more etymologically accurate word for that would be *factule*.

-ite, "one connected with, inhabitant of; a commercial product, a mineral"
> *sybarite*, an inhabitant of Sybaris (one devoted to luxurious living; a hedonist)
> *lucite* (< Latin *lux, luc-*, light), a clear, transparent) commercial product
> *Joesmithite*, a mineral named after Joe Smith

-ism, "the belief in, profession or practice of"

hylozoism, belief in connection of life and matter

-ist, "one who believes in, professes, or practices, a follower of"

   dramatist, one who makes plays

-ast, "one who does or practices, one who believes in"

   dicast, one who does justice, judge, juror

   ecdysiast, stripper

   iconoclast, one who breaks images

-isk, -iscus, "small"

   asterisk, a little star

   meniscus, a little moon

-ia, -y, act, state of [abstract noun forming suffix]

   polity, state of being a citizen: relation of citizens to the state

   utopia, no place (*ou*, not)

-sis, "act, state, condition of"

   kenosis, condition of being emptied

   thesis, act of putting, setting

-m, -me, -ma [base, -mat-], "result of"

   theorem, result of observing

   theme, result of setting

   plasma, result of forming

   mathematics, things having to do with the result of learning

And one more suffix: *-aster* a diminutive suffix from Latin that implies inferiority; "one who/that which has pretenses or dabbles in something"

   poetaster (a versifier), philosophaster (a false philosopher), criticaster (a poor critic), oleaster (a worthless olive).

EXERCISES

EXERCISE 12A. 1— USING SUFFIXES: make up or find at least three words using each suffix: Examples:

-isk, *-iscus*, small > asterisk, basilisk (a mythical serpent, "little king"), obelisk (a little spit), meniscus (small moon, crescent shaped body).

-oid, like > android, gynecoid, humanoid, anthropoid, droid, odontoid, crystalloid, planetoid, spheroid, adenoid, asteroid, thyroid, pyroid, colloid, dendroid, sarcoid.

-ast, one who does > iconoclast, dynast, pederast, dicast, osteoclast, gymnast, ecdysiast, scholiast, enthusiast. Words in *-plast* and *-blast* are not true *-asts*.

-ma, result of > plasma, protoplasm, coma, comma, axiom, anathema, biome, cinema, stigma (pl. stigmata), problem, lemma, pragmatic, dogma, dogmatic, drama, dramatic, gram, diagram, polygram, epigram, anagram, program, poem, rheum, schism, schismatic, enema, asthma, enigma, panorama, chrism, scheme, rhematic (pertaining to word formation).

EXERCISE 12A. 2—WORD FORMATION: using vocabulary from previous lessons, make up words meaning:

1. one who studies causes
2. one who studies winds
3. human-like
4. one who studies [what is] worthy [i.e., value judgments]
5. one afflicted with a mad desire for books
6. having to do with many colors
7. having to do with time
8. things having to do with written records concerning the people [i.e., populations]
9. having to do with nations
10. things having to do with customs
11. earthlike
12. one having many marriages
13. fishlike
14. having to do with the universe
15. having to do with rings
16. stonelike
17. things having to do with measures
18. state of single marriage
19. act of measuring earth
20. one who studies stories
21. one who studies birds
22. having to do with the birth of mountains
23. things having to do with the healing of children
24. having to do with one's father's name
25. of the study of the soul
26. belief in many gods
27. of/having another form
28. of recent life
29. of beautiful writing
30. having solid voice
31. toothlike
32. of suffering [experience] from afar
33. things having to do with the law of the household
34. measurements of the "Muse of History" (= Clio)
35. of government by a few
36. one concerned with the systematized study of burial

EXERCISE 12A. 3—WORD ANALYSIS: take apart and define:

1. chthonic
2. epic
3. oxytonic

4. orthodontist
5. necrosis
6. chiliast
7. android
8. misoneism
9. macrobiotic
10. kenosis
11. cryogenics
12. geopolitics
13. zodiac [< *zodiakos kuklos*] [< *zodion*, diminutive of *zoon*]
14. asterisk
15. gymnast
16. necrographist
17. axiologist
18. demotic
19. sophism
20. telepathy
21. monomaniac
22. typographical
23. prototypical
24. theism
25. telekinesis [< *kinein*, move]

EXERCISE 12A. 4—WORD FORMATION: find words from these bases using as many of the new suffixes as you can:

1. mimos
2. axios
3. chrōma, chromat-
4. ethos
5. cosmos
6. astēr
7. scholē
8. tupos
9. oikos
10. psuchē
11. hupnos [sleep]

Examples: *anthropos* (human being): anthropoid, philanthropic, philanthropist, misanthropy, anthropological, anthropomorphism, anthropopathism, anthropo-genesis, anthropophagy, anthropophobia.

graphein (write): pseudepigraphical, program, epigrammatic, graphics, graphologist, graphite, agraphia, graptolite, epigraphic, topography, tachygraphy, grammatical (grammar, glamor), brachygraphy.

B. VOCABULARY

Go over these words; concentrate on those marked with an asterisk (*)

* agros	*field, land* > agronomy, onager	
angos [angio-]	*vessel* > angiosperm, angioma	
*anthos	*blossom, flower* > anthology, anthesis, anther	
chemeia [chemo-]	*art of alloying metals; chemicals, chemical reactions*	
chloros	*green*	
chrusos	*gold*	
deinos [dino-]	*terrible*	
elektron	*amber*	
eremos	*lonely, desert*	
gala, galakto-	*milk*	
helix, helico-	*spiral*	
* hippos	*horse*	
hoplon	*armor*	
hugiēs	*healthy*	
* hulē	*material* [as suffix, -*yl* > ethyl, vinyl]	
* hupnos	*sleep*	
husteros	*later, behind*	
katharos	*clean, pure*	
keras	*horn*	
kolla	*glue*	
kuōn, kun-	*dog*	
magos	*enchanter, wizard*	
mēchanē	*contrivance, machine*	
mitos	*thread*	
oura	*tail*	
pelagos	*sea*	
phrēn [sometimes fren-]	*midriff, diaphragm, mind*	
* phulē	*tribe*	
* phullon	*leaf*	
polemos	*war*	
potamos	*river*	
* rhētōr	*orator*	
rhodon	*rose*	
sauros	*lizard*	
sklēros	*hard*	
* sema, semat-	*sign, signal*	
stear	*fat*	
toxon	*bow and arrows* > *arrow poison* > *poison*	
zumē	*yeast*	

PERIPHRASTICS are rewritten proverbs, maxims, or clichés with sesquipedalian words and pretentious phrases substituted for the energetic and epigrammatic expressions of the originals, for example:

—*Let it be interdicted to apply a stomatoscope to a donated hippic quadruped.*

—*A hiatus quickly develops between a fatuous or moronic individual and his (or her) pelf.*

—*A bursoklept obtains merely quisquilious matter from me.*

—*Chronotherapy is the optimal treatment for every trauma.*

EXERCISES

EXERCISE 12B. 1—USING THE NEW VOCABULARY: take these apart and define parts

1. colloid (< *kolla*)
2. agronomic
3. anthology
4. tyrannosaurus
5. intergalactic
6. phrenetic
7. sematic
8. hypnosis
9. hylozoism
10. hoplite
11. chemotherapy
12. chlorosis
13. helicoid
14. hipparch
15. cynophile
16. mitosis
17. polemics
18. eremite
19. rhetorical
20. panoply
21. catharsis
22. dinokeras
23. magic
24. phylum
25. sclerosis
26. chrysanthemum
27. electrotype
28. angiosperm
29. toxemia
30. stearic
31. phylogeny

EXERCISE 12B. 2—WORD FORMATION: make up words meaning:
1. terrible lizard
2. river horse
3. fear of dogs
4. passion for horses
5. tree rose
6. leaf green
7. poison-like
8. fish lizard
9. having to do with cleaning
10. state of flowering
11. study of vessels
12. leaflike

EXERCISE 12B. 3— INTERESTING WORDS AND NAMES DERIVED FROM THE NEW VOCABULARY: choose one or two and find out what they mean and how they come to be used as they are.
1. Hygeia
2. protocol
3. toxin
4. Mesopotamia
5. archipelago
6. alchemy
7. eohippus
8. hysteron proteron
9. helicopter
10. cynic
11. Philip
12. Phyllis

EXERCISE 12B. 4— PEOPLE AND PLACES:
1. A *biblioklept* would be most unwelcome a. in a shoestore b. at church c. in the library d. at a bar
2. A *necrophobe* would very likely avoid a. high places b. zoos c. the gymnasium d. mortuaries
3. The likeliest place to see a *lycanthrope* is a. at a charity ball b. at an art opening c. on creature features d. at tea
4. A *cynophile* might be met at a. a cat show   b. the animal shelter   c. the hippodrome d. a philosophers' convention
5. A *misologist* would be least likely to enjoy a. a public debate b. the superbowl c. grand opera d. a beauty contest

<h2 style="text-align:center">CHECK LIST FOR CHAPTER ELEVEN</h2>

1. Learn all suffixes.
2. Learn new vocabulary.
Make a chart of suffixes and use each in a word.

C. SUPPLEMENT TO CHAPTER ELEVEN: SOME MEDICAL WORDS & WORD ELEMENTS

1. Medical Suffixes

-acousia/acusia, -acousis/acusis *hearing*
-agra *violent pain*
-algesia *excessive sensitivity to pain*
-algia *pain*
-aphia *touch*
-asthenia *loss of strength*
-auxe *enlargement*
-be *life, organism*
-blast *embryonic cell*
-cele *herniation*
-centesis *surgical puncture*
-ceros/cerus *horn* [cf. corn-, Lat., *horn*]
-clasis *a breaking up, dissolution*
-clastic *pertaining to dissolution*
-clysis *irrigation, washing*
-col *glue, jelly, gelatin*
-cyesis *pregnancy*
-dipsia *thirst*
-ectasia, -ectasis *dilation, stretching*
-ectomy *excision*
-edema *swelling*
-emesis *vomiting*
-emia, -hemia *blood condition*
-esthesia *sensation, feeling*
-genesis *formation, development*
-geustia, -geusia, -geusis *taste*
-iatrics, -iatry *healing, medical art*
-itis *inflammation*
-kinesia *movement*
-lepsy *seizure*
-lite, -lith *stone*
-lysis *destruction, breaking down*
-malacia *softening*

-mania *madness*

-megaly *enlargement*

-odia, -osmia *smell*

-odynia *pain*

-oma *tumor*

-oncus *tumor*

-opis, -opsis, -opsy *vision*

-orexia, -orexis *appetite*

-orrhagia *rapid discharge*

-orrhaphy *suture*

-orrhea *flow, discharge*

-orrhexis *rupture*

-osis *abnormal condition*

-osmia *smell*

-osphresia, -osphresis *smell*

-ostomy *formation of a new opening*

-otomy *incision*

-pathy *disease*

-penia *deficiency*

-pepsia *digestion*

-pexy *fixation*

-phagia, -phagy *eating, swallowing*

-philia, -phily *love, affinity for*

-phobia *abnormal or morbid fear*

-phoria *feeling, bearing*

-phyma *swelling*

-plasia *formation, development*

-plasty *surgical repair, plastic surgery*

-plegia *stroke, paralysis*

-poiesis *formation, generation*

-ptosis *prolapse, sagging*

-schisis *splitting*

-sclerosis *hardening*

-sepsis *infection*

-spasm *twitching*

-stasis *controlling, checking, stopping*

-stat *device to check/stop*

-stenosis *stricture*

-therapy *treatment*

-tome *instrument to cut*

-tripsy *surgical crushing*

-trophy *development*

-uria *condition of urine*

EXERCISES

EXERCISE 12C 1— What seems to be the problem?
1. anorexia [*a-*, *an-*, not]
2. dyspepsia [*dys-* < *dus-* badly, ill]
3. cytopenia [< *cyto-*, cell]
4. anemia
5. diplopia
6. cephaloma
7. aerophagy
8. dactylospasm
9. cardiomegaly
10. odontalgia
11. podagra
12. neuromalacia
13. cephalalgia
14. megalomania
15. hemiplegia
16. hematuria
17. sclerosis
18. laryngalgia
19. hematocele
20. logorrhea
21. dysphoria
22. osteomalacia
23. cephalospasm
24. psychopathy
25. osteoma
26. osteoclasis
27. somatosmia
28. podosphresia

2. Some Human and Animal Body Parts

	English	Greek	Latin
A	ankle	sphyron	tarsus
	anus	proctos	anus
	arm	brachion	brachium
B	beak, snout	rhynchos	rostrum
	belly	gaster	venter
	bladder	cystis	vesica
	blood	haima, -at-	sanguis
	body	soma, -at-	corpus
	bone	osteon	os, oss-

	brain	encephalos	cerebrum
	breast	sternon, mastos	pectus, sternum, mamma
	bristle	chaite	seta
C	cartilage	chondros	cartilago
	cell	cytos	cella
	cheek	pareia, genys	bucca
	chest	stethos	
	claw	chele, onyx	unguis
	crest	lophos	crista
	crown	stephanos	corona
D	digit	dactylos	digitus
E	ear	ous, -ot-	auris
	egg	oon	ovum
	eye	omma,ophthalmos	oculus
	eyelash, -lid	blepharon	cilium
	eyebrow	ophrys	supercilium
F	face	ops, opsis	facies
	feather	pteron, ptilon	penna, pinna, pluma
	flesh	creas, sarx	caro, carn-
	foot	pous, pod-	pes, ped-
	forehead	metopon	frons, front-
G	gland	aden	glans, gland-
H	hair	thrix, trich-	capillus, crinis, pilus
	hand	cheir, chir-	manus
	head	cephale	caput, capit-
	heart	cardia	cor, cord-
	heel	pterna	talus, calx
	hip	ischion, hypokolion	coxa
	horn	keras, -at-	cornu
J	jaw	gnathos, genys	maxilla
	joint	arthron	artus, articulus
K	kidney	nephros	renes
	knee	gonu	genu
	knuckle	condulos	
L	leg	skelos	crus, crur-
	lip	cheilos	labium, labrum
	liver	hepar, hepat-	jecur, jecor-
	lung	pneumon	pulmo, pulmon-
M	membrane	hymen	membrana
	mouth	stoma, -at-	os, or-
	mucus	blenna, myxa	
	muscle	mys, myo-	
N	neck	auchen, dere, trachelos	cervix, -ic-, collum

	nose	rhis, rhin-	nares, nasus
R	rib	pleura, skelis	costa
S	scale	lepis, lepid-	squama
	shoulder	omos	scapula
	skin	derma, -at-	cutis
	skull	cranion	
	sperm/seed	sperma	semen, -in-
	stomach	gaster	venter
T	tail	oura, cercos	cauda
	thigh	ischion	femur, -or-
	thorax	thorax	
	throat	pharynx, laimos	gula, guttur
	tissue	istos	tela
	tongue	glossa	lingua
	tooth	odous, odont-	dens, dent-
V	vein	phleps, phleb-	vena
W	windpipe	tracheia, bronchos	
	wing	pteron	ala
	wrist	carpos	carpus

EXERCISES

EXERCISE 12C. 2— BODY PARTS: Fill in the blanks.

1. A person who is callisphyrous has beautiful _____ .
2. The metatarsal bones are behind the _____ [five bones
   between the tarsus and the toes, forming the instep].
3. Aproctous insects have no _____ .
4. A rhyncocephalian has a _____ on its head.
5. Binoculars are for both _____ .
6. The rostrum in the Roman forum was so called because it was decorated with the
   _____ of captured ships.
7. A gastric ulcer is an open sore in the _____ .
8. Cystitis is an inflammation of the _____ .
9. A hypochondriac experiences pain from imaginary illnesses arising from the
   region under the _____ of the breastbone [the seat of melancholy].
10. A hemorrhage is a copious discharge of _____ .
11. Encephalitis is inflammation of the _____ .
12. A brachiopod has a pair of _____ like tentacled structures on either side of its
   mouth.
13. Somatogenic compensations arise within the _____ in response to the
   environment.
14. A pectoral is worn over the _____ .
15. Osteomyelitis is an inflammation of the _____ marrow.

16. A pterodactyl is an extinct flying reptile, called wing-_____.
17. A rostrate biped has a pair of _____ and a _____.
18. A cristate helmet is _____.
19. A supercilious person often raises his/her _____ disdainfully.
20. Genyplasty is plastic surgery on the _____.
21. A pterosaur is a _____ lizard.
22. The oculomotor nerve controls the muscles of the _____.
23. The ootheca is the _____ case of certain insects.
24. A setaceous quadruped has _____ and four _____.
25. Oology is that branch of ornithology that deals with birds'_____.
26. A sarcophagus is a stone coffin; its name means _____-eating.
27. Surgeon comes from Greek *cheirurgus* which means working with the _____.
28. Carnal sin is of the _____.
29. Metopic wrinkles are creases on the _____.
30. A capillary resembles a _____.
31. A trichome is a _____like growth.
32. A depilatory removes _____.
33. An adenectomy is the surgical removal of a _____.
34. Myogenic growths arise from the _____ tissue.
35. An isosceles triangle has two equal _____.
36. An abscess of the myocardium would affect the _____ tissue around the

_____.
37. A cheirosopher is skilled in the _____.
38. The Rev. Mr. John Newton named his collected letters *Cardiophonia*, or "Utterances from the _____."
39. A myogram is a _____ of _____ contractions and relaxations.
40. A cardiognost is one who knows the _____: "As if they were cardio-gnosts and fully versed in his intentions."
41. A chiropodist treats diseases of the _____ and _____.
42. Nephrolithotomy is the removal of a _____ from the _____.
43. Keratin is a substance found in the _____.
44. Renal calculi are _____ _____.
45. Gnathopods are Crustaceans that have _____-_____.
46. Nephrorrhaphy is the operation of fixing a movable _____ by _____.
47. To chirotonize is to elect by show of _____.
48. The condyloid process is like a _____.
49. Arthrology is a) a treatise on _____ or b) the hand signs of the deaf and mute.
50. Pneumonoconiosis is a disease of the _____ caused by the inhalation of dust.
51. A chilocace is a canker of the _____.
52. Hymenoptera is a large order of insects having four _____ _____.
53. Maxillary glands are in the region of the _____.

54. A cervix is any _____-shaped anatomical structure.
55. Squamous creatures are covered with _____.
56. The cuticle is the strip of hardened _____ at the base of the finger- or toenail. In Botany, it is the layer of cutin [a waxlike, water-repellant material present in some plant cells] covering the epidermis [or _____ _____ layer] of plants.
57. The calcaneus is the quadrangular bone at the back of the tarsus and is also called the _____ bone.
58. An omophore bears a great weight on his or her _____.
59. Blennorrhea is discharge of _____.
60. A blenny is a small marine fish named for the _____ coating on its scales.
61. To genuflect is to bend the _____.
62. Another name for femur is the _____ bone.
63. Phlebotomy is the practice of cutting open a _____ to let the blood flow [also called bleeding or blood draw].
64. Ischiatic means pertaining to the _____.
65. A myxoma is a benign tumor composed of connective tissue and _____ elements.
66. The metacarpus is behind the _____.
67. Coxalgia is a _____ in the _____.
68. A costate leaf has _____.
69. A caudate variety of the human species would have a _____.
70. A coda is the conclusion [or _____] of a movement.
71. A guttural sound is produced in the _____.
72. Alate animals have _____.
73. Craniotabes is a wasting of the _____ bone.
74. The mastodon is named _____-_____ because of the nipple-like protuberances on its _____.
75. A histoblast is the primary element of a _____.
76. Bronchophony is the sound of the voice heard in the _____ by means of a stethoscope.
77. Narial hairs grow in the _____.
78. A pachyderm has a thick _____.
79. A rhapsode is a _____ of songs.
80. The crural nerve is in the _____.
81. The omoplate is the _____ or in Latin the _____.
82. A scapular is worn about the _____.
83. Phlebostenosis is abnormal _____ of the _____.
84. Histophyly is the history of _____ within the limits of a particular tribe [*phyle*] of organisms.
85. Apterous aphids have no _____.

ELIXIR

1. In common use *elixir* is a sweetened aromatic solution of alcohol and water, serving as a vehicle for medicine, as in Elixir of terpenhydrate with codeine.

2. A substance that was believed to have the power of turning base metal into gold, also called the philosopher's stone.

3. A panacea (or cure-all)

4. Elixir of life— a medicine that would bestow long life and eternal youth.

   Elixir comes to us through Old French from Arabic *al*, the and *iksir* from Greek *xērion*, a drying powder for putting on wounds, < *xēros*, dry (cf. xerox, xerophage, as in "My cat is a xerophage.").

Other words from Arabic and Greek mixed: acacia, alchemy, Almagest, antimony, burnoose, carat, caraway, jasper, moussaka, scarlet, surd, talisman, tarragon, typhoon, zircon.

WHICH DOES NOT BELONG?[1]

1. Muse mosaic amuse musicologist museum
2. crisis endocrine criticaster criminology hypocrite
3. allocate allograph parallel allogamy allochthon
4. athematic epithet synthetic atheism theme
5. apotheosis enthusiasm parenthesis theodicy henatheism
6. bipartite biopsy microbe cenobiarch bioscopy
7. cenogenesis Pliocene cenotaph cenozoicHolocene
8. ethics cacoethes antithesis ethology ethos
9. demonstrate democracy demographics endemic epidemiology
10. telepathy teleology telekinesis telegram telephone
11. ecology monoecious ectopic ecumenical economics
12. pantomime pantile Pan-Hellenic pantogram pancreas
13. ornithology orthoscopy orthodox orthoepy orthopedics
14. pederasty pediatrician pedant pedestrian pedagogue
15. nomenclature metronome nomad taxonomical
16. onomatopoetic heteronymous anonymity pseudonym nominative paronomasia

NOTE

1. Answers: 1. amuse; 2. criminology; 3. allocate ;4. atheism; 5. parenthesis; 6. bipartite; 7. cenotaph; 8. antithesis; 9. demonstrate; 10. teleology; 11. ectopic; 12. pantile; 13. ornithology; 14. pedestrian; 15. nomenclature; 16. nominative.

SECTION THREE: GREEK

CHAPTER THIRTEEN: GREEK PREFIXES

Like those from Latin, Greek prefixes are mostly derived from prepositions. A few like *a-* and *dys-* are inseparable (not used as discrete words); *eu-* is from an adverb.

* *a-* [*an-* before a vowel], not, un-, -less
    apathy, lack of feeling; *anechoic*, without echo
amphi-, both, on both sides, around, about
    amphimacer, long on both sides (a unit of verse, - --)
    amphibious, living on/in both (land and water)
* *ana-* [*an-* before a vowel], up, back, again
    anabasis, a going up/back; *anode*, a road up (a positively charged electrode)
* *anti-*, instead, against, in opposition to
    antithesis, a setting in opposition; *antidote*, something given against
* *apo-* [*ap-* before a vowel or h], from, away from, off, utterly, completely, lack of
    apostate, one who stands away (one who renounces a belief)
    aphesis, sending off (loss of an initial unaccented vowel)
    apophthegm, a speaking away (a terse saying)
* *cata-*, *cat-* [Greek, *kata*], down, against, completely [opp. *ana-*]
    catastrophe, a turning down
    cathode, a road down (a negatively charged electrode)
* *dia-*, *di-*, through, across, over, assunder
    diatom, cut through (a unicellular alga, having two symmetrical parts)
    diameter, a measure through
    Note: Be careful not to confuse *dia* with *di-*, two (diode, dimeter, dicotyledon) or *dicho-* which indicates division into two parts (dichotomy) or with Latin *dis-* in different directions (dissect, dismiss).
dys- [Greek, *dus-*], ill, un-, mis-, difficult, bad
    dysphoria, difficult bearing
    dysteleology, doctrine of the purposelessness of nature
* *ec-*, *ex-* [Greek, *ek*, *ex*], out, from, off

eccrine, secreting externally (as sweat glands do)

eczema, result of boiling out (inflammation of the skin)

exegesis, act of leading out (critical explanation)

ecto- [Greek, *ekto-*], on the outside

ectoderm, outer skin

* *en-, em-*, in

empathy, feeling in

enthusiasm, condition of having a god in one (< *en-theos*)

enantio- [*en- + anti-*], opposite

enantiobiosis, condition of living in opposition

endo-, within, inside, internal

endoscope, instrument for observing inside

eso-, inward, within

esoteric, more inward

exo-, outward, external

exobiology, search for and study of extraterrestrial life

exosphere, the outermost part of the atmosphere

* *epi-* (*ep-* before a vowel or h), upon, over, at, near

epicycle, an orbit over an orbit

ephebe, at youth (a young man between the ages of eighteen and twenty)

epexegesis, the addition of an explanatory note to a text

ephemeral, lasting for a day (*hemera*, day)

* *eu-* (rarely, *ev-*), well, good

euphoria, good bearing; *eulogy*, a good word/speech; *evangel*, the good message

* *hyper-* [Greek, *huper*, related to Latin *super*], above, beyond, exceedingly

hyperthyroid, above the doorlike gland

hypermetric, beyond the meter

hyperbole, a throwing beyond (exaggeration)

* *hypo-, hyp-* [Greek, *hupo*, related to Latin *sub*], under

hypotenuse, stretching under; *hypodermic*, under the skin

hypothesis, the act of setting under

* *meta-, met-*, among, between, change, behind, later

metamorphosis, the act of changing shape

metaphysics, the things after the physics

method, a going after

metadata, "data about other data" (*data* from Latin, things give)

palin-, pali-, back, again

palindrome, a running backward (a word or phrase that reads the same backwards or forwards)

* *para-, par-*, beside, beyond, near, incorrectly, like

paradox, beyond opinion

parabiosis, state of living beside (fusion of two organisms)

paraphernalia, what is brought besides the dowry (*phernē*)
* *peri-*, around, about
    perimorph, a form around (a mineral that encloses another mineral)
    peripatetic, walking around (of a school of philosophy, the Peripatetics)
    Note: Do not confuse with the Latin prefix *per-*, through.
* *pro-*, before, forward, for
    prologue, thing said before; *program*, something written for
    Note: Do not confuse with the Latin prefix *pro-*, forth, for, forward, instead of,
    publicly (proceed, procrastinate, progress, proscribe) or with the Greek prefix
    pros-, to, toward, besides (see next entry), or with the Greek adjective *protos*,
    first (protoplasm, protozoic), though they are all cognates.
pros-, to, toward, besides, in front
    prosody, accompanied song > study of metrical systems
    proselyte, one who comes to > a new convert
    prosthesis, attachment (putting besides)
* *syn-, sym-, syl-, sys-* [Greek, *sun*], with, together
    synagogue, a bringing together, assembly; *symbiosis*, a living together
    syllogism, the result of reasoning together
    system, the result of causing to stand (*histanai*, stand) together

Examples of PALINDROMES and other *palin-*, *pali-* words[1]
    ABLE WAS I ERE I SAW ELBA (Napoleon's lament)
    MADAM I'M ADAM
    A MAN A PLAN A CANAL: PANAMA
    NAOMI, DID I MOAN?
    GO HANG A SALAMI, I'M A LASAGNA HOG[2]
    BORROW OR ROB?
    CAMPUS MOTTO: BOTTOMS UP, MAC
    DAMMIT I'M MAD
    EGAD! AN ADAGE
    EVIL DID I DWELL LEWD DID I LIVE
    I PREFER PI
    OH NO, DON HO
    RUM, RUM I MURMUR
    RISE TO VOTE, SIR
    WONTON? NOT NOW
    palilalia, the repeating of a phrase faster and faster
    palinoia, compulsive repetition of an activity or task
    palingenesis, rebirth
    palimpsest, "scraped again" (a parchment that has been scraped of one text so
        that it can be used again)
    palinode, a retraction in verse

EXERCISES

EXERCISE 13 A 1— USING PREFIXES: take apart and define parts:
1. symbiosis
2. enantiobiosis
3. catholic
4. palinode [*ōdē*, song]
5. parody
6. antagonist [*agōn*, struggle, contest]
7. empathy
8. sympathy
9. analgesic
10. parallel [*allēlon*, each other]
11. amphibian
12. euthanasia [*thanatos*, death]
13. energetic
14. synergy
15. ephemeral [*hēmera*, day]
16. Eucharistic [*charis*, grace, thanks]
17. perimeter
18. anarchist
19. paragraph
20. dialogue
21. metamorphosis
22. analogy
23. endomorph
24. metempsychosis
25. encyclical
26. pseudepigrapha
27. evangelical
28. epigraphy
29. endemic
Some words using the base of * *hodos*, road, way
30. anode
31. cathode
32. method
33. period
34. episode (*epi-* + *eis-*, into)
35. exodos
36. eisodos (*eis-*, into)
37. parodos (side entrance; also entrance song of the chorus in Greek drama)
38. synod

39. odograph
40. odometer
Some words using the base of *ōdē*, song
41. parody
42. prosody
43. epode
44. palinode
45. odeon (a place for songs, music hall)
46. monody
47. rhapsode (*rhaptein*, sew: stitcher of songs)
48. odist
49. melodic (*melos*, tune)
50. tragedy (*tragos*, goat)
51. comedy (*komos*, revel)

EXERCISE 13A 2— PRODUCTIVE PREFIXES: Choose one *prefix and find as many words as you can using it. Make sure they are all legitimate (actually use that prefix; see pitfalls, below).

> Example: *kata-*: catholic, cathode, cathedral, cathexis, cation, catheter, catechism, catechumen, category, catastrophe, catalogue, catabolic, catachresis, catadromous (migrating downstream), catalepsy (muscular rigidity), catalyst, catastasis (intensified action before a catastrophe), catarrh, catapult, catalectic, cataract, catatonic.

PITFALLS:

NOT from *kata-*: catalpa [from Creek, not Greek], catamaran [from Tamil], catamount ["cat of the mountains"], catalo [cattle + buffalo], catenary [< Latin catena, chain], catamite [< the name Ganymede, Zeus' cup-bearer, etc.], catacomb [from Latin, but of obscure origin], catharsis [from *katharos*, pure]

NOT from *eu-*, eunuch but from *eune*, bed + *echein*, have, keep (Go figure or, better, look it up in a dictionary.)

NOT from *peri-*: periwig, periwinkle

NOT from *para-*: parasol, parachute, parade (from Latin *parare*); paradise (from a Persian word meaning "a pleasure garden"); parasang (also from Persian); paramour, parboil (both from Latin *per-*, through, respectively, "for love" and "boil thoroughly").

EXERCISE 13A 3—PRODUCTIVE COMBINING FORMS
1): Word-words [from *onoma*, using element *-onym*]: take apart and explain parts. Give an example of each or use it in a sentence.
  1. anonymous
  2. eponymous
  3. paronymous
  4. metonymy

5. synonym
6. antonym
7. homonym
8. acronym
9. pseudonymous
10. euonymous

2): House-words [from *oikos*, combining form, *eco-*]: Choose two, define, and use each in a sentence
1. metic (< *metoikos*)
2. parish (< *paroikos*)
3. diocese (< *dioikesis*)
4. synoikismos
5. monoecious
6. dioecious (*di-*, two)
7. ecesis (< *oikesis*) "habitation, establishment of a new environment"
8. heteroecious
9. autoecious

EXERCISE 13A 4— PRODUCTIVE BASES: make up compounds from these bases, using as many of the new prefixes as you can:
1. logos
2. kuklos
3. metron
4. ergon
5. pathos
6. demos
7. gram-, -graph
8. derma [skin]

EXERCISE 13A 5—WORD FORMATION: make up words meaning:
1. instrument for looking around
2. absence of feeling
3. without color
4. one bringing a good message
5. upon the people
6. having to do with writing on [stones]
7. good sound
8. measure through
9. at the same time [timed with]
10. of change in shape

EXERCISE 13A 6— REVIEW OF PREFIXES AND SUFFIXES. Fill in one word using the same prefix as the word given and one word using the same suffix or last combining element:

Ex. apathetic   atheist   archaeologist
           amphiarthrosis [*arthron*, joint]
           anarchy
           analytic [*luein*, loosen]
           antiphonal
           aposiopesis [*siope*, silence]
           diagnostics [*gno-*, perceive]
           dysteleological
           ecdysiast [*ekduein*, take off]
           ectoderm
           encephalitis [-*itis*, inflammation of]
           enantiomorph
           endocrinology [*krinein*, separate]
           esoterism [-*ter-*, more]
           exodontia
           epidermoid
           eupatrid [-*id*, son of > *Atreides*, son of Atreus]
           catalogue
           metaphysics [*physis*, nature]
           palindrome [*dromos*, a running]
           paradigmatic [*dig-* < *deik-*, show]
           periodical
           problem [*ball-*, *ble-*, throw]
           prosthesis [*the-*, put]
           symmetry
           hyperopia [*opia*, eye condition > diplopia]
           hypochondriac [*chondros*, cartilage]

CHECK LIST FOR CHAPTER TWELVE

Know all Greek prefixes
Make a chart using each prefix in a word

PARAPROSDOKIANS

A *paraprosdokian* (< Greek *para-* beyond + *prosdokia*, expectation) is a figure of speech in which the latter part of the phrase is humorously surprising or unexpected and causes the reader or listener to reframe or reinterpret the first part. (Based on the *Grammerly* Facebook page.) These are surprisingly like one-liners. A new word was needed since *paradox* was already taken. Examples include:

Where there's a will . . . I want to be in it.
The last thing I want to do is hurt you, but it's still on my list.

War doesn't determine who is right, it determines who is left.

Dance like no one is laughing.

Groucho Marx was a master of the *paraprosdokian*, for example:

"Time flies like an arrow. Fruit flies like a banana"

"Outside of a dog, a book is man's best friend. Inside of a dog, it's too dark to read."

"A child of five could understand this. Someone go fetch a child of five."

"The secret of life is honesty and fair dealing. If you can fake that, you've got it made."

"I was going to thrash them within an inch of their lives, but I didn't have a tape measure"

WORDS IN CONTEXT

Human history becomes more and more a race between education and *catastrophe*.
H. G. Wells, *Outline of History*, 1920

The speaking in perpetual *hyperbole* is comely in nothing but in love.
Francis Bacon, "Of Love," 1612

SUPPLEMENT FOR CHAPTER TWELVE

Greek and Latin prefixes compared with some English words or word elements that are cognate to them:

Greek	Latin	English cognate
a-, an- [not]	ne-, in-	no, none, nay, naught
amphi- [around]	ambi-	by, be-
ana- [on]		a- [as in aloft], on-
anti- [against]	ante- [in front]	un-, along, end
apo- [off, away]	ab-	of, off, ebb, after
dys- [bad]		= mis- [not cognate]
ec-, ex- [out]	ex-, extra-, extro-	
en- [in]	in-, intro, intra,	
endo-, eso-,	inter, intus	in, and
eis- [into]		
epi- [near]	ob- [to, against]	
eu- [well]		
cata- [down]	cf. catulus [young puppy < something thrown down]	
meta- [between]	cf. midwife	
para-, peri-,	per-, pro-, prae	far, for, fore-, first
pro-, pros-	cf. primus [basic meaning: forward]	
syn- [with]	cf. simul, semper	
hyper- [over]	super-, supra-	over
hypo- [under, up from under]	sub-, subter- cf. supinus	up, above, open; evil

WORD GAME: PREFIX PITFALLS

Which are from Greek?[3]

> parachute
> catalpa
> anaconda
> anticipate
> aport
> enmity
> ephah
> euchre
> meticulous
> palisade
> periwinkle
> proa
> syllabub
> hyson

[

Some interesting words using the new Greek prefixes: Choose one and explain it and find an example or picture.

> palimpsest
> aposiopesis
> apophthegm
> aphorism
> peristyle
> prostyle
> Peripatetic
> prosopopoeia
> catapult
> syllogism
> apostrophe
> synecdoche
> anaphora
> periodic style
> peripateia
> hysteron proteron
> hyperbole
> parataxis
> hypotactic
> anapest
> asyndeton
> epithalamium
> antistrophe

anagnorisis

Distinguish:

epigraph	epitaph	epithet
epigram	epitome	epode

SEMORDNILAPS

The other side of Palindrome is **semordnilap**. A semordnilap (the word *palindromes* in reverse) is a pair of words that spell each other backwards: for example, star/rats, drawer/reward, faced/decaf, avid/diva, live/evil, Harpo/Oprah, Dennis/sinned, God/dog, knits/stink. These are also called **anadromes**. Dylan Thomas' Welsh village **Llareggub** in *Under Milk Wood* is a famous semordnilap.

NOTES

1. For more palindromes, most of them pretty lame, see http://www.palindromelist.net/.

2. The title of a book on palindromes by Jon Agee.

3. Answer: none of these.

SECTION THREE: GREEK

CHAPTER FOURTEEN: GREEK VERBS

CHARACTERISTICS OF GREEK VERBS

Greek verbs like those in Latin are highly inflected: the endings and other changes show tense, voice, mood, person, and number. Greek has even more inflections: one more number, the DUAL (rare) for only two; one more tense, the AORIST for a single action in past time; one more mood, the OPTATIVE, for wishes and possibilities; and one more voice, the MIDDLE for subjects performing the action for or on themselves or in their own behalf. Vowel gradation is common in Greek verbs, as in English, in such verbs as *sing, sang, sung*, with the noun form *song; do, did, done*, with the noun form *deed*. Vowel gradation accounts for much of the variation in bases of Greek verbs. In vocabulary entries the bases that are used in English derivatives will be given along with the present infinitive.

VOCABULARY

Study the verb bases and meanings in the list below. The Greek present infinitive is given in brackets. Present infinitives end in *-ein* (thematic verbs), *-nai* (athematic verbs), *-esthai/asthai* (deponent verbs). THEMATIC and ATHEMATIC refer to the two conjugations (or patterns) and DEPONENT means that the verbs do not appear in the active voice but only in the middle/passive. Verbs ending in *-an* are *-a*-stems, that is, *-a*-contract verbs of the thematic type.

acou-, acu- [akouein] *hear* > acoustics, pseudacusis
aesth-, esth- [aisthanesthai] *feel, perceive* > aesthetic (esthetic), anaesthesia
ag- the base sometimes appears as *-eg-* [agein] *lead, bring* > strategy (*stratos*, army)
    -agogue [from *-agogos*] *one leading* > pedagogue
    or [from *-agogē*] *a leading, gathering* > synagogue
ba-, be- [bainein] *go, step, walk* > basis, diabetes
ball-, ble-, bol- [ballein] *throw* > ballistics, problem, hyperbole
chor- [chorein] *move*
    -chore: a plant distributed by a specific agency > anemochore, zoochore

cin-, kin- [kinein] *move* > kinesiology, kinescope, cinematography

cle- [kalein] *call* > Paraclete, ecclesiastical (related to Latin *clamare*)

clin-, cli- [klinein] *bend, make to slope* > geosyncline, climate

cop-, com- [koptein] *cut* > pericope, comma

crin-, cri- [krinein] *separate, judge, decide* > eccrine, apocrine, criterion, criticaster

crypt-, cryp- [kruptein] *hide* > cryptographer, apocrypha

do- [didonai] *give* > dose, anecdote

doc-, dog-, dox- [dokein] *seem, think* > Docetism, dogmatic, heterodox, paradox

    doxa, *opinion, praise, reputation* > doxology, paradox

dra- [dran] *do, act, perform* > dramaturgy, melodrama (< melos, *tune*)

drom- [dramein] *run* > dromedary, palindrome

dyn- [dunasthai] *be able, be powerful* > dyne, dynast

    dunamis, *power* > dynamometer, dynamic

glyph- [gluphein] *carve* > petroglyph, hieroglyphic

gno- [gignoskein] *know* > diagnosis, gnomic, agnostic

graph-, gram- [graphein] *draw, write* > topography, cartographer, programmatic,

    epigrammatist, graphic

histanai, see sta-

i- [ienai] *go* > ion, anion, cation

lab-, lep-, lem- [lambanein] *take, seize* > syllable, nympholepsy ("nymph-catching"

    the longing for what is impossible[1]), lemma, dilemma

leg-, lex-, lect-, log- [legein] *gather, say* > analects, eclectic, eclogue, catalogue,

    prolegomena (*-menos* passive participial ending), dyslexia, lexicon,

ly- [luein] *loose, break, destroy* > paralysis, catalyst, analyze

math- [manthanein] *learn* > polymath, mathematician,

    chrestomathy (a collection of useful learning)

nem-, nom- [nemein, cf. *nomos*] *assign, allot* > nemesis, nomad, -nomy

-ont-, -ous- [einai] *be* [root, -es] > ontological, palaeontology, ontic,

    Homoousian, Heteroousian, Homoiousian

    -ont- and -ous- are the masculine and feminine active participial endings and so

    mean *being*; -ousia is the noun form, meaning *substance, nature*

pau-, -pose (influenced by Latin *ponere*) [pauein] *cease, stop* > menopause,

    aeropause, pose, repose

pha-, phe- [phanai] *say, speak* (phēmē, *a saying*)

    aphasia, dysphasia, apophatic, euphemism, prophet, blasphemy

phag- [phagein] *eat*

    -phage *one who/that which eats* > xenophage

    -phagous *eating* > aerophagous

    -phagy *the habit or tendency to eat* > xerophagy

phen-, phan-, pha- [phainein] *show, cause to appear; appear*

    phenomenon, phenotype; epiphany, hierophant, sycophant, phantasy (fantasy);

    phase, emphasis

pher-, phor- [pherein] *bear, carry*

paraphernalia [< phernē, *dowry*, the things brought by the bride], periphery
anaphora, euphoria, phosphorescent, metaphor
phy- [phuein] *make to grow; grow, be by nature* > physics, neophyte, symphysis
poie-, poe- [poiein] *make, do*
  mythopoiesis, pharmacopoeia, poem, poet, poetaster, ONOMATOPOEIA:"making
  the name" used of words that imitate sounds like *murmur, twang, splat, fizz*
pol- [polein] *sell* > ichthyopole, aeropole, molopoly, oligopoly
  see also opsonein, *to buy* -opsony > monopsony, oligopsony
prag-, prac- [prattein] *do* > pragmatic; practical, chiropractor
rhe(u)-, rhy-, rho- [rhein] *flow* > rheumatic, rheostat, rhythm, rhyme, diarrhoea
  (diarrhea), logorrhoea, catarrh
schiz-, schis- [schizein] *split* > schizogenesis, schistosome, schism
scop-, scep-, skep- [skopein] *examine, look at* > scopomania, otoscope, episcopal,
  spectroscope,scepticism, skeptic or sceptic
sta-, ste- [histanai] *stand, cause to stand* > iconostasis, ecstasy, hemostat; system
stol-, stal-, stl- [stellein] *send, make ready* > apostolic, systalic, epistle, apostle
streph- (strep-), stroph- [strephein] *turn* > streptococcus, streptokinase,
  streptomyecin, strophe, antistrophe, catastrophe, apostrophe, diastrophism
tak-, tac-, tax- [tattein] *arrange, assign, assess* > tactician, tactics, taxidermy,
  taxonomy, tax, syntax, parataxis, hypotaxis
ten-, ta-, ton- [teinein] *stretch out, strain* > hypotenuse, protasis, epitasis,
  telangiectasia, tone, peritoneum
the- [tithenai] *put, place* > thesis, theme, epithet
tme-, tom- [temnein] *cut* > tmesis, anatomy, entomology, epitome, tome,
  dichotomy, atom,
  -tomy *surgical cutting* > lobotomy
  -ectomy *surgical removal* > appendectomy
troph- [trephein] *feed, nourish* > eutrophic, atrophy, dystrophy
trop(h)- [trepein] *turn* > tropic, heliotrope, entropy, trope, tropology, trophy
And a final verb, not for the fainthearted:
hec-, hex-, sche-, ech- och-, -uch- [echein] *have, hold*
  hectic, Hector; cathexis (holding down, a concentration of emotional energy),
  cachexia (bad keeping, *i.e.*, general wasting of the body)
  scheme, sketch; entelechy (completion, fulfilment; a thing's urge toward
  achieving its essence); epoch; eunuch
  From the same root comes scholē, *leisure* (< *a holding back*) > school,
  scholar, scholia, scholiast, scholasticism, scholastic.

EXERCISES

EXERCISE 14A 1— DERIVATIVES FROM VERBS: Study the verbs and examples; using
the suffixes and prefixes from the previous two lessons, make up several more words
using each verb (in any of its forms). Recommended for group work.

Examples:

akouein > acoustic, hyperacusia, anacusia, acoustician (possibly related to *kudos*, glory)

aisthanesthai > aesthetics, aestheticism, aesthete, kinesthesia, synesthesia, anesthetic, anestheticist, anesthesiology

ballein > ballista, ballistics; from *ballizein* (jump about) > ball (dance), ballet, ballad, balletomane, [but not ball or balloon]; catabolic, catabolism, diabolic, devil, emblem, symbol, symbolic, problem, problematic, metabolism, hyperbole, parabola, parable, parley, parlor, palaver, parole, parliament, amphibole, amphibology (ambiguity in language), Discobolus (the Discus Thrower)

gignoskein > gnostic, Gnosticism, agnostic, diagnostic, gnome (a maxim), gnomic, physiognomy, prognosis, prognosticate, gnomon (an indicator), gnosis (intuitive understanding of spiritual truths); cognate to Latin *(g)noscere* and to English *know, ken, can, cunning, uncouth*.

EXERCISE 14A. 2— COMMON VERB BASES: find the common verb in each group; choose 5, take apart and explain the meaning of the whole. (Recommended for group work.)

Example: problem, diabolic < *ballein* (ble-, bol-), throw: problem "result of something thrown in front (of one)"; diabolic "of throwing across" < *diaballein*, slander, > "of the slanderer" (i.e. the devil)

1. demagogue, pedagogue
2. aesthetic, anesthesia
3. acoustics, pseudacusis
4. acrobat, diabetes
5. emblem, metabolism
6. anemochore, anchorite
7. anecdote, apodosis
8. dogmatic, heterodox
9. dromedary, hippodrome
10. dramatic, drastic
11. dynasty, dynamite
12. cachexia, entelechy (hint < *echein*)
13. ion, cation
14. ontological, paleontology
15. agnosticism, diagnosis
16. hieroglyphic, petroglyph
17. seismograph, diagram [*seismos*, earthquake]
18. ecstatic, iconostasis
19. paraclete, ecclesiastical
20. cinema, hyperkinetic
21. enclitic, climate

22. pericope, syncope
23. critic, hypocrisy
24. apocryphal, cryptogram
25. dilemma, epilepsy
26. eclectic, prologue
27. dyslexia, catalogue
28. psychoanalytic, paralysis
29. polymath, mathematics
30. nomad, nemesis
31. pause, menapause [*men*- month]
32. sarcophagus, papyrophagy
33. epiphany, phenomenon, diaphanous
34. prophesy, dysphasia
35. euphoria, anaphora
36. physics, neophyte
37. onomatopoetic (or onomatopoeic), poem
38. bibliopole, monopoly
39. impractical, pragmatic
40. diarrhoea, logorrhoea, rheumatic
41. schismatic, schizogenesis
42. episcopal, telescope
43. epistle, apostolic
44. catastrophic, antistrophe
45. syntax, paratactic
46. atomic, dichotomy [*dicho*-, in two]
47. atrophy, entrophic
48. heliotrope, tropic
49. monotone, hypotenuse [-use is the participial ending,=-ing]
50. parenthetical, metathesis, anathema

EXERCISE 14A. 3—WORD FORMATION: make up words meaning

1. tending to go down
2. result of throwing in
3. thing given against
4. of right opinion
5. instrument for measuring power
6. running up
7. act of knowing before
8. far writing
9. act of standing away
10. act of calling upon
11. act of moving from afar
12. tending to judge under
13. a breaking up/down/through
14. book seller
15. fish, fowl, fire, flower, and foreigner eaters
16. one who makes
17. study of things beyond/after nature
18. a turning away
19. seller of paper, of fish, of air, of fire
20. of good nourishment
21. a putting under/against/together

EXERCISE 14A. 4—INTERESTING WORDS FROM GREEK VERBS: find one or one set that interests you and learn more about its etymology and meaning.

agein > strategy, pedant   ballein > devil, parable, parliament
echein > eunuch, hectic, entelechy   skopein > bishop
graphein > glamor, prolegomenon, hapax legomenon
koptein > comma, pericope   lambanein > nympholepsy, lemma
poiein > poetaster   mathein > chrestomathy
pherein > paraphernalia [*pherne*, dowry, that which is brought]
tithenai > boutique, bodega   prattein > barter
phainein > sycophant, phenomenon [-men- is a participial ending, also seen in
     prolegomenon, ecumenical, hapax legomenon[2]]
phanai > blame, blasphemy   kruptein > grotto, grotesque
dramein > dromadary   chorein > anchorite
nemein > nemesis   trepein > trophy

EXERCISE 14A. 5—WORD-WORDS: give examples of:
1. paradox
2. hyperbole
3. palindrome
4. anagram
5. protasis
6. euphemism
7. metaphor
8. boustrophedon ["as the ox turns"][3]
9. tmesis (see *saxo cere- comminuit -brum*, "he smashed his head (*cerebrum*) in two with a rock," Ennius, 2nd c. B.C.E. Roman poet.
10. epithet
11. onomatopoeia

EXERCISE 14A. 6—REVIEW OF VERBS
A. Match with meaning of base verb; fill in one additional English word using the same base.
1)

_x_	apocryphal	1. know	cryptology
___	mystagogue	2. go [use twice]	
___	esthete	3. run	
___	discobolus	4. be	
___	zoochore	5. have	
___	antidote	6. do	
___	doxology	7. lead	
___	catadromous	8. throw	
___	melodramatic	9. seem	
___	dynamic	10. give	

___ epoch		11. move
___ cation		12. hear
___ ontic		13. be able
___ gnostic		14. feel
___ acoustic		x. hide
___ basis		

2)

___ anaglyph	1. stop
___ program	2. learn
___ thermostat	3. gather
___ kinesthesia	4. hide
___ epiclesis	5. cut
___ proclitic	6. call
___ apocope	7. stand
___ endocrine	8. carve
___ cryptic	9. move
___ epilepsy	10. lean
___ analects	11. separate, judge
___ catalyst	12. take
___ monomath	13. loosen
___ anomy	14. write
___ diapause	15. assign

3)

___ anthropophage	1. put
___ phantasmagoria	2. sell
___ prophesy	3. eat
___ dysphoria	4. cut
___ physics	5. flow
___ pharmacopoeia	6. seem, appear
___ oenopole	7. arrange
___ catarrh	8. make
___ schismatic	9. speak
___ epistolary	10. turn
___ apostrophe	11. grow
___ hypotactic	12. carry
___ nephrolithectomy	13. send
___ prosthesis	14. split

B. Match words from same verb and give meaning of verb base:

a.	___ dialect	1. pericope
b.	___ schism	2. emblematic
c.	___ graphite	3. homoiousian
d.	___ system	4. epigram

e. ___ diacritical   5. poetry
f. ___ dilemma   6. anabatic
g. ___ dose   7. phantom
h. ___ paradoxical   8. dogmatic
i. ___ symbolic   9. criterion
j. ___ basis   10. schizogenesis
k. ___ stratagem   11. apostasy
l. ___ ontological   12. synagogue
m. ___ comma   13. dyslexia
n. ___ mythopoeic   14. astrolabe
o. ___ phenomenology   15. anecdotal

WORD GAME: WHICH DOES NOT BELONG?[4]

1. demagogue strategic pedagogy ago
2. acoustics pseudacusis acute
3. anabasis stylobate bass acrobat
4. devil ballistics metabolic balloon
5. dos-a-dos dose antidote anecdote
6. dramaturgy dromedary palindrome hippodrome
7. hectic hex eunuch cachexia
8. gnostic genesis prognosis gnomic
9. graffiti graminivorous grammar telegraph
10. cinerous cinema kinetic telekinetic
11. criticaster crinate criterion crisis
12. lyceum lysis catalyst paralytic
13. polyandry monopoly oligopoly oenopole
14. Prakrit practical pragmatic praxis
15. thesis thematic parenthetical theanthropism
16. epistle apostolic constellation systalic

CHECKLIST FOR CHAPTER THIRTEEN

Learn Greek verb stems
Review prefixes and suffixes

SUPPLEMENT TO CHAPTER THIRTEEN

Some Greek and Latin verb formations (with similar meanings) compared

dialysis	dissolution
hypostasis	substance
tmesis	caesura
synthesis	composition
anaesthetic	insensitive
acoustic	auditory
problem	project

dynast	potentate
syndrome	concourse
cachexia	disability
ontic	essential
diagram	transcript, description
ecclesiastic	evocative
pericope	circumcision
periphrasis	circumlocution
strophe	verse
apostle	missionary
episcopal	supervisory
epigraphic	inscriptional
erotic	amatory, amorous

Optional Exercise: Add to this list as a review of Greek and Latin elements.

WORDS IN CONTEXT

Poetry is not the proper *antithesis* to prose, but to science. Poetry is opposed to science, and prose to metre.
> Samuel Taylor Coleridge, "Definitions of Poetry," 1811

If you are anxious for to shine in the high *aesthetic* line...
> W. S. Gilbert, *Patience*, 1881

VERBUM SAPIENTI: A NOTE TO STUDENTS

Hangman

S_S_____N *

Students of etymology derive many academic benefits and we hope some fun as well. With words a **foot & a half long* you can gleefully garrotte your pals during dull meetings, improve your trivial pursuits, beat your profs at the dictionary game. With logomania you need never be bored.

The Dictionary Game

Equipment: A big dictionary; scrap paper; one pencil for each player
How to play: The player who is *It* finds an obscure [and if possible amusing] word in the Big Dictionary. He/she announces and spells the word for the other players who write it down on their pieces of scrap paper. If any player knows the word, that word is disqualified. The player with the dictionary then writes down the dictionary definition while each other player writes down a definition of his/her own invention, aiming at the greatest absurdity within the limits of dictionary diction. *It* then collects the definitions and reads them to the other players who vote for the definition of their choice. Play continues. Players receive points for votes for their false

definitions. A player receives a point for picking the right definition. The player who is *It* receives a point for each vote for a wrong definition.

Highlights from a Legendary Dictionary Game[5]

1. maxixe

a) The condition of feeling excruciating pain in the kidneys (especially of sheep).

b) In architecture, the topmost point of a gable in French neo-classical buildings.

c) One of several headdresses used in Colombian religious pageantry.

d) An herb of the madderwort family, used in flavoring a Flemish liqueur.

e) A Brazilian dance, similar to the two-step.

f) To sign the name by making the sign of a large X, said of an illiterate person.

2. rhopalic

a) An R-shaped mark or figure on an armorial design.

b) Of or pertaining to an eolithic member of the rose family, represented in fossils found on the island of Rhodes.

c) Verses in which each word contains one syllable more than the one preceding it.

d) In Etruscan, a P-shaped character, probably use in inventorying.

e) Member of an obscure religious sect in northern India, the members of which wear rose-colored vestments and paint their noses white.

f) Of or pertaining to an illness (rhopalgia) endemic to peoples of the southern Mediterranean area, a symptom of which is diplopia.

g) Linguistics, esp. psycholinguistics, a form of mild dyslexia especially common among students of the Hellenic language and culture, suffering from maenadism, in which the sufferer confuses the letters P and R (reading, for example, pose as rose); the opposite of rhotacism (*q.v.*).

3. cachelot

a) A whale having a very large head with small cavities.

b) A variety of woodbine native to Brittany.

c) A member of the leopard family, found principally in central Anatolia.

d) A member of the onion family, found in Poland, Germany, and parts of Russia.

e) Vulgarism: a successful streetwalker.

f) A type of small ceramic jar, commonly seen in Victorian parlors, in which tea or aromatic herbs were stored.

4. igasuric

a) Of or pertaining to a minute Mexican lizard of the family iguanilla igasaurides.

b) A geologic substratum in which fossils of extinct lizards are found.

c) A condition found in females of the lower economic strata in rural Transylvania.

d) Species of medicinal fern found only in the vicinity of Igassu Falls, used to heal wounds caused by poison darts.

e) An acid found in small quantities in St. Ignatius' bean.

f) Characteristic of reptiles with very small gastro-intestinal tracts.

5. cilice
a) Frosty build-up at the bottom of window frames.
b) In architecure: an outer frame for an artificial window.
c) A type of lace having floral patterns and no seams.
d) The sound made by vermin experiencing strong viverine emotions, especially among shrews in heat.
e) A coarse cloth, hair cloth, made from the hair of goat in Cilicia.
f) An herb, the seed of which is used as an ingredient in a type of curry powder.

6. mankeen
a) Pertaining to animals inclined to attack men; savage.
b) An especially small or young frequenter of Irish public houses.
c) Chinese dish of marinated shark livers.
d) An early, prehistoric hominid, found in England near Kent and on the isle of Man; a highly intelligent ancestor of *Homo Sapiens*.
e) A Japanese lantern of paper, painted with skulls and used in ancestor-worship.

> *I said it in Hebrew—I said it in Dutch—*
> *I said it in German and Greek;*
> *But I wholly forgot (and it vexes me much)*
> *That English is what you speak!*
>   Lewis Carroll, *The Hunting of the Snark*, 1876

NOTES

1. See also *paranymph*, a person "next to the bride" (< *numphē*, bride), a bridesmaid or the man who brought the bride from her home to the groom's house. In mythology, nymphs are female nature deities.

2. I'm surprised to find *hapax legomenon* in my dictionary: a word that is recorded only once in a language, author, or text < *hapax* ,once only, *legomenon* present passive participle, neuter of *legein* (say, speak): thing said. Plural: *hapaxes* or (more classically) *hapax legomena*.

3. See http://classicsenthusiast.tumblr.com/post/51416648113/boustrophedon

4. Answers: 1. ago 2. acute 3. bass 4. balloon 5. dos-a-dos 6. dramaturgy 7. hex 8. genesis 9. graminivorous 10. cinerous 11. crinate 12. lyceum 13. polyandry 14. Prakrit 15. theanthropism 16. constellation

5. Answers: 1. e; 2. c; 3. a; 4. e; 5. e; 6. a

SECTION THREE: GREEK

POSTLUDE
REVIEW OF GREEK— CHAPTERS NINE TO FOURTEEN

1. PRODUCTIVE BASES
Give meaning and form five English words from each of these:
Example: scholē, *leisure* > school, scholar, scholiast, scholophobia, scholology, scholasticism
1. anthrōpos
2. astēr
3. ergon
4. kosmos
5. tupos
6. chronos
7. lithos
8. oikos
9. morphē
10. zōon
11. autos
12. idios
13. isos
14. isos
15. mikros
16. monos
17. prōtos
18. tēle
19. anthos
20. theos
21. logos [words that are not -logy, *study of*, words]

2. SUFFIXES: Fill in meanings. Give two (or more) words using each, four for those marked with an asterisk.

Example: -isk, -iscus   *small* > asterisk, basilisk, obelisk, meniscus

-ic, -tic

* -ac

* -ics [Greek, -ika]

-ical < *-ic* + *-al* (from Latin)

* -oid

* -ite

-ism

-ist

* -ast

-ia, -y

* -sis

* -m, -me, -ma [base, -mat-]

3. PREFIXES: Find 4 words using each prefix marked with *; two using each of the others.

Example: * a- [an- before a vowel] *not, un-, -less* > atheist, amnesia, anarchy, amoral, assymetrical

amphi- *both, on both sides, around, about*

* ana- [an- before a vowel] *up, back, again*

* anti- *instead, against, in opposition to*

* apo- [ap- before a vowel or h] *from, away from, off, utterly, completely, lack of*

* cata-, cat- [Greek, kata] *down, against, completely* [opp. ana-]

* dia-, di- *through, across, over, assunder*

dys- [Greek, dus-] *ill, un-, mis-, difficult, bad*

* ec-, ex- [Greek, ek, ex] *out, from, off*

ecto- [Greek, ekto-] *on the outside*

* en-, em- *in*

enantio- [en- + anti-] *opposite*

endo- *within, inside, internal*

eso- *inward, within* > esoteric, esoterica

exo- *outward, external*

* epi- (ep- before a vowel or h) *upon, over, at, near*

* eu- (rarely, ev-) *well, good*

* hyper- [Greek, huper] *above, beyond, exceedingly*

* hypo-, hyp- [Greek, hupo] *under*

* meta-, met- *among, between, change, behind, later*

palin-, pali- *back, again*

* para-, par- *beside, beyond, near, incorrectly, like*

* peri- *around, about*

* pro- *before, forward, for*

pros- *to, toward, besides, in front*
* syn-, sym-, syl-, sys- [Greek, sun] *with, together*

4. VERBS. Study the verbs in Chapter 14. Give meaning of each verb; using the suffixes and prefixes from units IV and V, make up three or more words using each verb (in any of its forms).
Example: bainein *go, step*: basis, diabetes, catabatic, anabasis, acrobat, stylobate
* akouein: acou-, acu-
aisthanesthai: aesth-, esth-
* agein: ag- the base sometimes appears as -eg-
* bainein: ba-, be-
* ballein: ball-, ble-, bol-
chorein: chor-
kinein: cin-, kin-
kalein: cle-
klinein: clin-, cli-
koptein: cop-, com-
krinein: crin-, cri-
kruptein: crypt-, cryp-
didonai: do-
* dokein: doc-, dog-, dox-
dran: dra-
dramein: drom-
dunasthai: dyn-
gluphein: glyph-
* gignoskein: gno-
* graphein: graph-, gram-
echein: hec-, hex-, sche-, ech- och-, -uch-
ienai: i- *go* (cognate to Latin ire)
lambanein: lab-, lep-, lem-
* legein: leg-, lex-, lect-, log-
* luein: ly-
* manthanein: math-
nemein nem-, nom-
einai:-ont-, -ous-
pauein: pau-, -pose
* phanai: pha-, phe-
phagein: phag-
* phainein: phen-, phan-, pha-
* pherein: pher-, phor-
* phuein: phy-
poiein: poie-, poe-
polein: pol-

* prattein: prag-, prac-
rhein: rhe(u)-, rhy-, rho-
schizein: schiz-, schis-
* skopein: scop-, scep-, skep-
* histanai: sta-, ste-
* stellein: stol-, stal-, stl-
strephein: streph- (strep-), stroph-
tattein: tak-, tac-, tax-
teinein: ten-, ta-, ton-
* tithenai: the-
temnein: tme-, tom-
trephein: troph-
trepein: trop(h)-

5. WORD ANALYSIS—Divide into parts. Give meanings of parts. Choose ten and use each in a sentence.

Example: ornithocracy ornitho-cracy > bird power (government by birds). The characters in Aristophanes' *Birds* attempt to form an ornithocracy.

1. gynecocracy
2. xenoglossy
3. zoogeography
4. anemometer
5. anthropomorphic
6. androgyny
7. autobiography
8. pyromancy
9. topolatry
10. chromosome
11. plutonomy
12. psychosomatic
13. podiatry
14. xylography
15. theocracy
16. periscope
17. teleological
18. epidemic
19. gymnosophist
20. pseudepigrapha
21. autochthonous
22. orthography
23. theosophy
24. archetypical
25. demographics

26. telekinesis
27. stenography
28. stereoscope
29. isotherme
30. trachea
31. xerophil
32. telemetry
33. polychromatic
34. gymnophilia
35. holograph
36. isosceles [*skelos*, leg]
37. pliocene
38. megalomorph
39. monoecious [< *oikos*]
40. orthoscope

6. WORD-WORDS: give an example of each:
Example: *enantionyms* (called *contronyms*[1] if they are also spelled the same) are words that sound the same but have opposite meanings: cleave [cut, split], cleave [cling]; raise, raze; seed, seed.
 1. an anonymous work
 2. eponym
 3. paronymous words
 4. metonymy
 5. synonyms
 6. antonyms
 7. homonyms
 8. acronym
 9. pseudonym
10. euonym
11. hyperbole
12. palindrome
13. anagrams
14. euphemism
15 metaphor
16. epithet
17. heteronyms
18. oxymoron
19. cacoepy
20. homograph
21. homonyms
22. onomatopoeia

7. COMBINING FORMS: Choose 2 and give 20 words using each and tell what each is concerned with.

-logy

-meter

-phobia

8. List ten or more new words you have learned in Part Three, Chapters I-VI

VOCABULARY REVIEW

Be able to give two or more words from each.

A   aēr *air*

    agein: ag- the base sometimes appears as -eg- *lead, bring*

    agros *field, land*

    aisthanesthai: aesth-, esth- *feel, perceive*

    akouein: acou-, acu- *hear*

    akros [acro-] *topmost*

    algos [-algia] *pain*

    allos [allo-] *other*

    anemos *wind* [cf. Latin, animus/anima *breath, spirit*]

    anēr, andr- *man (male)*

    angelos *messenger*

    angos [angio-] *vessel*

    anthos blossom, *flower*

    anthropos *human being*

    arch- *chief, first*

    -archy [Greek archē, *rule, beginning*] *government, rule*

    aristos [aristo-] *best*

    astēr *star*

    atmos *steam, vapor*

    autos [auto-] *self*

    axios *worthy*

B   bainein: ba-, be- *go, step, walk*

    ballein: ball-, ble-, bol- *throw*

    barus [bary-, bari-, baro-] *heavy* bar a unit of pressure

    bathus [bathy-, batho-] *deep*

    biblion *book*

    bios *life*

    brachus [brachy-] *short* brachion *shorter* > upper *arm*

C   chorein: chor- *move* -chore indicates a plant *distributed by a specific agency*

    chrōma, chrōmat- *color*

    chronos *time*

    -cracy *government by*

D   daimōn *spirit, divinity*
     deinos [dino-] *terrible*
     demos *the people*
     dendron *tree*
     didonai: do- *give*
     dokein: doc-, dog-, dox- *seem, think*
     dramein: drom- *run*
     dran: dra- *do, act, perform*
     dunasthai: dyn- *be able, be powerful*
E   echein: hec-, hex-, sche-, ech- och-, -uch- *have, hold*
     eikōn *image, likeness*
     einai:-ont-, -ous- *be* (root, -es:)
     ergon *work*
     ethnos *nation, people*
     ethos *custom*
     etumos [etymo-] *true*
     eurus [eury-] *wide*
G   gamos *marriage, sexual union*
     gē [geo-] *earth*
     -genesis [Greek, genesis, *birth, origin*] *generation, birth* >
     gignōskein: gno- *know*
     glōssa/glōtta *tongue, language*
     gluphein: glyph- *carve*
     -gony, -geny [Greek goneia, *generation* < gonos, *offspring, seed*] *production of*
     -graph *means of writing/drawing; something drawn/written, to create the description of*
     graphein: graph-, gram- *draw, write*
     -graphic *having to do with method of writing / descriptive science*
     -graphy [Greek graphein, *to write*] *a method of writing; a descriptive science*
     gumnos [gymno-] *naked*
     gunē, gunaik- [gyneco-] *woman*
H   haima, haimat- [hem-/hemat-] *blood*
     hēlios *the sun*
     heteros [hetero-] *other, one of two*
     hieros [hiero-] *holy*
     hippos *horse*
     histanai: sta-, ste- *stand, cause to stand*
     histos *web, tissue*
     holos [holo-] *whole*
     homoios [homeo-, homoio-] *like*
     homos [homo-] *one and the same*
     hoplon *armor*

hōra *time, hour*
hudat- [< hudōr]; hydro- *water*
hugiēs *healthy*
hugros [hygro-] *wet, moist*
hupnos *sleep*

I   -iatrist, -iatrician *physician who treats*
-iatry [Greek iatreia, *healing*] *medical treatment*
ichthus *fish*
idios [idio-] *one's own, peculiar*
ienai: i- *go* (cognate to Latin ire)
isos [iso-] *equal*

K   kainos [ceno-, caeno-; -cene] *new*
kakos [caco-] *bad, ugly*
kalein: cle- *call*
kalos [kal-, calli-] *beautiful*
karpos *fruit*
kephalē *head*
kinein: cin-, kin- *move*
klinein: clin-, cli- *bend, make to slope*
kolla *glue*
koptein: cop-, com- *cut*
kosmos *order, universe, adornment*
krinein: crin-, cri- *separate, judge, decide*
kruptein: crypt-, cryp- *hide*
kuklos *circle*
kuōn, kun- *dog*

L   lambanein: lab-, lep-, lem- *take, seize*
-later *worshiper of*
-latry [Greek, *latreia, service for pay*] *worship of*
legein: leg-, lex-, lect-, log- *gather, say*
lithos *stone*
logos *word, reason*
-logy [Greek logos, *word*] *discourse, speech, the science, theory, study of*
luein: ly- *loose, break, destroy*
lukos *wolf*

M   makros [macro-] *long*
-mancy [Greek manteia, *prophecy*] *telling the future by*
-mania [Greek mania, *madness*] *madness, exaggerated craving*
-maniac *one displaying such an excessive craving*
manthanein: math- *learn*
megas, megal- [mega-, megalo-; -megaly] *big*
mētēr, mētro- *mother* [metra *womb*]
-meter [Greek, metron, *measure*] *an instrument for measuring, a measure*

metron *measure*
-metry, *the measurement of, science of measuring*
mikros [micro-] *small*
mimos *imitator*
miso- [Greek, misos, *hatred*] *hate of*
monos [mono-] *alone, only, single*
morphē *shape, form*
murios [myrio-] *countless, 10,000*
muthos *speech, story*
N naus *ship* -naut *sailor*
nekros *corpse*
nemein nem-, nom- *assign, allot*
neos [neo-] *new*
nephos/nephelē *cloud*
-nomy [Greek nomos, *law, custom, usage*] *systematized knowledge of, laws concerning*
O oikos [eco-] *house, environment*
oligos [oligo-] *few*
onoma, onomat- *name*
-onym [Greek onoma, *name*] *name*
ornis, ornitho- *bird*
oros *mountain*
orthos [ortho-] *straight*
osteon *bone*
oxus [oxy-] *sharp*
P pais, paid- [ped-] *child*
palaios [paleo-, palaeo-] *old*
pas, pant- [pan-, panto-] *all*
patēr, patro- *father*
pathos *suffering, experience* -pathy *illness*
pauein: pau-, -pose (influenced by Lat. ponere) *cease, stop*
petra *rock*
phagein: phag- *eat*
phainein: phen-, phan-, pha- *show, cause to appear; appear*
phanai: pha-, phe- *say, speak* (*pheme* a saying)
pherein: pher-, phor- *bear, carry*
philo- [Greek, philos, *loving, dear*] *love of* -phile *one loving*
philos *beloved, dear, loving*
-phobia [Greek phobos, *fear*] *fear of* -phobe *one who fears*
-phone [Greek, phonē, *voice*] *sound, sound emitting device*
phōnē *voice*
phōs, phōto- *light*
phōs, phōt- *light*

phuein: phy-   *make to grow; grow, be by nature*
phulē *tribe*
phullon *leaf*
platus [platy-] *wide, broad*
pleion [plio-, pleo-] *more, greater*
pleistos [pleisto-] *most, greatest*
poiein: poie-, poe-   *make, do*
polein: pol-   *sell*
polemos *war*
polis *city, city-state*
polus [poly-] *much, many*
potamos *river*
pous, pod-   *foot*
prattein: prag-, prac-   *do*
prōtos [proto-] *first*
pseudēs [pseudo-] *false*
psychē *soul, breath, life*
pur *fire*

Rh   rhein: rhe(u)-, rhy-, rho-   *flow*
rhētor *orator*
rhodon *rose*

S   sauros *lizard*
schizein: schiz-, schis-   *split*
scholē *leisure*
-scope [Greek skopein, to look at] *instrument for observing*
sēma, sēmat- *sign, signal*
sklēros *hard*
skopein: scop-, scep-, skep-   *examine, look at*
sōma, sōmato-   *body*
sophos *wise*
sta- see histanai (*stand*)
stellein: stol-, stal-, stl-   *send, make ready*
strephein: streph- (strep-), stroph-   *turn*

T   taphos *tomb*
tattein: tak-, tac-, tax-   *arrange, assign, assess*
technē *art, skill*
teinein: ten-, ta-, ton-   *stretch out, strain*
tektōn [-tect] *carpenter, builder*
tēle [tele-] *far away* [adverb]
telos [teleo-] *end*
temnein: tme-, tom-   *cut*
theos *god*
therapōn/theraps *attendant* therapeia *treatment*

thermos [thermo-] *warm, hot*
tithenai: the-   *put, place*
topos *place*
trepein: trop(h)-   *turn*
trephein: troph-   *feed, nourish*
tupos   *mark*
X   xenos   *foreigner, stranger*
    xēros [xero-] *dry*
Z   zōon   *animal, living thing*

CANVAS

A heavy, coarse, closely woven fabric of cotton, hemp, or flax, used for awnings, tents, sails and oil paintings.

Etymology: Middle English *canevas*, from Old French and from Medieval Latin *canavasium*, from Latin *cannabis*, hemp from Greek *kannabis*, Cannabis sativa. Possibly from Ugro-Finnish.

Herodotus, *Histories* 4.74-75, in writing about burial customs of the Scythians describes their use of hemp for vapor baths. [Paraphrased.]

> They carry the dead around from house to house for 40 days. Then they set up a space for a steam bath, enclosing it with wool mats. In the center they make a pit into which they throw hot stones. Then they throw the hemp seeds onto the hot stones. "No Greek steam could surpass its fumes. The Scythians howl in ecstasy."

Hemp was also used by the ancient Thracians and Scythians as a linen substitute.

Some things to leave with:

COLLECTING EGGCORNS

A new word for 2015 in the Merriam-Webster dictionary is *eggcorn*, defined as "A word or phrase that sounds like and is mistakenly used in a seemingly logical or plausible way for another word or phrase."[2] Examples are *eggcorn* itself which comes from a minority pronunciation of *acorn*, *idea card* for *ID card*, *ear bugs* for *ear buds*, *deluscious* for *delicious*, *laxidaisical* for *lackidaisical*, *earthquicks* for *earthquakes*, *paper towers* for *paper towels*, *pass mustard* for *pass muster*, *doggy-dog world* for *dog-eat-dog world*, *coming down the pipe* for *coming down the pike*, *exersizers* for *exercises*, *unchartered waters* for *uncharted waters*, *soredust* for *sawdust*, *carpool tunnel* for *carpel tunnel* and *for all intensive purposes* for *for all intents and purposes*. My personal favorite in the NPR list is *pre-Madonna* for *prima donna*.

Keep your ears open and try to collect eggcorns as they fall from the trees.

AND MONDEGREENS

Mondegreens are also fun. They are misheard lyrics. The name, coined by the writer Sylvia Wright in an essay, comes from lyrics of the ballad "The Bonnie Earl of Moray"
    They hae slain the Earl o' Moray,
    And *laid him on the green* (misheard as "Lady Mondegreen").

Among our favorites are "Gladly, the cross-eyed bear" and Jimi Hendrix' "Scuse me while I kiss this guy." But one we misheard is "people read books with Greek quotations" for "read books, repeat quotations" from the Bob Dylan song "Love Minus Zero / No Limit" (1965).

WORDNESIA

Even after studying etymology, *wordnesia* can strike out of nowhere. This happens when you cannot think of even the simplest word or when simple words look wrong to you. There is no need to worry because it happens to everyone. Is *wordnesia* just a portmanteau word made from *word + nesia* from *amnesia*? But *amnesia* is *a-*, not, un- + *mnesia*, memory. On the other hand -nesia means "group of islands," so do the letters of the word seem separate like the scattered islands of the Sporades?

NOTES

1. For a list of seventy-five contronyms or enantionyms, see the website:
 http://www.dailywritingtips.com/75-contronyms-words-with-contradictory-meanings/.

2. From NPR's Weekend Edition for Saturday, May 30, 2015. See also the follow-up, http://www.npr.org/sections/thetwo-way/2015/06/01/411231029/here-are-100-eggcorns-that-we-say-pass-mustard. It should be noted that eggcorn was already in the 2011 edition of the *American Heritage Dictionary*.

APPENDIX I: LATIN NOUN DECLENSIONS

Long marks are indicated only where needed to distinguish one case from another.

	I	II, m	II, n	III, m/f	III, n
	via,	modus	donum	rex	genus
	viae, f	modi, m	doni, n	regis, m	generis, n
	road	*manner*	*gift*	*king*	*birth*

SINGULAR

	I	II, m	II, n	III, m/f	III, n
Nominative	via	modus	donum	rex	genus
Genitive	viae	modi	doni	regis	generis
Dative	viae	modo	dono	regi	generi
Accusative	viam	modum	donum	regem	genus
Ablative	viā	modo	dono	rege	genere
Vocative	via	mode	donum	rex	genus

PLURAL

	I	II, m	II, n	III, m/f	III, n
Nom./ Voc.	viae	modi	dona	reges	genera
Genitive	viarum	modorum	donorum	regum	generum
Dative	viis	modis	donis	regibus	generibus
Accusative	vias	modos	dona	reges	genera
Ablative	viis	modis	donis	regibus	generibus

	IV m/f	IV, n	V
	manus	cornu	res
	manūs, f	cornūs, n	rei, f
	hand	*horn*	*thing*

SINGULAR

	IV m/f	IV, n	V
Nominative	manus	cornu	res
Genitive	manūs	cornūs	rei
Dative	manu(i)	cornu	rei
Accusative	manum	cornu	rem
Ablative	manu	cornu	re
Vocative	manus	cornu	res

PLURAL

	IV m/f	IV, n	V
Nom./ Voc.	manūs	cornua	res
Genitive	manuum	cornuum	rerum
Dative	manibus	cornibus	rebus
Accusative	manūs	cornua	res
Ablative	manibus	cornibus	rebus

Appendix II: Summary of Latin Plurals

First Declension
>   Nouns ending in -*a*, plural in -*ae* (most are feminine)
>>   alumna [*foster daughter*, female graduate], pl. alumnae (pronounced alúmnē [like knee] in English; in Latin -ae is pronounced like English *eye*)
>>   emerita [*retired*, but retaining an honorary title, used of a woman, as professor emerita], pl. emeritae

Second Declension
>   Nouns ending in -*us*, plural in -*i* (most are masculine)
>>   alumnus [*foster son*], pl. alumni (pronounced alúmnī [eye] in English; in Latin alumnē [like knee])
>>   emeritus [*retired*, but retaining an honorary title, used of a man, as professor emeritus), pl. emeriti
>>   When speaking of a mixed group of men and women the masculine plural form (alumni, emeriti) is used.
>   Nouns ending in -*um*, plural in -*a* — All these nouns are neuter.
>>   rostrum [*a speaker's platform* in Latin the original meaning is *beak*], pl. rostra or rostrums
>>   addendum [*something to be added*], pl. addenda

Third Declension
>   Nouns of this type vary widely in the nominative (or subject form) and a second form, showing the base, must be learned.
>>   appendix [f. *an addition*], base appendic-, pl. appendices or appendixes
>>   onus [n. *burden*], base oner-, pl. onera
>   Plurals:
>>   a) masculine and feminine, base + -*es*
>>>   index [*forefinger, pointer*], base indic-, pl. indices
>>>   cicatrix [*scar > scar tissue*], base cicatric-, pl. cicatrices
>>   b) neuter, base + -*a*
>>>   genus [*kind, birth*], base gener-, pl. genera
>>>   corpus [*body*], base corpor-, pl. corpora
>>>   opus [*work*], base oper-, pl. opera

Fourth Declension
>   Nouns end in -*us* [the few neuters end in -*u*]; the Latin plural is spelled the same as the singular [the neuters in -ua], but the Latin plurals of these are not much used in English, except in the sciences and other technical writing.
>>   hiatus [*gap*], pl. hiatuses or hiatus
>>   plexus [*network*], pl. plexuses or plexus

nexus [*bond*], pl. nexuses or nexus

apparatus [*preparation*], pl. apparatuses or apparatus

An *apparatus criticus* (usually placed at the bottom of a text) shows textual variants and scholarly emendations. The plural is *apparatus critici.*

Fifth Declension

Nouns in *-es*, the plural is the same as the singular

species [*appearance > kind*], pl. species

caries [*decay*], pl. caries

Glossary I: Latin

A

acer, acr-	*sharp, keen*
aequus [equi-]	*even, equal*
aevum [ev-]	*age*
ager, agr-	*field*
agere, actum	*do, drive, lead*
ala	*wing*
albus	*white*
alere, altum	*grow*
alienus	*belonging to another*
alter	*other*
altus	*high, deep*
amare	*love*
ambulare	*walk, go*
amicus	*friend*
amoenus [amen-]	*pleasant*
amplus	*large, spacious*
ancilla	*female servant*
anima	*breath*
animus	*spirit*
annus [-enn-]	*year*
antiquus	*old*
aperire, apertum	*open*
apis (pl. apes)	*bee*
aptus	*fitted to*
aqua	*water*
aquila	*eagle*
arbiter [-itr-]	*witness, judge*
arca	*chest*
arcus	*bow*
ardēre, arsum	*burn*
ars, art- skill,	*craft*
artus	*joint*
asper	*rough, bitter, harsh*
atavus	*ancestor*
audēre	*dare*
audire, auditum	*hear*
augēre, auctum	*increase*
augur	*soothsayer*
aura	*breeze*
auris, aur-	*ear*
auxilium	*aid*
avarus	*greedy*
avis (pl. aves)	*bird*
avus	*grandfather*

B

baca, bacca	*berry*
beatus	*happy, blessed*
bellum	*war*
bellus	*pretty, handsome*
bene	*well*
bi-, bin-, bis-	*two, by twos,*
bibere	*drink*
bonus	*good*
bos, bov-	*ox, bull, cow*
brevis	*short*

C

cadere, casum	*fall*
caedere, caesum	*cut, kill*
caelum	*sky*
calere	*be warm*
calx, calc-	*pebble*
campus	*open field*
candēre	*shine, be white*
canere, cantum	*sing*
canis, can(i)-	*dog*
capere, captum	*take, seize [-ceive]*
capsa	*box*
caput, capit-	*head*
carcer	*prison*
cardo, cardin-	*hinge*
caro, carn-	*flesh*
castra	*camp*
castus	*pure, chaste*
causa	*cause, reason*
cavus	*hollow*
cedere, cessum	*go, yield*
cella	*storeroom*
centum	*hundred*
cerebrum	*head, brain*
censēre, censum	*assess, rate*
cernere, cretum	*sift*
civis, civ(i)-	*citizen*
clamare, -atum	*shout [-claim]*
clarus	*bright, clear*
classis	*fleet*
claudere, clausum	*shut [-close]*
clavis	*key*
clinare, clinatum	*turn, bend*
codex, codic-	*tree trunk, book*
colere, cultum	*till, honor, dwell*
comis	*nice, courteous*
condere, -itum	*build, store, hide*
copia	*abundance, supplies*
cor, cordi-	*heart*
corium	*hide, skin*
cornu	*horn*
corona	*crown*
corpus, corpor-, n	*body*
creare, creatum	*create*
credere, -itum	*believe*
crescere, cretum	*grow*
crux, cruc(i)-	*cross*
culpa	*fault*
currere, cursum	*run*
cutis	*skin*

D

dare, datum	*give*
debere, debitum	*owe*
decem	*ten*
dens, dent-	*tooth*
deus, de-	*god*
dexter [-tr-]	*right hand*

dicere, dictum	*say*	fumus	*smoke, steam*
dies, di-	*day*	fundere, fusum	*pour*
difficilis	*hard*	fundus	*bottom, property*
dignus	*worthy*	fungi, functum	*perform*
diluvium	*flood*	funus, funer-	*death, rites for the*
discipulus	*pupil, disciple*		*dead*
divus	*of a god, divine*	G	
docēre, doctum	*teach*	garrire	*chatter*
dolēre, dolitum	*be in pain, grieve*	genus, gener-, n	*race, kind, birth*
dominus	*master*	gerere, gestum	*carry, wage*
domus [domes-]	*home, house*	germen, germin-	*sprout*
donum	*gift*	gladius	*sword*
dorsum	*back*	globus	*globe*
dubius	*doubtful*	gradi, gressum	*step, walk*
ducere, ductum	*lead*	gradus, gradu-	*step*
duo	*two*	granum	*grain*
E		gratia	*favor, thanks*
emere, emptum	*buy*	gratus	*grateful, thankful*
equ-, equi- see aequus		gravis	*heavy, serious*
equus	*horse*	grex, greg-	*flock*
errare, erratum	*go astray*	H	
esse, futurum	*be*	habēre, habitum	*have, hold*
experiri, -pertum	*try, test*	haerēre, haesum	*cling, stick* [-her-/hes-]
F		hamus	*hook*
facilis	*easy*	herba	*young plant, grass*
facere, factum	*do, make*	heres, hered-	*heir*
fama	*talk, rumor*	hibernus	*wintry, [of] winter*
fanum	*temple*	homo, homin-	*human being*
fari, fatum	*speak*	horrēre	*shudder, stand stiff*
fatēri, fassum	*acknowledge*	hospes, hospit-	*host*
fatum	*thing said, fate*	hostis, host(i)-	*enemy*
fatuus	*silly, foolish*	humanus	*human*
fecundus	*fertile*	humēre	*be moist*
felix, felic-	*happy*	humilis	*lowly*
femina	*woman*	humus	*the ground, soil*
fendere, fensum	*strike, hurt*	I	
ferre, latum	*bear, carry*	ignis, ign(i)-	*fire*
ferus	*wild*	imitari, imitatum	*copy*
fervēre	*boil*	immunis	*tax-exempt*
[-fici-, -fect-] see *facere*		index, indic-	*forefinger, pointer*
fidere	*trust, rely on*	insidiae	*ambush, trap*
findere, fissum	*split*	insula	*island*
fingere, fictum	*form*	ire, itum	*go*
finis	*end*	iter, itiner-	*journey*
flamma	*torch, fire, flame*	iterum	*again*
flectere, flexum	*bend*	J	
flos, flor-	*flower*	jejunus	*hungry*
fluere, fluxum	*flow*	jacere, jactum	*throw*
fluctus	*wave*	jacēre [no *ppp*]	*lie*
focus	*hearth*	jocus	*jest*
forma	*shape, beauty*	judex, judic-	*judge*
fortis	*strong, brave*	jungere, junctum	*join*
forum	*public space*	jus, jur-	*right, law*
frangere, fractum	*break*	L	
frater, fratr(i)	*brother*	labi, lapsum	*slip*
frustra	*in vain*	labor, labor-	*work*
fugere, fugitum	*flee*	lacrima	*tear*

lassus	*tired*	mordēre, -sum	*bite*
latēre	*lie hidden*	mors, mort-	*death*
latum [ferre]	*carried*	mortuus	*dead body*
latus, later-	*side*	mos, mor-	*custom, manner*
latus [adj.]	*wide*	movēre, motum	*move*
legere, lectum	*gather, choose,*	multus	*many*
	read	mundus	*world*
levis	*light*	murus	*wall*
lex, leg-	*law*	mus, mur-	*mouse*
liber, liber-	*free*	mutare, mutatum	*change*
liber, libr-	*book*	N	
libra	*balance*	nasci, natum	*be born*
limen, limin-	*threshhold*	navis, nav-	*ship*
linere, litum	*smear*	necesse	*unavoidable*
linquere, -lictum	*leave*	nepos, nepot-	*grandson, nephew*
liquēre	*be fluid*	nervus	*tendon*
littera	*letter*	nihil	*nothing*
livēre	*be black and blue*	nomen, nomin-	*name*
locus	*place*	nonus	*ninth*
longus	*long*	novem	*nine*
loqui, locutum	*speak*	novus	*new*
lucēre	*shine, be light*	nox, noct-	*night*
ludere, lusum	*play*	numerus	*number*
lumen, lumin-	*light*	nuntius	*message, messenger*
luna	*moon*	nutrire, nutritum	*nourish*
lupus	*wolf*	nux, nuc-	*nut*
lympha	*water*	O	
M		oculus	*eye*
magnus	*big, great*	octo	*eight*
major, majus	*greater, bigger,*	odium	*hatred*
	older	omnis, omni-	*all*
malus	*bad*	onus, oner-, n	*burden*
manēre, mansum	*remain*	ops, op-	*means, resources*
manus, manu-	*hand*	optare, optatum	*wish*
mare, mar-	*sea*	optimus	*best*
mater, matr(i)-	*mother*	opus, oper-, n	*work*
maximus	*biggest, greatest*	ordo, ordin-	*rank, row*
medius [adj.]	*[in the] middle*	oriri, ortum	*arise*
melior [see bonus]	*better*	os, or-	*mouth*
memor	*mindful*	os, oss-	*bone*
mens, ment-	*mind*	otium	*leisure*
mensa	*table*	P	
metus	*fear*	paene	*almost*
migrare, -atum	*move*	paenitēre	*repent*
miles, milit-	*soldier*	pagus	*village*
mille, mill(i)-	*thousand*	panis	*bread*
minimus	*smallest, least*	par	*equal*
minor, minus	*smaller, younger,*	parare, paratum	*get, get ready*
	less	parcus	*sparing*
mirari, miratum	*wonder at*	pars, part-	*part*
miscēre, mixtum	*mix, mingle*	pater, patr(i)-	*father*
miser	*wretched*	pati, passum	*suffer*
mittere, missum	*send, let go*	pauci [pl. adj.]	*few*
modus	*manner*	pax, pac-	*peace*
moles, mole-	*heap, mass*	pecunia	*money*
monēre, monitum	*warn, advise*	pejor	*worse*
mons, mont-	*mountain*	pellere, pulsum	*push*

pendere, pensum	*hang, weigh*	rogare, rogatum	*ask*
pes, ped-	*foot*	rota	*wheel*
pessimus	*worst*	ruga	*wrinkle*
pestis, pest(i)-	*plague*	rumpere, ruptum	*burst, break*
petere, petitum	*aim at, seek*	rus, rur-	*the country*
pingere, pictum	*prick, paint*	S	
pinna	*feather*	saeculum	*age, the times*
pius	*devoted to duty*	salire, saltum	*leap, jump*
placēre, placitum	*please*	salus, salut-	*health, safety*
plectere, plexum	*weave*	sanctus	*holy*
plenus	*full*	sanguis, sanguin-	*blood*
ponere, positum	*put, place*	sanus	*sound, healthy*
pontifex, pontific-	*high priest*	sapiens, sapient-	*wise*
populus	*a people*	satis	*enough*
portare, portatum	*carry*	scandere, -scensum	*climb*
posse [pot-]	*be able*	scire	*know*
posterus	*coming after*	scribere, scriptum	*write*
potens, potent-	*powerful, able*	scrupus	*stone*
praeda	*booty, prey*	secare, sectum	*cut*
prehendere,-sum	*seize*	secundus	*second*
premere, pressum	*squeeze*	sedēre, sessum	*sit*
pretium	*price*	semi	*one half*
prex, prec-	*prayer*	senex, sen-	*old*
primus	*first*	sentire, sensum	*feel*
prodigium	*portent, monster*	septem, sept-	*seven*
proles	*offspring*	sequi, secutum	*follow*
proprius	*one's own*	series	*row*
proximus	*nearest*	servare, servatum	*save*
puer, puer-	*boy, child*	servus	*slave*
pulcher, pulchr-	*handsome*	sesqui-	*one half more*
pugnare, -atum	*fight*	sex	*six*
pungere, punctum	*prick, sting*	signum	*mark*
putare, putatum	*think, consider*	similis	*like*
Q		sinus, sinu-	*wave, fold*
quaerere, -quisit-	*seek, ask*	sistere, statum	*set, stand*
qualis	*of what kind*	sobrius	*moderate*
quantus	*how much*	socius	*ally, companion*
quartus	*fourth*	sol, sol-	*sun*
quattuor, quadr-	*four*	solere, solitum	*become accustomed*
quēri	*complain*	solvere, solutum	*loosen*
quintus	*fifth*	somnus	*sleep*
quinque	*five*	soror	*sister*
quis, quid	*who, what*	specere, spectum	*look at*
quotus	*how many*	species	*sight, appearance*
R		spirare, spiratum	*breathe*
radius, radi-	*ray*	sponte	*of one's accord*
radix, radic-	*root*	squalere	*be stiff, be clotted*
ramus	*branch*	stare, statum	*stand*
rancere	*stink*	sternere, stratum	*spread*
rapere, raptum	*snatch*	stimulus	*goad*
ratio, ration-	*reason, reckoning*	stinguere, stinctum	*quench*
regere, rectum	*guide, direct, rule*	stringere, strictum	*draw tight*
rēri, ratum	*think*	struere, structum	*pile up, build*
rete	*net*	studēre	*be eager, study*
rex, reg-	*king*	studium	*eagerness, zeal*
rigēre	*be stiff*	stupēre	*be stunned*
rodere, rosum	*gnaw*	sumere, sumptum	*take up*

T

tabula	*plank, table*
tangere, tactum	*touch* [-ting-]
tegere, tectum	*cover*
templum	*sanctuary*
tempus, tempor-, n	*time*
tendere, tentum/ tensum	*stretch, aim at*
tenēre, tentum	*hold, keep*
tenuis	*thin*
terminus	*boundary, end*
terere, tritum	*rub away*
terra	*earth, land*
terrēre	*frighten*
testis	*witness*
texere, textum	*weave, build*
timēre	*fear*
tingere, tinctum	*dip*
tondere, tonsum	*shear, clip, shave*
torpēre	*be numb*
torquēre,tortum	*twist*
trahere, tractum	*drag*, draw
tremere	*quake, tremble*
tres, tri-	*three*
tumēre	*be swollen*
turba	riot, uproar

U

ultimus	*last*
unus	*one*
urbs, urb-	*city*
uti, usum	*use*

V

vacuus	*empty*
vadere, vasum	*go, make one's way*
valēre	*be well*
varius	*speckled, changing*
vehere, vectum	*convey*
vellere, vulsum	*pluck, pull*
vendere, -ditum	*sell*
venire, ventum	*come*
venter, ventr-	*stomach, belly*
venum	*sale*
ver	*spring*
verbum	*word*
vermis	*worm*
vertere, versum	*turn*
verus	*true*
vestigium	*trace, footprint*
vestis	*clothes*
vexare, vexatum	*shake*
via way,	*road*
vidēre, visum	*see*
vigēre	*thrive*
vigilare	*be wakeful*
vilis	*cheap*
vincere, victum	*win, conquer*
vinum	*wine*
vir, vir-	*man, male*
virus	*poison*
vis	*force, strength*
vita	*life*
vitium	*fault*
vivere, victum	*live*
vocare, vocatum	*call, use the* vox
volvere, volutum	*roll*
vorare, voratum	*devour, eat*
vovēre, votum	*vow, promise*
vox, voc-	*voice*

GLOSSARY II: ENGLISH TO LATIN

A: NOUNS AND ADJECTIVES FOR EXERCISES IN SECTION TWO A

abundance	*copia*	moon	*luna*
age	*saeculum*	mother	*mater*
all	*omnis*	mouse	*mus, mur-*
beautiful	*pulcher, pulchri-*	night	*nox, nocti-*
bigger	*major*	number	*numerus*
body	*corpus, corpor-*	nut	*nux, nuc-*
bone	*os, oss-*	old man	*senex, senect- sen-*
bright	*clarus*	older	*major, senior*
changing	*varius*	one	*unus*
clear	*clarus*	part	*pars, part-*
comrade	*socius*	people	*populus*
day	*dies*	plague	*pestis*
dead body	*mortuus*	rank	*ordo, ordin-*
devoted to duty	*pius*	root	*radix, radic-*
ear	*auris*	said, thing	*fatum*
earth	*terra*	sea	*mare, mar-*
end	*finis*	shape	*forma*
even	*aequus*	sharp	*acer, acri-*
father	*pater*	ship	*navis*
fault/flaw	*vitium*	short	*brevis*
few	*pauci*	side	*latus, later-*
first	*primus*	slave	*servus*
flesh	*caro, carni-*	sleep	*somnus*
foot	*pes, ped-*	smaller	*minor*
free	*liber*	soldier	*miles, milet-*
full	*plenus*	sound (healthy)	*sanus*
god	*deus, divus*	spirit	*animus, anima*
grain	*granum*	sun	*sol*
hatred	*odium*	supplies	*copia*
head	*caput, capit-*	thing said	*fatum*
healthy	*sanus*	time	*tempus, tempor-*
heap	*moles*	[these] times	*saeculum*
heart	*cor, cordi-*	unavoidable	*necesse*
herb	*herba*	voice	*vox, voc-*
holy	*sanctus*	water	*aqua*
home	*domus, domes-*	wicked	*malus*
human	*humanus*	wide	*latus*
large	*amplus, magnus*	witness	*testis*
law	*lex, leg-*	word	*verbum*
light	*levis*	worthy	*dignus*
like	*similis*	wretched	*miser*
long	*longus*	year	*annus (-enni-)*
lowly	*humilis*	younger	*minor*
mind	*animus, anima*		

B: VERBS: FOR EXERCISES IN SECTION TWO B

able, be	*posse (pot-)*	be afraid	*timēre*
add	*addere/additum*	be strong	*valēre*
afraid, be	*timēre*	be born	*nasci/natum*
all	*omnis*	be able	*posse (pot-)*
ask	*rogare/rogatum*	be shining white	*candēre*

bear	*ferre/latum*	pile	*struere/structum*
believe	*credere/creditum*	place	*ponere/positum*
bend	*flectere/flexum*	play	*ludere/lusum*
bite	*mordēre/morsum*	please	*placēre/placitum*
born, be	*nasci/natum*	pour	*fundere/fusum*
break	*frangere/fractum,*	push	*pellere/pulsum*
	rumpere/ruptum	put	*ponere/positum*
buy	*emere/emptum*	quiver	*tremere*
call	*vocare/vocatum*	read	*legere/lectum*
cause to stand	*sistere/statum*	remain	*manēre/mansum*
choose	*legere/lectum*	repent	*paenitēre*
climb	*scandere/scensum*	rise	*oriri/ortum*
close	*claudere/clausum*	rule	*regere/rectum*
come	*venire/ventum*	run	*currere/cursum*
cut	*secare/sectum*	save	*servare/servatum*
devour	*vorare/voratum*	see	*vidēre/visum,*
divide	*dividere*		*specere/spectum*
do/make	*facere/factum*	seek	*quaerere/-situm,*
do/drive	*agere/actum*		*petere/petitum*
draw/drag	*trahere/tractum*	seize	*prehendere*
estimate	*censēre/censum*	send	*mittere/missum*
fall	*cadere/casum*	shining white, be	*candēre*
feel	*sentire/sensum*	shout	*clamare/-atum*
flee	*fugere/fugitum*	sift	*cernere/cretum*
flow	*fluere/fluxum*	sing	*canere/cantum*
follow	*sequi/secutum*	sit	*sedēre/sessum*
get ready	*parare/paratum*	snatch	*rapere/raptum*
give	*dare (-d)/datum*	speak	*dicere/dictum,*
go	*cedere/cessum,*		*fari/fatum*
	ire/itum	stand	*stare/statum,*
hang	*pendere/pensum*		*sistere/statum*
have	*habēre/habitum*	stick	*haerēre/-haesum*
hear	*audire/auditum*	store	*condere/conditum*
hold	*tenēre/tentum*	stretch	*tendere/tensum,*
increase	*augēre/auctum*		*tentum*
join	*jungere/junctum*	strong, be	*valēre*
keep	*tenēre -tain/tentum*	take up	*sumere/sumptum*
know	*scire/scitum*	take	*capere/captum*
lead	*ducere/ductum,*	talk	*loqui/locutum*
	agere/actum	teach	*docēre/doctum*
lead/draw	*ducere/ductum*	throw	*jacere/jactum*
lead/drive	*agere/actum*	touch	*tangere/tactum*
leap	*salire/saltum*	trust	*fidere*
lie	*jacēre*	turn	*vertere/versum*
live	*vivere/victum*	twist	*torquēre/tortum*
look at	*specere/spectum*	use	*uti/usum*
loosen	*solvere/solutum*	walk	*gradi/-gressum*
make	*facere/factum*	warn	*monēre/monitum*
make one's way	*vadere/vasum*	weigh	*pendere/pensum*
move rapidly	*vadere/vasum*	win	*vincere/victum*
move	*migrare/migratum*	write	*scribere/scriptum*
paint	*pingere/pictum*	yield	*cedere/cessum*
perform	*fungi/functum*		

GLOSSARY III: GREEK WORDS, BASES, COMBINING FORMS

A			
acou, acu-	*hear*	bios	*life*
acusia, acusis	*hearing*	-blast	*embryonic cell*
aer	*air*	blenna	*mucus*
aesth-, esth-	*feel, perceive*	blepharon	*eyelash, eyelid*
ag-	*lead, bring*	botane	*pasture, herb*
agape	*love, agape*	bous	*bull, cow, ox*
agon	*contest, struggle*	brachion	*arm*
agora	*marketplace*	brachus, brachy-	*short*
agra	*violent pain*	bronchos	*windpipe*
agros	*field, land*	brotos	*mortal man*
ainigma	*riddle*	bruein, bry-	*grow*
aion	*age*	bursa	*pouch, sac*
aisth-/esth-	*feel*	C [K, Ch] [see also under K]	
aither	*upper air*	cardia	*heart*
aitia [etio-]	*cause*	centesis	*surgical puncture*
Akademeia	*Plato's school*	cephale	*head*
akos	*remedy*	ceros/cerus	*horn*
akros [acro-]	*topmost*	chaite	*bristle*
algia	*pain*	chaos	*empty space*
algos [-algia]	*pain*	charis	*grace, favor*
allos [allo-]	*other*	cheir, chir-	*hand*
anathema	*something set up*	chemeia	*art of alloying*
anemos	*wind*	chili-/chilo-/kilo-	*thousand*
aner, andr-	*man* (male)	chloros	*green*
angelos	*messenger*	chole	*gall, bile*
angos, angio-	*vessel*	chondros	*cartilage*
anthos	*blossom, flower*	chor-	*move*
anthropos	*human being*	choros	*dance*
aphia	*touch*	chroma/chromat-	*color*
arch-	*first*	chronos	*time*
arche	*beginning, rule*	chrusos	*gold*
archein	*begin, rule*	chthon	*earth*
-archy	*rule, government*	cin-, kin-	*move*
aristos [aristo-]	*best*	clasis	*a breaking up*
arithmos	*number*	cle- [kalein]	*call*
arktos	*bear; the north*	clin-	*bend, slope*
arthron	*joint*	clysis	*washing*
askein (asce-)	*exercise*	colla	*glue, jelly*
aspis, aspid-	*shield*	condulos	*knuckle*
aster	*star*	cop-, com-	*cut*
asthenia	*loss of strength*	cranion	*skull*
atmos	*steam, vapor*	creas	*flesh*
auchen	*neck*	crin-, cri-	*separate, judge*
autos [auto-]	*self*	crypt-, cryp-	*hide*
auxe	*enlargement*	cyesis	*pregnancy*
axios [axio-]	*worthy*	cystis	*bladder*
B		cytos	*cell*
ba-, be-	*go, step, walk*	D	
bakterion	*staff, cane*	dactylos	*digit, finger, toe*
ball-, ble-, bol-	*throw*	daimon	*spirit, divinity*
baptein	*dip*	deik-, dig-, deic-	*show*
barbaros	*non-Greek*	deinos [dino-]	*terrible*
bary-/bari-/baro-	*heavy*	deka-, deca-	*ten*
bathy-, batho-	*deep*	demokratia	*democracy*
-be	*life, organism*	demos	*the people*
biblion	*book*	dendron	*tree*
		derma, dermat-	*skin*

despotes	*master*
deutero-	*second*
di-, dy-, do-	*two*
diaita	*way of living, diet*
diakonos	*servant, attendant*
dicastes	*juryman, judge*
dicho-	*in two*
didaskein	*teach*
didonai	*give*
dike	*justice*
diplo-	*double*
dipsia	*thirst*
diskos	*plate*
do- [didonai]	*give*
doc-/dog-/dox-	*seem, think*
doulos	*slave*
doxa	*opinion, praise,*
dra- [dran]	*do, act, perform*
drakon	*serpent*
drom- [dramein]	*run*
dunamis	*power*
dyn-	*be able/powerful*
E [epsilon, eta, ai]	
echein	*hold, have*
echo	*sound, echo*
-ectomy	*excision*
edema	*swelling*
emesis	*vomiting*
eidos	*form, thing seen*
eikon	*image, likeness*
einai, ont-, ous-	*be*
eironeia	*affected ignorance*
ekleipsis	*a leaving out*
elaunein [ela-]	*drive*
eleemosune	*mercy, pity*
elektron	*amber*
elthein	*come*
-emia, -hemia	*blood condition*
enantios	*opposite*
encephalos	*brain*
ennea-	*nine*
enteros	*intestine*
epos	*word*
eran	*love*
eremos	*lonely, desert*
ergon	*work*
esthesia	*sensation, feeling*
ethnos	*nation, people*
ethos	*custom*
etumos [etymo-]	*true*
eu	*good, well*
eurus [eury-]	*wide*
G	
gala, galakto-	*milk*
gamos	*marriage, union*
gaster	*stomach, belly*
ge [geo-]	*earth*

genesis	*formation*
genos	*birth, race, kind*
genus	*cheek*
geustia/geusis	*taste*
glossa/glotta	*tongue, language*
glukus [glyc-]	*sweet*
glyph-[gluphein]	*carve*
gnathos, genys	*jaw*
gno-[gignoskein]	*know*
gonia, -gon	*angle*
gonu	*knee*
-gony	*production of*
gram	*line*
graph-, gram-	*draw, write*
gumnos[gymno-]	*naked*
gune, gunaik-	*woman*
H [rough breathing]	
hem-/hemat-	*blood*
hairein	*take, grasp, choose*
harmozein	*fit together*
hecato-	*hundred*
hedone	*pleasure*
hedron	*plane, seat*
hek- [echein]	*have, hold*
helios	*the sun*
helix, helico-	*spiral*
hemera	*day*
hemi-	*half*
hen-, en-	*one*
hepar, hepat-	*liver*
hepta-	*seven*
heteros	*other, one of two*
heuriskein	*find*
hex-	*six*
hienai	*send, throw*
hieros	*holy*
hippos	*horse*
histanai [sta-]	*stand*
historia	*inquiry*
histos	*web, tissue*
hodos	*road*
holos	*whole*
homoios	*like*
homos	*one and the same*
hoplon	*armor*
hora	*time*
horan	*see*
horkos	*oath*
hubris	*violence*
hudor, hydro-	*water*
hugies	*healthy*
hugros [hygro-]	*wet, moist*
hule [-yl]	*material*
humnos	*song, hymn*
hupnos	*sleep*
husteros	*later, behind*
hymen	*membrane*

hypsos	*height*	lithos	*stone*
hystera	*womb*	logos	*word, reason*
I		lophos	*crest*
i- [ienai]	*go*	luein [ly-]	*loose, break*
-iatrics, -iatry	*medical art*	lukos	*wolf*
iatros	*healer, physician*	lura	*stringed instrument*
ichthus	*fish*	ly-[luein]	*loose, break,*
icos-	*twenty*		*destroy*
idios	*one's own,*	lysis	*breaking down*
	peculiar	M	
ischion	*thigh, hip*	magos	*enchanter, wizard*
isos [iso-]	*equal*	makros	*long*
istos	*tissue*	malacia	*softening*
-itis	*inflammation*	mania	*madness*
K [see also under C]		martur	*witness*
kai	*and, plus*	mastos	*breast*
kaiein [kau-]	*burn*	math-	*learn*
kainos [-cene]	*new*	mechane	*contrivance*
kakos [caco-]	*bad, ugly*	-megaly	*enlargement*
kalein	*call*	megas, megal-	*big*
kalos	*beautiful*	meros	*part*
kaluptein	*hide*	meter, metro-	*mother*
kanon	*rod, standard*	metopon	*forehead*
karpos	*fruit*	metron	*measure*
katharos	*clean, pure*	mimos	*imitator*
kenos [ceno-]	*empty*	mikros [micro-]	*small*
kephale	*head*	misein	*hate*
kerannunai	*mix*	mitos	*thread*
keras, -at-	*horn*	mnasthai [mne-]	*remember*
kinesia	*movement*	monos [mono-]	*alone, only, single*
kinein	*move*	moros	*fool*
klan	*break*	morphe	*shape, form*
kleptein	*steal*	Mousa	*Muse*
kleros	*lot, legacy*	muein	*close the eyes*
koinos	*common*	murios [myrio-]	*countless, 10,000*
kolla	*glue*	muthos	*speech, story*
koma, -at-	*deep sleep*	mys, myo-	*muscle*
kosmos	*order, universe,*	N	
	adornment	narke	*numbness*
kreas	*flesh, meat*	naus	*ship*
krinein	*judge, separate*	-naut	*sailor*
kruos [cryo-]	*frost*	nekros	*corpse*
kruptein	*hide*	nem-, nom-	*assign, allot*
kuklos	*circle*	neos [neo-]	*new*
kuon, kun-	*dog*	nephos, nephale	*cloud*
kurios	*swollen, Lord*	nephros	*kidney*
L		neuron	*sinew, nerve*
lab-, lep-, lem-	*take, seize*	nomos	*law, custom*
laos	*the people*	nous	*mind*
-latry	*worship of*	nux, nukt-	*night*
legein	*gather, say*	O [omicron, omega]	
leipein [lip-]	*leave*	ochlos	*crowd, mob*
lepis, -id-	*scale*	octo-	*eight*
-lepsy	*seizure*	ode	*song*
lethe	*forgetfulness*	-odia, -osmia	*smell*
leukos	*white*	odous, odont-	*tooth*
-lite, lith	*stone*	-odynia	*pain*

oikos [eco-]	*house, environment*	-phage	*that which eats*
oligos	*few*	-phagia, -phagy	*eating/swallowing*
-oma	*tumor*	-phagous	*eating*
omma	*eye*	-phagy	*eating*
omos	*shoulder*	phain/phen/phan-	*show, appear*
onoma[-onym]	*name*	pharynx	*throat*
oncus	*tumor*	pher-, phor-	*bear, carry*
ont-, ous-[einai]	*be [root, -es]*	philia, -phily	*love, affinity for*
oon	*egg*	philos	*dear, loving*
ophrys	*eyebrow*	phleps, phleb-	*vein*
ophthalmos	*eye*	phobia	*fear*
opia, opsis, opsy	*vision*	phone	*voice*
ops, opsis	*face*	-phoria	*feeling, bearing*
-orexia, orexis	*appetite*	phos, photo-	*light*
ornis, ornitho-	*bird*	phren (fren-)	*diaphragm, mind*
oros	*mountain*	phule	*tribe*
-orrhagia	*rapid discharge*	phullon	*leaf*
-orrhaphy	*suture*	phy-[phuein]	*grow, be by nature*
-orrhea	*flow, discharge*	phyma	*swelling*
-orrhexis	*rupture*	planasthai	*wander*
orthos [ortho-]	*straight*	plasia	*development*
-osis	*abnormal*	-plasty	*surgical repair*
	condition	platus [platy-]	*wide, broad*
-osphresia/-is	*smell*	plegia	*stroke, paralysis*
osteon	*bone*	pleion [plio/pleo-]	*more, greater*
-ostomy	*formation of a new*	pleistos [pleisto-]	*most, greatest*
	opening	pleura	*rib*
ostrakon	*shell, potsherd*	ploutus	*wealth*
otomy	*incision*	pneumon	*lung*
oura	*tail*	poie-, poe-	*make, do*
ous, ot-	*ear*	poiesis	*formation*
oxus [oxy-]	*sharp*	pol-[polein]	*sell*
P [P, Ph, Ps]		-pole, -polist	*seller*
pais, paid- [ped-]	*child*	polemos	*war*
palaios [paleo-]	*old*	polis	*city, city-state*
palin	*again*	polus [poly-]	*much, many*
papuros	*a plant used for*	pompe	*sending*
	making paper	potamos	*river*
pareia	*cheek*	pous, pod-	*foot*
pas, pant-	*all*	prag-, prac-	*do*
pater, patro-	*father*	presbus	*old*
pathos	*suffering,*	proctos	*anus*
	experience	protos	*first*
-pathy	*disease, illness*	psallein	*play the lyre*
pau- [pauein]	*stop, cease*	pseudes	*false*
pedon	*soil, ground, plain*	psilos	*bare, plain*
peira	*attempt*	psyche	*soul, breath, life*
pelagos	*sea*	pteron	*wing*
pempein	*send*	pteron, ptilon	*feather*
-penia	*deficiency*	ptosis	*prolapse, sagging*
pente-	*five*	pur	*fire*
-pepsia	*digestion*	puxis	*boxwood, box*
petra	*rock*	R [Rh]	
-pexy	*fixation*	rhaptein	*sew*
pha-, phe-	*say, speak*	rhegnunai [rhag-]	*break*
pheme	*a saying*	rhe(u)-, rhy-, rho-	*flow*
phag-[phagein]	*eat*	rhetor	*orator*

rhis, rhin-	*nose*	techne	*art, skill*
rhiza	*root*	teinein	*stretch*
rhodon	*rose*	tekton [-tect]	*carpenter, builder*
rhynchos	*beak*	tele [tele-]	*far away*
S		telos [teleo-]	*end*
sarx, sark-	*flesh*	temnein	*cut (-tomy)*
sauros	*lizard*	ten-, ta-, ton-	*stretch out, strain*
schisis	*splitting*	tetra-	*four*
schiz-, schis-	*split*	thanatos	*death*
schole	*leisure*	the-[tithenai]	*put, place*
sclerosis	*hardening*	theatron	*place for viewing*
scop-/scep-/skep-	*examine, look at*	thema	*something set*
sema, semat-	*sign, signal*	theos	*god*
sepsis	*infection*	therapeia	*treatment*
sitos	*bread, food*	therapon/theraps	*attendant*
skelos	*leg*	therapy	*treatment*
skene	*tent*	thermos	*warm, hot*
skia	*shadow*	thesauros	*treasure*
skleros	*hard*	thorax	*thorax*
soma, somato-	*body*	thrix, trich-	*hair*
sophos	*wise, clever*	thronos	*armchair*
spasm	*twitching*	thumos	*spirit (thymus)*
sperma, spermat-	*sperm, seed*	tme-,tom-	*cut*
sphaira	*a ball*	tokos	*birth*
sphyron	*ankle*	-tomy	*cutting*
sta-, ste-	*stand*	tonos	*tone, accent*
stalassein	*drip*	topos	*place*
stasis	*controlling*	toxon	*poison*
-stat	*device to check*	tracheia	*windpipe*
stear	*fat*	trachus [trachy]	*rugged, harsh*
stellein	*send*	tri-	*three*
stenos [steno-]	*narrow*	-tripsy	*surgical crushing*
stenosis	*stricture*	trop(h)-[trepein]	*turn*
stephanos	*crown*	troph-[trephein]	*feed, nourish*
stereos [stereo-]	*solid, firm*	-trophy	*development*
sternon	*breast*	tupos	*mark*
stethos	*chest*	turannos *king*	
sthenos	*strength*	U	
stichos	*line, verse*	-uria	*condition of urine*
stoa	*porch*	X	
stol-, stal-, stl-	*send, make ready*	xenos	*stranger*
stoma, -at-	*mouth*	xeros [xero-]	*dry*
stratos	*army*	xulon	*wood*
strephein	*turn, twist*	Z	
stulos	*column*	zelos	*eagerness*
sukophantes	*informer, flatterer*	zone	*belt, girdle*
T [T, Th]		zoon	*animal*
tak-, tac-, tax-	*arrange, assign*	zume	*yeast*
taphos	*tomb*		

A–E	
afar, from afar	*tele*
air	*aer*
all	*pas (pan-, panto-)*
animal	*zoon*
another	*allos, heteros*
bad	*kakos*
beautiful	*kalos (calli-)*
being	*onto-, ous-*
best	*aristos*
bird	*ornis, ornitho-*
book	*biblion*
break	*luein (ly-)*
call	*kalein (kle-)*
cause	*aitia (etio-)*
child	*pais, paid- (ped-)*
clean	*katharos*
color	*chroma, chromat-*
craving	*mania*
custom	*ethos*
deep	*bathus, bathy-/o-*
demon	*daimon*
divination	*manteia*
dog	*kuon, kuno-/cyno-*
draw	*graphein*
dry	*xeros*
earth	*ge*
eat	*phagein*
empty	*kenos*
equal	*isos*
experience	*pathos*
F–J	
false	*pseudes*
father	*pater*
fear	*phobia*
few	*oligos*
fire	*pur*
first	*protos*
fish	*ichthus*
flower	*anthos*
foot	*pous, pod-*
form	*morphe*
fowl	*ornis, ornitho-*
from afar	*tele*
give	*didonai (do-)*
go	*bainein (ba-, be-), ienai (-i-)*
god	*theos*
government by	*kratia (-cracy)*
green	*chloros*
hate	*misos*
head	*kephale*
healer	*iatros*
healing	*iatreia*
heavy	*barus*

holy	*hieros*
horse	*hippos*
hour	*hora*
house	*oikos (eco-)*
household	*oikos (eco-)*
human being	*anthropos*
human	*anthropos*
humid	*hugros*
image	*eikon*
imitator	*mimos*
judge	*krinein (krin/kri-)*
K–O	
know	*gignoskein (gno-)*
knowledge of	*-nomy*
large	*megas, mega-/-al-*
law	*nomos*
leaf	*phullon*
life	*bios; -onto-, zoo-*
light	*phos, photo-*
line	*stichos*
living thing	*zoon*
lizard	*sauros*
look (at)	*skopein*
lover	*philos*
love	*philein*
make	*prattein, poiein*
many	*polus*
man	*aner, andr-*
mark	*tupos*
marriage	*gamos*
measure	*meter*
messenger	*angelos*
mother	*meter, metr-*
mountain	*oros*
move	*kinein*
naked	*gumnos*
name	*onomat-, -onym-*
nation	*ethnos*
nature	*phusis*
new	*neos*
old	*palaios (paleo-)*
one who fears	*phobe*
opinion	*doxa*
other	*allos, heteros*
P–S	
paper	*papuros, charte*
peculiar	*idios*
people	*demos*
poison	*toxon*
power	*dunamis*
pressure	*baros*
production	*genesis, goneia*
put	*tithenai (the-)*
recent	*kainos*
ring	*kyklos*

river	*potamos*	terrible	*deinos*
rock	*lithos, petra*	throw	*ballein*
rose	*rhodon*	time	*chronos*
rule	*archein, kratia*	tongue	*glotta, glossa*
run	*dramein (-drom-)*	tooth	*odous, odonto-*
same	*homos*	topmost	*akros*
self	*autos*	treatment	*therapeia*
sell	*polein*	tree	*dendron*
shadow	*skia*	true	*etumos*
shape	*morphe*	ugly	*kakos*
sharp	*oxus*	universe	*kosmos*
short	*brachus*	vessel	*angos (angio-)*
single	*monos*	voice	*phone*
small	*mikros*	wealth	*ploutos*
solid	*stereos*	weight	*baros*
soul	*psuche*	whole	*holos*
stand	*histanai (sta-/ste-)*	wind	*anemos*
star	*aster, astr-*	wise	*sophos*
steam	*atmos*	witness	*martur*
stone	*lithos*	wolf	*lukos*
story	*muthos*	woman	*gune, gynec-*
straight	*orthos*	wood	*xulon*
stranger	*xenos*	word	*logos, epos*
study of	*-logy, -nomy*	work	*ergon*
suffering	*pathos*	worship	*latreia*
sun	*helios*	worthy	*axios*
T–W		write	*graphein*

INDEX